D1250203

BASIC
READINGS
IN
INTERPERSONAL
COMMUNICATION

Under the Advisory Editorship of
J. Jeffery Auer

BASIC
READINGS
IN
INTERPERSONAL
COMMUNICATION

Kim Giffin
Professor of Speech Communication and Human Relations
The University of Kansas

Bobby R. Patton
Associate Professor of Speech Communication and Human Relations
The University of Kansas

HARPER & ROW, PUBLISHERS
NEW YORK, EVANSTON, AND LONDON

Cover photo by Michel Cosson

HM 132
.G52

INDIANA
PURDUE
LIBRARY.
JUN 1971
FORT WAYNE

WITHDRAWN

Basic Readings in Interpersonal Communication

Copyright © 1971 by Kim Giffin and Bobby R. Patton

Printed in the United States of America. All rights reserved. No part of
this book may be used or reproduced in any manner whatsoever without
written permission except in the case of brief quotations embodied in
critical articles and reviews. For information address Harper & Row,
Publishers, Inc., 49 East 33rd Street, New York, N.Y. 10016.

LIBRARY OF CONGRESS CATALOG CARD NUMBER: 70-129476

CONTENTS

JUN 3 0 1971

PREFACE

During the last decade there has developed a new wave of
human aspiration regarding the potential value of interpersonal
communication as the means by which a person may reach a
more satisfying relationship with other human beings. The
older, more traditional view of communication usually focused
on one (or a combination) of two objectives: (1) To tell them
what I know or believe, or (2) To get them to see things as I do.

By comparison, the more recent view of interaction places
much greater emphasis upon the desire to relate to other persons.
People with whom we are in daily contact are viewed as
potential warm personal friends, not just as co-workers or
possible competitors. In this way new importance has been given
to the phrase, "human relations." There is an increased sense
of personal justice. The other person has a right to be heard,
not just a need to be informed or persuaded. The real potential
of communication is seen in interaction, where listening as
well as talking occurs. The emphasis on the human element
reflects a very personal need of the individual in an automated
and highly specialized society. It reflects one's need to be in
personal touch with other persons as well as a greater willingness
to consider the needs of others. The hallmark of those who
express increased interest in human relations is that they care
about the other person—they want to understand him, to know
him better, and to reach out to him a friendly, helping hand.

This new aspiration regarding interpersonal communication
places special importance on the personal and interpersonal
facets of the communication process: how we perceive each other,

our orientation toward other people in general, our inter-personal response-sets, and those behavior patterns which become serious barriers to developing meaningful relationships with others. In addition, new emphasis is placed on understanding those human needs which a person tries to satisfy through interaction with others, needs which we have identified under the rubric of interpersonal imperatives.

Dean Barnlund complained in 1961 that the speech field had overemphasized public speaking, giving "the impression that the rostrum is the only setting where communication among men matters." He then added: "There is no reason, if scholarship supports it, why there should not be courses in interpersonal communication, in conflict resolution, in decision-making, in organizational communication, in psycholinguistics, in societal communication, in network theory and so on."[1] While we have been slow to respond to Barnlund's suggestions, there is no longer a problem regarding the abundance of available relevant writings; the problem is that of identifying, obtaining, evaluating, sorting, and selecting what is most useful for a particular group of readers. Consequently, the need for a book of the present type becomes quite obvious when one starts to review the scattered and rather specialized literature available. A glimpse at the original sources of the articles included in this collection will support that fact.

In making our selections we have started with those concepts that we view as basic to the study of interpersonal communication: a person's need for interaction, the process of person-perception, interpersonal response-sets, those situation variables that influence interaction, message variables that influence outcomes of interaction, and behaviors that may act as serious barriers to interactional goals. In our opening section we have presented a brief examination of the basic principles of interpersonal communication; the concluding section contains specific suggestions for improving interpersonal relationships.

These readings are basic in two senses: first, we presuppose

[1]Dean C. Barnlund, "Toward a Meaning-Centered Philosophy of Communication," **Journal of Communication, 11** (1962), p. 208.

no prior educational experience with the conceptual notions
or their applications. Although we have all engaged in interpersonal communication all of our lives, we may never have
paused to reflect upon the behavioral science involved. The
articles included are within the range of the college freshman
or the busy businessman seeking a sound guide to improved
communication. Secondly, the readings are basic in the sense
that they provide the foundation for appreciation and
understanding of the more sophisticated writings in the field.
Advanced students have access to the professional periodicals
and volumes that provide greater challenge and insight into the
complex process of human communication behavior.

To those persons who authored the selections contained in
this volume we owe a great debt, not only for originally
writing the selections, but for their contribution to our thinking
over the past few years. Many of their other writings have
been of great value to us, but could not be included in the
present volume. Any errors of judgment in making our selections
we must claim as our own; even so, to these authors we owe
a very deep sense of personal gratitude.

K.G.
B.R.P.

BASIC READINGS IN INTERPERSONAL COMMUNICATION

PRINCIPLES OF INTERPERSONAL COMMUNICATION
SECTION ONE

Effective public communication for centuries has been the concern of people in the field of speech. Focus remained upon the speaker as he attempted to elicit certain desired responses from his audience. The variables of effectiveness were sought out as means of enabling the speaker to manipulate his audience and be more persuasive.

The impetus toward a more humane, process-oriented view of our communication initially came from psychiatry and social psychology. This view of interaction places less emphasis on communication for task achievement: talking to others simply to "get on with the work at hand." Rather it emphasizes the possibility of enjoying our being together while we also do our work. By placing less value on trying to influence others to think the way we do, it makes the manipulation of others for selfish motives highly objectionable.

The article by Jurgen Ruesch that follows provides an excellent overview of the dimensions of interpersonal communication. This psychiatrist's view of the effects of messages upon the behavior of people describes the characteristics of normal communication behaviors as a backdrop for analysis of deviant behaviors. The channels, contexts, and systems that he discusses distinguish the broad area for interdisciplinary academic concern. Emphasis has been shifted from the sender of the message to the receiver.

The second article in this section, by Virginia Satir, further expands and delineates our current view of interpersonal communication. Her outline format provides varied examples of the roles of both verbal and nonverbal messages in the communication process. The inevitability of communication when we are in the presence of others has been a principle long ignored in theoretical explanations of communication behaviors.

Dean Barnlund has been a pioneer in attempting to expand the dimensions of the speech discipline. The paper included in this section attempts to refute some commonly held assumptions concerning the definition of communication, and presents one more appropriate to the design of this book.

We think that these three articles provide an excellent foundation for understanding the nature and scope of studies in interpersonal communication behaviors. We concur with the basic principles established by Barnlund and with his conclusion that "Research or instruction that disregards these characteristics of the communicative act would appear both unsound and of dubious value."

Jurgen Ruesch
Communication and Human Relations: An Interdisciplinary Approach

The field of communication is concerned with human related-ness. Every person, plant, animal, and object emits signals which, when perceived, convey a message to the receiver. This message changes the information of the receiver and hence may alter his behavior. Change in behavior of the receiver, in turn, may or may not perceptibly influence the sender. Some-times the effect of a message is immediate; at other times the message and its effect are so far apart in time and space that the observer fails to connect the two events. For purposes of our presentation however, we shall be concerned more with the immediate effects of messages and their influence upon the behavior of people.

Channels of Communication in Everyday Life

In order to familiarize the reader with the varieties of human communication, let us view the experiences of Mr. A as he proceeds with his daily activities. In the morning when Mr. A enters his office he reads his incoming mail (written communica-tion). In sorting his mail he encounters a number of pamphlets which are designed to describe the merits of various business machines (pictorial communication). Through the open window the faint noise of a radio is heard, as the voice of an announcer

Reprinted from COMMUNICATION, The Social Matrix of Psychiatry by Jurgen Ruesch, M.D., and Gregory Bateson. By permission of W. W. Norton & Company, Inc. Copyright © 1968, 1951 by W. W. Norton & Company, Inc.

clearly praises the quality of a brand of toothpaste (spoken communication). When his secretary enters the room she gives him a cheerful "good morning," which he acknowledges with a friendly nod of his head (gestural communication) while he continues with his conversation on the telephone (spoken communication) with a business associate. Later in the morning he dictates a number of letters to his secretary, then he holds a committee meeting (group communication), where he gathers the advice of his associates. In this meeting a number of new governmental regulations (mass communication) and their effect upon the policies of the firm are discussed. Later in the meeting a resolution to the employees of the firm concerning the annual bonus (mass and group communication) is considered. After the committee has adjourned, Mr. A, engaged in thoughts concerning unfinished business (communication with self), slowly crosses the street to his restaurant for lunch. On the way he sees his friend Mr. B, who in a great hurry enters the same luncheon place (communication through action), and Mr. A decides to sit by himself rather than to join his friend, who will probably gulp down his coffee and hurry on (communication with self). While waiting, Mr. A studies the menu (communication through printed word) but the odor of a juicy steak deflects his gaze (chemical communication); it is so appetizing that he orders one himself. After lunch he decides to buy a pair of gloves. He enters a men's store and with the tips of his fingers carefully examines the various qualities of leather (communication through touch). After leisurely concluding the purchase, he decides to take the afternoon off and to escort his son on a promised trip to the zoo. On the way there, John, watching his father drive through the streets, asks him why he always stops at a red light and why he does not stop at a green light (communication by visual symbol). As they approach the zoo, an ambulance screams down the street, and Mr. A pulls over to the side of the road and stops (communication by sound). As they sit there he explains to his son that the church across the street is the oldest in the state, built many years ago, and still standing as a landmark in the community (communication through material culture). After paying admission to the zoo (communication through action), they leisurely stroll over to visit the elephants. Here John laughs at the antics of an elephant who sprays water through his trunk at one of the spectators (communication through action), sending him into near flight. Later on in the afternoon Mr. A yields to the pressure of his son, and they enter a movie house to see a cartoon (communication through pictures). Arriving home, Mr. A dresses in order to attend a formal dinner and theater performance (communication through the arts).

These examples may suffice to illustrate the varieties of social situations in which communication occurs. Let us next consider how a scientist can conceptualize these various events in a more systematized fashion.

The Context in Which Communication Occurs

The scientific approach to communication has to occur on several levels of complexity. In a first step we shall be concerned with the definition of the context in which communication occurs. This context is summarized by the label which people give to specific social situations. Identification of a social situation is important both for the participant who wishes to communicate and for the scientist who aims at conceptualizing the processes of communication.

The Perception of the Perception

A social situation is established as soon as an exchange of communication takes place; and such exchange begins with the moment in which the actions of the other individual are perceived as responses—that is, as evoked by the sender's message and therefore as comments upon that message, giving the sender an opportunity of judging what the message meant to the receiver. Such communication about communication is no doubt difficult, because it is usually implicit rather than explicit, but it must be present if an exchange of messages is to take place. The perception of the perception, as we might call this phenomenon, is the sign that a silent agreement has been reached by the participants, to the effect that mutual influence is to be expected.

The mutual recognition of having entered into each other's field of perception equals the establishment of a system of communication. The criteria of mutual awareness of perception are in all cases instances of communication about communication. If a person "A" raises his voice to attract person "B's" attention, he is thereby making a statement about communication. He may, for example, be saying, "I am communicating with you," or he may be saying, "I am not listening to you; I am doing the talking"—and so on. Similarly, all punctuations of the stream of emitted signals are statements about how that stream is to be broken down into sections, and significantly all modifications of the stream of signals, which implicitly or explicitly assign roles either to the self or to the other, are statements about communication. If "A" adds the word "please" to a verbal request, he is making a statement about that request; he is giving instructions about the mood or role which he desires the listener to adopt when he interprets the verbal stream. He is adding a signal to cause a modification in the receiver's interpretation. In this sense the added signal is a communication about communication as well as a statement about the relationship between two persons.

The Position of the Observer
Within the System of Communication

Dependent upon whether an observer is a participant in a group discussion, or remains a scientific observer who, rather aloof and with a minimum of participation, proceeds to make scientific notes, the information about what happens is going to vary. The position of the observer, his viewpoints and foci of interest, his degree of participation, and his lucidity in interpreting rules, roles, and situations will determine that which he is going to report.

When a scientist endeavors to study such complicated matters as human relations, he conveniently divides the universe into segments small enough so that the events which occur within such a subdivision can be observed and recorded in a satisfactory manner. In proceeding from the larger to the smaller units of consideration, the scientist has to guard against pitfalls which may arise from his personal focus of endeavor, his personal views, and his particular perspectives. His position may be likened to that of a visitor to a museum of art, who never succeeds in seeing the front and back views of a statue at the same moment. From a position in back of the statue, for example, he will be unable to predict the facial expression until he has seen it from the front. To obtain a complete impression, he has to walk around the statue; and as he moves, a new perspective will open at every step until the combination of all impressions will enable the visitor to construct within himself a small-scale model of the marble figure. Matters get even more complicated if one considers that not all visitors go to the museum with the same purpose in mind. Some wish to obtain a quick impression of the treasures on hand; others want to undertake detailed studies in preparation for an artist's career; some want to meet people who have the same interests. Thus, varying with their purpose, any of several persons gathered around the statue might retain within himself a different view of the marble figure.

The scientist is very much in the same position as the spectator of the statue, with the exception that, to achieve a more complete understanding of what he is doing and of what happens in nature, he does not limit himself to perception and observation only. In order to satisfy his curiosity, he compensates for his human limitations of perception by creating a theory. In brief, he proceeds about as follows: First, he postulates that there are events. An event is defined as an occurrence which occupies a small part of the general four-dimensional, space-time continuum. If the scientist happens to observe such an event and if it can be verified by others, he refers to his statement of it as a fact. Sometimes he adds to his observations certain physical measurements; he makes observations on the relations between measurements: he makes observations on the relations between the event and his own measuring rod. In order to be able to measure or to experiment, however, the scientist needs a hypothesis; it is nothing but a provisional, tentative theory, a supposition that he adopts temporarily in order to add to the already well-established knowledge a series of new facts. Hypotheses thus guide all future research work. When a hypothesis—that is, an assumption without proof—can be substantiated by fact, it becomes a theory. The latter can be described as being the result of reasoning with the intent to derive from a body of known facts some general or abstract principles. Such principles can then be applied to other bodies of knowledge in order to finally interconnect the information about events in a larger time-space continuum. The scientist has to rely upon theory, because only few events are accessible to direct observation or measurement. The majority of processes in nature or within the human being himself are either so slow or so fast that they escape perception. Theory is then used to combine the known facts into a network, allowing for interpolation and extrapolation, reconstruction of past and prediction of future events.

At this point the reader will recognize that as soon as we talk or think about a social situation we have to define our own position as observers. Therefore, every individual becomes a scientific observer as soon as he engages in communication.

To evaluate daily events and to guide future actions, every single human being possesses a private scientific system. To students of human behavior, the private sytems of others are accessible only in a rather restricted manner. That which is assimilated by the human being in terms of stimuli—be it food, oxygen, sound, or light—and that which the individual produces in heat, waste materials, or purposive action is accessible to investigation. Whatever happens between intake and output is known on a restricted scale only; through introspection and, in recent years, by means of X-rays and radioactive tracer substances, scientists have been able to follow some of the processes which take place within the organism. For practical purposes, however, events occurring in other persons are accessible to an observer in terms of inference alone; all he observes is the stimuli which reach the other person and the latter's reactions; the rest is subject to conjecture. Furthermore, the observer, being a social stimulus for others, possesses knowledge about the origin and the nature of some of the stimuli which he feeds to other individuals. In such a system, which includes the observer as an integral part, the actions of the first person are stimuli for the second person and the responses of the second person are stimuli for the first person.

Identification of Roles and Rules

Once the position of the observing reporter is clearly defined and a social situation has been established because people have entered into communication, it is left to the participants to identify the social situation. The label which a person is going to give to a social situation is intimately connected with the rules which govern the situation, as well as the roles which the various participants are to assume. It is obvious that each person has his own views regarding the label of the situation and that much confusion results when people disagree as to what a situation is about. Through communication with others, roles are mutually assigned, and by means of mutual exploration agreement is frequently reached as to the nature of the situation. Used in connection with communication, the term "role" refers to nothing but the code which is used to interpret the flow of messages. For example, the statements of a person who wishes to see an automobile are going to be interpreted in a sense quite different from that which they would have if the person were to make the same statements in the role of an automobile buyer. Awareness of a person's role in a social situation enables others to gauge correctly the meaning of his statements and actions.

Once the roles of the self and of all other participants have been established, the code for interpreting the conversation is given. The number of roles which people can assume is limited, and elsewhere we have calculated that their number is probably about twenty-five.[1] A mature individual is capable of mastering this number of roles in the course of a lifetime.

[1] J. Ruesch and A. R. Prestwood, "Interactive Processes and Personal Codification," *Journal of Personality*, 18 (1950), 391–430, p. 405.

Any social situation is governed by explicit or implicit rules; these rules may be created on the spur of the moment for a particular situation, or they may be the result of centuries of tradition. In the context of communication, rules can be viewed as directives which govern the flow of messages from one person to another. Inasmuch as rules are usually restrictive, they limit the possibilities of communication between people, and above all, they restrict the actions of the participating persons. Rules can be viewed as devices which either stabilize or disrupt a given communication system, and they provide directives for all eventualities. The meaning of rules, regulations, and laws can be understood best if one thinks of a card game in which several persons participate: The channels of communication are prescribed, the sequence of messages is regulated, and the effects of messages are verifiable. The rules also explain that certain messages, at certain times, addressed to certain people, are not admissible, and that known penalties are imposed upon those who break the rules. Furthermore, regulations pertaining to the beginning of the game, the division of functions in terms of roles, and the termination of the game are always included.[2]

The Label of the Social Situation

A social situation is established when people have entered into communication; the state of communication is determined by the fact that a person perceives that his perception has been noted by others. As soon as this fact has been established, a system of communication can be said to exist. At that point selective reception, purposive transmission, and corrective processes take place and the circular characteristics and self-corrective mechanisms of the system of communication become effective. This implies that roles have been assigned and rules established. The participants in a social situation experience these events more or less consciously, and the experience

[2] *Ibid.*, p. 401. See also J. Von Neumann and O. Morgenstern, *Theory of Games and Economic Behavior* (Princeton, N.J.: Princeton University Press, 1941).

induces them to label a social situation. Such a label specifies not only the status assignment (roles) of the participants and the rules pertaining to the gathering, but also the task or the purpose to which a social situation is devoted. A funeral, for example, serves another purpose than a wedding, and communications vary accordingly. Elsewhere[3] we have advanced the idea that the social situations encountered by the average person number less than forty, a figure which the normally gifted person can master easily.

In identifying social labels it is obvious that external criteria are extremely helpful. If people are dressed in mourning, and others know the significance of the special clothing, they will all agree as to the label of the situation, and communications are therefore limited and interpreted under the seal of the situation. Different and difficult is the situation, however, when two strangers meet—for example, in a western frontier setting, around 1850. External cues of behavior might not have helped them recognize each other's roles. One man, for example, might have been intent on murder, or persecution, or trade. In such cases the label has to be worked out as time goes on, and new rules created. The interval which elapses between the establishment of a social situation and its definite label may vary. Some persons are very skillful in bringing about a clarification of the situation; others, especially neurotics, may experience great anxiety until roles, rules, and purpose have been defined.

The Simpler Systems of Communication

When a person is alone, the system of communication is confined to that one organism. If there are two people, then the communication network embraces both organisms. If there are many people, the network embraces the whole group, and if we consider many groups, we may talk about a cultural network. In a one-person communication system the signals travel along the established pathways of the body. In a two-or-more-

[3] *Ibid.*, p. 398.

person system the signals travel both along the pathways of the body and through the media which separate the bodies.

Let us now consider first the human instruments of communication and the bodily pathways used for communication. A man's organism as a whole can be conceived of as an instrument of communication, equipped with sense organs, the receivers; with effector organs, the senders; with internal transmitters, the humoral and nervous pathways; and with a center, the brain. However, the reader is warned not to think in anatomical terms when considering the internal network of communication; more appropriate is the comparison of the individual with a social organization. Within the organized confines of a state, for example, messages from the borders and from all parts of the nation are transmitted to the capital and to all other points by means of an intricate network. The messages can be conveyed by radio, telephone, telegraph, or word of mouth; printed messages may be carried by air, ship, rail, on wheels, on foot, or on horseback. The person that first reports an event usually does not engage in any extensive traveling to spread the news. Instead, through a system of relays the message is transmitted to other places and people. Each relay station may alter, amplify, condense, or abstract the original message for local use; and frequently after long transit any resemblances between the first and the last report are purely coincidental. This analogy applies well to the consideration of the human organism.

The sense organs, for example, are found scattered from head to toe on the external surface of the body and in or around internal organs as well. Sensitive to stimuli which originate in the surroundings as well as in the body itself, the end organs act as stations of impulse transformation. Regardless of whether the original stimulus consists of a series of light or sound waves or of a chemical reagent, the sense organs transform that which is perceived into impulses which are suitable for internal transmission within the organism. Likewise, it does not matter whether these impulses are conducted along afferent pathways from peripheral and cranial nerves to the brain or along humoral pathways, or perhaps contiguously from cell to cell within a given organ. The essence of the matter is that all living tissue is equipped with the ability to respond to the impact of specific stimuli; such responsiveness may be called irritability. The nature of this responsiveness is determined in part by the type of stimulus which is perceived and in part by the nature of the reacting tissues, organs, and systems of organs. For greater economy and efficiency the stimulus perceived on the surface of the body or within the organism itself is transformed in such a way that it can be transmitted properly; and likewise, the impulses originating in the brain and other regulatory centers are transformed in several stations before they reach the effector organs or, even more remotely, the sense organs of another person.

Our effector organs, the striped and smooth muscles of the body, react to stimuli originating in the organism itself. The irritability of the muscles, when stimulated, results in contractions which in turn may give rise to movements of the limbs, to motions of the body in space, to passage of air through the windpipe, and subsequently to sound or to internal movements of the intestinal tract or the circulatory system. Whenever activities of an organ or of the whole organism are perceived by the self or by others, they constitute communicative acts which warrant interpretation. The higher centers of the nervous systems and perhaps certain glands evaluate messages originating in single organs, and a person may respond automatically, sometimes not being consciously aware of this transmission. Such automatic responses are termed reflexes if the circuit, with the exception of the stimulus, is located entirely within one organism. In transmission of messages from person to person information pertaining to the state of the organism of the speakers is frequently transmitted without the awareness of the participants. In social situations, for example, people automatically evaluate the other person's attitude—that is, whether it is friendly or hostile. Without being conscious of their own responses they will be more cautious and alert when facing a hostile individual than when they encounter an apparently harmless person. More complex interpersonal messages, especially when coded in verbal form, require a more conscious evaluation and interpretation. But regardless of the complexity of the message or the extent of the network, the basic principles remain the same.

A neutral observer, for example, when perceiving that a person tumbles downstairs and remains motionless at the end of the fall, might be impressed by several different communicative aspects of this incident. Referring to the physical sphere, the conclusion may be warranted that the person was injured. With reference to the intrapersonal system of the victim, the inference is made that certain processes within the mind of the accident-bearer may have been altered or arrested, and that the person has lost consciousness. Pertinent to the interpersonal relation, the conclusion is warranted that the person needs help; and in social terms, though not immediately, certain repercussions can be expected which might deal with lawsuits, establishment of rules for accident prevention, and the like. Thus any change in the state of an organism can be viewed from varied standpoints and can be registered consciously or unconsciously.

If actions of human beings and animals have communicative aspects, so also do plants and objects convey a message to the person who perceives them. It takes but the fraction of a second for our organism to perceive a multitude of stimuli, and most scientific descriptions of perceptive phenomena run into insurmountable difficulties when an attempt is made to describe the processes involved. A brief illustration may serve as an example. When our attention is attracted by the sight of a red rose, we conceive its splendor under the influence of messages transmitted to us through several channels. First we see, then we smell, and eventually after approaching the rose, we can touch the flower. The scientific description of these three steps would run into many hundreds of pages. Starting with the assessment of the color, the wave length of the reflected light, for example, could be specified as being around 7,000 Angstrom units. Thereafter the tint or shade of the color, the angle of reflection, the position and nature of the original source of light, its brightness, the surface texture and the color of the contrasting background, and many other features would have to be studied to complete the scientific description of the processes related to light alone. Botanical specifications of the family and species of the rose bush, identification of the time and duration of the process of blooming, would embrace some of the plant biological aspects of the investigation. Specifications of the odor emitted by the blossom, the number and type of insects attracted, and their effectiveness in seed dispersion might follow next. Chemical analysis of the constituent parts of the rose tissues or an assessment of the soil or weather conditions might head other chapters of the scientific study. Finally, after exhausting consideration of the rose, and of the conditions under which it bloomed, the investigation would finally reach the human being who perceives the rose. Name, age, sex, and other specifications would be needed to identify us, the individual observer. Study of our physical health and assessment of our vital apparatus would probably precede the psychological investigation of our past experiences, in particular those with flowers and roses. Psychological probing might reveal traces of previous events which enabled us to focus upon the rose rather than upon the structure of the wall in the background or upon a dog playing near by. Further elaboration might reveal the purposes that we might have had in focusing upon roses, either as decoration of the buttonhole in the lapel, as an arrangement on our desk, or maybe as a present for a beloved one. And after all this long and tedious scientific preparation and accumulation of information regarding the rose and the human being who perceived it, we would have to be concerned with that split second which it took to see the rose, and those few seconds more which were necessary to walk towards it.

The reader will readily understand that no scientist is able to describe all the things that might have acted as stimuli or all the possible reactions that a person might have had in that situation. Nevertheless, a neutral observer, sitting on a bench near by, and observing the act of approach and of picking the rose, might infer a number of things from his own experiences in similar situations. He might conclude that we possess a readiness—or shall we say a preference—for that particular rose at that particular time in that particular situation. Let us say that the act of picking the rose had for us the significance of satisfying a desire and of providing us with a present, while for the observer it constituted an expressive act which transmitted to him information about ourself and the rose as well as about the total situation which was conducive to this act. To him, the observer, the only thing that was obvious was the combination of a particular stimulus, the rose, with a particular kind of response, the picking. This combination of a particular stimulus with a particular response we have called a value. For the observer, the choice of this act indicated to him that at that particular moment no other act could take place, though, for example, we might have walked by, heading for the dog without even noticing the rose. For ourselves who proceeded to pick the rose, the act created a precedent which might influence future actions and which in itself was a sequel to previous experiences of ours. Regardless of whether we were aware of our choice, and regardless of whether we knew the motivating reasons for our actions, we, as well as any observer, would agree that at the instant we picked the rose we conveyed a message to others. And this message certainly carried the meaning that within the context of this situation we valued—above all—a rose.

For purposes of communication, then, any action constitutes a message to ourselves as well as to others. Within the framework of communication, the expresion and transmission of values—that is, actions denoting a choice—occupy a central place. A value conveys not only information about the choice made, but also relays information about the things that could have been chosen but were not selected. The ability to select, to maximize or minimize certain aspects of perception, are features which characterize our communication center. Furthermore, this center possesses the faculty of retaining traces of past experiences. Obviously not the action itself, but a symbolic representation, is retained, which has the function of representing within the human organism a small-scale model of all the events which have been experienced in the past.

Creation of new things and adaptation through molding of the surroundings distinguishes man from all other creatures. This gift, which the organicist calls "brain" and which the mentalist refers to as "psyche," is localized nowhere. With no anatomical structure of its own, none the less it needs for its functioning the sum total of all the cells and properties of the organism. To integrate parts into a whole, to magnify, minimize, or discard events, to evaluate the past and to anticipate the future, to create that which never before existed, such are the functions of the center. The infant, when born, is vested with all these potentialities; their exploitation, however, depends upon experiences and circumstances. Equipped with an insatiable desire for a search for the new, the exploration of things and people grinds permanent and indelible grooves into the center of the child. Imprints become experiences when events are registered, and traces remain available for future reference. Little by little, information is acquired through representation of outside events in the mind of the child. Happenings in and around a person are recorded in codified form, and complementation of immediate impressions with traces of the past facilitates a selective response. The individual is said to have learned when discriminating reactions as well as anticipation of events indicate mastery of self and surroundings.

The expansion of the maturing individual is controlled by biological limitations which in turn delineate the extension in space of the system of communication. Man's genetic endowment forces him to seek social relations, while his early development and his first social contacts will in part determine the way he is going to use[4] and eventually refine his means of communication. Man is born of a mother. After his birth, certain death would embrace the infant unless it were fed, clothed, and sheltered. The severance of the umbilical cord is but the first step towards achieving independence. The infant's struggle to acquire an identity of his own requires some fifteen or twenty years. During this time, the growing child, at first helpless and immobilized, little by little learns to explore the world and to undertake ventures on his own. Tedious codification of events leading to the accumulation of a vast mass of information and acquisition of the "know-how" pertaining to the use of this information enables the child to relinquish gradually the help

[4] J. Ruesch, "Individual Social Techniques," *Journal of Social Psychology*, 29 (1949), 3–28.

received from parents and protectors. When biological matura-
tion and social learning have progressed sufficiently, the child
is equipped to set out on his own and to continue the battle for
life with a reasonable chance of survival. Now even more than
before, communication with fellow men becomes a necessity,
since information about the self, others, and the surroundings
has to be kept up to date. The state of maturity has been
reached when finally communication and cooperation with contemporaries has replaced the former reliance upon physical and
emotional assistance from elders.

Man's concept of the world is acquired through social interaction[5] and communication, and these acquired views are the
foundations upon which will rest the future organization of his
surroundings. The shaping of things in the environment distinguishes man from all other living creatures. Man has mastered his physical limitations by extension in space and time.
His voice, audible within a few hundred yards at best, now can
encompass the globe and perhaps beyond. His movements in
space, under primitive conditions, perhaps extended a few hundred miles; now they embrace the whole world and possibly
more. The creation of script, the construction of man-made
shelters, and the use of design enables messages from times
past to reach future generations. The invention of time-binding
mass communication led to the formation of a cumulative body
of knowledge. Information accumulated in the course of centuries became the ground upon which were erected new object
systems and events which eventually developed an existence of
their own. In contrast to the animal, the human being has to
face not only other people but messages and productions of
the past as well. The inventions of man, frequently designed in
the name of progress and survival, may undermine his biological foundations. Whether in the end the creations of man will
improve his lot or result in his own modification or in his total
annihilaton remains to be seen. Be that as it may, at the root of
all man-made events stands his ability to communicate, which
is the foundation upon which cooperation is built.

Cooperation is closely linked to those characteristics which

[5] N. E. Miller and J. Pollard, *Social Learning and Imitation* (New Haven,
Conn.: Yale University Press, 1941).

make man a gregarious creature. Thus man does not live alone. Usually he is surrounded by parents, mate, and offspring, and he seeks the company of contemporaries. In the fold of the family, the clan, the group, or, in the widest sense of the word, the herd, he feels secure. Here, the threatening experiences can be shared, and through pooling of information and cooperation of forces he can master adverse events. Reliance upon other members of the group increases his chances for survival in a troubled world. The first experience of being helped and raised by the mother or other members of the group induces man to trust or fear people. If trust and confidence prevail, he will seek the help of others; if fear predominates he will dominate or avoid others. But regardless of the motive, be it for the sake of sharing, avoiding, conquering, or destroying, he always needs other people.

Man has to move. As the infant acquires mastery of space, locomotion is soon supplemented by other means of transportation. In boats, on the backs of animals, on wheels, or on wings, the exploration of the world is carried on. Movement in space facilitates the acquisition and dissemination of information and the satisfaction of needs. Transportation and communication are thus so intimately linked that distinction is hardly possible.

In his exploration of space, in his quest for mastery, and in his need for food, shelter, and a mate, man will meet dangers and perhaps interference from others. Man and animal alike are alarmed at the sight of danger, and anything is threatening which, by their experiece, is not known to be harmless. In animals, alarm—that is, impending readiness for events to come— is told in many ways: the lion tosses his mane and roars, the fiddler crab brandishes a bright red claw, while the moor hen utters a harsh "krek." A cat when chased by a dog seeks refuge in a tree, its fur erect, claws thrust into the bark, hissing at the growling canine below. The cat's body spells readiness for any future action if a change in the situation should occur; when prowling and stalking a mouse, it will patiently wait for hours for the opportune jump which will spell doom to the outwitted rodent.

While the alarmed animal has the choice of fight, flight, or playing possum, the human being has one additional opportunity. Constructive action, designed to eliminate the source of danger, long-term planning with the intent of preventing a recurrence of the danger, and pooling of information with subsequent cooperation with other humans are the unique privileges of man. Communication for the purpose of sharing and transmission of information to obtain the views of others provides help for the alarmed person. When fight, flight, playing possum, and communication are barred, the readiness of the body for action cannot be consummated. The continuous alarm becomes a permanent state, which is referred to as anxiety. Eventually the overtaxation of mind and body will gradually lead to a breakdown of integrated functioning. The individual is then psychologically and physically sick; the focusing of protracted attention upon the impending danger monopolizes the mental resources, and perpetual readiness of the body results in anxiety and fatigue. Unawareness of other circumstances which might require immediate attention and the inability to mobilize the worn-out body for maximal effort eventually defeat the individual in situations which otherwise he could easily have mastered. Even then, communication is a helpful procedure. The process of talking, though not an act of great physical expenditure for the individual, will absorb the overflow of readiness, and eventually a person is again enabled to find his bearings. This interpersonal process constitutes the core of any type of psychotherapy.

The human being's need for social action is the moving force which compels him to master the tools of communication. Without these his ability to gather information is imperiled and gratification of vital needs is threatened. The superiority of a person within his group is determined in the first instance by skillful use of his means of communication; to receive information and to give that which others need, to possess a workable concept of events, and to act accordingly, marks the successful man.

Virginia Satir
Communication:
A Verbal and Nonverbal Process
of Making Requests
of the Receiver

1. When judging whether a communication is clear, one must
   also remember that people communicate in a variety of
   ways in addition to using words.
   a. A person simultaneously communicates by his gestures,
      facial expression, body posture and movement, tone of
      voice, and even by the way he is dressed.
   b. And all this communication occurs within a context.
      When does it take place? Where? With whom? Under
      what circumstances? What is the contract between the
      persons carrying on the interchange?
2. Because of all these factors, communication is a complex
   business. The receiver must assess all the different ways in
   which the sender is sending messages, as well as being
   aware of his own receiving system, that is, his own interpretation system.
   a. When A talks, B assesses the verbal meaning of A's mes-
      sage.
   b. He also listens to the tone of voice in which A speaks.
   c. He also watches what A does; he notes the "body lan-
      guage" and facial expressions which accompany A's
      message.
   d. He also assesses what A is saying within a social con-
      text. The context may be how B has seen A respond to

Reprinted by permission of the author and the publisher from Virginia
Satir, *Conjoint Family Therapy*, rev. ed., Palo Alto, Calif.: Science and Behavior
Books, 1967, pp. 75–90.

him and to others in the past. It may also be B's expectations about what the requirements of the situation are.

e. In other words, the receiver (B) is busy assessing both the verbal and the nonverbal content of A's message so that he can come to some judgment about what A meant by his communication.

3. What A meant by his communication can be said to have at least two levels:

a. *The denotative level:* the literal content.

b. *The metacommunicative level:* a comment on the literal content as well as on the nature of the relationship between the persons involved.

4. Animals other than man can send metacommunications. For example, as Gregory Bateson describes it:

a. Cats may go through all their battery of fighting motions yet at the same time withhold their claws.

b. By this metacommunication the cat clues other cats as well as people to the fact that he is not "really" fighting; he is playing at fighting. (1)

5. Metacommunications is a message *about* a message.

a. It conveys the sender's attitude toward the message he just sent: "The message I sent was a friendly one."

b. It conveys the sender's attitude toward himself: "I am a friendly person."

c. It conveys the sender's attitude, feelings, intentions toward the receiver: "I see you as someone to be friendly with."

6. Humans are especially versatile at metacommunication.

a. Humans, like other animals, can send nonverbal metacommunications. But the variety of these is wide; humans can frown, grimace, smile, stiffen, slump. And the context in which humans communicate is, itself, one way of communicating.

b. As a matter of fact, humans cannot communicate without, at the same time, metacommunicating. Humans cannot *not* metacommunicate.

c. Humans can also send verbal metacommunications. They can verbally explain their message-sending.

7. When a person verbally explains his message-sending, he is thus denotatively speaking at a metacommunicative level. And these verbal metacommunications are, themselves, at various abstraction levels.

   a. A person can label what kind of message he sent telling the receiver how seriously he wishes him to receive it and how he should respond to it. He can say:

   "It was a joke." (laugh at it)

   "It was just a passing remark." (ignore it)

   "It was a question." (answer it)

   "It was a request." (consider it)

   "It was an order." (obey it)

   b. He can say why he sent the message, by referring to what the other did.

   "You hit me. So I hit you back."

   "You were kind to me. I was returning the favor."

   c. He can say why he sent the message, by referring to what he thinks the other's wishes, feelings, intentions toward him are.

   "I thought you were mad and were going to hurt me."

   "I thought you were tired and wanted me to help you."

   "I thought you were discouraged and wanted me to reassure you."

   d. He can say why he sent the message by referring to a request made by the other:

   "You were ordering me to do something, and I don't take orders."

   "You were requesting something from me, and I was considering it."

   e. He can say why he sent the message by referring to the kind of response which he was trying to elicit from the other:

   "I was trying to get your goat."

   "I was trying to get you to love me."

   "I was trying to get you to talk."

   "I was trying to make you laugh."

   "I was trying to get you to agree with me."

   f. He can say why he sent the message by specifically referring to what he was trying to get the other to do or say or *not* do and *not* say:

   "I wanted you to go to the store for me."

   "I was asking you to phone her for me."

   "I was asking you to leave the room."

   "I didn't want you to tell her about my illness."

   "I wanted you to tell him that I was home."

8. Since humans can "metacommunicate" both verbally and nonverbally, they can give the receiver quite an assortment of messages to sort and weigh, as he tries to figure out what is meant by the communication.

   a. Perhaps A makes the following denotative statement: "The dog is on the couch."

   b. He automatically comments, nonverbally, on this statement, by the irritable tone in which he makes it.

   c. He can then verbally explain what he meant by what he said. Out of the welter of choices, he may say: "I wanted you to take the dog off the couch."

9. The receiver of these messages (B) must balance what A said, with how he said it, with what he then said about it.

   a. B balances the nonverbal and the verbal metacommunications (within the context) and compares them to the denotative statement.

   b. If they are all congruent (seem to jibe with each other) he has little difficulty in deciding that A meant what he said he meant.

   c: Whether or not they jibe, he will attend more to the nonverbal metacommunications and to context than he will to the verbal metacommunications. For one thing, the nonverbal is a less clear or explicit communication, so it requires greater attention.

10. Whenever a person communicates he is not only making a statement, he is also asking something of the receiver and trying to influence the receiver to give him what he wants. This is the "command aspect" of a message. Such requests, however, may have various degrees of explicitness and intensity.

    a. The sender may be simply asking the receiver to show, by response, that his message was heard: "Just listen to me."

    b. Or he may be asking for a specific kind of response: "Tell me where the store is" or, "Go to the store for me."

11. The receiver, in turn, must respond, because people cannot *not* communicate.

    a. Even if the receiver remains silent, he is still communicating.

    b. And, incidentally, symptoms are one way of communicating in a nonverbal way.

12. But even though all messages have requests in them, they are not always expressed verbally. Thus, the receiver must rely on metacommunications for his clues as to what the sender wants. He asks himself:

    a. What is the sender verbally saying?

    b. What, specifically is he requesting? Is the request fully expressed at the denotative level?

    c. If not, perhaps the way in which he communicates and the context in which he is communicating will give me clues to what he is asking of me.

13. If the communication, or message, and the metacommunication or meta-message do not fit, the receiver must somehow translate this into a single message. In order to do this satisfactorily he needs to be able to comment on the presence of the discrepancy. Let us take a trivial example. A husband who is working on a household fixture says, in an irritable tone, "Damn it, the fixture broke!" The wife, in this relationship, may go through the following process (with greater agility and speed, of course, than the snail's pace described here):

    a. He is telling me about the condition of the electrical fixture he is working on.

    b. But he is doing more than that. He is telling me that he is irritated. His "Damn it," along with his tone, helps me decide this.

    c. Is he criticizing me? Is he telling me that I am responsible for the condition of the fixture?

    d. If he is criticizing me, what does he want me to do? Take over the job for him? Apologize? Or what?

    e. Or is he criticizing himself, irritated that he is having a frustrating time with the job, and that he only has himself to blame for the fact that the fixture broke?

    f. If he is primarily criticizing himself, what is he asking me to do? Sympathize with him? Listen to him? Or what?

    g. I know, from living with him, that he prides himself on his tool dexterity and that he considers electrical maintenance his special forte. Evidently, his view of himself is being put to the test. So he must be criticizing himself. And he must primarily be asking me to sympathize with him.

    h. But sympathize *how?* Does he want me to help him with the job, bring him coffee, or what? What behavior on my part that he could see and hear would mean to him that I am sympathizing with him?

14. Let us take another example. A husband says, in an irritable tone, "The dog is on the couch." The wife, in this relationship, may go through the following process:

    a. He is telling me where the dog is.

    b. But he is doing more than that. He sounds irritated.

    c. Why is he telling me about his irritation? Is he criticizing me for the fact that the dog is on the couch?

    d. If he is not criticizing me, what does he want me to do? Just listen to him? Sympathize with his irritation? Take the dog off the couch? Or what?

    e. I wanted a dog. He didn't. I went ahead and got one without his agreement. Now, when he shows his irritation at the dog, he is complaining about what I did. He is criticizing me for disobeying him. He undoubtedly wants me to take the dog off the couch, but does he also want me to get rid of the dog and apologize to him for going against his wishes

15. Let us return to the first example. Instead of saying, "Damn it, the fixture broke," the husband could say, "Damn it, I'm having a hard time with this job. Bring me a cup of

coffee." The wife, in this case, would have little trouble assessing his message. He would be telling her overtly what he wanted from her and why. In other words, his request that she sympathize with him by bringing coffee would be clear.

16. In the second example, instead of saying, "The dog is on the couch," the husband could say, "Take the dog off the couch and get rid of him. You never should have bought a dog. I told you I didn't want one." The wife in this case would have little trouble assessing his message.
   a. He would be telling her specifically what he wanted from her and why. In other words, his request that she agree to obey him would be clear.
   b. In both cases, the wife is still in the position of deciding whether or not to agree to her husband's request that she obey him. But at least she is in no doubt about what it really is that her husband wants of her.

17. In other words, the request, which is part of every message, may or may not be expressed denotatively. And there are degrees to which requests can be spelled out denotatively.
   a. "Damn it, the fixture broke," and "The dog is on the couch," are very indirect requests, requests not expressed at the denotative level.
   b. "Bring me a cup of coffee," and "Take the dog off the couch and get rid of him," are direct requests, requests expressed at the denotative level.
   c. Or, if these specific requests had been expressed at a more abstract level, they would also be direct: "Sympathize with me" or, "Do what I want."

18. However, all messages, when viewed at their highest abstraction level can be characterized as "Validate me" messages. These are frequently interpreted as "Agree with me," "Be on my side," "Validate me by sympathizing with me," or "Validate me by showing me you value me and my ideas."

19. When people communicate, they rarely go around verbally requesting that others agree with them or requesting that

others want what they want. They don't, because they are forced by the wish to be valued, and by the wish for co-operation, to persuade or at least try to elicit the wished-for response. Many persons feel embarrassed about their wish to get validation from outside themselves.

a. As I have said, communication is a necessarily incomplete process. But we can now see why this process becomes even more incomplete than pure logic or inadequacy of words would dictate.

b. Incomplete (indirect) communication can serve many interpersonal purposes which are not necessarily dysfunctional.

—It can help camouflage such requests.

—It can prevent embarrassment in case one's requests (of any kind) are refused.

20. Up to now, I have been discussing the problems posed for human receivers by the complexity and the incompleteness of human communication.

a. Just because this communication *is* complex and incomplete to differing degrees, all receivers are required to fill in or complete the sender's message by clairvoyance or guesswork.

b. Receivers can and do achieve this, sometimes with amazing accuracy, considering all the fancy footwork they have to go through.

c. But there are times when even the most clairvoyant of receivers guesses incorrectly. When this happens, the sender's next message usually lets him know his error.

21. The messages I have listed in this chapter have all been relatively *congruent* within the context; they have jibed with each other.

a. A congruent communication is one where two or more messages are sent via different levels but none of these messages seriously contradicts any other. For example, the huband says, "The dog is on the couch," in an irritable tone, in a context which tells the wife that he is irritated and why he is irritated.

b. An incongruent communication is one where two or

more messages, sent via different levels, seriously do contradict each other. One level of communication is context itself. For example, the husband says, in a delighted tone, that the dog is on the couch, but from the context the wife knows that he hates dogs; whether they are on couches or anywhere else.

22. Simple contradictory communication is where two or more messages are sent in a sequence via the same communication level and oppose each other.

   a. Perhaps A says the following:
   > "Come here. . . . No, go away."
   > "I love you. . . . No, I hate you."
   > "I'm happy. . . . No, I'm sad."
   > "My wife is tall. . . . No, my wife is short."

   b. Perhaps A does the following:
   —Pushes B away. Pulls B back.
   —Buys a ticket to the movie, but doesn't go see it.
   —Puts his coat on, then takes it off.

23. But such simple contradictions cannot occur without some accompanying metacommunication, since one cannot *not* metacommunicate.

   a. Although the self-contradictions listed above are relatively clear, they are also accompanied by smiles or frowns or tone of voice, and in a context.

   b. When contradictions occur between different levels of communication, they become *incongruent.**

24. Messages differ in the degree to which they are incongruent. Relatively simple incongruent communication sounds and looks like this:

   a. A says, "It's cold in here," and takes off his coat.
   b. A says, "I hate you," and smiles.
   c. A wears an evening dress to a funeral.
   d. A wears tennis shoes to a board of directors' meeting.
   e. A says, "Come closer, darling," and then stiffens.

25. Incongruent communication can become even more so

---

*"Incongruent" refers to a discrepancy between the report and the command aspects of a message; for the system for analyzing this devised by Bateson, Jackson, Haley and Weakland, see 2, 4, 5, 6, in the bibliography.

when the sender's nonverbal metacommunication does not jibe with his verbal metacommunication.

a. The sender may say "Come closer, darling," then stiffen, and then say, "I want to make love."

—In this case, should the receiver respond to the sender's denotative statement ("Come closer, darling.")?

—Or should he respond to the sender's nonverbal statement (the stiffness)?

—Or should he respond to the sender's words explaining his intentions ("I want to make love.")?

—This is called being presented with a double-level message.

b. As usual, the receiver relies heavily on context, and on the nonverbal signals to help him in his clairvoyance process. In this case, the nonverbal signals and the context contradict each other. But, being an especially trusting and courageous receiver, he says to himself:

"Let's see. The sender and I are courting. Yet other people are around.

"I have learned from past experience with the sender that she is nervous about showing amorous feelings publicly. But that doesn't mean she doesn't have amorous feelings toward me.

"I will live dangerously and ignore her nonverbal metacommunication in this case. I will rely on context alone and accept her verbally-stated intention.

"In other words, her verbal statement 'I want to make love' carries greater weight with me. All I do is add to it the proviso which she did not add: '. . . but other people are around, so I am just nervous.' In other words, the sender is willing to be nervous, with a little assistance."

c. The freedom to comment and question immediately takes the receiver out of the clairvoyant dilemma. When this freedom is not present, the chances for misunderstanding are great. In the case of a child, as we have seen, there is a likelihood that such messages will be built up to the point where a "double bind" occurs.

26. Incongruent communication like that just described puts an extra burden on the receiver. But, whether or not the sender's message is incongruent, the receiver can still go through various checking-out procedures in order to find out what is being reported, what requested, and why.

    a. For example, when the wife heard her husband say, in an irritable tone, "Damn it, the fixture broke," she could have decided that she still didn't have enough data, even from the content of the message, to find out what her husband was requesting from her and why.

    b. She might have gone to where he was and stood there for a minute, continuing to pick up clues from him.

      —If she had done this, she would, of course, have been communicating with him. By her presence she would be saying: "I heard you. I am attending."

      —He would also continue to communicate with her, as he jabbed at the fixture, grunted, sighed, etc.

    c. The wife might then have asked, "Is there anything I can do?"

      —The minute she did this, she would be asking her husband to be specific in what he was requesting.

      —Perhaps he would have said, "No, I just have to work it out."

      —By this response, the wife would have succeeded in narrowing her unknowns. She would now be more certain that he was distressed with himself but she still could not be sure what he specifically wanted from her. Did he want her to listen? Attend? Sympathize?

    d. The wife might go on to ask, "Would you like a cup of coffee" And he might answer, "Yes, damn it, I would." The communication sequence would now be relatively closed or complete. (Of course, it is more complete if she actually brings the coffee!)

27. If, instead, the wife had been fairly confident about her clairvoyance, she might have simply assumed that she knew what his implied request was. She might have put it in words herself and seen how he responded.

    a. She could have asked outright, "Would you like a cup

of coffee?" and he might have said, "Yes, damn it, I would." If she had guessed correctly enough, the sequence would have been relatively closed.

b. But he might have said, "Hell, no, what would I want coffee for, at a time like this?" Then she would have known that her clairvoyance process wasn't working very well. She would have been required to check out further, perhaps by going through the clue-getting procedures already described.

28. Receivers vary in their ability to perceive the needs and wishes of others.

a. Although all receivers put great weight on the metacommunicative aspects, they vary in their ability to assess what the sender is asking of them.

   —The wife may mistake her husband's irritation with himself for a criticism of her, and end up trying to take over the job for him instead of sympathizing with him.

   —The wife may mistake her husband's criticism of her for irritation over the specific behavior of the dog, and end up trying to sympathize with him instead of taking the dog off the couch or getting rid of the dog.

   —The lover, in the third example, may mistake the woman's stiffening for distaste, and end up rejecting her instead of making love.

b. We even have psychiatric labels for people who are not able to accurately weigh a message for its meaning. They are not able to guess attitudes, intentions, feelings (as expressed in metacommunication) accurately.

c. If this wife, in all contexts, in all relationships, and at all times within a relationship, decides that senders are criticizing her or praising her, we would readily label her paranoid or egocentric.

d. Also, although receivers put great weight on the metacommunicative aspects to help tell them what the sender is requesting, they vary in their ability to attend to denotation in spite of, or along with, metacommunication. For example, perhaps a person attends a lecture for the purpose of receiving denotative content from the speaker. But perhaps the speaker speaks in such a frightened tone that the receiver cannot hear what the speaker is saying because he is so concerned about the speaker's fright.

29. Senders vary in their ability to send clear requests, so that the receiver has to guess as little as possible.

    a. For example, let us say that a wife wants to see a movie with her husband. If she communicates in a functional way, she might say, "Let's see a movie," or, more overtly, "I would like to see a movie with you."

    b. But, if she communicates in a dysfunctional way, she might say any of the following things:

        "It would do you good to see a movie."

        "You would like to see a movie, *wouldn't* you."

        "If you want to see a movie, we'll see one."

        "We might as well see a movie. It's Saturday night."

        "There's a new movie house down the street."

        "My voices are ordering me to see a movie."

30. These are some of the covert ways in which this wife can request something from her husband without acknowledging that she is making a request.

    a. She does not clearly label her wish which is behind her request, as *her* wish.

    b. Or, she may fail to label her wish *as a wish*. It becomes not a wish but a "must," something one is commanded to do. (The commander may be the other person or people in general, or "one's duty" or "voices" or something foreign inside of the self.)

    c. Or, she may label her wish as not a wish but as "the lesser of two evils."

31. The husband, in this case, could do some checking out. He could say: "Do *you* want to see a movie?" or "Do you want to see a movie *with me?*"

    a. But here is what can happen if the husband does ask his wife what she meant by her communication. She might go on to explain her message in any one of the following statements:

"No, I thought *you* wanted to go."

"No, I just thought we *should*."

"No, I don't necesarily want to go. I want to do what you want."

"There are times when I want to see a movie, but this isn't one of them."

"I don't particularly want to go. My voices are ordering me."

32. By denying that she had a wish, the wife is also denying that her wish was expressed toward her husband. She denies that she has made a request of him. If he pursues his questions, she may go on to deny further.

"You can go or not. I don't care."

"If you want to be a stay-at-home, that's your business."

"If you go to the movies, you go to the movies."

"Nobody asked you to go. If you want to go, then go."

33. The wife, when replying to her husband's request (in this case, a request to clarify), denies any or all parts of her message.

a. The Bateson group, and Jay Haley, in particular, has defined four parts of every message:

—I (the sender)

—am saying something (message)

—to you (the receiver)

—in this situation (context). (3)

b. All messages are requests, yet the wife may deny this, in so many words, by saying:

"I didn't care one way or the other." (*I* didn't request. anything.)

"I just threw out a suggestion for whatever it was worth." (I didn't *request* anything.)

"Whether or not you go to the movies is immaterial to me." (I didn't request anything *of you*.)

"At one time, I might have wanted to go with you. But I know better now." (I didn't request anything of you *just now*.)

34. We note how defensive the wife is, as she sends her highly incomplete message. (These messages are incomplete because they do not clearly label *"I, want this, from you, in this situation."*) She makes it hard for her husband to find out what she wants.

   a. She covers herself as she sends her request, almost as though she anticipated refusal.

   "Voices are ordering me. . ."

   "I am doing this for you. . ."

   "There's a new movie house down the street."

   b. She covers herself after she is asked to clarify: "I thought *you* wanted me to go," or, "Nobody asked you to go."

35. We also note how offensive the wife is, as she sends her request and responds to requests to clarify. She makes it hard for her husband to want to do what she wants.

   a. She disparages him in anticipation of refusal:

   "A person should see a movie at least once a month if he professes to be cultured."

   "We might as well see a movie. I'm bored."

   b. She disparages him after he asks her to clarify (and this very disparagement reveals her disappointment over the fact that he does not seem influenceable):

   "I can't *make* you do anything."

   "You'll do exactly what you *feel* like doing."

   "Ask anything of you? I know better!"

36. One could decide, on first thought, that this wife is a dysfunctional communicator and that she puts unnecessary burdens on her functional husband who, in this case, tries to check out the meaning of her message.

   a. But when people communicate, they are sending a message to a receiver.

   b. The wife tailors her message to the way she thinks her husband will respond to it.

   c. Once we note how he does respond to her, we will see that her messages are tailored to a kind of response which she has learned to expect from her husband.

   d. Her husband, in his response, does the same.

37. One cannot view messages separate from interaction, as I have been doing, and receive the full picture.
    a. One must at least note what A says, how B responds, how A responds to B's response. Communication is a two-sided affair; senders are receivers, receivers are also senders.
    b. One must note whether or not these interaction sequences repeat themselves over time and in different content areas.
    c. If they do repeat themselves, these sequences represent how these two people characteristically communicate with one another.
38. However, before analyzing interaction, one can profit from analyzing isolated messages. Such an analysis:
    a. Highlights different principles about messages and message-sending.
    b. Highlights the kind of problems which highly defensive communication poses for the receiver.
    c. Helps document inferences about what inner wishes and fears dictate and how they perpetuate dysfunctional communication.
39. This husband's communication does have something to do with the wife's characteristic way of asking for something from him.
    a. But even before analyzing this, we can guess that this wife fears that her husband will reject her request.
    b. Behind her denials that she has a wish and has made a request, is the wish that her husband would not only want to go to the movies with her, but would want to do what she wants because he loves her: "You'll do what you *feel* like doing."
    c. She is not unusual in having this want. But if she cannot come to terms with it, she can easily trap herself and husband in an impossible dilemma.
       —No two people think alike on everything.
       —No two people feel the same way at all times within a relationship.

—No two people want the same things or want them at the same time. People operate from different time-tables.

—We are, in fact, autonomous, different, and unique beings.

—Yet we are, at the same time, dependent on others. We need them to help us get many of the things we want (or not prevent us from getting them). We are also dependent on others to validate our existence and worth.

40. Therefore, even though people are making requests of others when they communicate, there are some things that cannot be requested. Yet these are the very things people also want.

   a. We cannot ask that others feel as we do or as we want them to. As Bateson and Watzlawick have pointed out, feelings are spontaneous; they are not subject to self-request or to the requests of others. (1, 7)

      —All we can do is try to elicit feelings.

      —Failing to elicit, we can accept our disappointment and try again.

   b. We cannot ask that others think as we do. Thoughts are not subject to the requests of others.

      —All we can do is try to persuade others, and present our arguments in the clearest, most cogent form possible.

      —Failing to persuade, we can accept our disappointment and compromise, or "agree to disagree."

   c. We can, of course, *demand* that others say or do (or not say or not do) what we want. But if we succeed in this, our success will be questionable.

      —We shall have validated our power but not our lovability or worth, since we have "had to ask."

      —Also, since such a tactic challenges the other's autonomy, it is likely that he will feel devalued and will devalue back.

41. Evidently man is insatiable. He can never be loved enough,

valued enough. Yet he can never be safe enough, powerful enough.

a. These two wants are contradictory if viewed on the same continuum. Man seems to have a built-in potential for defeating himself.

—If he sees these two wants as an either/or proposition, he puts them in conflict with each other and loses out on both.

—If he allows them to coexist, each in its proper time and place, he will not only gain both, but will find that each enhances the other.

b. The way he communicates with other persons will take its form from whichever of these two approaches he adopts.

—If he takes the first approach, it indicates that he will handle the different-ness of others in terms of *war* and *who is right*.

—If he takes the second, he will handle different-ness on the basis of *exploration* and *what fits*.

—The former leads to stalemating, retardation and pathology.

—The latter leads to growth, individuality and creativity.

Bibliography

1. Bateson, G., "A Theory of Play and Fantasy," *Psychiat. Res. Rep.*, 2:39–51, 1955.

2. Bateson, G., D. D. Jackson, J. Haley, and J. H. Weakland, "Toward a Theory of Schizophrenia," *Behav. Sci.*, 1:251–264, 1956.

3. Haley, J., "The Family of the Schizophrenic: A Model System," *J. Nerv. Ment. Dis.*, 129:357–374, 1959.

4. Haley, J., "Control in the Psychotherapy of Schizophrenics," *Arch. Gen. Psychiat.*, 5:340–353, 1961.

5. Jackson, D. D., "Family Interaction, Family Homeostasis, and Some Implications for Conjoint Family Psychotherapy." In J. Masserman (Ed.), *Individual and Familiar Dynamics.* New York, Grune and Stratton, 1959.

6. Jackson, D. D., J. Riskin, and V. M. Satir, "A Method Analysis of a Family Interview," *Arch. Gen. Psychiat.*, 5:321–329, 1961.

7. Watzlawick, P. *An Anthology of Human Communication.* Palo Alto, Calif., Science and Behavior Books, 1963.

Dean C. Barnlund
Toward a Meaning-Centered Philosophy of Communication

Aim of Communication

We begin by asking why men communicate? What human need does it, or should it, satisfy? While there is almost universal agreement that communication is tied to the manipulation of symbols, there is widespread disagreement as to what constitutes effectiveness in this endeavor. A brief review of some abortive explanations of communication is essential because, in spite of repeated criticism, these conceptions continue to influence current training in speech.

One of these theories is that the aim of communication is to transmit information. Success hinges on mastery of the facts, effective arrangement of materials and strength of expression. It is a message-centered philosophy of communication. And it is largely amoral. Critical standards for determining the effectiveness of communication, as in the critical evaluation of literature, are internal; they are found within the message itself. When a writer or speaker or critic asks, "Was it well said?" he is usually viewing communication as a mode of expression. The training in communication that follows from this premise and perspective is destined to be truncated and unrealistic. Talk is not a guarantee of communication. Facts and

Reprinted by permission of the author and the publisher from Dean C. Barnlund, "Toward a Meaning-Centered Philosophy of Communication," *Journal of Communication, 11* (1962), pp. 198—202. This paper was presented originally at the SAA Convention in New York in 1961 under the title "A Philosophy of Communication Training."

ideas are not shared because they are articulated loudly or even well. Messages do not influence automatically because of being broadcast on the mass media. The inadequacy of this approach lies in its neglect of the listener as terminus of the communicative act, in its failure to provide an explanation of how meaning arises through communication and in its disregard for all but public and continuous discourse.

A second theory is that the aim of communication is to transfer ideas from one person to another. Here the listener is admitted as part of the communicative situation. The focus, however, in research and training, is upon the message formulator. Effectiveness in communication is thought to turn not only on the content and phrasing of the message, but on the intelligence and credibility of the source. Relatively little attention is paid to the listener other than to note that messages should be adapted to his interests. It ends by becoming a speaker-centered philosophy. Communicative events are explained largely in terms of the experiential milieu that shaped the mind of the speaker and find expression in his messages.

As an explanation of communication it, too, fails in several important respects. First, the listener tends to be regarded as a passive object, rather than an active force in communication. Unfortunately, it is not that simple to deposit ideas in another mind. Teachers of great intelligence and high purpose often find their lessons disregarded or misapplied. Messages flowing through an industrial complex are not received undistorted like images in a hall of mirrors. Second, this approach also fails to provide a satisfactory theory of meaning, and of how messages from highly credible sources can provoke so many and such contradictory meanings. Finally, it is too parochial. It neglects man's communication with himself—an area that is fast becoming one of the most vital in communication research—and it fails to account for the fact that communication is as often a matter of hiding or protecting what is in men's minds as it is a matter of revealing their thoughts and intentions.

Neither of these schools of thought, of course, omits the constituent elements in communication altogether. It is, rather, a question of emphasis. Questions of emphasis, however, are not irrelevant or inconsequential in establishing a productive orientation for a discipline. The pedagogical consequences of both of these approaches is to place a disproportionate emphasis (in research, courses and textbooks) on the source and message elements in communication. Both schools of thought tend, also, to minimize or overlook completely, the interactive and dynamic nature of the communicative process.

Communication, as I conceive it, is a word that describes the process of creating a meaning. Two words in this sentence are critical. They are "create" and "meaning." Messages may be generated from the outside—by a speaker, a television screen, a scolding parent—but meanings are generated from within. This position parallels that of Berlo when he writes, "Communication does not consist of the transmission of meaning. Meanings are not transmitted, nor transferable. Only messages are transmittable, and meanings are not in the message, they are in the message-user."[1] Communication is man's attempt to cope with his experience, his current mood, his emerging needs. For every person it is a unique act of creation involving dissimilar materials. But it is, within broad limits, assumed to be predictable or there could be no theory of communication.

The second, and more troublesome word, is "meaning." Meaning is not apparent in the ordinary flow of sensation. We are born into, and inhabit a world without "meaning." That life becomes intelligible to us—full of beauty or ugliness, hope or despair—is because it is assigned that significance by the experiencing being. As Karl Britton put it, "A world without minds is a world without structure, without relations, without facts."[2] Sensations do not come to us, sorted and labeled, as if we were visitors in a vast, but ordered, museum. Each of us, instead, is his own curator. We learn to look with a selective eye, to classify, to assign significance.

Communication arises out of the need to reduce uncertainty,

[1] David Berlo, *The Process of Communication* (New York: Holt, Rinehart, Winston, 1960), p. 175.
[2] Karl Britton, *Communication: A Philosophical Study of Language* (New York: Harcourt, Brace, 1939), p. 206.

to act effectively, to defend or strengthen the ego. On some occasions words are used to ward off anxiety. On other occasions they are means of evolving more deeply satisfying ways of expressing ourselves. *The aim of communication is to increase the number and consistency of our meanings within the limits set by patterns of evaluation that have proven successful in the past, our emerging needs and drives, and the demands of the physical and social setting of the moment.* Communication ceases when meanings are adequate; it is initiated as soon as new meanings are required. However, since man is a homeostatic, rather than static, organism, it is impossible for him to discover any permanently satisfying way of relating all his needs; each temporary adjustment is both relieving and disturbing, leading to successively novel ways of relating himself to his environment.

To say that communication occurs whenever meaning is assigned to internal or external stimuli is to enlarge greatly the span of our discipline. Communication, in this sense, may occur while a man waits alone outside a hospital operating room, or watches the New York skyline disappear at dusk. It can take place in the privacy of his study as he introspects about some internal doubt, or contemplates the fading images of a frightening dream. When man discovers meaning in nature, or in insight in his own reflections, he is a communication system unto himself. Festinger refers to this as "consummatory communication." The creation of meanings, however, also goes on in countless social situations where men talk with those who share or dispute their purposes. Messages are exchanged in the hope of altering the attitudes or actions of those around us. This can be characterized as "instrumental communication," as long as we remember that these two purposes are not mutually exclusive.

What I am describing is a meaning-centered philosophy of communication. It admits that meaning in the sender, and the words of the messages are important, but regards as most critical the state of mind, the assumptive world and the needs of the listener or observer. The impact of any message from "See me after class" to "What's good for General Motors is good for the country" is determined by the physical, personal and social context, the most critical ingredient of which is the mind of the interpreter. Communication, so defined, does not require a speaker, a message, or a listener, in the restricted sense in which these terms are used in the field of speech. All may be combined in a single person, and often are.

A theory that leaves out man's communication with himself, his communication with the world about him and a large proportion of his interactions with his fellowman, is not a theory of communication at all, but a theory of speechmaking. Indeed, it seems applicable to speechmaking only in the most formal and restricted sense of that word. There is little in the traditional view of speech that is helpful in the analysis of conversation, interviewing, conflict negotiations, or in the diagnosis of the whole span of communicative disorders and breakdowns that are receiving so much attention currently. Upon so limited a view of communication it is unlikely that there can develop theories of sufficient scope and stature to command the respect of other disciplines or of the larger public that ultimately decides our role in the solution of man's problems. The field of speech seems to be fast approaching what the airlines call a "checkpoint" where one loses the freedom to choose between alternative flight plans, between a limited interest in speechmaking and a broad concern with the total communicative behavior of man. By defining communication operationally, by examining a wider range of communicative acts, the way might be prepared for making the startling theoretical advances that have, so far, not characterized our field.

The Communication Process

A satisfactory philosophy should also provide a starting point for the technical analysis of communication. One way of accomplishing this to to ask what characteristics would have to be built into a scientific model that would represent at the same time and equally well, the entire spectrum from intrapersonal to mass communication. It should not be a model that is mechanically or structurally faithful, but one that is symbolically and functionally similar. Space is too limited here to more than suggest a few of the principles that would have to be reflected in such a model.

1. Communication is not a thing, it is a process. Sender, message and receiver do not remain constant throughout an act of communication. To treat these as static entities, as they often are in our research, is questionable when applied to the most extreme form of continuous discourse, is misleading when used to analyze the episodic verbal exchanges that characterize face-to-face communication, and is totally useless in probing man's communication with himself. Changes in any of these forces, and few forces remain constant very long, reverberate throughout the entire system. Students of communication are not dissecting a cadaver, but are probing the pulsing evolution of meaning in a living organism.

2. Communication is not linear, it is circular. There are many situations in life where a simple, linear, causal analysis is useful. One thing leads to another. A, then B, then C. I push over the first domino and the rest, in turn, topple over. But this sort of thinking is not very helpful, though quite appealing in its simplicity, in studying communication. There is not first a sender, then a message and finally an interpreter. There is, instead, what Henderson calls "mutual dependence" or what I have termed "interdependent functionalism." The words "sender" and "receiver" no longer name the elements in a communicative act, but indicate the point of view of the critic at the moment.

3. Communication is complex. Someone once said that whenever there is communication there are at least six "people" involved: The person you think yourself to be; the man your partner thinks you are; the person you believe your partner thinks you are; plus the three equivalent "persons" at the other end of the circuit. If, with as few as four constants, mathematicians must cope with approximately fifty possible relations, then we, in studying communication, where an even greater number of variables is concerned, ought to ex-

pound with considerable humility. In this age of Freudian and non-Freudian analysts, of information theory specialists, of structural linguists, and so on, we are just beginning to unravel the mysteries of this terribly involved, and therefore fascinating, puzzle.

4. Communication is irreversible and unrepeatable. The distinction being suggested here is between systems that are deterministic and mechanical, and those that are spontaneous and evolutionary. One can start a motor, beat a rug, or return a book. But you cannot start a man thinking, beat your son, or return a compliment with the same consequences. The words of a teacher, even when faithfully repeated, do not produce the same effect, but may lead to new insight, increased tension, or complete boredom. A moment of indifference or interest, a disarming or tangential remark, leave indelible traces.

5. Communication involves the total personality. Despite all efforts to divide body and mind, reason and emotion, thought and action, meanings continue to be generated by the whole organism. This is not to say that some messages do not produce greater or lesser dissonance, or shallower or deeper effects on the personality; it is only to hold that eventually every fact, conclusion, guilt, or enthusiasm must somehow be accommodated by the entire personality. The deeper the involvement produced by any communication, the sooner and more pervasive its effects upon behavior.

Research or instruction that disregards these characteristics of the communicative act would appear both unsound and of dubious value.

The Moral Dimension

The perennial and legitimate concern with ethics in the field of speech arises out of the inherent moral aspect of every interpersonal communication. As was noted earlier, the aim of communication is to transform chaotic sense impressions into some sort of coherent, intelligible and useful relationship. When men do this privately, either in confronting nature or in assessing their own impulses, they are free to invent whatever meaning they can. But when men encounter each other, a moral issue invades every exchange because the manipulation of symbols always involves a purpose that is external to, and in some degree manipulative of, the interpreter of the message. The complexity of communication makes it difficult to know in advance, and with certainty, the impact of any bundle of words upon the receiver of them. The irreversibility of communication means that whatever meaning is provoked by a message cannot be annulled. A teacher may erase a blackboard, a colleague apologize, or an employer change his mind, but there is no way of erasing the effect of a threatening ultimatum, a bitter remark, or a crushing personal evaluation.

Meaning, in my opinion, is a private preserve and trespassers always run a risk. To speak of personal integrity at all is to acknowledge this. Any exchange of words is an invasion of the privacy of the listener which is aimed at preventing, restricting, or stimulating the cultivation of meaning. Briefly, three types of interference may be distinguished. First, there are messages whose intent is to coerce. Meaning is controlled by choosing symbols that so threaten the interpreter that he becomes incapable of, and blind to, alternative meanings; second, there are messages of an exploitative sort in which words are arranged to filter the information, narrow the choices, obscure the consequences, so that only one meaning becomes attractive or appropriate; third, there is facilitative communication in which words are used to inform, to enlarge perspective, to deepen sensitivity, to remove external threat, to encourage independence of meaning. The values of the listener are, in the first case, ignored, in the second, subverted, in the third, respected. While some qualification of this principle is needed, it appears that only facilitative communication is entirely consistent with the protection and improvement of man's symbolic experience. Unless a teacher is aware of these possibilities and appreciates the differences in these kinds of communication, it is unlikely that he will communicate responsibly in the classroom.

Questions
for
Reflection
and
Discussion
Section One

1. Why does Ruesch place special emphasis upon specific social situations in communication?
2. What factors does Ruesch consider significant components of the communication act? What are the physiological considerations in human communication?
3. Why is the metacommunicative level of meaning critical in interpersonal relations?
4. Is Satir's view of communication more restrictive than Ruesch's view?
5. Compare and contrast a "speaker-centered" philosophy of communication with the "meaning-centered" view of Barnlund.
6. What concerns are shared by Ruesch, Satir, and Barnlund? Do you feel that any portions of the articles are "at odds" with others?

THE
INTERPERSONAL
IMPERATIVE
SECTION TWO

It is our carefully considered and deliberately chosen position that an individual has personal needs within himself that can only be satisfied by interaction with other people. It appears that people—all people—are born with these needs.

The basic interactional needs apparently are: (1) to be able to show interest in others and to have others show interest in us; (2) to show respect for the competence and responsibility of others and to have others show respect for our competence and sense of responsibility; and (3) to be able to show warmth or affection for *at least one* other person and to have *at least one* other person show warmth or affection for us.

The satisfaction of these basic needs is imperative for human growth and development. When one or another of these needs remains significantly unsatisfied, a certain amount of anxiety is generated. This degree of personal anxiety is an index of a person's condition of mental health. Continued lack of satisfaction of these basic needs can produce mental illness and eventually psychological or physical death of the individual. To some extent, and in certain ways, these needs may be met by communication which is not interpersonal—aged people and those who are ill, for example, can meet these needs, in part, by watching television. However, ultimately and inevitably these needs can be met completely only by direct interpersonal communication.

A secondary interactional need is to negotiate with others on a contractual basis wherein we offer our assistance to others when they need it, in return for which we may obtain their assistance when we need it. Our American culture places special emphasis on this process. Almost daily we go shopping in the interactional marketplace in order to satisfy this interpersonal need. Our complex and specialized society makes this need imperative.

The first article in this section is a summary of theoretical essays and research which supports the precept that human interaction is necessary for the growth and development of the individual. Since this article was written (1967), Heider has obtained additional data tending to show that communication suppression is related to inadequate social development.[1]

The second article, "Interpersonal Needs," presents Schutz's theory of fundamental interpersonal relations orientations; it is an analysis of the individual's needs that must be satisfied by interaction with other people. These basic needs are identified as *inclusion, control,* and *affection.* A case is made for the proposition that these needs, as described, constitute a conceptual system that is helpful in the prediction and explanation of interpersonal behavior.

In the third selection, Berlo identifies interaction as the primary goal of interpersonal communication. This interaction is viewed as interdependent: a person *acts* (communicates), and another person *reacts;* in turn, the first person also then reacts. This interaction (or perhaps *inter-reaction*) is viewed as the primary goal of the communication process. As we *react,* we tell the other person both something about ourselves and something of our view of him. Through this feedback process we come to know ourselves as well as others. When we respond to such new information, we grow and develop, thus satisfying a deep personal need. The readings in this section show how interpersonal communication meets our needs on the intrapersonal, interpersonal, and interactional levels.

[1] Heider, Mary (1968). "An Investigation of the Relationship between Speech Anxiety in Adults and Their Indication of Parental Suppression of Communication in Childhood," Unpublished M.A. Thesis, University of Kansas.

Kim Giffin and
Mary Heider
**The Relationship Between
Speech Anxiety and the Suppression of
Communication in Childhood**

The exploration of factors producing speech anxiety generally has been neglected in communication research; yet programs for its alleviation cannot offer effective and lasting results until basic causal factors have been determined. While there is a strong likelihood of multifaceted etiology, this paper aims to establish a theoretical basis for one possible cause for a lack of speaker confidence: parental suppression of a child's communication. Here we are speaking primarily of verbal communication.

The Role of Communication in Child Development

A child relates to the world through interpersonal communication. His communication allows perception and reception of the world around him; it also is his means for revealing himself to the world.

The significance of early communication is evident in the widely accepted view that a child's basic personality, which remains an intrinsic part of his adult self, is formed early in a child's life. Eric Erikson (1963), Gordon Allport (1955), and Eric Berne (1964) believe that an individual's mental attitude toward himself and his world is taken and fixed as early as one or two

Reprinted by permission of the authors and the publisher from Kim Giffin and Mary Heider, "The Relationship between Speech Anxiety and the Suppression of Communication in Childhood," *The Psychiatric Quarterly Supplement,* Part 2, 1967, Utica, N.Y., State Hospitals Press.

years of age, and at least by age seven. Berne maintains that the type of childhood a person has had can easily be determined from his mental attitude. Allport (1955) holds that a child's character and mental health depend to a considerable degree upon his early childhood relationships, particularly with his mother (p. 31).

The healthy development of a child rests upon early experiences in communication. Specifically, the maturity level which a child can possibly reach is limited by his communication in the formative years; in addition, the self-concept of the child is shaped during this time.

Maturity development can be viewed as the formation of a series of personality characteristics, with the establishment of two in particular which are necessary for successful development of all the others. These two traits—trust and initiative—are developed in early relationships.

Communication and Trust Formation

In their theories of child and personality development, Erik Erikson (1963), Abraham Maslow (1962), and J. Church and L. J. Stone (1957) postulate the development of a basic attitude of trust within a child as the first necessary step toward the development of a mature person. An infant's orientation toward the world is gained through the way in which his needs are met. If his desires and needs are fulfilled, he finds the world a reliable, stable, good place which can be trusted and relied upon to fulfill his needs (Church and Stone, 1957, p. 58). To Erikson (1963, p. 248), basic trust

implies not only that one has learned to rely on the sameness and continuity of the outer providers, but also that one may trust oneself and the capacity of one's own organs to cope with urges; and that one is able to consider oneself trustworthy enough so that the providers will not need to be on guard lest they be nipped.

Maslow (1962) sees the development of a child as a never-ending process of choosing between the need for safety and the delight of new experiences which lead toward change and growth. When the delights of change do not jeopardize the infant's need for safety, he chooses the delights of change and moves forward; this is the basis of Maslow's "growth-through-delight" concept of child development (p. 45).

The love and approval of others is vital to an infant; he must rely upon his parents (or substitutes) not only for physical security, but also for emotional security. Consequently, when a child is forced to choose between two clear-cut alternatives—new experiences involving self-trust and safety resting upon the approval of others—need for safety remains dominant over need for change. He will choose the approval of others and be forced to repress or ignore his delight motives, let them die, or control them consciously. Thus, according to Maslow, his spontaneous wishes and delights will be cut off when he cannot risk loss of parental love and approval (p. 49). Growth through change requires trust in oneself as well as trust in others.

The child development theories of Erickson, Allport, and Church and Stone start with a foundation of basic trust. Maslow's "growth-through-delight" notion involves interpersonal and intrapersonal trust. Here we are dealing with trust as conceptualized by Giffin (1967, p. 105): ". . . reliance upon the characteristics of an object, or the occurrence of an event, or the behavior of a person in order to achieve a desired but uncertain objective in a risky situation." The risky situation involves the child's need for love, approval and basic physical necessities.

Since communication is the child's tie with his parents, it is vital that he be able to rely upon the communication behavior of his parents. Interpersonal trust in the communication process is defined by Giffin (1967, p. 105) as "reliance upon the communication behavior of another person in order to achieve a desired but uncertain objective in a risky situation." Trust in oneself, *intrapersonal trust*, is essential for the child, and can logically be viewed as reliance upon oneself to achieve a desired but uncertain objective in a risky situation.

Communication and Initiative Development

Erikson (1963) sees the development of initiative as vital to achievement of maturity. Initiative is present when the child begins to contemplate goals, to initiate acts, to act spontaneously, or as Erikson calls it, to develop a sense of "being on the make" (p. 255); this is possible only if self-trust and environmental trust exist. The opposite of initiative development is a sense of guilt arising over abortive attempts to assert oneself, attempts which sometimes appear to the individual as inappropriately aggressive. Guilt may also arise from merely *wanting* to initiate.

Communicating constitutes initiating. Not only does it allow a child to reveal himself, but it involves self-assertion. If the parent-child relationship is one that permits the child to initiate communication, maturity development is furthered. In other words, the parent-child communication relationship becomes a determinant of freedom to initiate communication and to move in a healthy direction.

Communication as an Influence upon Self-Concept

A healthy child has a positive self-concept. The development of self-concept is based in part upon communication with other people. A theoretical basis for this rests in Mead's (1934) conceptualization of the language process as essential for the development of the "self." In this sense the "self" that an individual perceives is largely determined by his interaction with the world, primarily through interpersonal communication.

Not only is one's self-concept largely formed through social interaction, but this interaction allows continued validation of one's "self" through the process of checking with others. This human need to evaluate one's own opinions and abilities is described by Festinger (1954) in his theory of socal comparison.

Since the mental attitude which a person carries through life is formed in the early parent-child relationships, early communication will determine the self-concept a child forms. Positive early communication experiences are likely to produce a positive self-concept.

Communication Suppression in Child Development

Essentially, the role of communication in child development is one of allowing the child to relate to the world in order to develop the characteristics of trust and initiative and to form a positive self-concept.

The Concept of Communication Suppression

Negative parent-child communication will undoubtedly be detrimental to the child's development. One form of negative communication experience is communication suppression. Suppression of communication in the authors' conceptualization occurs when a child who desires to express himself obtains negative reactions from his parents.*

Communication Suppression and the Formation of Trust and Initiative

When his communication meets parental suppression, the child's trust of others (interpersonal trust) is undermined. He cannot put himself forth with the assurance that he will be accepted, nor is he allowed to feel the security of trusting that his needs will be met. Consider the effects of suppression upon a child's spontanous communication if the child, as Maslow claims, chooses the approval of others over fulfilling his growth-oriented motives. It appears to the authors that communication and resultant growth can thus become repressed, controlled, halted, or even feared.

Furthermore, if a child delights, to use Maslow's term, in taking initiative by asserting himself through communication and then meets negative feedback, he is likely to identify his motives as selfish and experience feelings of guilt. He may come to tell himself: I should not want to talk so much, to be a leader, to "push" my own ideas. The suppressed child most likely becomes shy, introverted, submissive, unwilling to assume leadership in his observable actions. Anxiety may accom-

---

* Used throughout this paper in the sense also of parent surrogates.

pany guilt feelings about wanting to exercise initiative. His desire to manipulate or assert control over others will likely be fulfilled by over-manipulation of himself which will be detrimental to his own healthy development.

Communication Suppression and the Formulation of a Self-Concept

Communicating constitutes revealing oneself to the world; this interaction determines one's sense of "self" (Mead, 1934) and allows for validation of one's "self" (Festinger, 1954).

If a child's communication encounters negative feedback, negative feelings about himself are likely to follow. He evaluates his opinions by checking with others and finds his ideas negatively received. Continued attempts at self-expression, met by parental suppression, are likely to produce an undesirable self-concept. The child will tend to guard against situations where he is expected to reveal a part of himself and to avoid experiences that might validate a negative self-concept. Slowly communication lessens, a positive self-concept disappears, and the child's social health is undermined.

Communication Suppression and Speech Anxiety

The authors have theorized that healthy parent-child communication will produce a healthy child with a positive self-concept, thus providing a maturity development established through exercise of trust and initiative. From this conceptualization, the effect of communication suppression upon trust, initiative and self-concept formation has been viewed harmful.

The Speaker Experiencing Anxiety

Research shows that speakers experiencing anxiety are characterized by lack of trust, initiative and a poor self-concept.

1. Trust: Related Research Findings.
Using the Guilford-Martin Personality Inventories (1948), S. Ainsworth (1949) found that college students in the lower quar-

tile of speaker effectiveness revealed significantly more seclusiveness. A biographical questionnaire devised by Gordon Low
(1950) revealed that "high stage fright" students reported being
on guard in social relationships significantly more (p>.01) than
students experiencing "low stage fright." A significant number
of low-confidence speakers felt their ideas were not worth saying or would not be found interesting by an audience. Gordon
Low also found the expression of feelings difficult for this
group.

E. Wilkinson (1938) attempted to relate speech experience
with submissiveness or dominance as measured by the Bernreuter Personality Inventory (Bernreuter, 1932) and with introversion and extroversion determined by the Miller-Murray Personal-Social Adjustment Test (Miller and Murray, 1938). Her
results with the Bernreuter Personality Inventory revealed that
students with submissive tendencies showed significantly more
fear of laughter, forgetting, and evaluation by others than
speakers possessing dominance trends. Her use of the Miller-
Murray Test showed speakers with introversion tendencies reporting also a fear of the opinions of others "just as frequently
or more frequently than" speakers showing trends of extroversion.

Seclusiveness, being on guard, and negating one's ideas
show a lack of self-trust; this intrapersonal trust is a factor in
one's expression of feelings and confidence in remembering.
A lack of interpersonal trust is evident in the fear of audience
reaction to one's communication.

2. Initiative: Related Research Findings.

Ainsworth (1949) devised a case history questionnaire which
revealed some significant trends about the lower quartile of
speaker effectiveness. These students had made fewer acquaintances and were less likely to assume leadership in activities
with friends. Use of the Guilford-Martin Personality Inventories
(1948) found these speakers experiencing significantly more
shyness and withdrawal from social situations than speakers in
the upper quartile. The lower quartile tended to have more
periods of depression, often accompanied by feelings of guilt

and unworthiness. They were characterized by an inhibited disposition and a tendency to over-control their impulses. A high degree of social passivity and an inclinaton toward emotional instability were found.

Ainsworth's study supports the initiative-versus-guilt concept previously described. He specifically states that the lower quartile group tended to over-control their impulses, a characteristic of suppressed initiative.

Low's (1950) biographical questionnaire found that those students experiencing "high stage fright" had participated in fewer extra-curricular activities in high school, had their first date at a later age, reported qualities of shyness and withdrawal significantly more ($p > .01$) than students with "low stage fright." These students found relations with the opposite sex difficult. Rarely or never had the "high stage fright" group been chosen leaders in their childhood and were chosen leaders during high school only "occasionally, seldom, or never."

Findings about the "low stage fright" group showed they were eager to voice their opinions *whether others liked it or not.* Also more "friction" existed between students with "low stage fright" and their fathers. One might view the increased "friction" as possibly resulting from increased self-assertion; however, Low does not specifically explain what is meant by "friction."

On the Minnesota Multiphasic Personality Inventory (Hathaway and McKinley, 1942) Low found no significant difference between the high or low speaker confidence group at the .01 level of confidence; however, the "high stage fright" group had tendencies toward worrying, a narrow range of interest, and introversion trends.

An early study by Mimms (1939) investigated the relationship between frequency of participation in a one-hour daily class period for thirty days and the dominance-submission characteristic measured by the Bernreuter Personality Inventory. Mimms found a significant relationship between participation and dominance-submission. Her results showed that 92.6% of the dominant pupils participated frequently in class discussions while only 35% of the submissives participated frequently.

The frequent participation of the dominant students can be interpreted as evidence of initiative development in a child who early felt free to put forth his ideas.

Findings by Chenoweth (1940) support Mimms' study. Using the Bernreuter Personality Inventory, Chenoweth found a tendency toward dominance in the well-adjusted speakers, while a greater tendency toward submission existed in the maladjusted speakers.

Wilkinson (1938) found that those speakers possessing submissive and introversion tendencies, measured by the Bernreuter Personality Inventory and the Miller-Murray Personal-Social Adjustment Test (Miller and Murray, 1938), showed more limited experience in self-expression than those speakers showing dominance and extroversion.

The authors' interpretation of these findings is that speech anxiety tends to correlate with shyness, introversion, submission, unwillingness to assume leaderhip or to express oneself. These reactions suggest a deficiency in initiative development.

3. Self-Concept: Related Research Findings.

The self-concept of the speaker experiencing anxiety has been found to be poor in a number of studies. Gilkinson's (1943) study found a generalized low self-evaluation in the more fearful speakers questioned. Ainsworth's (1949) case history questionnaires showed that the students with less confidence were raised in larger families, and if they were the middle child, a tendency existed for these persons to rate themselves as slightly inferior in verbal fluency when compared to other children in the family. Trends showed that students with less confidence were more likely to choose terms such as worry, uncertainty, or embarrassment as a *common reflection of their feelings.*

Using the Guilford-Martin Personality Inventories (1948), Ainsworth found that students lacking speaking effectiveness had more feelings of unworthiness, inadequacy, and inferiority than effective speakers. As previously stated, Low (1950) found that a significant number of low-confidence speakers felt that their ideas were not worth saying or would not be interesting to an audience.

The Early Social Environment of the Person Who Has Speech Anxiety

As we have seen, a number of studies reveal a correlation between the degree of speaker anxiety and degree of trust, initiative and positive self-concept; research also shows that the environment of speakers experiencing anxiety is not conducive to the development of trust, initiative and a positive self-concept.

The study of Crowell, Katcher, and Miyamoto (1955) ties together the elements of self-concept development and parental encouragement to communicate. This study included a case history questionnaire on background factors relating to the speaker's performance in small group discussion.

The findings suggest "that family influences play a part in determining self-concepts with respect to communicator skills" (p. 24). Specifically, the questionnaire indicated that parents of children with "high self-concepts" placed more emphasis on accurate phrasing of ideas, the importance of everyone expressing his opinion, and the importance of having witty and interesting speech. Also, a wider variety of topics had been discussed by the families of "high self-concept" speakers. Most notable is the evidence of apparently less suppression of verbal expression by parents of "high self-concept" speakers. While an unsatisfactory level of confidence was obtained, it appeared to the researchers that "high self-concept" children had received more training and practice in communication skills and practiced them under more favorable conditions than did the "low self-concept" speakers.

It should be pointed out that, although the variables of speech experience and a "high self-concept" tend to be correlated, causality could proceed in either direction: Because a child lacks a "high self-concept," he could have avoided opportunities for gaining speech experience; or a lack of speaking experience could have contributed to a "low self-concept." However, a child's very early speech environmental conditions, especially since they occur at a time when he has very little control over his social environment, probably are more cause than effect of a lack of a "high self-concept" as a speaker.

The submissive and introverted speakers in Wilkinson's (1938) study were described as having dominating parents, a lack of social contacts because of limited environment and older people, and poor English and speech environment more frequently than speakers showing extroversion and dominance. These appear to be factors hindering initiative development.

Elwood Murray's (1936) early work on the speech personality included detailed case histories showing unfavorable conditions present during the childhood and adolescence of poor speakers. Usually they lived in homes and localities of low social and cultural status and received little or no speech training. Their parents lacked speech training and were not effective speakers. Murray concluded (p. 108)

the attitudes and habits of thinking and feeling characterizing a person's adjustment to the speech situation are directly the outgrowth of the social, emotional, and speech experiences and influences he had undergone in his past history.

Chenoweth's (1940) study found that well-adjusted speakers had experienced not only more speech training and experience in the grades and high school, but that they received more speech training, experience and encouragement at home. Gilkinson (1943) found that the less confident speakers had less formal training and experience in speech activities than confident speakers, supporting Chenoweth's finding. Early encouragement to assert oneself, to initiate, seems to characterize well-adjusted speakers.

Low's (1950) study found that the "high stage fright" group knew less about their early infancy; this may indicate that their parents told them less about their behavior during childhood, but numerous other reasons may be the basis for such a finding, such as a wish to forget childhood experiences. Low also found that students with "high stage fright" considered their "early" speech experiences to be disagreeable.

*   *   *

Healthy development of a child rests upon initial parent-child communication which encourages the development of trust, initiative, and a positive self-concept—all factors that play a part in adult communication. The probable effect of suppression of a child's communication has been described, revealing how mistrust, a lack of initiative and guilt, and a poor self-image can result. Since the early parent-child relationship shapes the future adult, the child is likely to show the results of these experiences throughout his life.

Research shows that speakers experiencing speech anxiety lack the trusting and initiating tendencies related to confidence in a speech situation. They tend to be on guard, seclusive, unwilling to trust their memories and express their feelings; audience reaction to their communication is feared. Guilt, shyness, introversion, submissiveness, plus an unwillingness to assert oneself through leaderhip activities characterize these students; all are traits characteristic of a lack of initiative development. In addition, they tend to possess negative self-concepts, with feelings of inferiority, unworthiness, and inadequacy.

Furthermore, the childhood environmental conditions reported by speakers who lack confidence reveal conditions not conducive to the emergence of trust, initiative, and a good self-concept. They were not encouraged to speak, had dominating parents, or lacked experience in speech activities.

It appears that parental suppression of a child's communication can produce speaker anxiety which can be carried into adult speech situations; it seems quite probable that the foundation of maturity development and the basis for a positive self-concept are undermined when a child's communication meets suppression. The authors would like to encourage scholars to explore this hypothesis in future research.

Bibliography

Ainsworth, Stanley H.: A study of fear, nervousness, and anxiety in the public speaking situation. Unpublished Ph.D. dissertation, Northwestern University. Chicago. 1949.

Allport, Gordon: *Becoming.* Yale University Press. New Haven. 1955.

Baird, A., and Knower, F. H.: *General Speech.* (3rd ed.) McGraw-Hill. New York. 1963.

Berne, Eric: *Games People Play.* Grove Press. New York. 1964.

Bernreuter, R. H.: *Personality Inventory.* Stanford University Press. Stanford, Calif. 1932.

Buehler, E. C., and Linkugel, W. A.: *Speech: A First Course.* Harper & Row. New York. 1962.

Chenoweth, Eugene: The adjustment of college freshmen to the speaking situation. *Quart. J. Speech,* 26: 585, 1940.

Crowell, Laura; Katcher, Allan; and Miyamoto, S. Frank: Self-concepts of communication skill and performance in small group discussions. *Speech Monog.,* 22: 20–27, 1955.

Erikson, Erik H.: *Childhood and Society.* (2nd ed.) Norton. New York. 1963.

Festinger, Leon: A theory of social comparison processes. *Human Relations,* 7: 117–140, 1954.

Giffin, Kim: The contribution of studies of source credibility to a theory of interpersonal trust in the communication process. *Psychol. Bull.,* 68: 104–120, 1967.

Giffin, Kim, and Bradley, Kendall: Group Counseling for Speech Students with Low Self-Confidence: An Approach and a Rationale. Research Monograph P/16. The Communication Research Center, The University of Kansas. Lawrence, Kansas. 1967 (a)

———: An exploratory study of group counseling for speech anxiety. *J. of Clin. Psychol.* (in press)

Gilkinson, Howard: A questionnaire study of the causes of social fears among college speech students. *Speech. Monog.,* 10: 74–83, 1943.

Greenleaf, Floyd I.: An experimental study of social speech fright. Unpublished M.A. thesis, State University of Iowa. 1947.

Guilford, J. P., and Martin, H. G.: *The Guilford-Martin Inventory of Factors GAMIN.* (Abridged ed.) Sheridan Supply Company. Beverly Hills, Calif. 1948.

Hathaway, Starke R., and McKinley, J. C.: *Minnesota Multiphasic Personality Inventory.* Psychological Corporation. New York. 1942.

Low, Gordon M.: The relationship of psychometric factors to stage fright. Unpublished M.S. thesis, University of Utah. 1950.

Low, Gordon M., and Sheets, B. V.: The relation of psychometric factors to stage fright. *Speech Monog.,* 18:266–271, 1951.

Maslow, A. H.: *Toward a Psychology of Being.* Van Nostrand. Princeton, N.J. 1962.

Mead, George H.: *Mind, Self and Society.* University of Chicago Press. Chicago. 1934.

Miller, Laurence, and Murray, E.: *Miller-Murray Personal-Social Adjustment Test.* University of Denver. Denver, Colo. 1938.

Mimms, Louise: A study of the relations of dominance-submission to speech participation. Unpublished M.A. thesis, University of Denver. 1939.

Murray, Elwood: A study of factors contributing to the maldevelopment of the speech personality. *Speech Monog.,* 3: 95–108, 1936.

Paulson, Stanley F.: Changes in confidence during period of speech training: transfer of training and comparison of improved and non-improved groups on the Bell Adjustment Inventory. *Speech Monog.,* 18: 260–265, 1951.

Ross, Raymond S.: *Speech Communication.* Prentice-Hall. Englewood Cliffs, N.J. 1964.

Stone, L. J., and Church, J.: *Childhood and Adolescence.* Random House. New York. 1957.

Wilkinson, Esther R.: A study of disintegrating background factors in the development of effective speech personalities. Unpublished M.A. thesis, University of Denver. 1938.

William C. Schutz
**The Postulate of
Interpersonal Needs:
Description**

Postulate 1. The Postulate of Interpersonal Needs.
(a). Every individual has three interpersonal needs:
inclusion, control, and affection.
(b). Inclusion, control, and affection constitute a
sufficient set of areas of interpersonal behavior for the
prediction and explanation of interpersonal phenomena.

Explanation: In studying interpersonal behavior it is important to isolate the relevant variables. "People need people"
serves as a good starting point, but, if the frontiers of knowledge are to recede, the next question must be investigated:
"*In what ways* do people need people?"

The literature is not lacking in contestants for the mantle of
"basic interpersonal variables." French[1] in a recent report summarizes the factors found in the factor analysis of various personality tests; he was able to reduce the number of apparently
unrelated factors to forty nine! Clearly this number is unmanageable for use in future investigation.

If the strictly statistical techniques for reducing variables still
leaves forty nine, some other exploratory method must be employed or at least added. A developmental approach to isola-

Reprinted by permission of the author and the publishers from William
C. Schutz. *The Interpersonal Underworld*, Palo Alto, Calif.: Science and Behavior
Books, 1966., pp. 13–33.

[1] T. French, *Summary of Factor Analytic Studies of Personality* (Princeton,
N.J.: Educational Testing Service, 1956).

ting variables has several appealing features. It seems promising to attempt to trace the developing individual through his sequence of typical interpersonal dealings, as a method of identifying the most basic interpersonal areas from which others are derivable. A consideration of this developmental process (discussed in more detail below), and some formulations presented by certain investigators, notably Bion, led the author to the conclusion that three interpersonal areas seemed to cover most interpersonal behavior. Later analysis of certain relevant literature (see Chapter 3) lent weight to the proposition that three areas would prove adequate for fruitful investigation.

As the description of these three areas, here called inclusion, control, and affection, progressed the fable came to mind of the blind men who disagreed over the characteristics of an elephant because each was exploring a different sector. It seems that various investigators are describing different aspects of the elephant—the three need areas—but apparently they are describing the same elephant. Thus clinicians discuss unconscious forces, small-group investigators describe overt behavior, child psychologists report on early interpersonal relations, and sociologists are interested in roles and group structures. But there seems to be heartening convergence toward the same set of variables, even though the approaches differ. The problem, then, is to give a complete description of the "elephant" and point out which aspects are being described by each observer. This chapter attempts to provide a complete description of the three basic interpersonal areas as basic needs, by showing how they appear in personality structure, in overt behavior, and in pathological behavior: In Chapter 3 a brief summary is given of selected studies which seem to fit into various parts of this schema.

Interpersonal Need

The concept of interpersonal need, often called "social need," has been discussed by many authors[2] but because it forms the

---

[2] N. E. Miller and J. Pollard, *Social Learning and Imitation* (New Haven, Conn.: Yale University Press, 1941).

central part of this book it is important to describe in what sense the term will be used.

The term "interpersonal" refers to relations that occur between people as opposed to relations in which at least one participant is inanimate. It is assumed that, owing to the psychological presence of other people, interpersonal situations lead to behavior in an individual that differs from the behavior of the individual when he is not in the presence of other persons. An optimally useful definition of "interpersonal" is one such that all situations classified as interpersonal have important properties in common—properties that are in general different from those of noninterpersonal situations. With this criterion for a definition in mind, the following specifies the meaning of "interpersonal situation." (The term "interpersonal" shall be used as equivalent to the term "group.")

An *interpersonal situation* is one involving two or more persons, in which these individuals take account of each other for some purpose, or decision, D. It is described from a particular point of reference, usually either that of one of the participants or of an outside observer. It is also specified as existing during a stated time interval. Thus a complete statement of an interpersonal situation has the form:

"From the standpoint of O (or A, or B), A takes account of B for decision D during time interval t_1 to t_n."

"A takes account of B for decision D" means that when A considers what alternative to select for decision D one criterion for his choice is his expectation of B's response to his choice. This expectation does not require that A make a different decision because of the influence of B; it simply means that his criteria for making the decision are supplemented.

For example, if a man who is sitting on a bus trying to decide whether or not to give up his seat to an elderly lady considers the reaction of the attractive young woman across the aisle, he is taking account of the young woman whether or not he gives up his seat. From *his* point of view the relation is interpersonal, since he takes account of her. From the standpoint of the young woman the situation may not be interpersonal at all, since she may not even be aware of his presence. Further, A

may take account of *B* for one decision, for example, giving up a bus seat, as in the previous example, but not for another, for example, deciding which cobbler to patronize a week later. In addition, the degree to which *A* takes account of *B* varies with time. Our bus rider may be taking account of the lady during the bus ride (i.e., t_1 to t_n) but not at all when watching television that evening (i.e., after t_n).

The type of investigation will determine which point of reference for defining the term "interpersonal" will be most useful. Sometimes it is useful to consider an interpersonal situation from the standpoint of an individual, as when we speak of an interpersonal need. Sometimes it is more advantageous to consider a situation interpersonal only if the "taking account of" relation is reciprocal, that is, perceived by both members of a dyadic (two-person) relation (see Chapter 7). Sometimes the point of view of observers will decide whether a situation is interpersonal, regardless of the reports of the individuals involved in the relation. For conceptual clarity the important requirement in describing an interpersonal relation is that the point of reference be specified.

The phrase "face-to-face" used frequently by other writers when defining "interpersonal" or "group" has been omitted from the present definition. As shall be elaborated below, the property of physical presence is an important variable within the scope of interpersonal behavior, closely related to the area of inclusion. Further, it is often useful to consider situations as interpersonal in which behavior is determined by *expectations* of the behavior of others, even if the others are not physically present. It therefore seems more useful to leave the term "interpersonal" free of the face-to-face condition and consider as a separate problem the effect of that condition on behavior.

The other term in the phrase under discussion is "need." A "need" is defined in terms of a situation or condition of an individual the nonrealization of which leads to undesirable consequences. An interpersonal need is one that may be satisfied only through the attainment of a satisfactory relation with other people. The satisfaction of a need is a necessary condition for the avoidance of the undesirable consequences. An interpersonal need is one that may be satisfied only through the attainment of a satisfactory relation with other people. The satisfaction of a need is a necessary condition for the avoidance of the undesirable consequences of illness and death. A discrepancy between the satisfaction of an interpersonal need and the present state of an organism engenders a feeling in the organism that shall be called *anxiety*.

There is a close parallel between biological needs and interpersonal needs, in the following respects:

1. A biological need is a requirement to establish and maintain a satisfactory relation between the organism and its *physical* environment. An interpersonal need is a requirement to establish a satisfactory relation between the individual and his *human* environment. A biological need is not satisfied by providing unlimited gratification. An organism may take in too much water and drown, as well as too little water and die of thirst. The need is satisfied by establishing an equilibrium between the amount of water inside and outside the organism. The same is true for the "commodities" exchanged between people. An individual's needs may be unfulfilled either by having, for example, too much control over his human environment and hence too much responsibility, or too little control, hence not enough security. He must establish a satisfactory relation with his human environment with respect to control.

2. Nonfulfillment of a biological need leads to physical illness and sometimes death. Nonfulfillment of an interpersonal need leads to mental (or interpersonal) illness and sometimes death. Unsatisfactory personal relations lead directly to difficulties associated with emotional illness. Death, either through suicide or resulting from the more general loss of motivation for life, results when interpersonal dissatisfaction is prolonged.

3. The organism has characteristic modes, which are temporarily successful, of adapting to lack of complete satisfaction of biological needs. The organism also has characteristic ways, which are temporarily successful, of adapting to nonsatisfaction of interpersonal needs. For the interpersonal situation the terms "conscious" and "unconscious" needs are sometimes used to describe the phenomena at issue.

The distinction between a conscious and an unconscious need

finds a parallel in a biological condition such as drug addiction. In drug addiction the immediate (conscious) need is to satisfy the immediate craving and to adjust the body chemistry so that the pain is reduced. The more basic (unconscious) need is to adjust the body chemistry back to the state where the drug is no longer required. The pain or anxiety felt when the organism is in a situation which does not allow for the satisfaction of these two needs is different in each case. In the first there is the immediate deprivation, analogous to an interpersonal situation in which an individual's characteristic psychological adjustment mechanisms (for example, defenses) cannot operate. To illustrate, if denial were the defense used by an individual in the affection area and he were placed in a situation in which close personal relations were called for, he would feel an *immediate anxiety* caused by the discrepancy between the demands of the situation and his most comfortable behavior pattern. The more *basic anxiety* or interpersonal imbalance stemming from the general inadequacy of the defense to ward off the need for affection is analogous to the physical discomfort caused by the discrepancy between the chemical balance produced by the drug addition and the normal chemical balance.

This analogy assumes a particular interpersonal relation that optimally satisfies interpersonal needs, parallel to an optimal chemical balance. This assumption is made, although it is difficult to test. Perhaps it parallels the condition in which the psychoanalyst attempts to place his patient. The analyst has a conception of an optimal psychological condition for a given individual toward which the person strives. This condition goes deeper than the reinforcement of the patient's defense mechanisms, which protect him from undesirable impulses. The optimal state is one in which defenses are only minimally required. It is this psychological state that is analogous to the concept of an optimal interpersonal relation.

These parallels between the interpersonal and biological needs will be specified more precisely in the following discussion. Other aspects of this problem could be mentioned at this point, such as the phylogenetic continuity of interpersonal needs, their universality cross-culturally, and possible physiological correlates. However, this would take the discussion too far afield. The main point is that in many important ways interpersonal needs have properties closely parallel to those of biological needs.

Inclusion, Control, and Affection

Now comes the problem of describing the elephant, that is, providing a complete description of interpersonal variables sufficient to provide a framework for integration and future investigation in the field.

To construct such a schema it is necessary to determine the most relevant parameters for describing important aspects of the interpersonal variables. These parameters may then be used as the classification variables for generating a matrix to encompass the interpersonal behavior of interest. This process is called "substructing" by Lazarsfeld and Barton,[3] and "facet analysis" by Guttman.[4] It has the virtue of providing all possible combinations of parameter values so that omissions or duplications are easily recognized.

The parameters chosen should delineate salient differences worthy of preservation in personality description. Differences on these parameters represent important behavioral differences which are helpful, even necessary, when behavioral characteristics are related to external factors, for example, childhood experiences, productivity, compatibility, leadership. The matrix generated by the parameters represents the *types of available data*. The methods of obtaining the data (such as introspection, questionnaire, observation, projective test) are independent of the matrix. Any method of data collection is permissible for any type of data. The parameters:

1. *Observability*—the degree to which an action of an individual is observable by others. This parameter is dichotomized

[3] P. Lazarsfeld and A. Barton, "Qualitative Measurement in the Social Sciences," in D. Lerner and H. Lasswell, *The Policy Sciences* (Stanford, Calif.: Stanford University Press, 1951).

[4] L. Guttman, "Principal Components of Scalable Attitudes," in *Mathematical Thinking in the Social Sciences*, ed. by P. Lazarsfeld (Glencoe, Ill.: Free Press, 1954).

TABLE 1. MATRIX OF RELEVANT INTERPERSONAL
DATA—"THE ELEPHANT"

			Inclusion		
			Self to Other (Actions)	Other to Self (Reactions)	Self to Self
Desired Interpersonal Relations (Needs)		Act	Satisfactory relation re interaction and inclusion behavior 1		Feeling that I am significant
		Feel	Satisfactory relation re feelings of mutual interest 2		
Ideal Interpersonal Relations		Act	Social 3	People include me 4	
		Feel	I am interested in people 5	People are interested in me 6	15
Anxious Interpersonal Relations (Anxieties)	Too much activity	Act	Over-social 7	Social-compliant 8	I am insignificant (I don't know who I am; I am nobody)
		Feel	I am not *really* interested in people 9	People aren't *really* interested in me 10	
	Too little activity	Act	Under-social 11	Counter-social 12	
		Feel	I am not interested in people 13	People are not interested in me 14	16
Pathological Interpersonal Relations	Too Much				17
	Too Little		Psychotic (Schizophrenia)		18

Control			Affection		
Self to Other (Actions)	Other to Self (Reactions)	Self to Self	Self to Other (Actions)	Other to Self (Reactions)	Self to Self
Satisfactory relation re power and control behavior 19		Feeling that I am responsible	Satisfactory relation re love and affection behavior 37		Feeling that I am lovable
Satisfactory relation re feelings of mutual respect 20			Satisfactory relation re feelings of mutual affection 38		
Democrat 21	People respect me 22		Personal 39	People are friendly to me 40	
I respect people 23	People respect me 24	33	I like people 41	People like me 42	51
Autocrat 25	Rebel 26	I am incompetent (I am stupid, irresponsible)	Over-personal 43	Personal-compliant 44	I am unlovable (I am no good, rotten bastard)
I don't trust people 27	People don't trust me 28		I don't *really* like people 45	People don't *really* like me 46	
Abdicrat 29	Submissive 30		Under-personal 47	Counter-personal 48	
I don't *really* respect people 31	People don't *really* respect me 32	34	I don't like people 49	People don't like me 50	52
Obsessive-compulsive		35	Neurotic		53
Psychopath		36	Neurotic		54

into *action* and *feeling*. An action is usually more observable to outsiders, a feeling usually more observable to the self.

2. *Directionality*—the direction of the interaction with respect to originator and target. This parameter is trichotomized into (a) self toward other, (b) other toward self, and (c) self toward self. The last category is interpersonal in the sense that it represents interaction between the self and others who have been interiorized early in life.

3. *Status of Action*—whether the behavior is in the inclusion, control, or affection area.

4. *State of Relation*—whether the relation is desired, ideal, anxious or pathological.

Table 1 summarizes the terms and concepts discussed in this chapter. This table, in a sense, is the "elephant."

The Three Interpersonal Needs

The interpersonal need for inclusion is defined behaviorally as the need to establish and maintain a satisfactory relation with people with respect to interaction and association. "Satisfactory relation" includes (1) a psychologically comfortable relation with people somewhere on a dimension ranging from originating interaction with all people to not initiating interaction with anyone; (2) a psychologically comfortable relation with people with respect to eliciting behavior from them somewhere on a dimension ranging from always initiating interaction with the self to never initiating interaction with the self.

On the level of feelings the need for inclusion is defined as the need to establish and maintain a feeling of mutual interest with other people. This feeling includes (1) being able to take an interest in other people to a satisfactory degree and (2) having other people interested in the self to a satisfactory degree.

With regard to the self-concept, the need for inclusion is the need to feel that the self is significant and worth while.

The interpersonal need for control is defined behaviorally as the need to establish and maintain a satisfactory relation with people with respect to control and power. "Satisfactory relation" includes (1) a psychologically comfortable relation with people somewhere on a dimension ranging from controlling all the behavior of other people to not controlling any behavior of others and (2) a psychologically comfortable relation with people with respect to eliciting behavior from them somewhere on a dimension ranging from always being controlled by them to never being controlled by them.

With regard to feelings, the need for control is defined as the need to establish and maintain a feeling of mutual respect for the competence and responsibleness of others. This feeling includes (1) being able to respect others to a satisfactory degree and (2) having others respect the self to a satisfactory degree.

The need for control, defined at the level of perceiving the self, is the need to feel that one is a competent, responsible person.

The interpersonal need for affection is defined behaviorally as the need to establish and maintain a satisfactory relation with others with respect to love and affection. Affection always refers to a two-person (dyadic) relation. "Satisfactory relation" includes (1) a psychologically comfortable relation with others somewhere on a dimension ranging from initiating close, personal relations with everyone to originating close, personal relations with no one; (2) a psychologically comfortable relation with people with respect to eliciting behavior from them on a dimension ranging from always originating close, personal relations toward the self, to never originating close, personal relations toward the self.

At the feeling level the need for affection is defined as the need to establish and maintain a feeling of mutual affection with others. This feeling includes (1) being able to love other people to a satisfactory degree and (2) having others love the self to a satisfactory degree.

The need for affection, defined at the level of the self-concept, is the need to feel that the self is lovable.

This type of formulation stresses the interpersonal nature of these needs. They require that the organism establish a kind of equilibrium, in three different areas, between the self and other people. In order to be anxiety-free, a person must find a comfortable behavioral relation with others with regard to the exchange of interaction, power, and love. The need is not wholly satisfied by having others respond toward the self in a particular way; nor is it wholly satisfied by acting toward others in a particular fashion. A satisfactory balance must be established and maintained.

Inclusion, Control, and Affection Behavior

Thus far these key terms have been discussed only from the standpoint of their status as interpersonal needs. Since the value of the theory is dependent to a large extent on the cogency and clarity of these terms, it is important to describe them as fully as possible. In later chapters many different ways of describing these terms will be introduced, including

1. Examples;

2. Synonyms (Chapter 2);

3. A description of aspects of these behaviors at various levels of personality (Chapter 2);

4. A description of the interconnection between these terms and other terms in the theory, such as "compatibility" (Chapter 6);

5. A description of the relations between these areas and factors found by other investigators (Chapter 3);

6. A description of these areas as applied to literary works (Chapter 9); and

7. A measuring instrument FIRO—B (Fundamental Interpersonal Relations Orientation—Behavior), which measures two aspects of each of the three areas (Chapter 4).

Inclusion behavior is defined as behavior directed toward the satisfaction of the interpersonal need for inclusion.

Control behavior is defined as behavior directed toward the satisfaction of the interpersonal need for control.

Affection behavior is defined as behavior directed toward the satisfaction of the interpersonal need for affection.

In general, *inclusion behavior* refers to association between people. Some terms that connote a relation that is primarily positive inclusion are "associate," "interact," "mingle," "communicate," "belong," "companion," "comrade," "attend to," "member," "together," "join," "extravert." Some terms that connote lack of, or negative, inclusion, are "exclusion," "isolate," "outsider," "outcast," "lonely," "detached," "withdrawn," "abandoned," "ignored."

The need to be included manifests itself as wanting to be attended to, to attract attention and interest. The classroom hellion who throws erasers is often objecting mostly to the lack of attention paid him. Even if he is given negative affection he is partially satisfied, because at least someone is paying attention to him.

In groups, people often make themselves prominent by talking a great deal. Frequently they are not interested in power or dominance but simply prominence. The "joker" is an example of a prominence seeker, very much as is the blond actress with the lavender convertible.

In the extreme, what is called "fame" is primarily inclusion. Acquisition of fame does not imply acquisition of power or influence: witness Marilyn Monroe's attempt to swing votes to Adlai Stevenson. Nor does fame imply affection: Al Capone could hardly be considered a widely loved figure. But fame does imply prominence, and signifies interest on the part of others.

From another standpoint, behavior related to belonging and "togetherness" is primarily inclusion. To desire to belong to a fraternal organization by no means necessarily indicates a liking for the members or even a desire for power. It is often sought for its "prestige value," for increase of "status." These terms are also primarily inclusion conceptions, because their primary implication is that people pay attention to the person, know who he is, and can distinguish him from others.

This last point leads to an essential aspect of inclusion, that of identity. An integral part of being recognized and paid attention to is that the individual be identifiable from other people. He must be known as a specific individual; he must have a particular identity. If he is not thus known, he cannot truly be attended to or have interest paid to him. The extreme of this identification is that he be understood. To be understood implies that someone is interested enough in him to find out his particular characteristics. Again, this interest need not mean that others have affection for him, or that they respect him. For example, the interested person may be a confidence man who is exploring his background to find a point of vulnerability.

At the outset of interpersonal relations a common issue is that of commitment, the decision to become involved in a given relation or activity. Usually, in the initial testing of the relation, individuals try to identify themselves to one another to find out which facet of themselves others will be interested in. Frequently a member is silent for a while because he is not sure that people are interested in him. These behaviors, too, are primarily in the inclusion area.

This, then, is the flavor of inclusion. It has to do with interacting with people, with attention, acknowledgement, being known, prominence, recognition, prestige, status, and fame; with identity, individuality, understanding, interest, commitment, and participation. It is unlike affection in that it does not involve strong emotional attachments to individual persons. It is unlike control in that the preoccupation is with prominence, not dominance.

Control behavior refers to the decision-making process between people. Some terms connoting a relation that is primarily positive control are "power," "authority," "dominance," "influence," "control," "ruler," "superior officer," "leader." Some terms that connote primarily a lack of, or negative, control are "rebellion," "resistance," "follower," "anarchy," "submissive," "henpecked," "milquetoast."

The need for control manifests itself as the desire for power, authority, and control over others and therefore over one's future. At the other end is the need to be controlled, to have responsibility taken away. Manifestations of the power drive are very clear. A more subtle form is exemplified by the current magazine advertising campaign featuring the "influential." This is a person who controls others through the power he has to influence their behavior.

The acquisition of money or political power is a direct method of obtaining control over other persons. This type of control often involves coercion rather than more subtle methods of influence like persuasion and example. In group behavior, the struggles to achieve high office or to make suggestions that are adopted are manifestations of control behavior. In an argument in a group we may distinguish the inclusion seeker from the control seeker in this way: the one seeking inclusion or prominence wants very much to be one of the participants in the argument, while the control seeker wants to be the winner or, if not the winner, on the same side as the winner. The prominence seeker would prefer to be the losing participant; the dominance seeker would prefer to be a winning nonparticipant. Both these roles are separate from the affectional desires of the members.

Control behavior takes many subtle forms, especially among more intellectual and polite people. For example, in many discussion groups where blackboards are involved, the power struggle becomes displaced onto the chalk. Walking to the blackboard and taking the chalk from the one holding it, and retaining possession, becomes a mark of competitive success. Often a meeting is marked by a procession of men taking the chalk, writing something, and being supplanted by another man for a further message. In this way propriety is maintained, and still the power struggle may proceed.

In many gatherings, control behavior is exhibited through the group task. Intellectual superiority, for one thing, often leads to control over others so that strong motivation to achieve is often largely control behavior. Such superiority also demonstrates the real capacity of the individual to be relied on for responsible jobs, a central aspect of control. Further, to do one's job properly, or to rebel against the established authority structure by not doing it, is a splendid outlet for control feelings. Doing a poor job is a way of rebelling against the structure and showing that no one will control you, whereas acquiescence earns rewards from those in charge which satisfies the need to be respected for one's accomplishments.

Control is also manifested in behavior toward others controlling the self. Expressions of independence and rebellion exemplify lack of willingness to be controlled, while compliance, submission, and taking orders indicate various degrees of accepting the control of others. There is no necessary relation between an individual's behavior toward controlling others, and his behavior toward being controlled. The domineering sergeant may accept orders from the lieutenant with pleasure and gratefulness, while the neighborhood bully may also rebel against his parents; two persons who control others differ in the degree to which they allow others to control them.

Thus the flavor of control is transmitted by behavior involving influence, leadership, power, coercion, authority, accomplishment, intellectual superiority, high achievement, and independence, as well as dependency (for decision making), rebellion, resistance, and submission. It differs from inclusion behavior in that it does not require prominence. The concept of the "power behind the throne" is an excellent example of a role that would fill a high control need and a low need for inclusion. The "joker" exemplifies the opposite. Control behavior differs from affection behavior in that it has to do with power relations rather than emotional closeness. The frequent difficulties between those who want to "get down to business" and those who want to get to "know one another" illustrate a situation in which control behavior is more important for some and affection behavior for others.

In general, *affection behavior* refers to close personal emotional feelings between *two* people. Affection is a dyadic relation; it can occur only between pairs of people at any one time, whereas both inclusion and control relations may occur either in dyads or between one person and a group of persons. Some terms that connote an affection relation that is primarily positive are "love," "like," "emotionally close," "positive feelings," "personal," "friendship," "sweetheart." Some terms that connote primarily lack of, or negative, affection are "hate," "dislike," "cool," "emotionally distant."

The need for affection leads to behavior related to becoming emotionally close. An affection relation must be dyadic because it involves strong differentiation between people. Affectional relations can be toward parental figures, peers, or children figures. They are exemplified in friendship relations, dating, and marriage.

To become emotionally close to someone involves, in addition to an emotional attachment, an element of confiding innermost anxieties, wishes, and feelings. A strong positive affectional tie usually is accompanied by a unique relation regarding the degree of sharing of these feelings.

In groups, affection behavior is characterized by overtures of friendship and differentiation between members. One common method of avoiding a close tie with any one member is to be equally friendly to all members. Thus "popularity" may not involve affection at all; it may often be inclusion behavior, whereas "going steady" is usually primarily affection.

A difference between affection behavior, inclusion behavior, and control behavior is illustrated by the different feelings a man has in being turned down by a fraternity, failed in a course by a professor, and rejected by his girl. The fraternity excludes him and tells him, in effect, that they as a group don't have sufficient interest in him. The professor fails him and says, in effect, that he finds him incompetent in his field. His girl rejects him, and tells him, in effect, that she doesn't find him lovable.

Thus the flavor of affection is embodied in situations of love, emotional closeness, personal confidences, intimacy. Negative affection is characterized by hate, hostility, and emotional rejection.

In order to sharpen further the contrast between these three types of behavior, several differences may be mentioned.

With respect to an interpersonal relation, inclusion is concerned primarily with the formation of the relation, whereas control and affection are concerned with relations already formed. Basically, inclusion is always concerned with whether or not a relation exists. Within existent relations, control is the area concerned with who gives orders and make decisions for whom, whereas affection is concerned with how emotionally close or distant the relation becomes. Thus, generally speaking, inclusion is concerned with the problem of *in or out*, control is concerned with *top or bottom*, and affection with *close or far*.

A further differentiation occurs with regard to the number of people involved in the relation. Affection is *always* a one-to-one relation, inclusion is *usually* a one-to-many relation, and control may be either a one-one or a one-many relation. An affectional tie is necessarily between two persons, and involves varying degrees of intimacy, warmth, and emotional involvement which cannot be felt toward a unit greater than one person. Inclusion, on the other hand, typically concerns the behavior and feelings of one person toward a group of people. Problems of belonging and membership, so central to the inclusion area, usually refer to a relatively undifferentiated group with which an individual seeks association. His feelings of wanting to belong to the group are qualitatively different from his personal feelings of warmth toward an individual person. Control may refer to a power struggle between two individuals for control over each other, or it may refer to the struggle for domination over a group, as in political power. There is no particular number of interactional participants implied in the control area.

Control differs from the other two areas with respect to the differentiation between the persons involved in the control situation. For inclusion and affection there is a tendency for participants to act similarly in both the behavior they express and the behavior they want from others; for example, a close, personal individual usually likes others to be close and personal also. This similarity is not so marked in the control area. The person who likes to control may or may not want others to control him. This difference in differentiation among need areas is, however, only a matter of degree. There are many who like to include but do not want to be included, or who are not personal but want others to be that way toward them. But these types are not as frequent as the corresponding types in the control area.

Types of Interpersonal Behavior

For each area of interpersonal behavior three types of behavior will be described: (1) deficient—indicating that the individual is not trying directly to satisfy the need, (2) excessive—indicating that the individual is constantly trying to satisfy the need, (3) ideal—indicating satisfaction of the need, and (4) pathological.

In delineating these types it is assumed that anxiety engendered by early experiences leads to behavior of the first, second, and fourth types, while a successful working through of an interpersonal relation leads to an individual who can function without anxiety in the area. The development origins are dealt with in Chapter 5. For simplicity of presentation the extremes will be presented without qualifications. Actually, of course, the behavior of any given individual could be best described as some combination of behavior incorporating elements of all three types at different times, for instance, the oversocial, undersocial, and social.

Inclusion Types

The Undersocial
The interpersonal behavior of the undersocial person tends to be introverted and withdrawn. Characteristically, he avoids associating with others and doesn't like or accept invitations to join others. Consciously he wants to maintain this distance between himself and others, and insists that he doesn't want to get enmeshed with people and lose his privacy. But unconsciously he definitely wants others to pay attention to him. His biggest fears are that people will ignore him, generally have no interest in him, and would just as soon leave him behind.

Unconsciously he feels that no one ever will pay attention to him. His attitude may be summarized by, "No one is interested in me. I'm not going to risk being ignored. I'll stay away from people and get along by myself." There is a strong drive toward self-sufficiency as a technique for existence without others. Since social abandonment is tantamount to death, he must compensate by directing his energies toward self-preservation; he therefore creates a world of his own in which his existence is more secure. Behind this withdrawal lie anxiety and hostility, and often a slight air of superiority and the private feeling that others don't understand him.

The direct expression of this withdrawal is nonassociation

and noninteraction with people, lack of involvement and commitment. The more subtle form is exemplified by the person who for one reason or another is always late to meetings, or seems to have an inordinate number of conflicting engagements necessitating absence from people, or the type of person who precedes each visit with, "I'm sorry, but I can't stay very long."

His deepest anxiety, that referring to the self concept, is that he is worthless. He thinks that if no one ever considered him important enough to receive attention, he must be of no value whatever.

Closely allied with this feeling is the lack of motivation to live. Association with people is a necessary condition for a desire to live. This factor may be of much greater importance in everyday interaction than is usually thought. The degree to which an individual is committed to living probably determines to a large extent his general level of enthusiasms, perserverance, involvement, and the like. Perhaps this lack of concern for life is the ultimate in regression: if life holds too few rewards, the prelife condition is preferable. It is likely that this basic fear of abandonment or isolation is the most potent of all interpersonal fears. The simple fear that people are not interested in the self is extremely widespread, but in scientific analyses it, too often, is included as a special type of affectional need. It is extremely useful, however, to make clear the distinction between inclusion and affection.

The Oversocial

The oversocial person tends toward extraversion in his later interpersonal behavior. Characteristically, he seeks people incessantly and wants them to seek him out. He is also afraid they will ignore him. His interpersonal dynamics are the same as those of the withdrawn person, but his overt behavior is the opposite.

His unconscious attitude is summarized by, "Although no one is interested in me, I'll make people pay attention to me in any way I can." His inclination is always to seek companionship. He is the type who "can't stand being alone." All of his activities will be designed to be done "together." An interesting illustration of this attitude occurs in the recent motion picture, "The Great Man." José Ferrer, as a newspaper man, is interviewing a woman about her reasons for attending the funeral of a television celebrity.

"Because our club all came together," she replies.
"But," Ferrer persists, "why did you come *here?*"
"I came here because the rest came here."
"Were you fond of the dead man?"
"Not especially," she replies, "but we always do things together."

This scene (the dialogue is from memory) nicely illustrates the importance of being together presumably as an end in itself. The interpersonal behavior of the oversocial type of person will then be designed to focus attention on himself, to make people notice him, to be prominent, to be listened to. There are many techniques for doing this. The direct method is to be an intensive, exhibitionistic participator. By simply forcing himself on the group he forces the group to focus attention on him. The more subtle technique is to try to acquire status through such devices as name dropping, or by asking startling questions. He may also try to acquire power (control) or try to be well liked (affection), but for the primary purpose of gaining attention. Power or friendship, although both may be important (depending on his orientation in the other two interpersonal areas), is not the primary goal.

The Social

To the individual for whom the resolution of inclusion relations was successful in childhood, interaction with people presents no problem. He is comfortable with people and comfortable being alone. He can be a high or low participator in a group, or can equally well take a moderate role, without anxiety. He is capable of strong commitment and involvement to certain groups and also can withhold commitment if he feels it is appropriate.

Unconsciously, he feels that he is a worthwhile, significant person and that life is worth living. He is fully capable of being genuinely interested in others and feels that they will include him in their activities and that they are interested in him.

He also has an "identity" and an "individuality." Childhood feelings of abandonment lead to the absence of an identity; the person feels he is nobody. He has no stable figures with whom to identify. Childhood feelings of enmeshment lead to confusion of identity. When a child is nothing but parts of other people and has not had sufficient opportunity to evaluate the characteristics he observes in himself, he has difficulty knowing who he is. The social person has resolved these difficulties. He has integrated aspects of a large number of individuals into a new configuration which he can identify as himself.

Inclusion Pathology

Failure to be included means anxiety over having no contact with people. Unsuccessful resolution of inclusion relations leads to feelings of exclusion, of alienation from people, of being different and unacceptable, and usually the necessity of creating a phantasy world in which the nonincluded person is accepted. Inclusion, because it is posited to be the first of interpersonal relations to be dealt with by the infant, has strong narcissistic elements and other close similarities to the description by psychoanalysts of the interpersonal characteristics in the oral stage. Hence a pathological difficulty in the inclusion area leads to the most regressed kind of behavior, that concerned with belonging to people, being a significant individual. This syndrome is very much like the functional *psychoses*. In Ruth Munroe's description of the Freudian explanation of psychoses these points are made clear:

The essential feature of Freud's explanation of psychotic conditions may be stated as the greater depth of regression. The adult never lapses back to infancy all of a piece of course. . . . Freud felt, however, that the truly psychotic manifestations belong to the pre-oedipal period—indeed to the stage of narcissism before the ego has properly developed. The mechanisms of

psychoses are the archaic mechanisms of the infant before
secure object relations have been established.[5]

The last line of this quotation is especially pertinent to
demonstrating the close relations between the Freudian discussion of the psychosis and the area of inclusion. The phrase,
"before secure object [interpersonal] relations have been
established," certainly bears a close resemblance to the preceding discussion of the problems of becoming included in the
social group.

It appears, then, that difficulty in establishing a satisfactory
relation with other persons, with regard to inclusion or contact,
when difficulty reaches a pathological state, leads to psychosis,
especially schizophrenia. This statement does not mean that
all conditions now called psychosis are caused by difficulties in
the inclusion area, nor does it necessarily mean that all inclusion problems will, if pathological, become psychoses; nor
does it even imply that there are "pure" inclusion problems
uncontaminated with other areas. It implies only that there is a
close relation between disturbance in the inclusion area and
psychosis.

Psychosis, especially schizophrenia, appears to be related
more to the undersocial pattern than the oversocial. The lack
of identity and inability to be alone, if carried to the extreme,
would correspond to the pathological extreme of the oversocial.

Control Types

The Abdicrat

The abdicrat is a person who tends toward submission and
abdication of power and responsibility in his interpersonal behavior. Characteristically, he gravitates toward the subordinate
position where he will not have to take responsibility for
making decisions, and where someone else takes charge.

[5] Ruth Munroe, *Schools of Psychoanalytic Thought* (New York: Dryden, 1956),
p. 288.

Consciously, he wants people to relieve him of his obligations. He does not control others even when he should; for example, he would not take charge even during a fire in a children's schoolhouse in which he is the only adult; and he never makes a decision that he can refer to someone else. He fears that others will not help him when he requires it, and that he will be given more responsibility than he can handle. This kind of person is usually a follower, or at most a loyal lieutenant, but rarely the person who takes the responsibility for making the *final* decision. Unconsciously, too, he has the feeling that he is incapable of responsible adult behavior and that others know it. He never was told what to do and therefore never learned. His most comfortable response is to avoid situations in which he will feel helpless. He feels that he is an incompetent and irresponsible, perhaps stupid, person who does not deserve respect for his abilities.

Behind this feeling are anxiety, hostility, and lack of trust toward those who might withhold assistance. The hostility is usually expressed as passive resistance. Hesitancy to "go along" is a usual technique of resistance, since actual overt rebellion is too threatening.

The Autocrat

The autocrat is a person whose interpersonal behavior often tends toward the dominating. Characteristically, he tries to dominate people and strongly desires a power hierarchy with himself at the top. He is the power seeker, the competer. He is afraid people will not be influenced or controlled by him—that they will, in fact, dominate him.

Commonly, this need to control people is displaced into other areas. Intellectual or athletic superiority allows for considerable control, as does the more direct method of attaining political power. The underlying dynamics are the same as for the abdicrat. Basically the person feels he is not responsible or capable of discharging obligation and that this fact is known to others. He attempts to use every opportunity to disprove this feeling to others and to himself. His unconscious attitude may be summarized as, "No one thinks I can make decisions for myself, but I'll show them. I'm going to make all the decisions for everyone, always." Behind this feeling is a strong distrust that others may make decisions for him and the feeling that they don't trust him. This latter becomes a very sensitive area.

The Democrat

For the individual who has successfully resolved his relations with others in the control area in childhood, power and control present no problem. He feels comfortable giving or not giving orders and taking or not taking orders, as is appropriate to the situation. Unconsciously, he feels that he is a capable, responsible person and therefore that he does not need to shrink from responsibility or to try constantly to prove how competent he really is. Unlike the abdicrat and autocrat, he is not preoccupied with fears of his own helplessness, stupidity, and incompetence. He feels that other people respect his competence and will be realistic with respect to trusting him with decision making.

Control Pathology

The individual who does not accept control of any kind develops pathologically into a psychopathic personality. He has not been adequately trained to learn the rules of behavior established for respecting the rights and privileges of others. Ruth Munroe says,

The major Freudian explanation for this condition is that there has been a serious failure of superego development. The practical image has not been adequately internalized in the form of conscience but remains the policeman at the corner—an external force. Truly, the behavior of the psychopath is childish without the limited experience of the child. When the resources of adulthood are used without the inner controls of adulthood the resultant behavior is very likely to be deplorable. Object relations generally are poor of necessity since good early object relations would have led to more adequate superego development.[6]

Affection Types

The Underpersonal

The underpersonal type tends to avoid close personal ties with others. He characteristically maintains his dyadic relations on a superficial, distant level and is most comfortable when others do the same to him. Consciously, he wishes to maintain this emotional distance, and frequently expresses a desire not to get "emotionally involved"; unconsciously he seeks a satisfactory affectional relation. His fear is that no one loves him. In a group situation he is afraid he won't be liked. He has great difficulty genuinely liking people. He distrusts their feeling toward him.

His attitude could be summarized by the "formula," "I find the affection area very painful since I have been rejected; therefore I shall avoid close personal relations in the future." The direct technique for maintaining emotional distance is to reject and avoid people to prevent emotional closeness or involvement activity, even to the point of being antagonistic. The subtle technique is to appear superficially friendly to *everyone*. This behavior acts as a safeguard against having to get close to, or become personal with, any *one* person. ("Close" and "personal" refer to emotional closeness and willingness to confide one's most private concerns and feelings. It involves the expression of positive affection and tender feelings.) Here the dyadic relation is a threatening one. To keep everyone at the same distance obviates the requirement for treating any one person with greater warmth and affection.

The deepest anxiety, that regarding the self, is that he is unlovable. He feels that people won't like him because, in fact, he doesn't "deserve" it. If people got to know him well, he believes, they would discover the traits that make him so

[6] *Ibid.,* p. 292.

unlovable. As opposed to the inclusion anxiety that the self is of no value, worthless, and empty, and the control anxiety that the self is stupid and irresponsible, the affection anxiety is that the self is nasty and bad.

The Overpersonal

The overpersonal type attempts to become extremely close to others. He definitely wants others to treat him in a very close, personal way. His response may be summarized by the formula, "My first experiences with affection were painful, but perhaps if I try again they will turn out to be better." He will be striving in his interpersonal relations primarily to be liked. Being liked is extremely important to him in his attempt to relieve his anxiety about being always rejected and unlovable. Again, there are two behavorial techniques, the direct and the subtle. The direct technique is an overt attempt to gain approval, be extremely personal, intimate, and confiding. The subtle technique is more manipulative, to devour friends and subtly punish any attempts by them to establish other friendships, to be possessive.

The underlying dynamics are the same as those for the underpersonal. Both the overpersonal and the underpersonal responses are extreme, both are motivated by a strong need for affection, both are accompanied by strong anxiety about ever being loved, and basically about being unlovable, and both have considerable hostility behind them stemming from the anticipation of rejection.

The Personal

For the individual who successfully resolved his affectional relations with others in childhood, close emotional relations with one other person present no problem. He is comfortable in such a personal relation, and he can also relate comfortably in a situation requiring emotional distance. It is important for him to be liked, but if he isn't liked he can accept the fact that the dislike is the result of the relation between himself and one other person—in other words, the dislike does not mean that he is an unlovable person. Unconsciously, he feels that he is a lovable person who is lovable even to people who know him well. He is capable of giving genuine affection.

Affection Pathology

Neuroses are commonly attributed to difficulties in the area of affection. Ruth Munroe says,

The early bloom of sexuality, which cannot possibly come to fruition, is called the phallic stage to differentiate it from true genitality leading to mature mating and reproduction. At this period attitudes are formed which are crucial for later hetero-sexual fulfillment and good relations with people generally. For this reason it is the stage most fraught with potentialities for neurotic distortion.[7]

The discussion of pathology in this chapter should be supplemented with the discussion of the childhood origins of various adult behavior patterns presented in Chapter 5. Combining the early experience and present behavior with the pathological classification will provide a more complete picture of the process of personality development and disintegration.

Summary

To summarize, difficulties with initiating interaction range from being uncomfortable when not associating with people ("can't stand to be alone"—the *oversocial*) to not feeling comfortable initiating interaction ("can't stand being with people"—the *undersocial*). Difficulties with controlling others range from not feeling comfortable controlling the behavior of anyone ("can't tell anyone what to do"—the *abdicrat*) to not feeling comfortable when unable to control everyone ("always have to be in charge"—the *autocrat*). Difficulties with originating close, personal relations range from being uncomfortable when unable to establish a sufficiently close, personal relation ('can't get close enough"—the *overpersonal*) to being uncomfortable when

[7] *Ibid.,* p. 199.

getting too close and personal with someone ("don't like to get emotionally involved with people"—the *underpersonal*).

This description could be stated in psychoanalytic terms with little if any difference in meaning. In the struggle between the id and the superego to determine the individual's behavior the excessive response in each area represents the triumph of the id. The restrained response results from the triumph of the superego. The ideal response represents the successful resolution of the id impulses, the demands of the superego, and external reality; it therefore corresponds to the triumph of the ego.

In each of the nonideal (extreme) types described there are anxiety, hostility, and ambivalence. (One outcome of this analysis is to suggest that each of these widely used terms could be divided profitably into three types.) Anxiety arises from a person's (a) anticipation of a nonsatisfying event (for instance, being ignored, dominated, rejected) and (b) fear of exposure, both to self and others, of what kind of person he "really" is— his inadequate self-concept. The anxiety indicates that these behavior patterns are inflexible, since anxiety usually leads to rigid behavior. The threat involved in changing behavior is too great to allow for much flexibility. Hostility also follows from anxiety; so the hostility, too, may arise in three ways.

Finally, ambivalence is also present in the nonideal behaviors, since the behavior pattern being utilized is necessarily unsatisfactory. In many instances an overpersonal individual, for example, will occasionally become underpersonal, and vice versa. Complete reversals are to be expected more than slight modifications, especially for the extreme behavior patterns. The characterization of a person's behavior can describe only his most usual behavior, not his invariable behavior.

David K. Berlo
Interaction:
The Goal of
Interpersonal Communication

We have spent a good deal of time talking about the ways in which communication sources and receivers behave. At the beginning, we defined communication as a process, and pointed out that it is on-going, dynamic, without starting and stopping points. This is true. Yet, we necessarily have talked at times as if communication were static, nondynamic. This has not been intentional, but it is impossible to avoid when we *talk about* communication, when we take it apart to see how it works.

At this point, we might profit from another look at the process viewpoint of communication. The behaviors of the source do not occur independently of the behaviors of the receiver or vice versa. *In any communication situation, the source and the receiver are interdependent.*

The concept of interdependence is itself complex and can be illustrated by defining the possible relationships between any two concepts, such as *A* and *B*. A *and* B *are independent if and only if neither affects the other.* For example, the color of a person's hair (*A*) and his left- or right-handedness (*B*) are independent. They do not affect each other. Blondes are just as likely to be right-handed as they are left-handed. So are brunettes or red-heads. Right-handed people are just as likely to be blondes as they are to be brunettes or red-heads. The same is true for left-handed people. Neither affects the other.

From *The Process of Communication* by David K. Berlo. Copyright © 1960 by Holt, Rinehart and Winston, Inc. Reprinted by permission of Holt, Rinehart and Winston, Inc.

There is a dependency relationship between A *and* B *if* A *affects* B *but* B *does not affect* A, *or vice-versa.* For example, the production of the ragweed flower (**A**) and the incidence of hay-fever (**B**) are dependently related. The presence of ragweed affects some people by producing hay-fever. Hay-fever is dependent on the existence of ragweed. Ragweed is not dependent on the existence of hay-fever. People who have hay-fever do not affect the existence of ragweed. *A* is not affected by *B*, but *B* is affected by *A*; therefore, *A* and *B* are dependently related.

Interdependence can be defined as *reciprocal* or *mutual* dependence. If *A* affects *B and B* affects *A*, then *A* and *B* are interdependent. For example, in this country the farmer and the grocer are interdependent. The food the farmer grows affects the product the grocer can sell. On the other hand, the sales of the grocer affect the kind and amount of crops the farmer will grow. Each is dependent on the other, each affects the other.

There are varying levels of interdependence among concepts or events. Maximum interdependence is found in concepts that we have referred to as dyadic. For example, the concepts of father and child are interdependent for their existence, neither can exist without the other. The same is true for husband-wife, leader-follower, supervisor-supervisee, etc. This can be called *definitional interdependence.* Dyadic concepts refer to relationships between events which cannot exist alone.

Communication between two or more people requires an interdependent relationship; however, the levels of communicative interdependence vary from situation to situation. How do these levels differ?

Levels of Communicative Interdependence

For purposes of discussion, we shall distinguish four levels of communicative interdependence. Again, it must be emphasized that we are distorting the process of communication when we do this. The four levels discussed are themselves not independent. Any communication situation probably includes some aspect of each; however, there are differences in emphasis from situation to situation.

If we remember that we are distinguishing among levels to point out differences in emphasis rather than differences in kind, we will not be misled. If we assume that communication at one level of interdependence is *not* related to the other levels, we will *not* be taking the process aspect of communication into account.

Definitional-Physical Interdependence

If we reflect for a moment, it becomes clear that the communication concepts of source and receiver are dyadic. They depend on each other for their very definition. You cannot define a source without defining a receiver. You cannot define a receiver without defining a source.

In addition to their definitional interdependence, the functions of the source and receiver are *physically* interdependent, although the functions may be performed at different points in time and space. When two people are communicating, they rely on the physical existence of the other for the production or reception of messages. Occasionally, this is the only kind of mutual interdependence involved to any appreciable extent. For example, let us look at the following hypothetical conversation between an industrial foreman (Harry) and a plant worker (John). John and Harry work in the same department. They meet when they get to work in the morning, and have the following "conversation":

John: Harry, let me tell you about what happened last night at home . . .

Harry: Fine, John. You know, things aren't going well on that experimental assembly job on the line . . .

John: I came in last night, and everything hit me. The wife said that the kids had ruined some of the plants in the yard . . .

Harry: If we don't get into full production pretty soon on that job, I don't see how . . .

John: the plumbing stopped up in the basement . . .

Harry: we can fulfill the contract we're working on.

John: and the dog tried to bite the little boy down the street.

Harry: Things are sure rough.
John: They sure are.

This set of messages is exaggerated slightly to demonstrate a point, but most of us have heard conversations like this one, or even participated in a few. John and Harry were interdependent. Without the presence of the other, neither would have encoded the messages that he did; however, their major functions were to serve as receivers for the other's messages.

The kind of interdependence emphasized in this kind of situation is merely definitional-physical. The two communicators were not even reacting to each other's message. They were only waiting their turn to encode.

We probably would not want to label this "good" or "effective" communication. It *is* a frequent kind of communication.

When we communicate this way, we are not talking *to* each other, we are merely talking. We do not feel right in encoding certain messages unless we are in the presence of another. We cannot continue to do this when we are with another unless he puts up with it, or uses the situation for his own purposes. We are interdependent—but only because of the dyadic nature of the concepts of source and receiver.

Action-Reaction Interdependence

In explaining what is meant by action-reaction interdependence, we can use any of several servo-mechanisms as an illustration. For example, take the relationship between the modern furnace and the thermostat which we keep in our living rooms. We can look on thermostat-furnace behaviors as a communication relationship. Both the thermostat and the furnace serve as a source and a receiver. Each encodes messages, each receives messages from the other. Each affects the other. They are interdependent, and this relationship is more than mere physical interdependence. The responses that each make are determined by the responses of the other. We can describe the communication situation between the thermostat and the furnace as follows: The thermostat has an intention, a purpose: to maintain the temperature of the room at a specific level, such as 68°. As long as the temperature remains at that level, the thermostat is silent. It encodes no message. When the temperature drops below that level, the thermostat transmits a message to the furnace—"turn on." *The thermostat acts.*

When the furnace receives the message "turn on," it decodes it and *reacts* to the message. The furnace allows oil or gas to enter its chambers, it increases the force of the pilot, it produces heat. When the air at the top of the furnace reaches a certain level, such as 150°, another thermostat starts.

None of these messages are transmitted to the thermostat. They are internal (covert) responses of the furnace. When the blower starts, however, the furnace begins to transmit a message to the thermostat—heat. The thermostat receives this message (a reaction by the furnace), decodes it and decides that its original purpose has been accomplished. The room temperature is now at the desired level.

On making this decision, the thermostat reacts to the heat it received by encoding another message—"turn off." The furnace reacts to this message by reducing oil or gas flow, lowering the pilot, shutting off the blower, and stopping the transmission of heat. In time, the thermostat reacts to the absence of heat, decides the temperature has dropped below the desirable level, and encodes another message—"turn on." The cycle begins again. Continual communication occurs between the furnace and the thermostat. Each transmits messages, each receives messages. Each reacts to the messages it receives.

The thermostat-furnace relationship is illustrative of many communication situations. Take the earlier example of the dinner table discussion between Bill and John. Bill had a purpose, he wanted John to pass him the salt. He encoded a message ("Pass me the salt, please.") He performed some *action.* John decoded the message and *reacted* to it. He responded by producing the salt. His action was taken as a result of decoding Bill's message.

When Bill perceived John's reaction, he reacted to it by reaching his hand out for the salt and saying "Thank you" to John. Each of these behaviors was dependent on the behavior preceding it. Bill acted, John reacted, Bill reacted, and so on. Bill and John were interdependent. Each was affected by the action of the other.

Feedback

Communication terminology includes a term related to action-reaction interdependence to which we have already referred: "feedback." It is correct to say that the furnace reacted to the thermostat; however, if we analyze the situation from the thermostat's point of view, we can say that the reaction of the furnace was *fed back* to the thermostat. The thermostat can utilize the reaction of the furnace in determining its next message.

Feedback from the furnace was useful because it affected the next message that the thermostat produced. Without feedback from the furnace, the thermostat would not be able to determine whether it should tell the furnace to keep providing heat or to turn itself off. The thermostat needed feedback to ascertain whether it was being successful in its communication, whether it was having the desired effect.

The term "feedback" names a special aspect of receiver reaction. It names the use which the source can make of this reaction in determining its own success. For example, when Bill asked John to pass the salt, he could watch John to see if he did it. John's response was useful to Bill as feedback. It told him whether he had been successful in accomplishing his objective. If John did not pass the salt, Bill could have asked him again. If the furnace did not turn on, the thermostat would have repeated its message.

The source can use the reaction of the receiver as a check of his own effectiveness and a guide to his own future actions. The reaction of the receiver is a *consequence* of the response of the source. As a response consequence, it serves as feedback to the source.

Feedback provides the source with information concerning his success in accomplishing his objective. In doing this, it exerts control over future messages which the source encodes.

In the thermostat-furnace example, the reaction of each to the behavior of the other serves as feedback; however, these reactions can be utilized only in a limited way. The thermostat can repeat its message of "turn on" or "turn off." The furnace can repeat its message of "heat" or "no heat." No other alternative is available to either. Neither can communicate a different message, neither can alter the code, content, or treatment of its message. All feedback can do in this illustration is affect the repetition of a message.

In human communication, we can utilize feedback to a much greater extent. John's response to Bill was usable by Bill as feedback. It told him whether he had been successful or not. If John did not pass the salt, Bill could have changed his message, changed the code, the content, or the treatment. Bill could have changed receivers and asked someone else. He even could have changed his purpose and eaten his food without salt.

John also could get feedback. When he passed Bill the salt, he could observe Bill's response. If Bill smiled, and said "Thanks," or began to use the salt, that would be one thing. If Bill frowned, looked confused, said "What's that for," that would be another thing. All these responses could be used by John as feedback. *One consequence of a communication response is that it serves as feedback—to both the source and the receiver.*

In summary, communication often involves an action-reaction interdependence. The action of the source affects the reaction of the receiver, the reaction of the receiver affects the subsequent reaction of the source, etc. The source or the receiver can make use of the reactions of the other.

Reactions serve as feedback. They allow the source or receiver to check up on himself, to determine how well he is doing in accomplishing his purpose. Feedback also affects subsequent behavior, if the source and receiver are sensitive to it.

When a source receives feedback that is rewarding, he continues to produce the same kind of message. When he gets nonrewarding feedback, he eventually will change his message. In responding to a message, the receiver exerts control over the source. The kind of feedback he provides determines in part the next set of behaviors of the source. Speakers and audiences, actors and theatre-goers, sources and receivers generally can be interdependent through the mutual effects of their reactions on the other.

For example, suppose you are giving a talk, making a speech. At one point in your talk, you tell a joke. The audience is supposed to laugh. If they laugh, this can serve as feedback to you. It tells you that you were successful. It tells you to keep going, your messages are having an effect. On the other hand, suppose the audience does not laugh. Suppose it just sits. This, too, serves as feedback. It tells you that you are not getting what you want, your messages are not meeting with success. You might change your jokes, or stop telling jokes. *The audience exerts control over your future messages by the responses it makes.* These are fed back to you. You are dependent on the audience for feedback.

At the same time, members of the audience are dependent on feedback. If one person does not laugh at your jokes and all the other members of the audience do, these responses are fed back to the nonlaughing receiver. He begins to question his sense of humor—and often begins to laugh at succeeding jokes, whether they strike him as funny or not. Eventually, they may even begin to strike him as funny.

Communication sources and receivers are mutually interdependent, for existence and for feedback. Each of them continually exerts influence over himself and others by the kinds of responses that he makes to the messages he produces and receives. A newspaper affects its readers by selecting the news they are allowed to read. On the other hand, the readers also affect the newspaper (although probably not as much as some publishers would have us believe). If readers do not buy the paper (negative feedback), it may change its selection and presentation of news.

Advertisers control the reasons given to the public for buying this or that product. But the consumer affects the advertiser —through feedback. If the public buys more (positive feedback), the advertiser keeps his messages. If the public quits buying the product (negative feedback), the advertiser changes his messages—or the stockholders get a new advertising manager.

We can separate one communication situation from another

by the ease with which feedback is obtained. Clearly, person-to-person communication permits maximum feedback. All available communication channels can operate. The source has an opportunity to change his message on the spot as a result of the feedback he gets. On the other hand, communication forms that we refer to as the public media (newspaper, television, magazines, etc.) have minimum opportunities for feedback. The source and the receiver are separated in time and space. They have little opportunity to get feedback from the responses of the other.

The difficulty of obtaining feedback for sources who use the public media has given rise to an entire industry: the public opinion pollster, the audience rating service, people who measure the amount of readership of a magazine, researchers who study the impact of advertising copy, organizations that interview receivers to check their responses to the source's message in an immediate and personal way. All these professionals attempt to provide feedback for a communication source. They are paid to help the source determine who is receiving his messages and what reactions are being made.

As communication receivers, we often overlook our affecting power on the source. In a competitive market, it is amazing how much influence ten letters to the manager of a television station can have on his future policy decisions. Our decisions to turn off the television set affect future program decisions; i.e., audience ratings serve as feedback. The battle of audience ratings is of great importance in the broadcasting industry. Major policy decisions are often made solely on the basis of feedback on how many people are listening to or viewing a given program.

Even in our own person-to-person communication situations, we overlook the importance of feedback. As students, we fail to realize the extent to which we can affect the teacher. When we indicate that we do not understand, he repeats, if he is sensitive to feedback. When we let him know we think he is a good teacher, he may become a better teacher. Any performer would testify that he gives a better performance when his audience reacts favorably, when they make responses which he can use as positive feedback.

We underestimate the value of feedback when we communicate with our friends and families. We neglect to tell them when we think they have done a good job or when we like them. These kinds of responses are useful to them as feedback. They affect future actions toward us.

Action-reaction relationships are significant in analyzing communication. Feedback is an important instrument of affect. The reactions of the receiver are useful to the source in analyzing his effectiveness. They also affect his subsequent behaviors because they serve as consequences of his prior responses. If the feedback is rewarding, he perseveres. If it is not rewarding, he changes his message to increase the chances of being successful.

An awareness and utilization of feedback increase the communication effectiveness of the individual. The ability to observe carefully the reactions others make to our messages is one of the characteristics of the person we designate as being good at "human relations," or "sensitive as a communicator."

It is true to say that one can find communication situations that fit this action-reaction level of interdependence between the source and the receiver. Granted, too, that it is useful to retain the action-reaction concept and the corresponding concept of communication feedback. Yet there are at least two possible pitfalls into which this kind of analysis can lead.

First, the concept of feedback is used to reflect a *source orientation* to communication, rather than a receiver orientation or a process orientation. When we talk about the receiver's responses as feedback for the source, we are observing communication situations from the point of view of the source. We are perceiving through his eyes, not as an external observer.

As we shall show, there are levels of interdependence higher than action-reaction. We do not have to look at the source-receiver relationship as a one-way relationship; however, the feedback concept emphasizes one-wayness, at the expense of a two-way analysis. When people are taught about feedback, they are likely to take a source orientation to communication. We talk about "getting feedback" to the source, or "using the receiver's behavior" as feedback for the source.

The term "feedback" implies a point of view. We have said

that one individual makes a response, performs an act. This response is perceived by a second individual and responded to. We say that the second individual reacts to the original message. When we call this reaction "feedback," we are structuring it as if we were the original source. We are talking about a use we can make of a reaction, not the reaction itself. There is nothing inherently wrong with this kind of terminology. In fact, it is useful to think this way. Nevertheless, if we are not careful, we begin to think about all of the processes from the source's point of view, and ignore the basic interdependence that produced the term "feedback" in the first place.

The second pitfall in the use of the action-reaction concept is concerned with our continuing reference to communication as a process. The terms "action" and "reaction" deny the concept of process. They imply that there is a beginning to communication (the act), a second event in communication (reaction), subsequent events, etc., with a final end. They imply an interdependence of events within the sequence, but they do not imply the kind of dynamic interdependence that is involved in the communication process.

People are not thermostats or furnaces. They have the capacity to make trial responses within the organism, to use symbols to anticipate how others will respond to their messages, to develop expectations about their own behavior and the behavior of others. The concept of *expectations* is crucial to human communication. It requires analysis at a third level of communication interdependence.

Interdependence of Expectations: Empathy

All human communication involves predictions by the source and receiver about how other people will respond to a message. Even in the minimal-interdependence situation that we have called physical interdependence, Bill and John had some expectations about each other. They made predictions about the language facility of the other, the length of time the other would tolerate listening rather than speaking, the social relationships that existed between them, etc. We can analyze expectations as a distinctive level of interdependence; however, to some extent this kind of interdependence is involved in all communication.

Every communicator carries around with him an image of his receiver. He takes his receiver (as he pictures him to be) into account when he produces a message. He anticipates the possible responses of his receiver and tries to predict them ahead of time. These images affect his own message behaviors. For example, the Madison Avenue advertiser has an image (accurate or inaccurate) of the American public. The Hollywood producer has an image of the movie-goer. Newspapers have expectations about how their readers will react to messages. Magazines can be distinguished on the basis of the images they have of their subscribers. Personnel managers have an image of the typical factory worker. Teachers have expectations about students.

The development of expectations of the receiver by the source has its counterpart in the development of expectations of the source by the receiver. Receivers have expectations about sources. When we observe the President, we expect him to behave in certain ways and not in others—because he is the President. Magazine readers have an image of the magazines they read. The public image of the *Ladies Home Journal* is not the same as the image of *Fortune, Playboy,* or *True Story*. We expect different message treatments.

Communication receivers select and attend to messages in part because of their images of the sources and their expectations as to the kind of message these sources would produce. The public has an image of business corporations, labor union leaders, educators, doctors, etc. One of the major missions of the public relations expert is the development of expectations about his client. People in this profession are paid to manipulate the receiver's image of a company, a public figure, a product.

As sources and receivers, we have expectations about each other that affect our communication behaviors. Behavior is also affected by our images of *ourselves*. Our self-images influence the kinds of messages we create and the treatment we give our messages. Our expectations about our own behavior affect which messages we attend to. Subscribers to *Harper's* may have self-images different from those of subscribers to **The Reader's Digest**. Republicans have different expectations about their own behavior than do Democrats—at least in some behavioral areas.

As sources and receivers, we carry around images of ourselves and a set of expectations about other people. We use these expectations in encoding, decoding, and responding to messages. We take other people into account in framing messages. We frame messages to influence a receiver, but our expectations about the receiver influence us and our messages.

Some of the more interesting studies in communication analyze the images which individuals or communicative organizations have of their receivers, and how these expectations affect the source's behavior. For example, what image does Madison Avenue have of the typical Iowa farmer, of Madison Avenue itself? What image does the corporation executive have of himself, of the average factory worker, etc.? These are research questions, and important ones. Their answers can help us explain why people treat their messages as they do, because a source's expectations influence the way he communicates.

In approaching the concept of expectations, we can return to our basic model of the communication process. The communication source and receiver each possess certain communication skills, attitudes, and knowledges. Each exists within a social system and a cultural context. These affect how they will react to messages. Communication represents an attempt to couple these two individuals, these two psychological systems. Messages are used to accomplish this coupling of the organisms.

In one sense, messages are all that the organisms have available to them. By using messages, we come to "know" other men, to know ourselves. We believe that we can understand in part what is going on *within* another person. We develop expectations about what is going on within others and what will go on within ourselves. The basic question is, how do we develop these expectations?

To put it another way, we often make statements of the order, "I know John," or "He won't accept that argument—I know him inside and out." How do we come to "know" other people, inside and out? For that matter, how do we come to "know" ourselves? What is the process underlying our ability to develop expectations about others, to predict how they will behave before a situation arises?

Clearly, we frequently face decisions requiring this kind of knowledge. We decide whether we should promote Jones, whether we should marry Mary, whether we should recommend Bill for a responsible job. When we make these kinds of decisions, we operate on the assumption that we "know" Jones or Mary or Bill. We make decisions which imply that we understand people, that we can predict how they will behave.

When we say that we "know" somebody, we mean more than that we can recognize him physically when we see him. We mean that we can predict correctly that he will believe certain things and not others, he will behave in certain ways and not in others, he will react in certain ways and not in others.

When we say we "know" somebody, including ourselves, we are saying that we understand how he operates as a psychological entity—as a person with thoughts, feelings, emotions, etc. In making these predictions, we have physical behaviors as our basic data. Each of us perceives how others behave. We can observe these behaviors. They are overt, public. Expectations involve more than this. They involve the private behaviors of man, his covert responses, his internal states, his beliefs, his meanings. When we develop expectations, when we make predictions, we are assuming that we have skill in what the psychologists call *empathy—the ability to project ourselves into other people's personalities.* How do we develop empathic ability?

This is a basic question for students of communication. Unfortunately, there is no definitive answer to the question. In any complete sense, we are still without enough research evidence to substantiate one position or another. There are theories of empathy which are plausible—and at least consistent with research evidence. Tomorrow may provide an adequate answer—but we have to operate on what we know today. *We can define empathy as the process through which we arrive at expectations, anticipations of the internal psychological states of man.* How does this occur?

There are three major points of view on empathy. One school of thought argues that there is no such thing, that we cannot develop expectations. Supporters of this position for the most part are believers in a simple one-stage (S-R) theory of learning. This kind of learning theorist argues that all we have in communication is a set of messages. A message is produced by one person, and perceived by another. In other words, there are stimuli and responses. And that is that. We argued in Chapter 4 that a simple S-R theory of learning may account for nonhuman animal learning, but not for the more complex learning behaviors of man. By the same argument, a simple S-R theory of empathy does not seem to account for man's communication behavior.

We *do* develop expectations, we *do* have the ability to project ourselves into the internal states of others. We cannot accept the argument that empathy does not have meaning for us, that we cannot develop expectations and predictions. Some kind of *interpretative* process occurs.

The development of expectations requires a special kind of talent. We need to be able to think about objects that are not available. *Expectations require decisions about the not-here and the not-now.* In order to have expectations, to talk about the not-here and the not-now, we create arbitrary symbols to represent the objects that are not available. We need to be able to produce these symbols and manipulate them.

Man is distinguished from other animals in that he has developed both of these talents. He can receive and manipulate arbitrary symbols. He can produce these symbols to serve his purposes. Because of this, he can represent the nonavailable, the not-here and not-now. As Thorndike put it, the use of arbitrary symbols allows "humans to think *about* things, not merely to think things." Man clearly has these talents, although there are individual differences among people.

Some of our games involve this kind of skill, the development of empathic ability. Chess is an example. A successful chess-player cannot rely on action-reaction. He develops expectations about the consequences of his behavior, and operates under those expectations. He predicts how the other man will react—often several events in advance. He debates moving a pawn. He reasons, if I move this pawn, my opponent probably will take my knight with his bishop—but if he does that, then I will checkmate his king with my queen, etc.

The same thing occurs in contract bridge. The good bidder anticipates possible answering bids from his partner or opponents before he makes his own bid. He also predicts how others will play their hands. The inclusion of this kind of skill is what prevents bridge from becoming a mechanical game that can be described in books. We differ in empathic ability. Some of us are better predictors than others.

We can reject the argument that we have no meaning for the concept of empathy. All of us anticipate the future, we make predictions about the relationships between (a) certain behaviors on our parts, (b) subsequent behaviors of other people, and (c) subsequent behaviors of our own. We do more than act and react. We develop expectations about others which affect our actions—before we take them. This is what we mean by empathy.

Theories of Empathy

There are two popular theories about the basis for empathy. Both theories agree that the basic data of expectations are physical behaviors produced by man, i.e., messages. Both theories agree that man's predictions about the internal psychological states of man are based on observable physical behaviors. Both agree that man makes these predictions by using symbols to represent these physical behaviors and by manipulating these symbols. At this point, the two theories of empathy differ sharply. We can best discuss them separately.

Inference Theory of Empathy[1]

An inference theory of empathy is psychologically oriented. It argues that man can observe his own physical behavior directly,

[1] The major source of this theory is Solomon Asch, *Social Psychology,* Prentice-Hall, 1952, pp. 139–169.

and can relate his behavior symbolically to his own internal psychological states—his feelings, thoughts, emotions, etc. Through this process, man comes to have meanings (interpretations) for his own physical behavior. He develops a concept of *self*, by himself, based on his observations and interpretations of his own behavior.

Given a self-concept, he communicates with other people. He observes their physical behaviors. On the basis of his prior interpretations of himself, he makes *inferences* about the internal states of others. In other words, he argues to himself that if behavior on his part represented such and such a feeling, a similar behavior produced by somebody else would represent a similar feeling.

This view of empathy assumes that man has first-hand knowledge of himself and second-hand knowledge of other people. It argues that man has the ability to understand himself, through analysis of his own behaviors. From this analysis, man can make inferences about other people based on the similarities between their behavior and his own.

Let us take a simple example of this argument. Suppose you observe yourself making certain gestures; e.g., you repeatedly pound your hand on a table. You analyze how you felt when you performed this behavior. You conclude that you were angry, that you were upset. You discover a relationship between your overt behavior (table-pounding) and an internal state or feeling of anger. Then you observe somebody else pounding his hand on the table. From this behavior, you infer that he too is angry. You make assumptions about his internal state from (a) observing his behavior, and (b) comparing his behavior with similar behavior on your part which reflected anger in you.

This is the position of an *inference* theory of empathy. What are its assumptions?

1. Man has first-hand evidence of his own internal states. He can only have second-hand evidence of other people's internal states.

2. Other people express a given internal state by performing

the same behaviors that you perform to express the same state.

3. Man cannot understand internal states in other people which he has not experienced himself. Man cannot understand emotions which he has not felt, thoughts which he has not had, etc.

Let us take these assumptions one at a time. First, an inference theory of empathy says that man's first-hand knowledge is of himself. All other knowledge is second-hand. As we shall find, the other major view of empathy contradicts this assumption directly. From currently available research evidence, we cannot resolve this issue; the assumption can be neither accepted nor rejected.

There is considerable evidence that conflicts with the second assumption, that all people express the same purposes by the same behaviors, that all people mean the same things by the behaviors they perform. Many breakdowns in communication stem from this belief. We often assume that another person attaches the same meaning to a word that we do, that a smile by another person expresses the same internal state as does a smile by us, that other people see the world in the same way that we do—just because they perform many of the physical behaviors that we perform.

It is true that we often get our ideas about the internal states of other people by inferring them from our own internal states, as related to our own behavior. But in so doing, we often err. We often fail to "know" the internal workings of others when we assume they are the same as ours.

When we look at the success we have in predicting and anticipating the behavior of others, it seems likely that we need to add another approach to empathy to provide a complete explanation of our success. We need an approach which does not assume that man's first-hand knowledge is always of use. People are not the same.

There also is evidence that contradicts the third assumption of inference theory: that we cannot understand internal states which we have not experienced ourselves. Few theorists would dispute the point that man understands best those things which he has experienced himself. Yet we can find many examples of the understanding (at least in part) of emotions which have not been experienced. For instance, we can empathize with a mother who has just lost her baby. We can have expectations about how she will behave, what her internal states are, even though we have never lost a baby. We can empathize with people who are in a state of great happiness over their coming marriage, even though we have not been married ourselves. Experience increases our understanding, but it does not seem to be essential to understanding.

These are the essential arguments of an inference theory of empathy. There seems to be some merit in the arguments; however, inference theory does not seem to explain empathy in terms that are completely satisfying. We can turn our attention to the second point of view, popularized by Mead and usually considered to be a sociological point of view. Mead labeled his theory as *role-taking*.

Role-Taking Theory of Empathy[2]

Let us not assume that man's first-hand knowledge is of himself, or even that man *has* a concept of self before he communicates with other people. We can examine some of the behaviors of man, and try to interpret their implications for empathy.

Let us look at the very young child, the infant. How does he behave, how does he develop his ability to empathize? The basic data that are observable to the infant are physical behaviors, message behaviors. The infant, like everyone else, can observe and produce physical behavior. The question is, how does the child develop interpretations of self and others, given observable physical behaviors?

Role-taking theorists argue that the new-born infant cannot distinguish himself from other people, cannot tell one person from another. In order to develop the concept of self, the infant

[2] The major source of this theory is the work of George H. Mead. Much of the discussion is taken from George H. Mead, *Mind, Self and Society*. University of Chicago Press, 1934.

must first look on himself as an object—must act toward himself as he acts toward other objects, other people. *In other words, the concept of self does not precede communication. It is developed through communication.*

The young child exhibits a good deal of imitative behavior. He observes other people's behavior. He tries to repeat the behavior as well as he can. Some of the behavior he imitates is behavior directed toward him. His mother makes sounds (speaks) in his presence. He begins to imitate the sounds. The father moves his face (smiles) in his presence. He begins to imitate these facial movements.

In imitating behaviors directed toward him, the infant begins to act toward himself as others act toward him, but he has no interpretation for these actions, no meaning for the actions. This is the beginning of role-taking, the beginning of the development of a concept of self. *In the first stage of role-taking, the infant actually plays other people's roles without interpretation.* He imitates the behavior of others. He is rewarded for these role-playing responses; therefore he retains them.

As the child develops, he increases his role-playing behavior. He increasingly acts toward himself in the same way that other people act toward him. At the same time, he learns to produce and manipulate a set of symbols, significant symbols, symbols for which he and other people have meanings. Equipped with a set of significant symbols, the infant can begin to understand the roles that he takes. He can understand how other people behave toward him. He can begin really to put himself in other people's shoes, to look at himself as other people do.

Those of you who have watched small children know what is meant by this. The child at age two or three will play by having a make-believe tea party. At the tea party, he will reprimand himself—produce messages such as "Todd, you mustn't do that or I'll send you up to bed," or "No, no, Sandy, that's not the way to sit at the table." When the child behaves like this, he is looking at himself as an object of behavior—as an external object. He is playing the role of the parent, putting himself in the shoes of the parent. *This is the second stage of role-taking, in which the infant plays other people's roles—with understanding.*

As the child matures, he engages in more complex role-playing. He begins to play games with several other people. In playing games, the child must take a large number of roles at the same time. In hide-and-seek, the child must put himself in the shoes of the person who is "it," must, simultaneously, take the roles of all the other children who are hiding.

It now becomes impossible physically to *play* all these roles. The child cannot imitate all the related behaviors. Through the use of symbols, however, he hypothesizes what it would be like to behave as the other children do. He infers their roles, he takes their roles in his own mind, rather than playing the roles physically. *This is the third stage of role-taking, in which the child begins to put himself in other people's shoes symbolically, rather than physically.*

By putting himself in the places of all the other children, the child develops expectations about his own behavior—about what is expected of him in this situation. He then behaves according to his expectations, as determined by *taking* the roles of others. If he has done a good job of role-taking, his behavior conforms to the expectations the others have, and they reward him, they let him play, they like him. If he has not done a good job of role-taking, his behavior does not conform to the expectations of the other children and he is not rewarded. He is rejected, punished.

As the child continues to participate in group activity, he takes the roles of many other people. In so doing, he looks on himself as a receiver, as an object of behavior. Gradually, he begins to *generalize* the roles of others. He starts to get a general concept of how other people behave, how they interpret and how they act toward him. We can call this the concept of the generalized other. *The generalized other is an abstract role that is taken, the synthesis of what an individual learns of what is general or common to the individual roles of all other people in his group.*

Each of us develops a concept of the generalized other, based on our experiences in a specific social environment and in the successive roles of other people that we take. The generalized other provides us with a set of expectations as to how we should behave. This is our meaning for the concept of self. *Our self-concept is the set of expectations that we have as to how we should behave in a given situation.* How do we develop a self-concept? Through communication, through taking the roles of others, through acting toward ourselves as an object of communication, through the development of a generalized other.

Inference theory *assumes* a concept of self, and suggests that we empathize by using the self-concept to make inferences about the internal states of other people. Inference theory suggests that the self-concept determines how we empathize. Role-taking theory argues the other way around. It suggests that the concept of self does not determine empathy. Rather, communication produces the concept of self and role-taking allows for empathy. Both theories place great importance on the nature of language, significant symbols, in the process of empathy and the development of a concept of self.

Which are we to believe? How does man empathize? Here, we will take the position that *man utilizes both these approaches to empathy.* We can argue that man's first approach is through role-taking. Each of us takes roles of other people. Each of us develops a concept of the generalized other. The way that we look on ourselves, our definition of ourselves, is determined by our concept of the generalized other, the social context in which we exist, the expectations which we perceive others to have about our own behaviors.

As we develop and mature, we construct a concept of self. Then we operate on it. We now begin to make inferences about other people, based on our concept of self. We lessen our use of role-taking, and increase our use of inferences. We make the assumption that other people are like us, and that their behaviors reflect the same internal states that our behavior reflects. We do this until we do not find it rewarding.

When we empathize by making inferences and are not rewarded, we are forced to do one of two things. Either (1) we distort the behaviors of others that we perceive, and make them correspond to our expectations, or (2) we take another look at our images of ourselves, we redefine self, we return to role-taking.

If we take the first solution, distorting the world that we perceive, we become mentally ill, we have "delusions," we end up in an institution. This is not desirable. Yet we can predict that much of the problem of mental health is related to man's inability or unwillingness to change his own image of himself when he finds that it is not rewarded in his social environment.

What about the second alternative, a redefinition of self? To do this, we have to return to role-taking, we again have to take the role of others, to develop a new concept of the generalized other, a new set of expectations for our own behavior. In so doing, we redefine ourselves, change our behaviors accordingly, and again begin to make inferences about other people.

We often engage in role-playing when we are revising our role-taking or self concepts. Again, the mentally ill can use role-playing as a technique to increase their ability to make useful hypotheses about how others would react, and how they should react in a given situation.

As we play the role of another, we combine the inference and role-taking points of view. When we role-play, we actually perform certain behaviors. From these, we can infer our own internal states, we can make inferences from our own behavior which are pertinent to the behavior of another. We then can use these inferences in taking the role of another.

This process of role-taking, inference, role-taking, inference goes on continually. It is what we mean when we say that man is adjustable, adaptable, able to alter his behavior to fit the situation, the social environment in which he finds himself. He develops expectations by taking the roles of others, or by making inferences about himself, or both.

When do we often find it necessary to redefine self? When we enter a new social situation, a new group, a different social environment. For example, when a teen-ager enters the university, he finds himself in a new social situation. His inferences about other people are no longer valid. He makes false predictions, has hazy expectations. Often, he begins to ask himself who he really is.

What does the teen-ager begin to do? He reverts to role-playing, often at a primitive stage. He begins to imitate the behavior of others—without meaning. Gradually, he takes the roles of others (students, teachers, etc.) and is able to put himself in other people's shoes, to look at himself through their eyes. In so doing, he develops a new concept of the generalized other, a new set of expectations about his own behavior. He redefines self and begins to behave in accord with his new definition.

This kind of process is required of us many times in our lives. When we enter a new community, join a new group, travel to a different culture, our predictive power is weakened. We find it difficult to make inferences from self-knowledge. If we are to operate effectively in a changing social situation, we need to be able to take other people's roles, to redefine ourselves. In part, this is the mark of the adjusted man.

Interaction: The Goal of Human Communication

One necessary condition for human communication is an interdependent relationship between the source and the receiver. Each affects the other. At one level of analysis, communication involves only a physical interdependence; i.e., source and receiver are dyadic concepts, each requires the other for its very definition, each requires the other for its existence.

At a second level of complexity, interdependence can be analyzed as an action-reaction sequence. An initial message affects the response that is made to it, the response affects the subsequent response, etc. Responses affect subsequent responses because they are utilized by communicators as feedback—as information that helps them determine whether they are achieving the desired effect.

At a third level of complexity, communication analysis is concerned with empathic skills, the interdependence produced by expectations about how others will respond to a message. Empathy names the process in which we project ourselves into the internal states or personalities of others in order to predict ourselves in the other person's shoes, to perceive the world as he sees it. In doing this, we develop the concept of self that we how they will behave. We infer the internal states of others by comparing them to our own attitudes and predispositions.

At the same time, we engage in role-taking. We try to put

use to make inferences about others. In communicating, we shift from inferences to role-taking as a basis for our predictions. The expectations of the source and receiver are interdependent. Each affects the other, each is in part developed by the other.

A final level of interdependent complexity is interaction. The term *interaction* names the process of reciprocal role-taking, the mutual performance of emphatic behaviors. *If two individuals make inferences about their own roles and take the role of the other at the same time, and if their communication behavior depends on the reciprocal taking of roles, then they are communicating by interacting with each other.*

Interaction differs from action-reaction in that the acts of each participant in communication are interrelated with each other, they affect each other through the development of hypotheses about what these acts will be, how they fit the purposes of the source and receiver, etc.

The concept of interaction is central to an understanding of the concept of process in communication. Communication represents an attempt to couple two organisms, to bridge the gap between two individuals through the production and reception of messages which have meanings for both. At best, this is an impossible task. Interactive communication approaches this ideal.

When two people interact, they put themselves into each other's shoes, try to perceive the world as the other person perceives it, try to predict how the other will respond. Interaction involves reciprocal role-taking, the mutual employment of empathic skills. The goal of interaction is the merger of self and other, a complete ability to anticipate, predict, and behave in accordance with the joint needs of self and other.

We can define interaction as the ideal of communication, the goal of human communication. All communication is not interactional, or at least does not emphasize this level of interdependence. As we shall see in the following chapter, much of our social behavior involves attempts to find substitutes for interaction, to find less energy-consuming bases for communication.

We can communicate without interacting to any appreciable

extent; however, to the extent that we are in an interactional situation, our effectiveness, our ability to affect and be affected by others increases. As interaction develops, expectations become perfectly interdependent. The concepts of source and receiver as separate entities become meaningless, and the concept of process becomes clear.

Questions
for
Reflection
and
Discussion
Section Two

1. What major theories of child development can be cited to show that human interaction is necessary for adequate personal growth and development?
2. To what extent have you experienced suppression by others of your communication efforts? What have been your thoughts and reactions to these experiences? To what extent was such suppression justified?
3. Can you suggest additional personal needs for interaction with others not included among those postulated by Schutz: *inclusion, control,* and *affection?*
4. Note Schutz's table entitled "Matrix of Relevant Interpersonal Data." To what extent is graphic representation inadequate as a model of personal needs for human interaction and useful ways of meeting these needs?
5. Berlo makes the point that a person does not just talk *to* another person, but *interacts,* i.e., the other person's responses and behavior *influence* what the first person says and the way he says it. How does this principle relate to our efforts to satisfy our need to interact with others? Does it influence our attempts to *initiate* interaction? To choose to talk with some persons and not others? To ignore some persons who seem to want to talk with us? Can you name other factors in human interaction which are thus influenced?
6. Relate Berlo's concept of "Levels of Interdependence" to Giffin and Heider's description of communication suppression. Is it likely that such suppression occurs at some "levels" more than others? If so, why?

INTERPERSONAL
PERCEPTION
SECTION THREE

As we come into contact with one another, we receive sensory signals that establish the basis for our communication. The attempts at communication will be guided by our interpretation of these signals. These signals and the interpretations establish the basis of our "interpersonal perception." By "interpersonal perception" we mean the way individuals view and evaluate one another in direct interaction; this encompasses the inter-relationships between the perceiver, the person perceived, and the external contextual variables.

While all of our sense receptions form the basis for a variety of perceptual cues, interpersonal perception differs from our perception of objects in at least two ways: first, unlike objects, other people are perceived as having motives which influence their behaviors, and second, the person being perceived is simultaneously perceiving the other person and may alter his behaviors accordingly.

There has been much research and theorizing on the nature and consequences of interpersonal perceptions. In this section we have included three articles intended to encompass a wide range of research conclusions. The article by Hadley Cantril discusses some of the significant research findings on the assumptions that affect our perception. The report by William V. Haney provides a model of perception that identifies the interrelated variables and the behavioral results. Finally, the essay by George Orwell provides a case study for the applications of the theories suggested. As you read the Orwell essay, attempt to analyze the effects that the varying interpersonal perceptions have on the behaviors described.

Hadley Cantril
Perception and
Interpersonal Relations

It is with a very profound feeling of humility that I, as a psychologist, offer any comments for the consideration of psychiatrists on the subject of perception and interpersonal relations. For the more one studies perception, the more one sees that what we label "perception" is essentially a process which man utilizes to make his purposive behavior more effective and satisfying, and that this behavior always stems from and is rooted in a personal behavioral center. Thus perception involves numerous aspects of behavior which we rather artificially and necessarily differentiate in order to get a toe-hold for understanding, but which, in the on-going process of living, orchestrate together in a most interdependent way.

This means, then, that the nature of perception can only be understood if somehow we manage to start off with what some of us call a "first person point of view" as contrasted to the "third person point of view" represented by the traditional psychological investigator. And so my very genuine feeling of humility in accepting an invitation of psychiatrists derives from the fact that the psychiatrist, perhaps more than any other specialist concerned with the first-person point of view, is skilled in the art of uncovering what this may be for his patient, and

Reprinted by permission of the author and the publisher from Hadley Cantril, "Perception and Interpersonal Relations," *American Journal of Psychiatry,* Vol. 114, pp. 119–126, 1957. Copyright 1957, the American Psychiatric Association. This was read at the A.P.A. Regional Meeting in Montreal, Nov. 8–11, 1956.

knows from his own experience the wide gap that exists between this first-person experience and the abstractions we have created as scientists in order to analyze, conceptualize, and communicate. A very nice expression of this last state of affairs was, incidentally, recently made by Aldous Huxley in his book *The Genius and the Goddess:*

What a gulf between impression and expression! That's our ironic fate—to have Shakespearian feelings and (unless by a billion-to-one chance we happen to be Shakespeare) to talk about them like automobile salesmen or teen-agers or college professors. We practice alchemy in reverse—touch gold and it turns to lead; touch the pure lyrics of experience, and they turn into the verbal equivalents of tripe and hogwash.

Background

Most of you are probably familiar to some extent with a point of view that has developed rather recently in psychology and has been dubbed "transactional psychology." While I do not want to spend time here repeating what has been published in a variety of sources, I might at least very briefly note some of the major emphases of transactional psychology before discussing certain aspects and some experimental results which may be of particular interest to psychiatrists (1, 2, 3, 4).

Here, then, are some of the emphases of transactional psychology which may give us a take-off for discussion:

Our perception depends in large part on the assumptions we bring to any particular occasion. It is, as Dewey and Bentley long ago pointed out, not a "reaction to" stimuli in the environment but may be more accurately described as a "transaction with" an environment.

This implies that the meanings and significances we assign to things, to symbols, to people, and to events are the meanings and significances we have built up through our past experience, and are not inherent or intrinsic in the "stimulus" itself.

Since our experience is concerned with purposive behavior,

our perceptions are learned in terms of our purposes and in terms of what is important and useful to us.

Since the situations we are in seldom repeat themselves exactly and since change seems to be the rule of nature and of life, our perception is largely a matter of weighing probabilities, of guessing, of making hunches concerning the probable significance or meaning of "what is out there" and of what our reaction should be toward it, in order to protect or preserve ourselves and our satisfactions, or to enhance our satisfactions. This process of weighing the innumerable cues involved in nearly any perception is, of course, a process that we are generally not aware of.

Creating Constancies

Since things in the world outside us—the physical world and more especially the social world—are by no means static, are not entirely determined and predictable, experience for most of us carries at least some mild overtone of "concern" which we can label "curiosity," "doubt" or "anxiety" depending on the circumstances involved.

One of my favorite illustrations of this point is an incident described by Carl Sandburg in his autobiography, *Always the Young Strangers.*

I have always enjoyed riding up front in a smoking car, in a seat back of the 'deadheads,' the railroaders going back to the home base. Their talk about each other runs free. . . . Once I saw a young fireman in overalls take a seat and slouch down easy and comfortable. After a while a brakeman in blue uniform came along and planted himself alongside the fireman. They didn't say anything. The train ran along. The two of them didn't even look at each other. Then the brakeman, looking straight ahead, was saying, 'Well, what do you know today?' and kept looking straight ahead till suddenly he turned and stared the fireman in the face, adding, 'For sure.' I thought it was a keen and intelligent question. What do you know today—for sure?' I remember the answer. It came slow and honest. The fireman made it plain what he knew that day for sure: 'Not a damn thing!' . . .

Thus we seldom can count on complete 100% surety in terms of a perfect correspondence between our assumptions concerning the exact experience we may have if we do a certain thing and the experience we actually do have as the consequence of the action we undertake.

In an attempt to try to minimize our potential lack of surety concerning any single occasion and thereby maximize our sense of surety concerning the effectiveness of our action in achieving our intent, we build up "constancies" and begin to count on them. While a great deal of experimental work has been done on "constancies" in the psychological laboratory, we still have much more to learn. And above all, we have a great deal to learn about constancy as we extend this concept into the field of our interpersonal relations.

Parenthetically, one of the most important things we have to learn is that the "constancy" we create and that we describe usually by means of some word, symbol, or abstract concept *is* man's creation, the validity of which can only be tested and the meaning of which can only be experienced in terms of some behavior which has consequences to us and signals to us what the concept refers to.

We create these constancies by attributing certain *consistent* and *repeatable* characteristics to what they refer to, so that we can guess with a fair degree of accuracy what the significances and meanings are of the various sensory cues that impinge upon us. We do this so that we will not have to make fresh guesses at every turn.

These significances we build up about objects, people, symbols, and events, or about ideas all orchestrate together to give us what we might call our own unique *"reality world."* This "reality world" as we experience it includes, of course, our own fears and hopes, frustrations and aspirations, our own anxiety and our own faith. For these psychological characteristics of life—as the psychiatrist knows better than anyone else— are just as real for us in determining our behavior as are chairs, stones or mountains or automobiles. It seems to me that any-thing that takes on significance for us in terms of our own per-sonal behavioral center *is* "real" in the psychological sense.

Assigning Significances

Let me illustrate with reference to a few recent experiments the way in which the significance we attach to others "out there" seems to be affected by what we bring to the situation. Incidentally but important: I do want to underscore that the experiments mentioned here are only exploratory; are only, I believe, opening up interesting vistas ahead. I am in no sense attempting to indicate what their full theoretical implications may be. But I mention them to show how experiments de-signed to get at the first person point of view may suggest to the experienced psychiatrist ways of using experimental pro-cedures in his diagnosis and possibly even in therapy. And I also mention them because of my deep conviction that psy-chology can be both humanistic and methodologically rigorous.

A whole series of most promising experiments now seems possible with the use of a modern adaptation of an old-fashioned piece of psychological equipment, the stereoscope. Dr. Edward Engel who devised the apparatus has already published a description of it and reported some of his first findings (5). As you know, the stereoscope in a psychological laboratory has been used to study binocular rivalry and fusion but the material viewed almost always consisted of dots and lines or geometrical patterns. Engel was curious to see what would happen if meaningful figures were used instead of the traditional material.

The results are really most exciting. In Engel's experiments he prepares what he calls "stereograms" consisting of photo-graphs 2 × 2 inches, one of which is seen with the left eye, the other with the right. The photographs he used first were those of members of the Princeton football team just as they appeared in the football program. Although there were slight differences in the size and position of the heads and in the characteristics of light and shadow, still there was sufficient superimposition to get binocular fusion. And what happens? A person looks into the stereoscope and sees one face. He describes this face. And it almost invariably turns out that he is describing neither the face of the man seen with the left eye nor the face of the man seen with the right eye. He is describing a new and different face, a face that he has created out of the features of the two he is looking at. Generally the face seen in this particular case is made up of the dominant features of the two individuals. And generally the face created by the observer in this situation is more attractive and appealing than either of those seen separately. When the observer is shown the trick of the experiment by asking him to close first one eye and then the other and to compare the face he originally saw with the other two, he himself characterizes the face he created as more handsome, more pleasant, a fellow he'd like better, etc.

I hasten to add, however, that we should by no means jump to the conclusion that an individual picks out the "best" or "most attractive" features of figures presented to him in a situation of binocular fusion. For example, Professor Gordon Allport recently took one of Engel's stereoscopes with him to South Africa and initiated some experimental work there, using photographs of members of the different racial groups which make up that complex community.

While the experiments in South Africa have only just begun and no conclusion should be drawn, it is significant to note that in recent letters communicating the early results, Allport reported that when the stereograms consist of a European paired with an Indian, a colored person compared with an Indian, etc. the Zulus see an overwhelming preponderance of Indians. For the Zulu is most strongly prejudiced against the Indian who represents a real threat to him. Allport also reports that when Europeans in South Africa view the stereogram they tend to see more colored faces than white. It would seem, then, that a person sees what is "significant," with significance defined in terms of his relationship to what he is looking at.

One pair of slides we use in demonstrating this piece of

equipment consists of two stereograms, each a photograph of a statue in the Louvre. One of the statues is that of a Madonna with Child, the other a lovely young female nude. While I am unable so far to predict what any given individual will "see," no doubt such a prediction might be made after some good psychiatric interviewing. But let me describe what happened in a typical viewing of these stereograms. The viewers happened to be two distinguished psychologists who were visiting me one morning, one from Harvard, the other from Yale. The first looked into the stereoscope and reported that he saw a Madonna with Child. A few seconds later he exclaimed, "But my God, she is undressing." What had happened so far was that somehow she had lost the baby she was holding and her robe had slipped down from her shoulders and stopped just above the breast line. Then in a few more seconds she lost her robe completely and became the young nude. For this particular professor, the nude never did get dressed again. Then my second friend took his turn. For a few seconds he could see nothing but the nude and then he exclaimed, "But now a robe is wrapping itself around her." And very soon he ended up with the Madonna with Child and as far as I know still remains with that vision. Some people will never see the nude; others will never see the Madonna if they keep the intensity of light the same on both stereograms.

In the situation described above, we do not have conditions for genuine fusion, but rather a condition which introduces conflict and choice in the possible meaning of the content represented. In order to learn whether or not there might be differences in choice that would be culturally determined, a cross cultural comparison was made by Dr. James Bagby (6). He constructed pairs of stereograms that would create binocular rivalry: in one stereogram of each pair he had a picture of some individual, object or symbol that would be of particular interest to Mexicans; in the other stereogram he had a picture that would be of particular significance to Americans. For example one pair of slides consisted of a picture of a bull fighter matched with a stereogram picturing a baseball player. When these pairs were shown to a sample of Mexican school teachers, an overwhelming proportion of them "saw" the Mexican symbol; when the same slides were presented to a group of American school teachers, the overwhelming proportion "saw" the American symbol.

Incidentally, the Engel stereoscope is so constructed that one can get some idea of the relative "strength" of each of the stereograms by adjusting the intensity of the lighting on each. Hence, if the lighting is equivalent on two stereograms in a rivalry situation, one can reduce the amount of lighting on the one that originally predominates, increase the amount of light on the one that was not "seen" and find the point where the first one disappears and the second one "comes in."

A modification of the stereoscope has just been completed by Mr. Adlerstein in the Princeton laboratory. Our thought was that it might be extremely useful both in the clinical and social areas, if instead of having to use photographs of objects or people, a person could view the real thing—that is, the faces of real, live individuals or pairs of actual objects. So by means of prisms and mirrors, this device was constructed and I have only very recently had the opportunity of experiencing the resulting phenomena. I must say it is strange and wonderful. For example, when I viewed Mr. Adlerstein and Mrs. Pauline Smith, Curator of our Demonstration Center, I seemed to be looking at a very effeminate Mr. Adlerstein who was wearing Mrs. Smith's glasses. Though weird, he was extremely "real." At one point while I was observing them Mrs. Smith began to talk yet it was Adlerstein's lips that were moving! Tingling with excitement and with a certain amount of anxiety, I drove home and asked my wife and daughter to come down to the laboratory so that I could take a look at them. I was, of course, fearful that I might see only one or the other. But fortunately, again I got an amazing fusion—a quite real and lovely head composed of a blending of my daughter's hair and chin and my wife's eyes and mouth—an harmonious composition that would do justice to any artist and which I created almost instantaneously and without any awareness of what was going on. These pieces of apparatus seem to me to have enormous potential usefulness for studying the way in which we create the world around us. I am hoping, for example, that before long someone in a position to do so may use this sort of equipment in a study of disturbed children. The child—having two eyes and two parents—might in some situations and in a very few seconds reveal a good bit about his inner life and his interpersonal family relations.

An interesting series of experiments on perception and interpersonal relations began systematically a few years ago after an observation I made one Sunday morning in our laboratory. An old friend of mine, who was a distinguished lawyer in New York and has since died, called me at home to say that he and his wife had been in town for the weekend and would I be willing to show them some of the Ames' demonstrations about which he had heard. It is important for this story to emphasize the fact that the gentleman in question was really a most unusual man in terms of his ability, charm, accomplishments, and his devotion to his family and friends.

Many of you are familiar, I am sure, with the "distorted room" designed by Albert Ames, Jr., which produces the same image on the retina as a regular square room if it is viewed monocularly from a certain point. Since the room is seen as square, persons or objects within the room or people looking through the windows become distorted. I had shown this room to hundreds of individuals and among other phenomena had demonstrated that when two people look through the back windows, the head of one individual appeared to be very large, the head of the other to be very small. When the individuals reversed the windows they were looking through, the size of their heads appeared to the observer to change. But on this Sunday morning when my friend's wife was observing him and me, she said, "Well, Louis, your head is the same size as ever, but Hadley your head is very small." Then we changed the windows we were looking through and she said, "Louis, you're still the same, but Hadley you've become awfully large." Needless to say this remark made a shiver go up my spine and I asked her how she saw the room. It turned out that for her—unlike any other observer until then—the room had become somewhat distorted. In other words, she was using her husband—to whom she was particularly devoted—as her standard. She would not let him go. His nickname for her was "Honi" and we have dubbed this the "Honi phenomenon."

This observation was followed systematically in a series of experiments on married couples by Dr. Warren Wittreich. He found that if couples had been married less than a year there was a very definite tendency not to let the new marital partner distort as quickly or as much as was allowed by people who had been married for a considerable time (7). But, again, I hasten to add that it is not a simple matter of how long one has been married that determines how willing one is to distort the size or shape of one's marital partner! The original observation was made on a couple who were already grandparents. Preliminary investigation also seems to show that parents of young children will not allow their children to distort as readily as will parents of older children.

We could continue at some length reporting experiments which seem to show that what we "perceive" is, as already emphasized, in large part our own creating and depends on the assumptions we bring to the particular occasion. We seem to give meaning and order to sensory impingements in terms of our own needs and purposes and this process of selection is actively creative.

Social Constancies and Self-Constancy

It is clear that when we look for constancies in other people either as individuals or as members of a group a variety of complications is introduced. For when people are involved, as contrasted to inorganic objects or most other forms of life, we are dealing with purposes, with motives, with intentions which we have to take into account in our perceptual process—the purposes, motives and intentions of other people often difficult to understand. The purposes and intentions of these other people will, of course, change as conditions change; and they will change as behavior progresses from one goal to another. Other people's purposes will be affected by our purposes, just as our purposes will be affected by theirs.

It is by no means a quick and easy process, then, to endow the people with whom we participate in our interpersonal relations with constancies and repeatabilities that we can always rely on. And yet we must, of course, continue the attempt to do so, so that our own purposeful action will have a greater chance of bringing about the satisfying consequences we intended. So we try to pigeonhole people according to some role, status, or position. We create constancies concerning people and social situations. These provide us with certain consistent characteristics that will ease our interpretation and make our actions more effective so long as there is some correspondence between the attribution we make and the consequence we experience from it in our own action.

The "social constancies" we learn obviously involve the relationships between ourselves and others. So if any social constancy is to be operational, there must also be a sense of "self-constancy." The two are interdependent. Since the human being necessarily derives so much of his value satisfaction from association with other human beings, his conception of his "self," his own "self-constancy" and "self-significance" is determined to a large extent by the significance he has to other people and the way they behave toward him. This point is, of course, a familiar one to the psychiatrist and has been eloquently illustrated in literature as, for example, in Shaw's *Pygmalion*.

But it seems to me of paramount importance in any discussion of perception and interpersonal relations that we should not slip into the error of positing an abstract "self" or "ego" that can somehow be isolated, pointed to, analyzed, or experienced apart from any social context. It is only through the life setting and the process of participation with others that meaning and continuity are given to the "self." If the constancy of "self" is upset, it becomes difficult for us to assess changes in our interpersonal relations and accommodate to them. We lose the compass that keeps us going in a direction. "We" are lost.

This does not mean in any sense that for self-constancy to be maintained there can be no development or growth. On the contrary, self-development and growth are themselves aspects of social constancy. But this development must, as the psychiatrist knows better than anyone, flow from form if it is to be recognized, if there is to be continuity, and if there is to be a standard for comparison. Obviously, each of us surrounds himself with anchoring points of one kind or another which help to maintain this self-constancy in the process of ceaseless change around us. In this connection I think, for example, of Konrad Lorenz' interpretation of why people like dogs. In his book *King Solomon's Ring,* he writes that we should

not lie to ourselves that we need the dog as a protection for our house. We do need him, but not as a watch-dog. I, at least in dreary foreign towns, have certainly stood in need of my dog's company and I have derived, from the mere fact of his existence, a great sense of inward security, such as one finds in a childhood memory or in the prospect of the scenery of one's own home country, for me the Blue Danube, for you the White Cliffs of Dover. In the almost filmlike flitting-by of modern life, a man needs something to tell him, from time to time, that he is still himself, and nothing can give him this assurance in so comforting a manner as the 'four feet trotting behind.'

This interdependent problem of social constancy and self-constancy has been submitted to some preliminary investigation. For example, when a person is wearing a pair of aniseikonic spectacles, which greatly distort the shape of the environment when familiar monocular cues are ruled out, he will generally see another person as distorted if that person is standing in an environment which has itself already become distorted. With a certain pair of these spectacles, for example, an individual will be seen as leaning forward with the upper and lower half of his body distorted in length. Dr. Wittreich set up such a situation at the Naval Training Center at Bainbridge, Maryland to see what might happen when the relationship of the person who was doing the viewing and the person being viewed was altered. His subjects were 24 white male Navy recruits. They first observed an authority figure dressed up as a first class petty officer and, second, a non-authority figure dressed up in a white enlisted uniform with the marks of a recruit. Wittreich found that the authority figure did not distort nearly as much as the non-authority figure. In other words, the disciplinary training imposed in an organization that depends for effective functioning on the rigid acceptance of roles had produced a "constancy" which over-powered physiological changes in the optical system.

Another finding using the aniseikonic spectacles may be of interest to psychiatrists: namely, that a person tends to report much less distortion of his own image when he looks at himself in a full-length mirror while wearing aniseikonic spectacles than he reports when he is looking at a stranger. When one looks at one's self, the changes that appear seem to be minor and detailed—for example, slight distortions in the hands or feet; when one looks at a stranger, there is the more general bodily distortion plus the leaning one way or another, depend-ing on the kind of spectacles used.

A subsequent study by Wittreich and one which I em-phasize is only suggestive, was made comparing 21 subjects obtained from the patient roster of the neuro-psychiatric unit at the Bethesda Naval Hospital. When these disturbed in-dividuals were wearing aniseikonic spectacles and saw their own image in the mirror, they tended to see the gross distor-tions that the "normal" population attributed to others; and, conversely, when the disturbed clinic population looked at others, they tended to see the more detailed and minor distor-tions which the "normal" population had seen in themselves. All I should like to conclude about this particular experiment so far is that there seems to be some difference between the normal individual and the clinical patient in the functional importance assigned to his bodily image; the patient may conceivably be operating in terms of a relatively fixed and homogeneous image of himself which does not alter readily with the demands of the environment.

Perceptual Change

Laboratory experimentation as well as research in the field of opinion and attitude change seems to demonstrate beyond a shadow of a doubt that the major condition for a change in

our perception, our attitudes or opinions is a frustration experienced in carrying out our purposes effectively because
we are acting on the basis of assumptions that prove "wrong."
For example, Dr. Kilpatrick has demonstrated that apparently
the only way in which we can "learn" to see our distorted
room distorted is to become frustrated with the assumption
that the room is "square" in the process of trying to carry
out some action in the room (8). It is clear that an "intellectual," "rational," or "logical" understanding of a situation
is by no means sufficient to alter perception. The psychotherapist has taught us how successful reconditioning requires
a therapy which simplifies goals so that their accomplishment
can be assured through an individual's action as he experiences the successful consequences of his own behavior and
thereby rebuilds his confidence in himself.

In this connection I recall a conversation I had in 1948 in
Paris with an extremely intelligent woman who was at that
time a staff member of the Soviet Embassy in Paris. We were
at some social gathering and she began to ask me about
American elections and the two-party system. She just couldn't
understand it. She wasn't trying to be "smart" or supercilious.
She was simply baffled. She couldn't "see" why we had to
have 2 parties. For, obviously, one man was better than
another and why wasn't he made President and kept as
President as long as he proved to be the best man? It was a
difficult argument for me to understand, just as my argument
was impossible for her to understand. It was much more than
a matter of opinion, stereotype or prejudice on either side.
We were simply living in different reality worlds, actually
experiencing entirely different significances in happenings
which might appear to "an objective" "outside" observer to be
the same for both of us.

Parenthetically, while one of the outstanding characteristics
of man is often said to be his amazing capacity to learn, it
seems to me that an equally outstanding characteristic is man's
amazing capacity to "unlearn" which is, I think, not the exact
opposite. Because man is not entirely a creature of habits, he

has the fortunate ability to slough off what is no longer of use to him.

The Reality of Abstractions and the Commonness of Purposes

In order to ease our interpersonal relations and to increase the commonness of the significances we may attribute to the happenings around us, man has created abstractions in his attempt to bring order into disorder and to find more universal guides for living no matter what the unique and individual purposes and circumstances of an individual may be. Such abstractions are represented by our scientific formulations, our ethical, political, legal and religious systems. The abstractions can be recalled and repeated at will. They can be communicated. They are repeatable because they are static and have fixed characteristics.

The value of these abstractions for us in our interpersonal relations seems to be that when the tangibles of our personal reality world break down, we can turn to the intangible—to the abstractions we have learned that have been created by others and have presumably proved useful to them. We can begin to check our own particular situation, possibly a frustrating one, against the abstraction and thereby, perhaps experience for ourselves what the abstraction is referring to. Only then will the abstraction become real for us. For when it does become functional for us in our own individual lives, it *is* real as a determinant of our experience and behavior.

I will close this discussion of perception and interpersonal relations with a story which seems to sum a good deal of what I have been talking about. The story concerns three baseball umpires who were discussing the problems of their profession. The first umpire said, "Some's balls and some's strikes and I calls 'em as they is." The second umpire said, "Some's balls and some's strikes and I call 'em as I sees 'em." While the third umpire said, "Some's balls and some's strikes but they ain't nothin' till I calls 'em."

Bibliography

1. Cantril, Hadley. *The "Why" of Man's Experience*. New York: Macmillan, 1950.

2. Kilpatrick, F. P. (ed.). *Human Behavior from the Transactional Point of View*. Hanover, N. H.: Institute for Associated Research, 1952.

3. Kilpatrick, F. P. Recent Transactional Perceptual Research, a summary. Final Report, Navy Contract N6onr 27014, Princeton University, May, 1955.

4. Cantril, Hadley. *ETC: A Review of General Semantics,* 12: No. 4, 278, 1955.

5. Engel, Edward. *Amer. J. Psychol.,* 69: No. 1, 87, 1956.

6. Bagley, James. A Cross Cultural Study of Perceptual Predominance in Binocular Rivalry. 1956.

7. Wittreich, Warren. *J. Abnorm. Soc. Psychol.,* 47:705, 1952.

8. Kilpatrick, F. P. *J. Exp. Psychol.,* 47: No. 5, 362, 1954.

William V. Haney
Perception and Communication

yerry marcus

"This is nothing. When I was your age the snow was so deep it came up to my chin!" Reprinted from Redbook with permission.

Dad is right, of course—*as he sees it*. And in this seemingly innocuous self-deception lies one of the most interesting and perhaps terrifying aspects of human experience: *We never*

Reprinted by permission of the publisher, from William V. Haney, *Communication and Organizational Behavior Text and Cases*, rev. ed., Homewood, Illinois, Richard D. Irwin, Inc., 1967, pp. 51–77.

really come into direct contact with reality. Everything we experience is a manufacture of our nervous system.

For practical purposes we should acknowledge that there is a considerable range of similarity between reality and one's perception of it. When an engineer is measuring, testing, and the like, usually with the aid of precise gauges and instruments, his perceptions may be an extremely close approximation of reality. This is basically why bridges, tunnels, and skyscrapers not only get built but generally stay built.

But when the engineer, or anyone else, is relating to and communicating with other human beings—when he is operating in a world of feelings, attitudes, values, aspirations, ideals, and emotions—he is playing in a very different league and the match between reality and perceptions may be far from exact.

Just what is going on and just what is this concept "perception" we have been alluding to so casually? "Perception" is a term we perhaps shouldn't be using at all. There seems to be very little agreement as to what it entails. It evidently is a complex, dynamic, interrelated composite of processes which are incompletely and variously understood. Allport, for example, describes some 13 *different* schools of thought on the nature of perception, listing, among others, core-context theory, gestalt theory, topological field theory, cell-assembly, and sensory-tonic field theory.[1] In the face of such irresolution I will be so bold as to define perception in unsophisticated language as the process of *making sense out of experience—of imputing meaning to experience.*[2]

Obviously what kind of "sense" one makes of a situation will have great bearing on how he responds to that situation so let us examine the phenomenon more closely.

[1] F. H. Allport, *Theories of Perception and the Concept of Structure* (New York: John Wiley & Sons, Inc., 1955).

[2] Perception has been defined as "the more complex process [as distinguished from sensation] by which people select, organize, and interpret sensory stimulation into a meaningful and coherent picture of the world." B. Berelson and G. A. Steiner, *Human Behavior: An Inventory of Scientific Findings* (New York: Harcourt, Brace & World, Inc., 1964), p. 88.

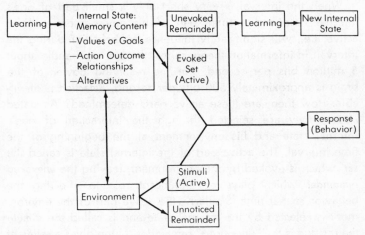

Figure 1.

A Model of Perception

March and Simon suggest a model (see Figure 1) which seems well supported by research. First of all, they regard man as a complex, information-processing system—"a choosing, decision-making, problem-solving organism that can do only one or a few things at a time, and that can attend to only a small part of the information in its memory and presented by the environment."[3]

They argue that one's behavior, through a short interval of time, is determined by the interaction between his *internal state*[4] (which is largely a product of one's previous *learning*) at the beginning of the interval and his *environment*.

[3] J. G. March and H. A. Simon, *Organizations* (New York: John Wiley & Sons, Inc., 1958), p. 11.

[4] His internal state is mostly contained in his memory which "includes [but is not limited to] all sorts of partial and modified records of past experiences and programs for responding to environmental stimuli." Thus, the memory consists, in part, of:

  a) Values or goals: criteria that are applied to determine which courses of action are preferred among those considered.

  b) Relations between actions and their outcome; beliefs, perceptions, and

When the interval is very short only a small part of one's internal state and a small part of his environment will be active, i.e., will significantly influence his behavior during the interval. In information theory terms, the eye can handle about 5 million bits per second, but the resolving power of the brain is approximately 500 bits per second. *Selection* is inevitable. How then, are these active parts determined? As stated above, they are selected through the interaction of one's internal state and his environment at the beginning of the time interval. The active part of the internal state is called the *set*[5] which is evoked by the environment, leaving the *unevoked remainder* which plays no significant role in affecting the behavior at that time. Similarly, the active part of the environment is selected by the internal state and is called the *stimuli;* the residue is the "unnoticed" remainder. Munn gives a relevant illustration:

I once had a colony of white rats in the attic of the psychology building. One afternoon I found several rats outside of their cages. Some were dead and partly eaten. It occurred to me that, however the rats had escaped, they must have been eaten by wild rats. I went downstairs to get some water and was climbing the stairs again when I saw before me, and directly in front of the cages, a large wild gray rat. It was standing tense and trembling, apparently having heard me ascend the stairs. Very slowly I raised a glass jar that was in my right hand, and aimed it at the rat. Much to my surprise, the animal failed to move. Upon approaching the object, I discovered it to be a piece of crumpled-up-grayish paper. Without the set induced by my suspicion that gray rats were in the attic, I should undoubtedly have seen the paper for what it was, assuming that I noticed it at all.[6]

---

expectations as to the consequences that will follow from one course of action or another. . . .

c) Alternatives: possible courses of action.

Ibid., pp. 10—11.

[5] *Set* is generally regarded as the readiness of the organism to respond in a particular way.

[6] Norman L. Munn, *Psychology: The Fundamentals of Human Adjustment* (Boston: Houghton Mifflin Co., 1947), p. 327.

Let us examine Munn's behavior, asserting a chain of *sets* and *stimuli*. To start at an arbitrary point, he was *set* to notice the white rats among other reasons because they were presumably why he went to the attic in the first place. Thus, the partly eaten white rats readily became *stimuli* which in turn triggered still another *set*—the expectation of wild gray rats. Any part of his environment which bore a reasonable resemblance to a wild gray rat thus became a candidate for becoming his new *stimuli*. The crumpled paper qualified. It was not only selected as a *stimulus* (supposedly it had been part of the "unnoticed remainder" of the environment on his first trip to the attic) but was interpreted as a wild gray rat.

The result of the interplay of environment and internal state is one's *response* (behavior) and his *internal state* at the beginning of the next time interval. This new internal state can be considered as modified by the *learning* derived from the experience of the previous interval.

Just what is active or passive in one's internal state and environment is a function of time, among other factors. For a very short period, there will be very few active elements in set and stimuli. For a longer period, a larger portion of the memory content will likely be evoked and a large number of environmental events will influence behavior at some time during the interval. Thus, phrases such as "definition of the situation" and "frame of reference" are more appropriate than "set" in discussing longer time periods.

If one's response is a function of interrelated variables it follows that a variation in any or all of them would normally affect the response. Therefore we shall examine some of these variables in greater detail.

Differing Environments

Hold up a die between us. If you see three dots I will see four. As obvious as it should be, the phenomenon of differing environments, which would preclude our receiving the same stimuli, seems to contribute to a great deal of unnecessary and destructive conflict.

I have had the rewarding experience of serving for several years as a consultant to the Federal Mediation and Conciliation Service. Any number of the commissioners, men who are constantly concerned with union-management controversies, have asserted to me that a significant portion of the lack of communication, understanding, and harmony between the two parties stems from the simple fact that neither side is given full and direct access to the private environment—including the pressures, complexities, and restrictions—of the other. Thus, from the very outset of the negotiation the parties are exposed to substantially different environments and therefore are, in many respects, responding to different stimuli.

Differing Stimuli

Presume a mutual environment and there is still no guarantee that your responses and mine will be influenced by the same stimuli. Our respective evoked sets will have a considerable bearing on which parts of the environment will significantly impinge upon us as stimuli. Munn's story of the rat is a case in point.

Differing Sensory Receptors

Another reason why parts of the environment either never become stimuli or are experienced differently is that our sensory "equipment" varies. It has long been recognized that individuals differ markedly in sensory thresholds and acuity. While there has been gratifying progress in the prevention, correction, and amelioration of sensory limitations there is still much to be learned.

An interesting demonstration of differing sensory equipment is to give a bit of paper to each person in a group and request each to determine the taste of the paper. The group does not know it but the paper is impregnated with phenylthiocarbamide (PTC). If the group is representative, a significant portion will experience a distinctly bitter sensation. But some will taste it as sweet, others as sour, and still others as salty. And about half will find it utterly tasteless!

PTC, a chemical used by geneticists to trace heredity traits, reveals dramatically that we simply do not all inherit identical sensory apparatus. Add to this variations of the nervous system due to disease and injury and it is clear that our senses are inclined to be neither infallible nor uniform. I have a personal example to contribute in this regard. I have had a few mild disputes with my wife who "alleged" a shrill whistle in the television set. Since I did not hear it I denied that it existed. Somewhat later I had an autiometric examination and discovered that, like many others who were around artillery during the war, I had lost the capacity to hear tones of extremely high pitch.

Differing Internal States

One's *internal state* is the product of his *learning processes* and it is obvious that the "lessons" acquired by one person can differ markedly from those of another. Imagine a number of individuals observing a man drinking liquor. If the observers are candid and sufficiently representative we can expect a gamut of reactions. Some will regard the man as sinful; others as extravagant. Others will associate his drinking with friendliness and congeniality. Some will view it as a character flaw— a way of avoiding unpleasantness, running from problems. Still others may perceive it as a relaxant. And people in the distilling industry—and the Alcohol and Tobacco Tax Division of the Internal Revenue Service—may relate it to a job!

For a more dramatic example of the role of learning compare cultures. One's culture is an extraordinarily effective teacher. First, it teaches us unrelentingly—every waking moment. Second, it is a most subtle, even insidious teacher—which detracts not at all from its effectiveness. Immersed in it constantly, we are seldom conscious of what it has been teaching us until we contrast its lessons with those taught by other cultures. The perceptive traveler, for example, as he visits countries learns a good deal about *himself* and the special lessons his culture has taught him.

For example, anthropologists tell us that we learn from our respective cultures how to perceive a misbehaving child. This is revealed by how we speak to the child. English-speaking people generally consider misbehavior as "bad" or "naughty," a suggestion of immorality, and admonish the child with "Johnny, be *good!*" Italian- and Greek-speaking people say the equivalent. The French, however, tend to say "Jean, sois sage!" —be *wise.* Their culture teaches that the child who misbehaves is being stupid, foolish, imprudent, injudicious. The Scandinavians have another concept expressed by the Swedish, "Jan, var snell!" and the Norwegian, "Jan, ble snil!"—be *friendly,* be *kind.* Germans have learned still differently. With them it is "Hans, sei artig!"—*get back in step. Sei artig* is literally "be of your own kind"—in other words, "conform to your role as a child."[7]

Clearly, individuals from these various cultures could observe the same child misbehaving but regard him very differently because they had been *trained* to do so. Grant that different people learn different "lessons" from life and it is readily apparent that individualized learning plays a subtle but critical role in one's communication with others.

Differing Evoked Sets

One's set, according to the model, is dependent upon three other variables: that which is available in the internal state, the stimuli which trigger the set, and, though less directly, the processes of learning. March and Simon clarify the role of learning in this regard:

When one of these elements (values or goals, action-outcome relationships and alternatives) is evoked by a stimulus, it may also bring into the evoked set a number of other elements with which it has become associated through the learning process. Thus, if a particular goal has been achieved on previous occasions by execution of a particular course of action, then evocation of

---

[7] L. Sinclair (ed.), "A Word in Your Ear," *Ways of Mankind* (Boston: Beacon Press, 1954), pp. 28–29. For a fascinating account of cultural differences interfering with interpersonal communication see E. T. Hall, *The Silent Language* (Garden City, N.Y.: Doubleday & Co., Inc., 1959).

*that goal will be likely to evoke that course of action again.
Habitual responses are extreme instances of this in which the
connecting links between stimulus and response may be suppressed
from consciousness. In the same way, the evocation of a course
of action will lead by association to evocation of consequences
that have been associated with the action.*[8]

This helps to account for the apparent self-perpetuating
nature of sets which others have observed.

*Our concept of causal texture implies that definitions and relations,
once they have been adopted, influence interpretations of
subsequent events. Early definitions of the conditions under which
a task will be accomplished are apt to take precedence over
later definitions.*[9]
*. . . the tendency to distort messages in the direction of identity
with previous inputs is probably the most pervasive of the
systematic biases.*[10]

Sebald confirmed a hypothesis "that largely only those
meanings are being perceived and recalled which reinforce
images."[11] He also suggested "that selective distortion takes
place in order to screen out dissonant features—features which
are apt to disturb pre-conceived images."[12]

The concept of differing sets helps to explain the abyss
which so frequently separates superiors and subordinates. A
man looking downward in an organization may often have a
very different set from the man below him looking up. For
example, Likert reports that 85 percent of a sampling of
foremen estimated that their men 'felt very free to discuss
important things about the job with my superior." However,

[8] March and Simon, *op. cit.*, p. 11.
[9] H. B. Pepinsky, K. E. Weick, and J. W. Riner, *Primer for Productivity*
(Columbus, Ohio: The Ohio State University Research Foundation, March, 1964),
p. 54.
[10] D. T. Campbell, "Systematic Error on the Part of Human Links in Communication Systems," *Information and Control*, Vol. 1 (1958), p. 346.
[11] H. Sebald, "Limitations of Communication: Mechanisms of Image Maintenance in Form of Selective Perception, Selective Memory and Selective Distortion,"
Journal of Communication, Vol. XII, No. 3 (September, 1962), p. 149.
[12] *Ibid.*

only 51 percent of their men shared this view.[13] Seventy-three percent of the foremen felt they "always or almost always get subordinates' ideas" on the solution of job problems. Only 16 percent of their subordinates agreed with this appraisal.[14] Ninety-five percent of the foremen said they understood their men's problems well but only 34 percent of the men felt that they did.[15]

The gulf between superiors' and subordinates' sets is documented further by Maier[16] who reports a study of 35 pairs from four large firms. A pair consisted of a manager, third echelon from the top, and one of his immediate subordinates. Each partner in each pair was questioned regarding the subordinate's job. On only one aspect was there substantial agreement—the content of the subordinate's duties. However, there was little agreement on the order of importance of these duties. There was only fair agreement on the job's requirements and almost complete disagreement on their priority ranking. Finally, there was virtually no agreement on the problems and obstacles of the subordinate. These findings were discussed with all participants. Several months later a questionnaire was sent to each participant asking if the superior and his respective subordinate had gotten together to discuss their differences. Only 22 pairs replied. Six of them agreed that they had gotten together; nine agreed that they had not; and seven pairs could not agree on whether they had or had not gotten together![17]

In Summation

The perception model suggests why it is impossible for one to be in simple, direct contact with reality, why he lives in a per-

[13] Rensis Likert, *New Patterns in Management* (New York: McGraw-Hill Book Co., 1961), p. 47.

[14] *Ibid.,* p. 53.

[15] *Ibid.,* p. 52.

[16] N. R. F. Maier, "Breakdown in Boss-Subordinate Communication," *Communication in Organizations* (Ann Arbor, Mich.: The Foundation for Research on Human Behavior, 1959).

[17] The reader may wish to test the influence of sets upon him by viewing perceptual *(not optical)* illusions.

sonalized world and why, in the words of St. Paul, "We see through a glass darkly." Indeed, there are a number of inter-related variables (differing environments, stimuli, sensory receptors, internal states, and evoked sets) which intervene between perception and reality. Thus, individuals are led to respond differently to events and, in general, complicate the process of communication enormously—particularly *if the role of such factors is ignored or misunderstood.*

. . . the prime obstacle of every form of communications . . . is simply the fact of difference. *On this point most serious students of communication are in agreement, the great gap in background, experience, and motivations between ourselves and those with whom we would communicate.*

It is a gap that will remain. . . . But if we cannot close the gap, we must at least acknowledge it. For this acknowledgement *of difference is the vital preface to all the efforts that follow. . . .*[18]

Defensiveness

The "acknowledgement of difference"—a simple phrase but how difficult to practice! Perhaps the most appropriate adjective to describe much of the behavior of people communicating and relating to one another in organizational settings would be *defensive.* A fundamental reason for defensive behavior appears to be the inability of so many people to *acknowledge differences* —differences between their perceptions and reality and differences between their perceptions and those of others. Their prevailing, albeit largely unconscious, presumption is that "the world is as I see it." He who harbors this notion will find life continuously threatening for there are many others who share his notion—but not *his "world!"* Such people find it perpetually necessary to protect their "worlds" and to deny or attack the other fellow's.

Admittedly, the premise that one deals only indirectly and often unreliably with reality can be disturbing. To those who

[18] "Is Anybody Listening," *Fortune,* September 1950, p. 83. The emphasis is mine.

crave a certain, definite, and dependable world (and that includes all of us in varying degrees) the admission that we respond only to *what it appears to be* rather than *what it is* necessarily lessens our *predictability* about the "real world." Even those who *intellectually accept* the perception model and the roles that stimuli, set, learning, and so on, play in determining responses may have difficulty converting the concept into performance. A good test of the extent to which one has truly internalized such awareness occurs when he becomes emotionally involved with others.

For instance, suppose you and I work in the same organization and we observe one of our colleagues, taking home company supplies—such as paper pads, paper clips, and pencils—not in large quantities but it is obvious to us that he will not use them exclusively for official purposes. He will let the children have them, use them for his private affairs, and so on.

Now, let us say that you are the product of a rigorous, religious upbringing. It is likely that you will be *set* to regard Joe as dishonest. But suppose that I have had none of your training and that the only part of my background that is particularly relevant was the three years I spent in the Army in World War II. There I learned a code that was unwritten but very pervasive. It was in effect, "You may rob the Army blind! but you must not steal a nickel from another serviceman." I would be quite inclined to regard Joes as honest and could readily consider his acquisitions as normal perquisites.

Let us examine the *communication* issue. (Permit me to disregard the moral issue without denying that there is one.) Consider the tremendous difficulty you and I would have in discussing Joe if in our increasingly vehement statements— "Joe's dishonest!" "No, he's not!"—we failed to realize that neither of us was talking about *Joe*. We were talking about *you* and *me* and our *respective* "inside-the-skin" experiences. Our respective worlds were different from the outset and there was no reason to expect them to be identical—and no *rational* reason to have to protect them. Why, then, did we protect them so ardently?

Let us begin with an assertion: Most reasonably mature people can tolerate fairly well differences in value judgments, opinions, attitudes, points of view—*so long as they can recognize them as such.* If I can realize that your "reality" is not the same as mine then your statement about *your* "reality" is no threat to *mine.*

But no one can tolerate differences on matters of objectivity —matters which submit to corrobable measurement and are capable of general agreement. To illustrate, suppose you and I have a mutual superior and he comes to us and says: "This may sound silly but I'm serious. I want you two to estimate the length of that 2 × 4 over there (about 20 feet away) on the ground. You have to estimate because you can't use any kind of measuring device and you can't get any closer to it than you are now. Now, I want a good estimate and only one between you—so get to it!"

(Now suppose the piece of lumber is actually 7 feet long but neither of us knows this.) So we start sizing up the situation and you say, "Looks about 6½ or 7 feet." And I say, "No, no— you're way short—that's a lot closer to 14 feet!" Unless you had admirable constraint you would probably blurt out, "You're crazy!"

Now, why were you moved to feel I was crazy?

Was it not partly because my statement was at least a slight threat to your sense of reality and, therefore, your sanity? In other words if (I said *if*) I were indeed right—i.e., if the board actually were 14 feet and everything were twice as big as you perceive it—would you not begin to have serious misgivings about *your* "contact with reality"? "You're crazy!", then, is your understandable if impulsive way of defending yourself against an attack on your sanity.

Actually, we would be unlikely to have such a disparity (unless one or both of us *were* losing touch with reality) because our perceptual lessons, when we initially learned to perceive the inch, the foot, and the yard, were likely to have been very similar regardless of where or when we learned them. And even if we were to disagree on matters such as distance, speed, and weight we could resolve our differences by using standardized measuring devices.

But when we encounter Cezanne and Dali, Tolstoi and Faulkner, Mozart and Cole Porter, we are unlikely to have had identical learning experiences and where is the "standardized measuring device"? Will someone resolve a controversy with "Why, that Van Gogh is 87 percent beautiful!"? Even professional critics are unable to provide universally acceptable and applicable criteria.

The point is that not only can we not tolerate differences in matters of objectivity (but what differences there may be are generally minor or resolvable by objective measurement) but we cannot accept differences on matters of subjectivity (value judgments, opinions, and so on) if we unconsciously *treat them* as matters of objectivity. There are many important aspects of our lives such as art, music, architecture, religion, politics, morals, fashions, food, economic and political theory, which (1) are taught to us in standardized lessons and (2) are not, by and large, measurable by standardized scales or gauges. It is in such areas that we find it easiest to threaten one another. And when one is threatened he tends, if he does not run, to fight back—the threatener is now threatened and bootless conflict generally follows.

Defensiveness appears to be so pervasive and potentially so destructive to organizational communication and interpersonal relationships that we shall examine it in more detail in terms of the communicator's *frame of reference.*

Frame of Reference

Frame of reference is the term March and Simon used for longer intervals of time in lieu of "set." It has been defined as:

A system of standards or values, usually merely implicit, underlying and to some extent controlling an action, or the expression of any attitude, belief, or idea.[19]

Carl Rogers offers several propositions[20] which serve as a

[19] H. B. English and A. C. English, *A Comprehensive Dictionary of Psychological and Psychoanalytical Terms* (New York: Longmans, Green & Co., 1958).

[20] Paraphrased from C. R. Rogers, *Client-Centered Therapy* (Boston, Mass.: Houghton Mifflin Co., 1951, pp. 483, 484, 487, 494.

rationale for the validity and utility of the frame of reference construct.

1. *Every individual exists in a continually changing world of experience of which he is the center.*

Rogers holds that each of us is at the core of his own world and everything else is happening, developing, occurring about him (not unlike Ptolemy's homocentric notion of the earth as the center of the universe). It is painfully obvious that man is the most egocentric organism on earth, and surely no one can be more self-centered than the human infant. The baby will outgrow much of this, of course, but hardly all of it. But it would seem that one who is approaching emotional maturity has already recognized that egocentrism is a substantial part of being human. Once one accepts this frailty he is in an excellent state to begin to compensate for it and to grow beyond it. The truly arrogant person, however, is the man or woman who has never made and perhaps cannot make this admission. For so long as one can shield himself from a recognition of his fallibility, he need not expend energy in growing and he need not submit to the unknowns and possible pain of *change*.

2. *The individual reacts to his world as he experiences and perceives it and thus this perceptual world is, for the individual, "reality."*

Rogers put quotes around *reality* to indicate that it is not the "real" reality. Consider these definitions of perception: "The point of reality contact, the door to reality appraisal";[21] the "structuring of stimuli"[22] and the "organization of stimuli";[23] and "the way in which the person structures his world and himself."[24] But regardless of how invalid and incomplete it may be, one's personalized reality is the only one he has and therefore the only one to which he responds.

[21] G. S. Klein, "The Personal World through Perception," *Perception, An Approach to Personality,* ed. R. R. Blake and G. V. Ramsey (New York; The Ronald Press Co., 1951), pp. 328–329.

[22] C. M. Solley and G. Murphy, *Development of the Perceptual World* (New York: Basic Books, Inc., Publishers, 1960), p. 26.

[23] F. A. Beach, "Body Chemistry and Perception," Blake and Ramsey, *op. cit.,* p. 56.

[24] U. Bronfenbrenner, "Toward an Integrated Theory of Personality," *ibid.,* p. 207.

3. *The individual has one basic tendency and striving which is to actualize, maintain, and enhance himself.*

Rogers writes of the *actualizing tendency* as "the inherent tendency of the organism to develop all its capacities in ways to serve to maintain or enhance the organism. It involves not only the tendency to meet . . . 'deficiency needs' for air, food, water, and the like, but also more generalized activities. . . . It is development toward autonomy and away from heteronomy, or control by external forces."[25] He subscribes to Angyal's statement: "Life is an autonomous event which takes place between the organism and the environment. Life processes do not merely tend to preserve life but transcend the momentary status quo of the organism, expanding itself continually and imposing its autonomous determination upon an ever increasing realm of events."[26]

More specifically, Rogers refers to *self*-actualization. We will discuss his concept of the self-image later in this chapter and for the moment will merely suggest that much of the individual's perceiving is in the service of preserving or enhancing his self-image.

According to Frenkel-Brunswik:

It would appear that we do not always see ourselves as we are but instead perceive the environment in terms of our own need. Self-perception and perception of the environment actually merge in the service of these needs. Thus, the perceptual distortions of ourselves and the environment fulfill an important function in our psychological household.[27]

The role of *needs* and *motivation* in influencing perception and therefore behavior is clearly important enough to require the separate chapter which follows this one.

[25] C. R. Rogers, "A Theory of Therapy, Personality, and Interpersonal Relationships, as Developed in the Client-Centered Framework," *Psychology: The Study of a Science*, Vol. 3, *Formulations of the Person and the Social Context,* ed. Sigmund Koch (New York: McGraw-Hill Book Co., 1959), p. 196.

[26] A. Angyal, *Foundations for a Science of Personality* (New York: Commonwealth Fund, 1941).

[27] Else Frenkel-Brunswik, "Personality Theory and Perception" chap. 13 in Blake and Ramsey *op. cit.,* p. 379.

4. Therefore, the best vantage point for understanding another's behavior is from that person's internal frame of reference.

This conclusion follows logically from Rogers' preceding propositions but this does not necessarily make it easy to utilize the frame of reference concept. The individual's internal frame of reference *is* his subjective world. "Only he knows it fully. It can never be known to another except through empathic inference and then can never be perfectly known."[28]

Probably the greatest single deterrent to one's accurately visualizing another's frame of reference is his *own*. An analogy will suggest why this is so.

Analogy of the Box

Visualize each of us as the sole and constant tenant of a box with a top, a bottom, and four sides. There is just one window in this box—one's frame of reference, loosely speaking—through which he views the outside world.

A Restricted Window. This suggests immediately that one's view is restricted—he cannot see what is happening in back of him, above, to the sides, and so forth. One obviously cannot be ubiquitous and therefore his view is inevitably limited. But there is another restriction that he can overcome to an extent— the *size* of the window. We all have our "narrownesses"—our areas of naïveté. I, for example, was born and reared in a suburb. Suppose you are a country boy and we go out to a farm. We could share the same environment but I would expect that your stimuli and evoked sets would greatly outnumber mine. You would have the preparation, the memory content, to make so much more significance out of the experience than I.

But I have the capacity to learn. Given the time and provided I have the motivation I can acquire some of your sophistication. In short I can *expand* my window.

Stained-Glass Window. Not only is one's window frame restricted (but expandable largely at his will) but it also does not

28 C. R. Rogers, "A Theory of Therapy . . . ," *op. cit.*, p. 210.

contain a pane of clear glass. It is rather like a stained-glass church window with various, peculiarly shaped, tinted, and refracting lenses. In one's frame of reference these lenses are his experiences, biases, values, needs, emotions, aspirations, and the like. They may all be distorting media to an extent but are we powerless to overcome these distortions? Hardly, but let us establish one point first.

Does anyone grow up with a clear window? Can anyone be without bias for example? Quite unlikely, for everyone had to be born at a particular time and in a particular place. Thus he was exposed to particular people and situations all of whom and which taught him *special* lessons regarding values, customs, mores, codes, and so on.

But again man has viability and the capacity to adjust and compensate—he can *clarify* his window. A pencil in a glass of water appears to bend abruptly but if one *understands* something about the nature of refraction he can compensate for the distortion, aim at where the pencil appears not to be, and hit it. So it is more profoundly with a man himself—if he can *understand himself* he can *compensate* for his distorted frame of reference and, in effect, clarify his window.

The Self-Image

But there is at least one extremely formidable obstacle in the way of a man's truly understanding himself. We return to Carl Rogers for this. A key concept of the Rogerian therapeutic approach is the premise that as a person grows up he develops a *self-image* or *self-concept*—a picture of himself. Hayakawa asserted: "The mode of human behavior is not self-preservation but self-concept. The self-concept is who you think you are and the self is who you are. Values determine people's self-concept and self-concept determines social experience."[29] Rogers uses *self, concept of self,* and *self-structure* as terms to refer to

the organized, consistent conceptual gestalt composed of perceptions of the characteristics of the "I" or "me" and the

[29] S. I. Hayakawa, participating in the 1965 Student Symposium, "Spectrum of Perspectives," Northwestern University.

perceptions of the relationships of the "I" or "me" to others and to various aspects of life, together with the values attached to these perceptions. It is a fluid and changing gestalt, a process. . . . The term self or self-concept is more likely to be used when we are talking of the person's view of himself, self-structure when we are looking at this gestalt from an external frame of reference.[30]

On Coping with Guilt. The self-image helps to explain how one copes with guilt.

One of man's most compelling needs is the need to justify himself. Moreover, most of us tolerate guilt very poorly. Guilt is painful—acutely so. Therefore, as pain-avoidance organisms most of us have desired highly facile and sophisticated means for eliminating or diminishing the pain of guilt. Test this assertion, if you can tread a painful route, by tracing back to an event in which you did something that you *knew* was *wrong;* that you *could not justify* by rationalizing that the end warranted the means; and that *was not beyond your control.*

Most of us have great difficulty remembering such events objectively and yet almost all of us have been guilty of them. The pain of guilt is so noisome that we have developed great skill in justifying our behavior before, during, or after the act.

At the core of this behavior appears to be the overriding motive to "actualize, maintain, and enhance" one's self-image. It is clear that the individual can distort experience to satisfy this powerful need. For example, suppose Mike treats Tom unjustly—at least as Tom perceives it. Tom will likely become angry and want revenge. If Tom were to analyze himself he might find that what he wants most of all is for Mike to experience remorse, true contrition—the pain of guilt—at least commensurate with the pain he inflicted upon Tom. However, Mike as a pain-avoider, has already begun to justify his behavior and is unlikely, therefore, to tender a sincere apology. Failing to receive evidence of Mike's acceptance of his own guilt, Tom may be moved to retaliate in kind or to attempt to wrench an apology from Mike. In either event, Tom's behavior, as Mike

[30] C. R. Rogers, "A Theory of Therapy . . . ," *op. cit.,* p. 200.

perceives it, is sufficiently obnoxious to complete his self-justifi-
cation. "You see how Tom is acting? That _____ deserved to
be treated that way in the first place!"

No matter how unreasonable, irrational, or immoral another's
behavior may appear to us it is generally a good assumption
that it is quite reasonable, rational and moral *in his world.*
Epictetus wrote: "The appearances of things to the mind is the
standard of action of every man."

One's self-image is perhaps most profoundly important to
the individual in the sense that it serves as *his contact with himself.* In fact, when he talks or thinks about *himself* he is usually
not referring to his limbs, torso, and head but rather to an abstraction he usually labels as "my *self."* Thus, it is by his self-
image that he *knows* himself.

Images of Others. But we also need to know and understand
others and thus we form images of them as well—particularly
those with whom we are most interdependent—parents, spouse,
children, superiors, subordinates. Such image formation, whether one is conscious of it or not, requires considerable energy
output and the marshaling of much psychological intelligence
about the individual of whom one is forming an image. The
prime motive for the effort is that we need to build a good base
for understanding and predicting the behavior of the other
person. And only by predicting the other's behavior reasonably
accurately can we confidently control our own behavior and
deal effectively with the other person.[31] This helps to explain

[31] The process we call *forming impressions of personality* is sometimes called
person perception. Bruner [J. S. Bruner, "Social Psychology and Perception,"
Readings in Social Psychology, ed. E. Maccoby, T. M. Newcomb, and E. L.
Hartley (3rd.; New York: Henry Holt, Inc., 1958), pp. 85–94] has argued that the
"process of perception tends, in general, to accomplish two things: (1) a
recording of the diversity of data we encounter into a simpler form that
brings it within the scope of our limited memory; (2) a going beyond the
information given to predict future events and thereby minimize surprise."
Roger Brown, *Social Psychology* (New York: The Free Press, 1065), p. 611.

Social psychologists, in particular, have been concerned with how we
perceive or infer the traits and intentions of others. For a sampling of experimental and theoretical works in "social perception" or "person perception"
see: I. E. Bender and A. H. Hastorf, "On Measuring Generalized Empathic
Ability (Social Sensitivity)," *Journal of Abnormal and Social Psychology,* Vol. 48

why one becomes confused and upset when another's behavior suddenly contradicts his image of that other person. He has lost or risks the loss of his base for predicting and thus for controlling himself in dealing with the other.

And this holds even when the other's behavior is *more favorable* than anticipated. Suppose you have a superior—a father, a teacher, a boss—who is a versatile tyrant. And suppose one day he greets you with a broad smile, a friendly clap on the back, and an encouraging comment. Is your initial response—"Wonderful, the old buzzard has finally turned over a new leaf!"? Or is it—"What's he up to now!"? As a friend in business put it, "You can work for an s.o.b.—provided he's a *consistent* s.o.b.! It's the one who turns it on and off unpredictably that gives you the ulcers!"

Self-Image Challenged. Now if we are troubled by another person's jeopardizing our predictability about him then how much more traumatic is it for one to have his *own self*-image challenged. He stands the risk of losing the ability to predict, control, and *know himself.* It is difficult to imagine a greater internal upheaval than suddenly not to *know oneself—to lose contact with oneself.* It may not be inaccurate to say that our mental institutions are filled with people who have lost contact with themselves more or less permanently.

It is no wonder, then, that the loss of a self-image is generally warded off at almost any cost. And yet few of us have gone through life unscathed. Anyone who has experienced a deeply traumatic experience at one time or another—whether related to a parent, a spouse, a child, school, religion, vocation, narcotics, alcoholism, job security, illness, injury, lawsuit—will

(1958), pp. 503—506; V. B. Cline and J. M. Richards, Jr., "Accuracy of Interpersonal Perception—A General Trait?", *Journal of Abnormal and Social Psychology,* Vol. 60 (1960), pp. 1—7; F. Heider, *The Psychology of Interpersonal Relations* (New York: John Wiley & Sons, Inc. 1958); W. C. Schutz, *FIRO: A Three-Dimensional Theory of Interpersonal Behavior* (New York: Holt, Rinehart & Winston, Inc., 1960); R. Taft, "The Ability to Judge People," *Psychological Bulletin,* Vol. 52 (1955), pp. 1—23; R. Tagiuri and L. Petrullo (eds.), *Person Perception and Interpersonal Behavior* (Stanford, Calif.: Stanford University Press, 1958).

probably find on restrospection that his self-image was being severely threatened.

A Personal Case. My own experience is a case in point. As a high school freshman I hit upon chemical research for a career. I suppose this was encouraged by an older boy I admired who also aspired to chemistry. He had built a laboratory in his basement so, of course, I had to have one too. I remember collecting hundreds of jars and bottles and scores of other treasures that might somehow be useful in my lab. I can also recall spending hour after hour thoroughly enjoying mixing potions of every description—and some beyond description. (I recall without quite so much relish the time I brewed some chlorine and nearly gassed myself unconscious!)

I *devoured* the chemistry course in my junior year. I must admit feeling rather smug during this period for I had a ready answer to the recurrent question, What are you going to be? Most of my friends had either a hazy answer or none at all. My self-image in this regard was forming and solidifying.

I was graduated from high school during World War II and immediately entered the service. Somehow the Army gave little shrift to young men who were long on aspiration but short on experience and consequently I had three years of singularly nonchemical experience—but this did not dissuade me. Finally, the war ended and I was discharged. I immediately enrolled in a chemical technology program at a university reputed for this field.

Suddenly, reality began to catch up with my self-image. I had not realized that a chemist was also expected to be a pretty fair mathematician. I had done well enough in high school math courses but the last three years were nonmathematical as well as nonchemical. At any rate I foolishly disregarded the math refresher course (my self-image said I didn't need a "crutch") and charged headlong into college algebra where I was in competition with fellows fresh from high school math. While I was rusty, it would be unfair to say that I didn't get the math; I did get it but about a week after the exams, which is poor timing! Net result—the first *D* I had ever received in my life. What was the consequence—did I trade in my self-image for a new model? Hardly; rather than yield, I fought tenaciously and found a ready explanation for my plight: Aside from the Army's causing me to "forget my math" the instructor "had it in for me." Among other evidences he had a Scottish name and I was convinced he was anti-Irish!

I was practicing what some writers call "perceptual defense," a form of perceptual distortion which "demonstrates that when confronted with a fact inconsistent with a stereotype already held by a person, the perceiver is able to distort the data in such a way as to eliminate the inconsistency. Thus, by perceiving inaccurately, he defends himself from having to change his stereotypes."[32] Haire and Grunes suggest that we "blinder" ourselves to avoid seeing that which might trouble us.[33] As communication authority David K. Berlo paraphrased the Bible— "Seek and ye shall find—whether it is there or not!"

The next quarter? A C in math. This instructor had an Irish name but he didn't like me either! In the middle of the third quarter and another math *D,* my self-image had withstood all the onslaught from harsh reality that it could. And for two to three weeks (at the time it seemed like six months) I was in a state of unrelieved depression. I became very nervous and had difficulty eating, sleeping, and studying (which only intensified my problem). Figuratively, a large section of my self-image had been shot away and *I had nothing to replace it.* The most appalling aspect of the experience was that I realized that *I didn't know myself.* To give the story a happy ending I took a battery of aptitude tests, changed to another major, and very gradually began to construct another self-image.

Resistance to Image Change. Anyone who has undergone such a trauma will understand why the individual generally resists image change—particularly sudden change. And herein lies one

---

[32] S. S. Zalkind and T. W. Costello, "Perception: Some Recent Research and Implications for Administration," *Administrative Science Quarterly,* September, 1962, p. 227.

[33] M. Haire and W. F. Grunes, "Perceptual Defenses: Processes Protecting an Original Perception of Another Personality," *Human Relations,* Vol. 3 (1958), pp. 403–412.

of the greatest obstacles to the full development of an effective communicator and, for that matter, an effective person. The central premise of an excellent book[34] by psychiatrist Karen Horney is that the neurotic process is a special form of human development which is the antithesis of healthy growth. Optimally, man's energies are directed toward realizing his own potentialities. But, under inner stress, he becomes estranged from his *real self* and spends himself creating and protecting a false, idealized self, based on pride, but threatened by doubts, self-contempt, and self-hate. Throughout the book the goal of liberation for the forces that lead to true self-realization is emphasized.

Take the case of a high school friend. After graduation he, too, went into the service but was more fortunate (in a sense), for the Army put him through three years of an engineering curriculum. Then the war was over and he was discharged. But he decided he did not care for engineering and could not bring himself to take a final year of course work to earn an engineering degree. And yet he could not bear the thought of starting all over again in another field. The net result was that, for all practical purposes, he did nothing. He took a clerical job in a nearby insurance firm and has been there for 20 years. Through the years, his perhaps largely unconscious philosophy of life has evidently been: "I can't stand another failure [he probably regarded not completing the engineering degree as a failure] and one sure way not to lose a race is not to enter it." In sum, here is a man who apparently has protected his self-image at the cost of a stunted life.

The handicap of inaccurate self-knowledge and the unwillingness to reconstruct a more realistic self-image seem to be very widespread. In 15 years of organizational research and consulting I have known scores, if not hundreds of men, particularly in the middle echelons of their organizations, who seemed to have all the requisites for continued success: intelligence, education, experience, drive, ability, ambition. But they had one vital thing—*they did not know themselves*. The image they held of

[34] Karen Horney, *Neurosis and Human Growth: The Struggle toward Self-Realization* (New York: W. W. Norton & Co., Inc., 1950).

themselves was pitifully out of phase with that which they were projecting to others. They seemed chronically annoyed and/or bewildered by the reactions of others to them. What was happening? As unrealistic as their self-images were it was nevertheless too threatening to entertain contrary cues from other people. Fending off the reactions of others variously as "those malicious/crazy/misinformed/ornery/perverse/stupid people!" they had been successful in perpetuating and even reinforcing their respective self-myths. Thus, they ineffectualized themselves; squandered their nervous energies in a kind of internal conflict, protecting their fallacious self-images.[35] The masterful Robert Burns captured the poignancy of self-deception almost two centuries ago.

> Oh wad some power the giftie gie us
> To see oursels as ithers see us!
> It wad frae monie a blunder free us,
>   An' foolish notion.

On Coping with Defensiveness

We have discussed defensive behavior as a critical obstacle to effective interpersonal communication. What, in the final analysis, are people defending *against*? In a word, *perceived threat*—the threat of change or harm to their self-images, to their personalized worlds. This would suggest that whatever reduced perceived threat would reduce the need to defend against it—to enable one to reduce his defenses accordingly. What threat-reducing techniques or approaches, then, are available to us?

After an eight-year study of recordings of interpersonal discussions, Jack Gibb delineated two communication climates—one threatening ("defensive"); the other nonthreatening ("supportive"). (See Table 2.) Incidentally, Gibb's "supportive climate" is quite in keeping with Likert's "supportive relationship" and McGregor's Theory Y as discussed in Chapter 2.

[35] This is why Brouwer was moved to write: "Manager development means change in the manager's self-image." Paul J. Brouwer, "The Power to See Ourselves," *Harvard Business Review*, Vol. 42, No. 6 (November–December, 1964), p. 156.

TABLE 2   Categories of Behavior Characteristic of Supportive and Defensive Climates in Small Groups*

Defensive Climates	Supportive Climates
1. Evaluation	1. Description
2. Control	2. Problem orientation
3. Strategy	3. Spontaneity
4. Neutrality	4. Empathy
5. Superiority	5. Equality
6. Certainty	6. Provisionalism

* Jack R. Gibb. "Defensive Communication," *Journal of Communication*, Vol. 11, No. 3, Sept., 1961, p. 143.

Gibb defined his paired categories of perceived behavior as follows:[36]

Evaluation. *To pass judgment on another; to blame or praise; to make moral assessments of another; to question his standards, values and motives and the affect loadings of his communications.*

Description. *Nonjudgmental; to ask questions which are perceived as genuine requests for information; to present "feelings, events, perceptions, or processes which do not ask or imply that the receiver change behavior or attitude."*

Control. *To try to do something to another; to attempt to change an attitude or the behavior of another—to try to restrict his field of activity; "implicit in all attempts to alter another person is the assumption of the change agent that the person to be altered is inadequate."*

Problem Orientation. *The antithesis of persuasion; to communicate "a desire to collaborate in defining a mutual problem and in seeking its solution" (thus tending to create the same problem orientation in the other); to imply that he has no preconceived solution, attitude, or method to impose upon the other; to allow "the receiver to set his own goals, make his own decisions, and evaluate his own progress—or to share with the sender in doing so."*

Strategy. *To manipulate others; to use tricks to "involve" another, to make him think he was making his own decisions, and*

[36] "Defensive Communication," *Journal of Communication*, Vol. 11, No. 3, Sept., 1961, pp. 142–148. [The complete text of the article appears on pp. 366–374 of this volume.—*Editors' note*.]

to make him feel that the speaker had genuine interest in him; to engage in a stratagem involving ambiguous and multiple motivation.

Spontaneity. To express guilelessness; natural simplicity; free of deception; having a "clean id"; having unhidden, uncomplicated motives; straightforwardness and honesty.

Neutrality. To express lack of concern for the welfare of another; "the clinical, detached, person-is-an-object-of-study attitude."

Empathy. To express respect for the worth of the listener; to identify with his problems, share his feelings, and accept his emotional values at face value.

Superiority. To communicate the attitude that one is "superior in position, power, wealth, intellectual ability, physical characteristics, other ways" to another; to tend to arouse feelings of inadequacy in the other; to impress the other that the speaker "is not willing to enter into a shared problem-solving relationship, that he probably does not desire feedback, that he does not require help and/or that he will be likely to try to reduce the power, the status, or the worth of the receiver."

Equality. To be willing to enter into participative planning with mutual trust and respect; to attach little importance to differences in talent, ability, worth, appearance, status, and power.

Certainty. To appear dogmatic; "to seem to know the answers, to require no additional data"; and to regard self as teacher rather than as co-worker; to manifest inferiority by needing to be right, wanting to win an argument rather than solve a problem, seeing one's ideas as truths to be defended.

Provisionalism. To be willing to experiment with one's own behavior, attitudes, and ideas; to investigate issues rather than taking sides on them, to problem solve rather than debate, to communicate that the other person may have some control over the shared quest or the investigation of ideas. "If a person is genuinely searching for information and data, he does not resent help or company along the way."

It would appear that if one were to offer another the most supportive climate possible his behavior should be descriptive, problem oriented, spontaneous, and so on, and should avoid attempting to evaluate, control, employ stratagems, and so forth. But the situation is a bit more complex.

First of all, the above are *perceived* behaviors. Therefore, the *perceptions* of the *perceiver* rather than the *intentions* of the perceived will be the final arbiter as to how defensive or supportive the perceiver regards the climate. Moreover, as a person becomes more defensive he becomes less able to assess accurately the motives, values, and emotions of the other person. Conversely, as he grows less defensive, the more accurate his perceptions become.[37]

The more "supportive" or defense reductive the climate, the less the receiver reads into the communication distorted loadings which arise from projections of his own anxieties, motives, and concerns. As defenses are reduced, the receivers become better able to concentrate upon the structure, the content and the cognitive meanings of the message.[38]

Another qualification on Gibb's classifications is that while the defensive categories *generally* arouse defensiveness and the supportive categories *ordinarily* generate defense reduction, the degree to which these responses occur depends upon the *individual's level of defensiveness* as well as the *general climate of the group at the time.*[39]

Still another qualification is that the behavior categories are *interactive*. For example, when a speaker's behavior appears *evaluative* it ordinarily increases defensiveness. But if the listener feels the speaker regards him as an *equal* and was being direct and *spontaneous,* the evaluativeness of the message might be neutralized or not even perceived. Again, attempts to *control* will stimulate defensiveness depending upon the degree of

[37] J. R. Gibb, "Defense Level and Influence Potential in Small Groups," L. Petrullo and B. M. Bass (eds.), *Leadership and Interpersonal Behavior* (New York: Holt, Rinehart, and Winston, 1961), pp. 66–81.

[38] J. R. Gibb, "Defensive Communication," *op. cit.,* p. 142. [p. 367 of this volume.]

[39] J. R. Gibb, "Sociopsychological Processes of Group Instruction," N. B. Henry (ed.), *The Dynamics of Instructional Groups* (Fifty-ninth Yearbook of the National Society for the Study of Education) (1960), Part II, pp. 115–135.

openness of the effort. The suspicion of hidden motives heightens resistance. Still another example, the use of *strata-gems* becomes especially threatening when one attempt seems to be trying to make strategy *appear spontaneous.*

Openness

A central theme running throughout Gibb's findings is the importance of *openness*—the willingness to be receptive to experience. Rogers considered openness as the polar opposite of defensiveness.

In the hypothetical person who is completely open to his experience, his concept of self would be a symbolization in awareness which would be completely congruent with his experience. There would, therefore, be no possibility of threat.[40]

One who is open to experience evaluates threat more accurately and tolerates change more graciously. This is why the frame of reference concept can be so helpful in reducing defenses and in keeping them low. Because the frame of reference obviates the mine-is-the-only-valid-world presumption it makes defense of one's personalized world unnecessary. Nondefensive, one is not compelled to attack or counterattack—thus he is more able to contribute to a supportive climate in his relations with others.

In a supportive climate people are more able to explore their own and each other's decision premises[41] and thus get down to the real grounds of controversy (or to discover that there was no real basis for conflict). Even if there are genuine differences, under conditions of openness people find themselves more capable of dealing with them maturely.

Rogers offers this practical suggestion:

The next time you get into an argument with your wife, or your friend, or with a small group of friends, just stop the discussion

[40] C. R. Rogers, "A Theory . . . ," *op. cit.,* p. 206.
[41] H. A. Simon, *Administrative Behavior* (2d ed.; New York: The Macmillan Co., 1957).

for a moment and for an experiment, institute this rule. "Each person can speak up for himself only after he has first restated the ideas and feelings of the previous speaker accurately, and to that speaker's satisfaction." You see what this would mean? It would be necessary for you to really achieve the other speaker's frame of reference—to understand his thoughts and feelings so well that you could summarize them for him. Sounds simple, doesn't it? But if you try it you will discover it one of the most difficult things you have tried to do. However, once you have been able to see the other's point of view, your own comments will have to be drastically revised. You will also find the emotion going out of the discussion, the differences being reduced, and those differences which remain being of a rational and understandable sort.[42]

Summary

We have depicted human behavior as the product of the internal state of the individual and the environment in which he finds himself. His behavior, then, is only indirectly a response to reality. One who cannot tolerate this basic uncertainty of life and assumes *his world is the only real world* may find that "world" in almost constant jeopardy. Closed and defensive he may respond to the "threats" with irrational attack and/or flight.

We have conceded that many organizations are populated to an extent with more or less defensive (and thus often aggressive) people. Therefore, the challenge to anyone who aspires to be an effective leader or member of an organization (or more broadly, wishes to live an emotionally mature and deeply satisfying life) might be phrased as follows:

1. Can he come to accept that *his* and everyone else's "reality" is subjective, incomplete, distorted, and unique? Can he,

[42] C. R. Rogers, "Communication: Its Blocking and Its Facilitation," a paper originally prepared for delivery at the Northwestern University Contennial Conference on Communications, held in Evanston, Illinois, October 11–13, 1951. Reproduced here from the Northwestern University *Information*, Vol. XX, No. 25.

therefore, muster the courage to become open and nondefensive—to permit even contrary cues to reach him and to
begin to revise, update, and make more valid his self-image?
2. Having clarified his own frame of reference can he learn to
assess accurately the frames of reference of others? Can the
manager, for example, realize the simple but profound truth
that his subordinates' worlds have him in it as a boss—his
world does not?

George Orwell
Shooting
an Elephant

In Moulmein, in Lower Burma, I was hated by large numbers of
people—the only time in my life that I have been important
enough for this to happen to me. I was sub-divisional police
officer of the town, and in an aimless, petty kind of way anti-
European feeling was very bitter. No one had the guts to raise
a riot, but if a European woman went through the bazaars alone
somebody would probably spit betel juice over her dress. As a
police officer I was an obvious target and was baited whenever
it seemed safe to do so. When a nimble Burman tripped me up
on the football field and the referee (another Burman) looked
the other way, the crowd yelled with hideous laughter. This
happened more than once. In the end the sneering yellow faces
of young men that met me everywhere, the insults hooted after
me when I was at a safe distance, got badly on my nerves. The
young Buddhist priests were the worst of all. There were several thousands of them in the town and none of them seemed
to have anything to do except stand on street corners and jeer
at Europeans.

All this was perplexing and upsetting. For at that time I
had already made up my mind that imperialism was an evil
thing and the sooner I chucked up my job and got out of it the
better. Theoretically—and secretly, of course—I was all for the
Burmese and all against their oppressors, the British. As for the

From *Shooting an Elephant and Other Essays,* copyright 1945, 1946, 1949,
1950, by Sonia Brownell Orwell. Reprinted by permission of Harcourt, Brace
and World, Inc.

job I was doing, I hated it more bitterly than I can perhaps make clear. In a job like that you see the dirty work of Empire at close quarters. The wretched prisoners huddling in the stinking cages of the lock-ups, the grey, cowed faces of the long-term convicts, the scarred buttocks of the men who had been flogged with bamboos—all these oppressed me with an intolerable sense of guilt. But I could get nothing into perspective. I was young and ill-educated and I had to think out my problems in the utter silence that is imposed on every Englishman in the East. I did not even know that the British Empire is dying, still less did I know that it is a great deal better than the younger empires that are going to supplant it. All I knew was that I was stuck between my hatred of the empire I served and my rage against the evil-spirited little beasts who tried to make my job impossible. With one part of my mind I thought of the British Raj as an unbreakable tyranny, as something clamped down, in *saecula saeculorum,* upon the will of prostrate peoples; with another part I thought that the greatest joy in the world would be to drive a bayonet into a Buddhist priest's guts. Feelings like these are the normal by-products of imperialism; ask any Anglo-Indian official, if you can catch him off duty.

One day something happened which in a roundabout way was enlightening. It was a tiny incident in itself, but it gave me a better glimpse than I had had before of the real nature of imperialism—the real motives for which despotic governments act. Early one morning the sub-inspector at a police station the other end of the town rang me up on the phone and said that an elephant was ravaging the bazaar. Would I please come and do something about it? I did not know what I could do, but I wanted to see what was happening and I got on to a pony and started out. I took my rifle, an old .44 Winchester and much too small to kill an elephant, but I thought the noise might be useful *in terrorem.* Various Burmans stopped me on the way and told me about the elephant's doings. It was not, of course, a wild elephant, but a tame one which had gone "must." It had been chained up, as tame elephants always are when their attack of "must" is due, but on the previous night it had broken its chain and escaped. Its mahout, the only person who could manage it when it was in that state, had set out in pursuit, but had taken the wrong direction and was now twelve hours' journey away, and in the morning the elephant had suddenly reappeared in the town. The Burmese population had no weapons and were quite helpless against it. It had already destroyed somebody's bamboo hut, killed a cow and raided some fruit-stalls and devoured the stock; also it had met the municipal rubbish van and, when the driver jumped out and took to his heels, had turned the van over and inflicted violences upon it.

The Burmese sub-inspector and some Indian constables were waiting for me in the quarter where the elephant had been seen. It was a very poor quarter, a labyrinth of squalid bamboo huts, thatched with palm-leaf, winding all over a steep hillside. I remember that it was a cloudy, stuffy morning at the beginning of the rains. We began questioning the people as to where the elephant had gone and, as usual, failed to get any definite information. That is invariably the case in the East; a story always sounds clear enough at a distance, but the nearer you get to the scene of events the vaguer it becomes. Some of the people said that the elephant had gone in one direction, some said that he had gone in another, some professed not even to have heard of any elephant. I had almost made up my mind that the whole story was a pack of lies, when we heard yells a little distance away. There was a loud, scandalized cry of "Go away, child! Go away, child! Go away this instant!" and an old woman with a switch in her hand came round the corner of a hut, violently shooing away a crowd of naked children. Some more women followed, clicking their tongues and exclaiming; evidently there was something that the children ought not to have seen. I rounded the hut and saw a man's dead body sprawling in the mud. He was an Indian, a black Dravidian coolie, almost naked, and he could not have been dead many minutes. The people said that the elephant had come suddenly upon him round the corner of the hut, caught him with its trunk, put its foot on his back and ground him into the earth. This was the rainy season and the ground was soft, and his face had scored a trench a foot deep and a couple of yards long. He was lying on his belly with arms crucified and head sharply twisted to one side. His face was coated with mud, the eyes wide open, the teeth bared and grinning with an expression of unendurable agony. (Never tell me, by the way, that the dead look peaceful. Most of the corpses I have seen looked devilish.) The friction of the great beast's foot had stripped the skin from his back as neatly as one skins a rabbit. As soon as I saw the dead man I sent an orderly to a friend's house nearby to borrow an elephant rifle. I had already sent back the pony, not wanting it to go mad with fright and throw me if it smelt the elephant.

The orderly came back in a few minutes with a rifle and five cartridges, and meanwhile some Burmans had arrived and told us that the elephant was in the paddy fields below, only a few hundred yards away. As I started forward practically the whole population of the quarter flocked out of the houses and followed me. They had seen the rifle and were all shouting excitedly that I was going to shoot the elephant. They had not shown much interest in the elephant when he was merely ravaging their homes, but it was different now that he was going to be shot. It was a bit of fun to them, as it would be to an English crowd; besides they wanted the meat. It made me vaguely uneasy. I had no intention of shooting the elephant —I had merely sent for the rifle to defend myself if necessary —and it is always unnerving to have a crowd following you. I marched down the hill, looking and feeling a fool, with the rifle over my shoulder and an ever-growing army of people jostling at my heels. At the bottom, when you got away from the huts, there was a metalled road and beyond that a miry waste of paddy fields a thousand yards across, not yet ploughed but soggy from the first rains and dotted with coarse grass. The elephant was standing eight yards from the road, his left side towards us. He took not the slightest notice of the crowd's approach. He was tearing up bunches of grass, beating them against his knees to clean them and stuffing them into his mouth.

I had halted on the road. As soon as I saw the elephant I knew with perfect certainty that I ought not to shoot him. It is a serious matter to shoot a working elephant—it is comparable to destroying a huge and costly piece of machinery—and obviously one ought not to do it if it can possibly be avoided. And at that distance, peacefully eating, the elephant looked no more dangerous than a cow. I thought then and I think now that his attack of "must" was already passing off; in which case he would merely wander harmlessly about until the mahout came back and caught him. Moreover, I did not in the least want to shoot him. I decided that I would watch him for a little while to make sure that he did not turn savage again, and then go home.

But at that moment I glanced round at the crowd that had followed me. It was an immense crowd, two thousand at the least and growing every minute. It blocked the road for a long distance on either side. I looked at the sea of yellow faces above the garish clothes—faces all happy and excited over this bit of fun, all certain that the elephant was going to be shot. They were watching me as they would watch a conjurer about to perform a trick. They did not like me, but with the magical rifle in my hands I was momentarily worth watching. And suddenly I realized that I should have to shoot the elephant after all. The people expected it of me and I had got to do it; I could feel their two thousand wills pressing me forward, irresistibly. And it was at this moment, as I stood there with the rifle in my hands, that I first grasped the hollowness, the futility of the white man's dominion in the East. Here was I, the white man with his gun, standing in front of the unarmed native crowd—seemingly the leading actor of the piece; but in reality I was only an absurd puppet pushed to and fro by the will of those yellow faces behind. I perceived in this moment that when the white man turns tyrant it is his own freedom that he destroys. He becomes a sort of hollow, posing dummy, the conventionalized figure of a sahib. For it is the condition of his rule that he shall spend his life in trying to impress the "natives," and so in every crisis he has got to do what the "natives" expect of him. He wears a mask, and his face grows to fit it. I had got to shoot the elephant. I had committed myself to doing it when I sent for the rifle. A sahib has got to act like a sahib; he has got to appear resolute, to know his own mind and do definite things. To come all that way, rifle in hand, with two thousand people marching at my heels, and then to trail feebly away, having done nothing—no, that was impossible. The crowd would laugh at me. And my whole life, every white man's life in the East, was one long struggle not to be laughed at.

But I did not want to shoot the elephant. I watched him beating his bunch of grass against his knees, with that preoccupied grandmotherly air that elephants have. It seemed to me that it would be murder to shoot him. At that age I was not squeamish about killing animals, but I had never shot an elephant and never wanted to. (Somehow it always seems worse to kill a *large* animal.) Besides, there was the beast's owner to be considered. Alive, the elephant was worth at least a hundred pounds; dead, he would only be worth the value of his tusks, five pounds, possibly. But I had got to act quickly. I turned to some experienced-looking Burmans who had been there when we arrived, and asked them how the elephant had been behaving. They all said the same thing: he took no notice of you if you left him alone, but he might charge if you went too close to him.

It was perfectly clear to me what I ought to do. I ought to walk up to within, say, twenty-five yards of the elephant and test his behavior. If he charged, I could shoot; if he took no notice of me, it would be safe to leave him until the mahout came back. But also I knew that I was going to do no such thing. I was a poor shot with a rifle and the ground was soft mud into which one would sink at every step. If the elephant charged and I missed him, I should have about as much chance as a toad under a steam-roller. But even then I was not thinking particularly of my own skin, only of the watchful yellow faces behind. For at that moment, with the crowd watching me, I was not afraid in the ordinary sense, as I would have been if I had been alone. A white man mustn't be frightened in front of "natives"; and so, in general, he isn't frightened. The sole thought in my mind was that if anything went wrong those two thousand Burmans would see me pursued, caught, trampled on and reduced to a grinning corpse like that Indian up the hill. And if that happened it was quite probable that some of them would laugh. That would never do. There was only one alternative. I shoved the cartridges into the magazine and lay down on the road to get a better aim.

The crowd grew very still, and a deep, low, happy sigh, as of people who see the theatre curtain go up at last, breathed from innumerable throats. They were going to have their bit of fun after all. The rifle was a beautiful German thing with cross-hair sights. I did not then know that in shooting an elephant one would shoot to cut an imaginary bar running from ear-hole to ear-hole. I ought, therefore, as the elephant was sideways on, to have aimed straight at his ear-hole; actually I aimed several inches in front of this, thinking the brain would be further forward.

When I pulled the trigger I did not hear the bang or feel the kick—one never does when a shot goes home—but I heard the devilish roar of glee that went up from the crowd. In that instant, in too short a time, one would have thought, even for the bullet to get there, a mysterious, terrible change had come over the elephant. He neither stirred nor fell, but every line of his body had altered. He looked suddenly stricken, shrunken, immensely old, as though the frightful impact of the bullet had paralyzed him without knocking him down. At last, after what seemed a long time—it might have been five seconds, I dare say—he sagged flabbily to his knees. His mouth slobbered. An enormous senility seemed to have settled upon him. One could have imagined him thousands of years old. I fired again into the same spot. At the second shot he did not collapse but climbed with desperate slowness to his feet and stood weakly upright, with legs sagging and head dropping. I fired a third time. That was the shot that did for him. You could see the agony of it jolt his whole body and knock the last remnant of strength from his legs. But in falling he seemed for a moment to rise, for as his hind legs collapsed beneath him he seemed to tower upward like a huge rock toppling, his trunk reaching skywards like a tree. He trumpeted, for the first and only time. And then down he came, his belly towards me, with a crash that seemed to shake the ground even where I lay.

I got up. The Burmans were already racing past me across

the mud. It was obvious that the elephant would never rise again, but he was not dead. He was breathing very rhythmically with long rattling gasps, his great mound of a side painfully rising and falling. His mouth was wide open—I could see far down into caverns of pale pink throat. I waited a long time for him to die, but his breathing did not weaken. Finally I fired my two remaining shots into the spot where I thought his heart must be. The thick blood welled out of him like red velvet, but still he did not die. His body did not even jerk when the shots hit him, the tortured breathing continued without a pause. He was dying, very slowly and in great agony, but in some world remote from me where not even a bullet could damage him further. I felt that I had got to put an end to that dreadful noise. It seemed dreadful to see the great beast lying there, powerless to move and yet powerless to die, and not even to be able to finish him. I sent back for my small rifle and poured shot after shot into his heart and down his throat. They seemed to make no impression. The tortured gasps continued as steadily as the ticking of a clock.

In the end I could not stand it any longer and went away. I heard later that it took him half an hour to die. Burmans were bringing dahs and baskets even before I left, and I was told they had stripped his body almost to the bones by the afternoon.

Afterwards, of course, there were endless discussions about the shooting of the elephant. The owner was furious, but he was only an Indian and could do nothing. Besides, legally I had done the right thing, for a mad elephant has to be killed, like a mad dog, if its owner fails to control it. Among the Europeans opinion was divided. The older men said I was right, the younger men said it was a damn shame to shoot an elephant for killing a coolie, because an elephant was worth more than any damn Coringhee coolie. And afterwards I was very glad that the coolie had been killed; it put me legally in the right and it gave me a sufficient pretext for shooting the elephant. I often wondered whether any of the others grasped that I had done it solely to avoid looking a fool.

Section Three
Questions
for
Reflection
and
Discussion

1. What is the relationship between metacommunication and interpersonal perception?
2. How does "stereotyping" affect our interpersonal perceptions?
3. What potential problems arise as we attempt to create consistencies in our perceptions of others?
4. What are the assumptions concerning "reality" and the "nature of the world" that underlie Haney's analysis of perception theory?
5. If communication "stratagems" can be dangerous and potentially deceptive, how may we legitimately incorporate applications of perception theory into our interpersonal communication?
6. What are the analogical implications of Orwell's experience with interpersonal perception?

INTERPERSONAL
ORIENTATIONS
SECTION FOUR

More and more our environment is becoming one of people, less and less an environment of trees, fields, rivers, and sky. As our interpersonal environment crowds around us, it is very important to be able to predict how one or another person will ordinarily respond to us. We must be able to anticipate how they view their social environment, what their experiences with people mean to them, and how they will likely interact with us.

When one person responds in a specific way to another person, this manner of response might be termed a type of interpersonal orientation. However, the concern of this section is with the way in which a person or persons *generally* respond to other people—an interpersonal life-style, so to speak. We might say our interest is on the wholesale, rather than the retail, level. Sets of typical interpersonal responses may be identified, classified, observed, and analyzed.

Basic classifications of interpersonal response sets are commonly recognized by all of us: We note that a person is generally cooperative or competitive, generally open to new friends and ideas, or usually closed to these situations.

One of the early systematic classifications of interpersonal response patterns was developed by Karen Horney,[1] a noted psychiatrist. She identified three general tendencies: (1) moving *toward* others; (2) moving *against* others; and (3) moving *away from* others.

---

[1] Horney, Karen (1945). *Our Inner Conflicts* (New York: Norton Press).

According to this conceptual system, going *toward* others indicates a need for affection or approval—a need for a partner, friend, or lover. This interpersonal orientation provides responses ranging from mild support to close affiliation, trust, or love.

An orientation of going *against* others indicates a view of the world as an arena where, in the Darwinian sense, the strong overcome the weak and only the fittest survive. Such an orientation indicates a need to excell, to achieve, to attain prestige and recognition. Typical behavior ranges from a mild form of challenge to exploitation of others in a callous pursuit of self-interest.

An orientation of going *away from* others indicates a need to avoid becoming attached to anybody or anything; self-sufficiency and privacy both serve this need. Independence and detachment are prized: The goal is *not* to be involved, influenced, obligated, or challenged. Persons exhibiting this orientation may conform outwardly in order to avoid friction or obligation; inwardly, however, they reject rules and standards presented by other people. Typical behavior ranges from mild alienation to suspicion, withdrawal, and fear.

Most of us display more than one of these interpersonal response patterns at different times toward various people. However, it is quite surprising how easily we can classify our acquaintances on the basis of their choice of words: "Will they like me?"—"I wonder if I can beat him (or use him)?"—or, "Will they interfere with me or let me alone?"

Since Horney's early study, more elaborate and sophisticated analyses of interpersonal response patterns have been made. One rather elaborate classification system has been previously presented in Section Two: Schutz's "Fundamental Interpersonal Relations Orientation." It was included in the section, "The Interpersonal Imperative," because it delineates a series of interpersonal needs. However, it may be reviewed in conjunction with the present section. Schutz outlines the ways in which an individual may *orient himself toward other people* in order to satisfy these needs.

In "Games," a chapter from *Games People Play*, Eric Berne dis-

cusses certain types of interpersonal transactions which are recurring, repetitious, superficially plausible, and have a concealed motivation. Such "games" are identified as a series of
complimentary transactions which involve ulterior motives and
produce a payoff. One illustrative game played by wives with
their husbands—"If It Weren't For You"—is discussed in descriptive detail. As a model of many other interactional games, it is
analyzed in terms of thesis, antithesis, aim, roles, psychodynamics, moves, and payoffs. This chapter presents an intriguing
analysis of behavior employed by a person who views another
as his "patsy," someone to be *used* for personal advantage.
Although Berne's work is presented in a very engaging and
sometimes comical vein, it represents a most serious attempt
by an astute scholar to analyze in detail a certain type of
interpersonal orientation.

The chapter entitled, "Verbalizers," is taken from Stuart
Palmer's book, *Understanding Other People*. He describes in
detail the type of person who is hostile or aggressive toward
others and who practices mild aggression through arguing,
complaining, gossiping, or making the other person uncom-
fortably aware that somehow he has performed some (vague)
personal transgression. The case studies presented seem to
describe certain real-life people who are memorable.

The third item in this section presents an analysis of a very
important but somewhat complicated principle of interpersonal
transaction. It concerns relationships between the interpersonal
orientations of two people while they are interacting. Laing,
Phillipson, and Lee describe ways in which communication
problems can occur when two such people disagree in their
interpretations of one of their response patterns. The basic
idea is relatively simple, but may seem to be rather complicated. It concerns this question: Do you see me responding
to you in the same way I see me responding to you? Further,
will how I see you accepting (or not accepting) my view of me
affect my further responses to you? But, of course, you are also
responding to your view of my perception of you—thus the
title of the chapter, "The Spiral of Reciprocal Perspectives."
Perhaps you have heard about a person who fell in love

after "she looked back to see if I looked back to see if she looked back." Young people in love seem to spend quite a bit of time on such matters as, "I wonder if her not smiling at my remark means that she thought I was angry because she couldn't (or wouldn't) go to the game with me last night?" One may think that such thoughts among lovers are strictly reserved for puppy-love types. Laing, Phillipson, and Lee have found that the congruence of interpersonal views is significantly related to the understanding and happiness of adult married couples. This chapter should be read with care and courage, realizing that interpersonal relations really are complicated rather than simple, and that the understanding of such a process may take a little extra time and attention.

Eric Berne
Games

1. Definition

A game is an ongoing series of complementary ulterior transactions progressing to a well-defined, predictable outcome.
Descriptively it is a recurring set of transactions, often repetitious, superficially plausible, with a concealed motivation; or,
more colloquially, a series of moves with a snare, or "gimmick."
Games are clearly differentiated from procedures, rituals, and
pastimes by two chief characteristics: (1) their ulterior quality
and (2) the payoff. Procedures may be successful, rituals
effective, and pastimes profitable, but all of them are by
definition candid; they may involve contest, but not conflict,
and the ending may be sensational, but it is not dramatic.
Every game, on the other hand, is basically dishonest, and the
outcome has a dramatic, as distinct from merely exciting,
quality.

It remains to distinguish games from the one remaining
type of social action which so far has not been discussed. An
operation is a simple transaction or set of transactions undertaken for a specific, state purpose. If someone frankly asks
for reassurance and gets it, that is an operation. If someone
asks for reassurance, and after it is given turns it in some way
to the disadvantage of the giver, that is a game. Superficially,
then, a game looks like a set of operations, but after the payoff

Excerpt reprinted by permission of Grove Press, Inc., from Eric Berne,
Games People Play, New York, Grove Press, 1964, pp. 48–65. Copyright © 1964
by Eric Berne.

it becomes apparent that these "operations" were really *maneuvers;* not honest requests but moves in the game.

In the "insurance game," for example, no matter what the agent appears to be doing in conversation, if he is a hard player he is really looking for or working on a prospect. What he is after, if he is worth his salt, is to "make a killing." The same applies to "the real estate game," "the pajama game" and similar occupations. Hence at a social gathering, while a salesman is engaged in pastimes, particularly variants of "Balance Sheet," his congenial participation may conceal a series of skillful maneuvers designed to elicit the kind of information he is professionally interested in. There are dozens of trade journals devoted to improving commercial maneuvers, and which give accounts of outstanding players and games (interesting operators who make unusually big deals). Transactionally speaking, these are merely variants of *Sports Illustrated, Chess World,* and other sports magazines. ·

As far as angular transactions are concerned—games which are consciously planned with professional precision under Adult control to yield the maximum gains—the big "con games" which flourished in the early 1900's are hard to surpass for detailed practical planning and psychological virtuosity.[1]

What we are concerned with here, however, are the unconscious games played by innocent people engaged in duplex transactions of which they are not fully aware, and which form the most important aspect of social life all over the world. Because of their dynamic qualities, games are easy to distinguish from mere static *attitudes,* which arise from taking a position.

The use of the word "game" should not be misleading. As explained in the introduction, it does not necessarily imply fun or even enjoyment. Many salesmen do not consider their work fun, as Arthur Miller made clear in his play, *The Death of a Salesman.* And there may be no lack of seriousness. Football games nowadays are taken very seriously, but no more so than such transactional games as "Alcoholic" or "Third Degree Rapo."

The same applies to the word "play," as anyone who has

"played" hard poker or "played" the stock market over a long period can testify. The possible seriousness of games and play, and the possibly serious results, are well known to anthropologists. The most complex game that ever existed, that of "Courtier" as described so well by Stendhal in *The Charterhouse of Parma,* was deadly serious. The grimmest of all, of course, is "War."

2. A Typical Game

The most common game played between spouses is colloquially called "If It Weren't For You," and this will be used to illustrate the characteristics of games in general.

Mrs. White complained that her husband severely restricted her social activities, so that she had never learned to dance. Due to changes in her attitude brought about by psychiatric treatment, her husband became less sure of himself and more indulgent. Mrs. White was then free to enlarge the scope of her activities. She signed up for dancing classes, and then discovered to her despair that she had a morbid fear of dance floors and had to abandon this project.

This unfortunate adventure, along with similar ones, laid bare some important aspects of the structure of her marriage. Out of her many suitors she had picked a domineering man for a husband. She was then in a position to complain that she could do all sorts of things "if it weren't for you." Many of her women friends also had domineering husbands, and when they met for their morning coffee, they spent a good deal of time playing "If It Weren't For Him."

As it turned out, however, contrary to her complaints, her husband was performing a very real service for her by forbidding her to do something she was deeply afraid of, and by preventing her, in fact, from even becoming aware of her fears. This was one reason her Child had shrewdly chosen such a husband.

But there was more to it than that. His prohibitions and her complaints frequently led to quarrels, so that their sex life was seriously impaired. And because of his feelings of guilt, he frequently brought her gifts which might not otherwise have been forthcoming; certainly when he gave her more freedom, his gifts diminished in lavishness and frequency. She and her husband had little in common besides their household worries and the children, so that their quarrels stood out as important events; it was mainly on these occasions that they had anything but the most casual conversations. At any rate, her married life had proved one thing to her that she had always maintained: that all men were mean and tyrannical. As it turned out, this attitude was related to some daydreams of being sexually abused which had plagued her in earlier years.

There are various ways of describing this game in general terms. It is apparent that it belongs in the large field of *social dynamics.* The basic fact is that by marrying, Mr. and Mrs. White have an opportunity to communicate with each other, and such an opportunity may be called *social contact.* The fact that they use this opportunity makes their household a social aggregation, as contrasted with a New York subway train, for example, where people are in spatial contact but rarely avail themselves of the opportunity and so form a dis-social aggregation. The influence the Whites exert on each other's behavior and responses constitutes *social action.* Various disciplines would investigate such social action from different points of view. Since we are here concerned with the personal histories and psycho-dynamics of the individuals involved, the present approach is one aspect of *social psychiatry;* some implicit or explicit judgment is passed on the "healthiness" of the games studied. This is somewhat different from the more neutral and less committed attitudes of sociology and social psychology. Psychiatry reserves the right to say, "Just a moment!" which the other disciplines do not. Transactional analysis is a branch of social psychiatry, and games analysis is a special aspect of transactional analysis.

Practical game analysis deals with special cases as they appear in specific situations. Theoretical game analysis attempts to abstract and generalize the characteristics of various games, so that they can be recognized independently of their momentary verbal content and their cultural matrix. The theoretical analysis of "If It Weren't For You," Marital Type, for example, should state the characteristics of that game in such a way that it can be recognized just as easily in a New Guinea jungle village as in a Manhattan penthouse, whether it is concerned with a nuptial party or with the financial problems of getting a fishing rod for the grandchildren; and regardless of how bluntly or subtly the moves are made, according to the permissible degrees of frankness between husband and wife. The *prevalence* of the game in a given society is a matter for sociology and anthropology. Game analysis, as a part of social psychiatry, is only interested in describing the game when it does occur, regardless of how often that may be. This distinction is not complex, but it is analogous to the distinction between public health and internal medicine; the first is interested in the prevalence of malaria, while the latter studies cases of malaria as they come up, in the jungle or in Manhattan.

At the present time the scheme given below has been found the most useful one for theoretical game analysis. No doubt it will be improved as further knowledge accumulates. The first requisite is to recognize that a certain sequence of maneuvers meets the criteria of a game. As many samples as possible of the game are then collected. The significant features of the collection are isolated. Certain aspects emerge as essential. These are then classified under headings which are designed to be as meaningful and instructive as possible in the current state of knowledge. The analysis is undertaken from the point of view of the one who is "it"—in this case, Mrs. White.

Thesis. This is a general description of the game, including the immediate sequence of events (the social level) and information about their psychological background, evolution and significance (the psychological level). In the case of "If It Weren't For You," Marital Type, the details already given will serve (pp. 185–186). For the sake of brevity, this game will henceforth be referred to as IWFY.

Antithesis. The presumption that a certain sequence constitutes a game is tentative until it has been existentially validated.

This validation is carried out by a refusal to play or by under-cutting the payoff. The one who is "it" will then make more intense efforts to continue the game. In the face of adamant refusal to play or a successful undercutting he will then lapse into a state called "despair," which in some respects resembles a depression, but is different in significant ways. It is more acute and contains elements of frustration and bewilderment. It may be manifested, for example, by the onset of perplexed weeping. In a successful therapeutic situation this may soon be replaced by humorous laughter, implying an Adult realization: "There I go again!" Thus despair is a concern of the Adult, while in depression it is the Child who has the executive power. Hopefulness, enthusiasm or a lively interest in one's surroundings is the opposite of depression; laughter is the opposite of despair. Hence the enjoyable quality of therapeutic game analysis. The antithesis to IWFY is permissiveness. As long as the husband is prohibitive, the game can proceed. If instead of saying "Don't you dare!" he says "Go ahead!" the underlying phobias are unmasked, and the wife can no longer turn on him, as demonstrated in Mrs. White's case.

For clear understanding of a game, the antithesis should be known and its effectiveness demonstrated in practice.

Aim. This states simply the general purpose of the game. Sometimes there are alternatives. The aim of IWFY may be stated as either reassurance ("It's not that I'm afraid, it's that he won't let me") or vindication ("It's not that I'm not trying, it's that he holds me back"). The reassuring function is easier to clarify and is more in accord with the security needs of the wife; therefore IWFY is most simply regarded as having the aim of reassurance.

Roles. As previously noted, ego states are not roles but phenomena. Therefore ego states and roles have to be dis-tinguished in a formal description. Games may be described as two-handed, three-handed, many-handed, etc., according to the number of roles offered. Sometimes the ego state of each player corresponds to his role, sometimes it does not.

IWFY is a two-handed game and calls for a restricted wife

and a domineering husband. The wife may play her role either as a prudent Adult ("It's best that I do as he says") or as a petulant Child. The domineering husband may preserve an Adult ego state. ("It's best that you do as I say") or slip into a Parental one ("You'd better do what I say").

Dynamics. There are alternatives in stating the psychodynamic driving forces behind each case of a game. It is usually possible, however, to pick out a single psychodynamic concept which usefully, aptly and meaningfully epitomizes the situation. Thus IWFY is best described as deriving from phobic sources.

Examples. Since the childhood origins of a game, or its infantile prototypes, are instructive to study, it is worthwhile to search for such cognates in making a formal description. It happens that IFWY is just as frequently played by little children as by grown-ups, so the childhood version is the same as the later one, with the actual parent substituted for the restricting husband.

Transactional Paradigm. The transactional analysis of a typical situation is presented, giving both the social and psychological levels of a revealing ulterior transaction. In its most dramatic form, IWFY at the social level is a Parent-Child game.

Mr. White: "You stay home and take care of the house."
Mrs. White: "If it weren't for you, I could be out having fun."

At the psychological level (the ulterior marriage contract) the relationship is Child-Child, and quite different.

Mr. White: "You must always be here when I get home. I'm terrified of desertion."
Mrs. White: "I will be if you help me avoid phobic situations."

The two levels are illustrated in Figure 2.

Moves. The moves of a game correspond roughly to the strokes in a ritual. As in any game, the players become increasingly adept with practice. Wasteful moves are eliminated, and more

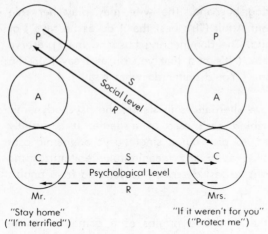

Figure 2. "If it weren't for you": A Game

and more purpose is condensed into each move. "Beautiful friendships" are often based on the fact that the players complement each other with great economy and satisfaction, so that there is a maximum yield with a minimum effort from the games they play with each other. Certain intermediate, precautionary or concessional moves can be elided, giving a high degree of elegance to the relationship. The effort saved on defensive maneuvers can be devoted to ornamental flourishes instead, to the delight of both parties and sometimes of the onlookers as well. The student observes that there is a minimum number of moves essential to the program of the game, and these can be stated in the protocol. Individual players will embellish or multiply these basic moves according to their needs, talents or desires. The framework for IWFY is as follows:

(1) Instruction-Compliance ("You stay home"—"All right").

(2) Instruction-Protest ("You stay home again"—"If it weren't for you").

Advantages. The general advantages of a game consist in its stabilizing (homeostatic) functions. Biological homeostasis is promoted by the stroking, and psychological stability is reinforced by the confirmation of position. As has already been noted, stroking may take various forms, so that the *biological advantage* of a game may be stated in tactile terms. Thus the husband's role in IWFY is reminiscent of a backhanded slap (quite different in effect from a palmar slap, which is a direct humiliation), and the wife's response is something like a petulant kick in the shins. Hence the biological gain from IWFY is derived from the belligerence-petulance exchanges: a distressing but apparently effective way to maintain the health of nervous tissues.

Confirmation of the wife's position—"All men are tyrants" —is the *existential advantage*. This position is a reaction to the need to surrender that is inherent in the phobias, a demonstration of the coherent structure which underlies all games. The expanded statement would be: "If I went out alone in a crowd, I would be overcome by the temptation to surrender; at home I don't surrender: he forces me, which proves that all men are tyrants." Hence this game is commonly played by women who suffer from feelings of unreality, which signifies their difficulty in keeping the Adult in charge in situations of strong temptation. The detailed elucidation of these mechanisms belongs to psychoanalysis rather than game analysis. In game analysis the end product is the chief concern.

Internal psychological advantage of a game is its direct effect on the psychic economy (libido). In IWFY the socially acceptable surrender to the husband's authority keeps the woman from experiencing neurotic fears. At the same time it satisfies masochistic needs, if they exist, using masochism not in the sense of self-abnegation but with its classical meaning of sexual excitement in situations of deprivation, humiliation or pain. That is, it excites her to be deprived and dominated.

External psychological advantage is the avoidance of the feared situation by playing the game. This is especially obvious in IWFY, where it is the outstanding motivation: by complying with the husband's strictures, the wife avoids the public situations which she fears.

Internal social advantage is designated by the name of the game as it is played in the individual's intimate circle. By her compliance, the wife gains the privilege of saying "If it weren't for you." This helps to structure the time she must spend with her husband; in the case of Mrs. White, this need for structure was especially strong because of the lack of other common interests, especially before the arrival of their offspring and after the children were grown. In between, the game was played less intensively and less frequently, because the children performed their usual function of structuring time for their parents, and also provided an even more widely accepted version of IWFY, the busy-housewife variation. The fact that young mothers in America often really are very busy does not change the analysis of this variation. Game analysis only attempts to answer this question without prejudice: given that a young woman is busy, how does she go about exploiting her busyness in order to get some compensation for it?

External social advantage is designated by the use made of the situation in outside social contacts. In the case of the game "If It Weren't For You," which is what the wife says to her husband, there is a transformation into the pastime "If It Weren't For Him" when she meets with her friends over morning coffee. Again, the influence of games in the selection of social companions is shown. The new neighbor who is invited for morning coffee is being invited to play "If It Weren't For Him." If she plays, well and good, she will soon be a bosom friend of the old-timers, other things being equal. If she refuses to play and insists on taking a charitable view of her husband, she will not last long. Her situation will be the same as if she kept refusing to drink at cocktail parties— in most circles, she would gradually be dropped from the guest lists.

This completes the analysis of the formal features of IWFY. In order to clarify the procedure further, the analysis of "Why Don't You—Yes But," which is the most common game played at social gatherings, committee meetings and psychotherapy groups the world over, should be consulted.

3. The Genesis of Games

From the present point of view, child rearing may be regarded as an educational process in which the child is taught what games to play and how to play them. He is also taught procedures, rituals and pastimes appropriate to his position in the local social situation, but these are less significant. His knowledge of and skill in procedures, rituals and pastimes determine what opportunities will be available to him, other things being equal; but his games determine the use he will make of those opportunities, and the outcomes of situations for which he is eligible. As elements of his script, or unconscious life-plan, his favored games also determine his ultimate destiny (again with other things being equal): the payoffs on his marriage and career, and the circumstances surrounding his death.

While conscientious parents devote a great deal of attention to teaching their children procedures, rituals and pastimes appropriate to their stations in life, and with equal care select schools, colleges and churches where their teachings will be reinforced, they tend to overlook the question of games, which form the basic structure for the emotional dynamics of each family, and which the children learn through significant experiences in everyday living from their earliest months. Related questions have been discussed for thousands of years in a rather general, unsystematic fashion, and there has been some attempt at a more methodical approach in the modern orthopsychiatric literature; but without the concept of games there is little possibility of a consistent investigation. Theories of internal individual psychodynamics have so far not been able to solve satisfactorily the problems of human relationships. These are transactional situations which call for a theory of social dynamics that cannot be derived solely from consideration of individual motivations.

Since there are as yet few well-trained specialists in child psychology and child psychiatry who are also trained in game analysis, observations on the genesis of games are sparse. Fortunately, the following episode took place in the presence of a well-educated transactional analyst.

Tanjy, age 7, got a stomach-ache at the dinner table and asked to be excused for that reason. His parents suggested that he lie down for a while. His little brother Mike, age 3, then said, "I have a stomach-ache too," evidently angling for the same consideration. The father looked at him for a few seconds and then replied, "You don't want to play that game, do you?" Whereupon Mike burst out laughing and said, "No!"

If this had been a household of food or bowel faddists, Mike would also have been packed off to bed by his alarmed parents. If he and they had repeated this performance several times, it might be anticipated that this game would have become part of Mike's character, as it so often does if the parents cooperate. Whenever he was jealous of a privilege granted to a competitor, he would plead illness in order to get some privileges himself. The ulterior transaction would then consist of: (social level) "I don't feel well" + (psychologist level) "You must grant me a privilege, too." Mike, however, was saved from such a hypochondriacal career. Perhaps he will end up with a worse fate, but that is not the issue. The issue is that a game *in statu nascendi* was broken up right there by the father's question and by the boy's frank acknowledgment that what he proposed was a game.

This demonstrates clearly enough that games are quite deliberately initiated by young children. After they become fixed patterns of stimulus and response, their origins become lost in the mists of time and their ulterior nature becomes obscured by social fogs. Both can be brought into awareness only by appropriate procedures: the origin by some form of analytic therapy and the ulterior aspect by antithesis. Repeated clinical experience along these lines makes it clear that games are imitative in nature, and that they are initially set up by the Adult (neopsychic) aspect of the child's personality. If the Child ego state can be revived in the grown-up player, the psychological aptitude of this segment (the Adult aspect of the Child ego state) is so striking, and its skill in manipulating people so enviable, that it is colloquially called "The Professor" (of Psychiatry). Hence in psychotherapy groups which concentrate on game analysis, one of the more sophisticated procedures is the search for the little "Professor" in each patient, whose early adventures in setting up games between the ages of two and eight are listened to by everyone present with fascination and often, unless the games are tragic, with enjoyment and even hilarity, in which the patient himself may join with justifiable self-appreciation and smugness. Once he is able to do that, he is well on his way to relinquishing what may be an unfortunate behavior pattern which he is much better off without.

Those are the reasons why in the formal description of a game an attempt is always made to describe the infantile or childhood prototype.

4. The Function of Games

Because there is so little opportunity for intimacy in daily life, and because some forms of intimacy (especially if intense) are psychologically impossible for most people, the bulk of the time in serious social life is taken up with playing games. Hence games are both necessary and desirable, and the only problem at issue is whether the games played by an individual offer the best yield for him. In this connection it should be remembered that the essential feature of a game is its culmination, or payoff. The principal function of the preliminary moves is to set up the situation for this payoff, but they are always designed to harvest the maximum permissible satisfaction at each step as a secondary product. Thus in "Schlemiel" (making messes and then apologizing) the payoff, and the purpose of the game, is to obtain the forgiveness which is forced by the apology; the spillings and cigarette burns are only steps leading up to this, but each such trespass yields its own pleasure. The enjoyment derived from the spilling does not make spilling a game. The apology is the critical stimulus that leads to the denouement. Otherwise the spilling would simply be a destructive procedure, a delinquency perhaps enjoyable.

The game of "Alcoholic" is similar: whatever the physiological origin, if any, of the need to drink, in terms of game analysis the imbibing is merely a move in a game which is carried on with the people in the environment. The drinking may bring its own kinds of pleasure, but it is not the essence of the game. This is demonstrated in the variant of "Dry Alcoholic," which involves the same moves and leads to the same payoff as the regular game, but is played without any bottles.

Beyond their social function in structuring time satisfactorily, some games are urgently necessary for the maintenance of health in certain individuals. These people's psychic stability is so precarious, and their positions are so tenuously maintained, that to deprive them of their games may plunge them into irreversible despair and even psychosis. Such people will fight very hard against any antithetical moves. This is often observed in marital situations when the psychiatric improvement of one spouse (i.e., the abandonment of destructive games) leads to rapid deterioration in the other spouse, to whom the games were of paramount importance in maintaining equilibrium. Hence it is necessary to exercise prudence in game analysis.

Fortunately, the rewards of game-free intimacy, which is or should be the most perfect form of human living, are so great that even precariously balanced personalities can safely and joyfully relinquish their games if an appropriate partner can be found for the better relationship.

On a larger scale, games are integral and dynamic components of the unconscious life-plan, or script, of each individual; they serve to fill in the time while he waits for the final fulfillment, simultaneously advancing the action. Since the last act of a script characteristically calls for either a miracle or a catastrophe, depending on whether the script is constructive or destructive, the corresponding games are accordingly either constructive or destructive. In colloquial terms, an individual whose script is oriented toward "waiting for Santa Claus" is likely to be pleasant to deal with in such games as "Gee You're Wonderful, Mr. Murgatroyd," while someone with a tragic script oriented toward "waiting for *rigor mortis* to set in" may play such disagreeable games as "Now I've Got You, You Son of a Bitch."

It should be noted that colloquialisms such as those in the previous sentence are an integral part of game analysis, and are freely used in transactional psychotherapy groups and seminars. The expression "waiting for *rigor mortis* to set in" originated in a dream of a patient, in which she decided to get certain things done "before *rigor mortis* set in." A patient in a sophisticated group pointed out what the therapist had overlooked: that in practice, waiting for Santa Claus and waiting for death are synonymous. Since colloquialisms are of decisive importance in game analysis, they will be discussed at length later on.

5. The Classification of Games

Most of the variables used in analyzing games and pastimes have already been mentioned, and any of them can be used in classifying games and pastimes systematically. Some of the more obvious classications are based on the following factors:

1. Number of players: two-handed games (Frigid Woman), three-handed games (Let's You and Him Fight), five-handed games (Alcoholic) and many-handed games (Why Don't You—Yes But).

2. Currency used: words (Psychiatry), money (Debtor), parts of the body (Polysurgery).

3. Clinical types: hysterical (Rapo), obsessive-compulsive (Schlemiel), paranoid (Why Does This Have to Happen to Me), depressive (There I Go Again).

4. Zonal: oral (Alcoholic), anal (Schlemiel), phallic (Let's You and Him Fight).

5. Psychodynamic: counterphobic (If It Weren't for You), projective (PTA), introjective (Psychiatry).

6. Instinctual: masochistic (If It Weren't for You), sadistic (Schlemiel), fetishistic (Frigid Man).

In addition to the number of players, three other quantitative variables are often useful to consider:

1. Flexibility. Some games, such as Debtor and Polysurgery, can be played properly with only one kind of currency, while others, such as exhibitionistic games, are more flexible.

2. Tenacity. Some people give up their games easily, others are persistent.

3. Intensity. Some people play their games in a relaxed way, others are more tense and aggressive. Games so played are known as easy and hard games, respectively.

These three variables converge to make games gentle or violent. In mentally disturbed people, there is often a noticeable progression in this respect, so that one can speak of stages. A paranoid schizophrenic may initially play a flexible, loose, easy game of first-stage "Ain't It Awful" and progress to an inflexible, tenacious, hard third stage. The stages in a game are distinguished as follows:

a. A First-Degree Game is one which is socially acceptable in the agent's circle.

b. A Second-Degree Game is one from which no permanent, irremediable damage arises, but which the players would rather conceal from the public.

c. A Third-Degree Game is one which is played for keeps, and which ends in the surgery, the courtroom or the morgue.

Games can also be classified according to any of the other specific factors discussed in the analysis of IWFY: the aims, the roles, the most obvious advantages. The most likely candidate for a systematic, scientific classification is probably one based on the existential position; but since knowledge of this factor is not yet sufficiently advanced, such a classification will have to be postponed. Failing that the most practical classification at present is probably a sociological one. That is what will be used in the next section.

Notes

Due credit should be given to Stephen Potter for his perceptive, humorous discussions of maneuvers, or "plays," in everyday social situations,[2] and to G. H. Mead for his pioneering study of the role of games in social living.[3] Those games that lead to psychiatric disabilities have been systematically studied at the San Francisco Social Psychiatry Seminars since 1958, and this sector of game analysis has recently been approached by T. Szasz.[4] For the role of games in the group process, the present writer's book on group dynamics should be consulted.[5]

References

1. Maurer, D. W. *The Big Con.* The Bobbs-Merrill Co., New York, 1940.

2. Potter, S. *Theory and Practice of Gamemanship.* Henry Holt & Company, New York, n.d.

3. Mead, G. H. *Mind, Self, and Society.* University of Chicago Press, Chicago, 1934.

4. Szasz, T. *The Myth of Mental Illness.* Harper & Brothers, New York, 1961.

5. Berne, E. *The Structure and Dynamics of Organizations and Groups.* J. B. Lippincott Company, Philadelphia and Montreal, 1963.

Stuart Palmer
Verbalizers

People frequently develop verbal habits which allow them to vent their aggression in reasonably acceptable ways and to gain approval or avoid disapproval at the same time.

For example, arguing is a verbal habit which often yields some satisfaction of both the needs to aggress and to gain approval. One of the most accomplished arguers in Madison is John Groats, a youngish junior executive. Most people agree that he will argue about practically anything. Here is a fairly typical instance of Groats in action.

The conversation is flowing smoothly in one of the ranch houses in the Glenhaven section of Madison when John Groats enters with his quiet wife. John sits down in the nearest chair and listens, pulling at his pipe. He always starts out that way.

Harry Walker has just returned from a trip to West Germany and has been talking about the German economy. "Well, as I was saying," Walker goes on, "the Germans have really gotten on their feet. What they've accomplished in the past ten years is simply unbelievable. And, say what you will, like them or not, it's all due to the innate German capacity and desire for hard, efficient work."

"Oh, I wouldn't say that." It is John Groats making his conversational gambit.

"Beg your pardon?" says Harry Walker. He does not know John Groats very well.

Reprinted from Stuart Palmer, *Understanding Other People.* Thomas Y. Crowell Company, Inc., New York. Copyright © 1955 by Stuart Palmer.

"I wouldn't say that at all," repeats John Groats. He knocks the ashes from his pipe.

"You didn't find Germany that way?" Harry Walker asks him.

"I never visit countries I'm interested in," says John Groats, shaking his head. "Destroys your perspective. But to get back to your statement. You miss the point entirely. You see—"

"John, please," says John Groat's wife. She knows Harry Walker considers himself, and some others consider him, a sort of minor expert on Germany.

"You miss the point completely there, fellow," John Groats goes on. "You see, it has nothing to do with innate capacity. Do you really believe that the capacity to work efficiently or otherwise is ever inborn?"

"Well, I won't quibble over whether it's inborn or not," Harry Walker says, "I'm simply saying that every German *has* this capacity for efficient work and—"

"*Every* German?" says John Groats.

"Yes, practically every German has—"

"Now, look, fellow. There's a whale of a difference between every German and practically every German. I'm not trying to argue the point with you, I'm simply explaining to you—"

"Now, boys, let's keep it light," someone says.

"You're wrong there." John Groats is just warming up. "You see, this matter of the German character is actually one of the most important problems with which we are confronted today. Centrally, it's a question of—"

"Pardon me. I have to get a refill," Harry Walker says and gets up quickly.

Someone else in the group says, "I was down looking at Bill Johnson's house yesterday. Never cared much for these modern houses, but this place of his really makes sense."

"I wouldn't say that," says John Groats. "To begin with it is not actually modern. You see—" He puffs twice, quickly, on his pipe and then really warms up to the task at hand.

One time you'll find John Groats arguing one side of a question and another time you'll find him arguing the opposite side. He doesn't care which side he takes as long as it's the other one.

John's arguing is directed toward trying to simultaneously

satisfy his needs to aggress and to gain approval. His need for approval is frustrated, not severely, but enough to cause in him a moderately strong need to aggress. His arguing is definitely a verbal form of aggression. He is always trying to put the other fellow in the wrong, make him seem somewhat stupid. At the same time, arguing is a fairly acceptable method of aggressing if not carried too far. It is not viewed with severe disapproval as is physical aggression. People get tired of it, yes, but they seldom strongly, disapprove of it. Furthermore, some people approve of it as a means of intellectual stimulation, which it sometimes is. Consequently, John Groats now and then gains some approval from his arguing. True, he overestimates and thinks he gains more approval than he actually does. But what he thinks is what counts to him.

John began to develop the arguing habit when he was an adolescent as a way of trying to cope with what was for him a frustrating situation. John had an older brother whom his parents considered to be a paragon. The brother was in fact quite an adolescent success in certain ways. He was president of the junior class in high school, he was a straight "A" student, and he was a star on the football team. He thought he could do no wrong and his parents agreed with him. One could hardly blame John for disagreeing—which he did.

John was an average enough boy. He did fairly well in school, but people always seemed to be comparing him to the older brother. By comparison, John looked pretty hopeless. The brother got the lion's share of approval. John's need for a spot of the limelight was frustrated and he began to feel a need to aggress.

The older brother was always making self-assured statements around the house which John's parents took as gospel. He did the same outside the home. A lot of the things the brother said would not particularly hold water but he said them with such assurance that people accepted them without examining them closely. John, however, examined them closely and he took to pointing out their weaknesses to the older brother and to anyone else who was on hand. His parents and the older brother deplored this. But as a matter of fact, John was often right. He often succeeded in making the older brother look a bit foolish. That was all John needed. He took to disagreeing with everything the brother said: John worked off some aggression and he got some approval from people outside the family who were beginning to think the older brother was just a little too big for his breeches. The foundation of John's arguing habit was thus firmly laid.

Since those early adolescent days when his brother got most of the approval, John has always been somewhat on the defensive. He still feels, as it were, that he is not gaining his share of approval. Whenever he sees someone seemingly gaining approval for speaking at all authoritatively on any given subject, the old aggressive feelings come over him and he resorts, for better or for worse, to the technique which worked against his brother.

A house on Chestnut Street shelters a lady, Mrs. Samuel Grull by name, who has another habit directed toward venting a little aggression and gaining a little approval: the habit of complaining. Chestnut Street, right in the city of Madison, is one of those streets where slightly rundown two-family houses predominate. The house on the corner stands out from the others, however. It has been newly painted a mustard yellow and it is a one-family house. The big screened porch extends almost to the sidewalk. The house is ugly but neat.

Mr. and Mrs. Grull have lived in this house for twenty years. There is Mrs. Grull, a round woman, and Mr. Grull, a man of few words. With them live their daughter Edna and her new husband, Sydney Powell. The young folks have a newly decorated apartment upstairs just until they can find exactly what they want.

It is after dinner. The two Grulls and the two Powells sit on the front porch.

"It's terrible hot," says Mrs. Grull fanning herself with the society page of *The Madison Times-Herald.*

"Yes, it is, Mother," says Edna. "Isn't it, Sydney?"

"Yes, it certainly is, Sydney says.

"Just right," Mr. Grull says from behind the sports page. Smoke curls slowly up from his pipe.

"You don't have to make dinner," says Mrs. Grull.

Mr. Grull does not answer.

"I could melt away in that kitchen and no one would care."

"Mother, of course we care," says Edna. "I'd help you, but we agreed I'd do the cleaning and you'd—"

"It doesn't matter. It doesn't matter. I'm just the hired woman around here."

"Mother!"

"I never thought the day would come when—"

"Oh, for Christ sakes, shut up!" says Mr. Grull from behind the sports page of *The Madison Times-Herald.*

Mrs. Grull takes a sharp breath, sniffles, gets up and goes into the house. "I never thought the day would come—"

Edna follows her.

Mrs. Grull seeks sanctuary in the dimness of the parlor. Edna sits down beside her.

Suddenly Mrs. Grull looks up and, peering at Edna, says, "Why does he hate me?"

"Who? Why does who hate you, Mother?"

"You know who. Sydney. Why does he hate me so?"

"Why, Sydney doesn't hate you, Mother. He loves you."

"He hates me. He hardly ever says a word to me."

"He's just quiet, Mother."

"Why doesn't he speak to me? Why does he hate me so?"

"But, Mother, Sydney doesn't hate you. You're just upset about dinner. From now on I'll help you and—"

"No. You'll be leaving me. I know. You and him looked at a house yesterday, didn't you?"

"Why yes, we did, Mother. But you know we planned to buy as soon as we could find a nice little house."

"After all I've done for you. I just don't understand it. I just don't understand it at all."

"Sadie!" It is Mr. Grull calling his wife. "Sadie. Where the hell's the rest of the paper?" Mr. Grull wants the funnies on the back of the women's page of *The Madison Times-Herald.*

Mrs. Grull gets up and goes out to the porch. "I don't even have time to look at the paper."

She gives Mr. Grull the part of the paper with which she has been fanning herself and he takes it wordlessly.

"Oh, it's so hot," says Mrs. Grull, sitting in her rocker once again. "I'll never live the summer out."

"It's awfully hot, Mother," says Edna.

"If we had a house outside of town, it wouldn't be so hot," says Mrs. Grull, slowly fanning her face with her hand. "Samuel, why don't we buy out in Breezy Acres? Or maybe even Beauty Hills?"

Her husband does not seem to hear.

"Why don't we, Samuel? Don't you care about me at all?"

"You'd find something wrong out there, too," says Mr. Grull from behind the newspaper.

"I certainly would not. We'd have neighbors that amounted to something out there. Not like the riffraff here."

"It's just as hot there as here," Mr. Grull says.

"You're at work all day. In a nice cool plant," says Mrs. Grull. "You don't have to broil in this hot box all day."

Mr. Grull, with considerable puffing, gets up, pads into the house, goes to the refrigerator for a can of beer, opens it, and pads upstairs to bed.

"Time for bed, Edna," says Sydney Powell and he, Edna and Mrs. Grull get up and go inside.

"I'll bring your lemonade up, children," says Mrs. Grull.

"Thank you, Mother. That would be nice," says Edna, and she and Sydney go up to their apartment.

Soon Mrs. Grull knocks on their door. Edna says, "Come in, Mother."

Mrs. Grull enters carrying a tray with two glasses of lemonade and four cookies on it. She looks very sad. She puts the tray on the bedside table, says "Good night, children," and then turns toward the door.

"What's the matter, Mother?" Edna says.

"Oh, it's nothing," answers Mrs. Grull. She continues slowly toward the door.

"What is it, Mother?"

"Oh, nothing. Nothing. I wish someone would bring me some lemonade, just once," says Mrs. Grull.

"But, Mother—"

"Good night, children," says Mrs. Grull and closes the door behind her.

"Poor Mother," says Edna. "She's so sensitive. What can be wrong with her?"

"Too much lemonade," says Sydney who, as a married man of twenty-two, prefers a glass of beer.

Well, Mrs. Grull's complaining is an unconscious habit she has developed as an attempt to satisfy her need for approval and her need to aggress, the latter having arisen as a result of frustration of the former.

The frustration of Mrs. Grull's need for approval is due to her relatively low position in the community and to her lack of material belongings, the possession of which stands for approval to her. Mrs. Grull's husband is a day laborer, they live in one of the less desirable sections of Madison, and they have a fifteen-year-old car and worn furniture. She feels that because of these facts she is denied the approval she deserves. She has always dreamed of serving tea in grand style in a rose garden and here she is living right in town in an old and ugly house and her husband on the front porch in his undershirt with a can of beer.

Mrs. Grull feels the need "to cut a fancy figure" in Madison. Since she does not do so, she feels she is not getting the approval of others. And she is somewhat right. The Grulls are not looked upon with much approval by the other people of Madison. Like many people in their walk of life they are neither approved of nor disapproved of.

Mrs. Grull's need for approval is obviously not satisfied in any degree by her husband, either. He used to give her a measure of approval but he has long since given that up. In the early days of their marriage he used to boast, to Mrs. Grull's delight, that "Sadie is full of beans and a yard wide." But Mr. Grull soon concluded that any such scraps of approval which he tossed out only created in Mrs. Grull an insatiable appetite for more of the same. So now he confines his comments to the fact that "she's gettin' wider all the time."

Because of the frustration of her need for approval Mrs. Grull feels vaguely aggressive toward her family and the world in general. Over the years she unconsciously nurtured the habit of complaining to her family and to others as a way of more or less acceptably venting her aggression and of gaining approval as well. The habit is acceptable in the sense that there is usually some semblance of truth in the things she complains about.

Mrs. Grull's complaining satisfies her need to aggress because it does hurt the members of her family, annoy them, and make them uncomfortable. She annoys Mr. Grull. And she definitely hurts her daughter, Edna, who is made to feel guilty for not being better to her mother although objectively the girl is all that a daughter should be. Mrs. Grull's complaining causes trouble between Edna and Sydney. Edna feels that they should do what her mother complains they don't do, and Sydney feels they should do what he wants to do.

Mrs. Grull unconsciously "realizes" this. She would not consciously hurt her family, but this is the kind of thing with which she can get away without worrying her conscience. She feels fine after a good session of complaining because she has vented her aggression.

The habit leads to some approval as well. Not from Mr. Grull it is true and not from Sydney either. But from Edna she gains quite a measure of a sympathetic sort of approval. Edna feels she has to agree with her mother when the latter specifies the nature of the burdens she bears. Edna feels compelled to tell her mother that yes, she does work too hard, that she must not work so hard, that she is the best mother in the world and so on.

It is often said that complainers like Mrs. Grull are only happy when they are complaining. There is a good deal of truth in this. They are satisfying their needs and so they are happy. If the habit were not rewarding, it would not thrive so heartily.

A third type of behavior which is directed toward both aggressing and attempting to gain approval is gossiping. Sometimes you can discover just a few faint traces of gossip riding the waves of conversation when three or four of the ladies of Madison get together for a few hours relaxation at the card table.

Last Friday, Leda Cole and Catherine Smith were at Helen Sheppard's in Glenhaven and Helen said, "I'm afraid we'll have to play canasta, girls. Sally called up a little while ago and said she couldn't come."

"Did she say why she couldn't come?" Leda asked.

"Said she didn't feel well."

"Oh. That's too bad," Catherine said. "I wonder if there's anything we can do for her." Catherine is twenty-two and the newest member of the Glenhaven set.

"Well, under the circumstances it's best not to ask. Might embarrass her," Leda said. "Of course you've heard—" She stopped and waited to be sure the others had not heard. Leda was one of the charter members of the Glenhaven set.

"Heard what, Leda?" Helen said.

"Oh, I thought you knew. I never would have mentioned it but I thought you knew by now." Leda glanced quickly to one side and then leaned over the table. "Well, don't repeat this and don't tell a soul I told you. Sally is pregnant."

"Oh, how nice," Catherine said..

"Oh, no, my dear. Not nice. Not nice at all. You've missed the point entirely, I'm afraid. Didn't you know her husband has only been back from that engineering job for two weeks?"

"Oh, I see. Well, maybe—"

"Leda, are you sure?" Helen said. "I simply don't believe that she—"

"Well, naturally, she didn't come right out and tell me if that's what you mean, dear," Leda said. "But I noticed last week that she wasn't looking well. And then the next day she hung out the wash much later than usual. So I decided I'd drop over for some coffee and see if she was all right. And do you know, she was just sitting there in a chair, the breakfast dishes weren't even washed, and she looked positively green. There's no doubt about it—she's pregnant."

"But, Leda, I don't see that that necessarily means she's pregnant," Helen said. "She might just—"

"Have I ever been wrong about something like this? Besides, I happened to drop over to Connie Bates' right afterward and Connie said she's noticed queer things about Sally lately too and that she'd been thinking the same thing I had. We both couldn't be wrong. Of course, Connie is an awful gossip, we all know that, but she doesn't miss a thing and you can hardly blame her for being a gossip with all the trouble she's had."

"Shall we draw for the deal?" Helen said. She spread the cards out on the table. They each took a card.

"Your deal, Leda," Helen said.

Leda began to shuffle the cards, slowly. "Poor Connie," she said. "It must be awful. That husband of hers—you know how I hate gossip and I wouldn't breathe a word of this to anyone but you and Catherine—but that husband of hers—Well, one night last week Caroline Johnson's sister was in a little bar in the city and she's sure she saw Jim Bates there at a corner table with the most awful looking peroxided blonde. And all this time poor Connie thinks Jim is going to night school. Of course she doesn't do a thing to fix herself up, you can hardly blame him I suppose, but still, after all—" Leda put down the cards and patted her new hairdo. "But on the other hand, Connie has other things to worry about, I suppose. Caroline Johnson says that little boy of Connie's is a half-wit at best."

"What a shame," Catherine said.

"I wondered about it myself," Leda said, "when I never saw him out playing with the other children and he's always so quiet when you go over there." She took out a cigarette and started looking in her handbag for a match.

"I'll get some matches and ashtrays," Helen said. "Go ahead and deal. I'll be right back." She went into the kitchen.

"Heavens, I never should have mentioned half-wits in front of Helen," Leda said to Catherine. "You know they say that Helen's brother—he's never been quite right, you know. Of around. Mary Danforth says he—I wouldn't dream of talking behind Helen's back, she's my dearest friend, but there are course, Helen never talks about it but things like that do get

some things you simply can't say to a person's face—Mary Danforth says—"

"Well, I guess we're all set now," Helen said, coming from
the kitchen with the ashtrays.

"Tell you later," Leda said to Catherine. "Why, Helen, what
lovely little ashtrays. I never saw these before." Then she
picked up the cards again and began to deal.

Leda goes on like this, gossiping about one person after
another, because by downing others she works off a little aggression and has a feeling, at least, of gaining a little approval.
Gossiping is a mild, acceptable form of aggression whereby
she hurts others' reputations. And, by making others seem
worse, she makes herself seem better in her own eyes. Also
she gets what seems to her to be some approval from those to
whom she gossips because they are interested in what she has
to say. After all, who can turn his back on a nice piece of
gossip? People listen to Leda, more or less admit she is on the
inside track; and it makes her feel important.

As is the case with many extreme gossips, Leda leads a
rather empty life. She has material security, but she has no
children and her husband is away on business a lot of the time.
She has no particular abilities which might win her approval.
She is not particularly good-looking. She has nothing which
makes it possible for her to enjoy, at least now and then, "a
place in the sun." In order to work off a little of the consequent
aggression and to gain what approval she can, she has developed the habit of gossiping to the point where it is fully automatic.

A fourth verbal type whose behavior is directed toward
venting aggression is the disquieting fellow who has a knack
for making you feel uncomfortable, for making you feel you've
hurt his feelings when you really haven't done anything at all.
But unlike the arguer, the complainer, and the gossip, he is not
trying to gain your approval at the same time that he works off
a little aggression. He is trying, rather, to avoid your disapproval.

One of those fellows with a knack for making you uncomfortable lives just down the street from us. We haven't been able to get to know him very well. Of course, we haven't tried very hard, but I don't suppose we would have gotten to know him very well even if we had tried. Take the other evening, for example, I turned from closing the garage door and he was standing there.

"Hello, Stanley," I said.

He stood his ground and coughed. "I don't suppose you'd want to give me a lift into town in the morning," he said solemnly.

"Why sure, Stanley, I'd be glad to."

"You don't have to," he said.

"What?" I asked him. I wasn't sure I understood.

"My car broke down but—you don't have to if it's too much trouble."

"It's no trouble, Stanley. The only thing is I have to be in town at eight-thirty tomorrow, so if you can be ready by—"

"Never mind, I'm sorry I asked."

"No, no. I'll be glad to give you a lift. It's just that I have to be in town at eight-thirty. What time do you usually leave in the morning?"

He was pointed toward his house. "About eight," he said.

"Well, that's when I'll be leaving anyway," I said. "No trouble at all."

"I can take the bus."

"No, Stanley, really, it's no trouble."

"It doesn't matter. Just forget about it.

"But I'll be glad to pick you up at eight."

He was still pointed toward his house but he nodded toward my garage. "How's the new car?"

"Oh, fine. Fine."

He nodded to himself and said, "Hmmm." Somehow or other he succeeded in making me feel that there was something sinful about my having bought a new car.

Then he started off toward home.

"See you in the morning, Stanley," I said.

"Well, if it's any trouble, just forget about it. It really doesn't matter," he said as he started doggedly toward home. Then he added, over his shoulder, "I can always take the bus."

Now, this fellow Stanley is fairly well educated and has a good job. There is nothing in his immediate situation for him to be defensive about. But every time I run into him he displays this knack for making me feel vaguely like a heel for no apparent reason at all. He does this regardless of whether he is asking a favor. The other neighbors tell me he acts the same way with them, which always makes me feel a little better.

The truth of the matter is, Stanley is pretty aggressive underneath that stolid exterior of his. He is also quite concerned about avoiding any possibility of face-to-face disapproval. By making other people vaguely uncomfortable, by making other people feel that they have somehow or other slighted him, Stanley works off a little aggression. At the same time, he avoids the possibility of disapproval because they are kept busy trying to figure out why he seems to be disapproving of them.

After Stanley graduated from high school he had no money for college, so he took a clerking job and worked for eight years at a low salary. He went to night school and eventually earned a college degree. During those eight years he lived alone, worked very hard, and had little time for relaxation. He was not getting approval from anyone; his approval lay in the future. He felt frustrated and envious of those who led a happier life. He developed feelings of aggression toward other people in general and he still has those feelings. It is true that he is no longer frustrated in his need for approval. He has a good job now, is married, and has a nice home. But the old feeling hangs on.

Stanley's disquieting ways are directed toward getting rid of some of that aggression in an acceptable manner. They are not directed toward gaining approval; he has that now. But he is trying to avoid disapproval as well as to release his aggression. This need to avoid disapproval concerns another aspect of Stanley's personality which we have not touched upon. He has always been a person who was awkward and stiff in social situations because he feared disapproval. This very awkwardness and stiffness brought him some mild disapproval in earlier years. He unconsciously developed his disquieting habits as ways of diverting attention from his awkwardness and uncertainty. His habits force other people to direct their attention toward whatever they may have said or done which seems to have slighted him rather than toward his basic ineptness in social situations.

The frustration of this need to avoid disapproval, which he used to experience, contributed to the development of aggression in him. But its contribution was less than the frustration of his need to gain approval. The sequence went like this: severe frustration of his need to gain approval plus mild frustration of his need to avoid disapproval led to a considerable need to aggress. The frustration of his need for approval ceased when he obtained a good job and a home. But he developed his disquieting habits as ways of venting the old aggression which remained and of avoiding the possibility of disapproval which also remained because of his awkward, uncertain personality.

Ronald D. Laing,
Herbert Phillipson, and
A. Russell Lee
**The Spiral of
Reciprocal Perspectives**

Human beings are constantly thinking about others and about
what others are thinking about them, and what others think
they are thinking about the others, and so on. One may be
wondering about what is going on inside the other. One desires
or fears that other people will know what is going on inside
oneself.

A man may feel that his wife does not understand him. What
may this mean? It could mean that he thinks she does not realize that he feels neglected. Or he may think that she does not
realize that he loves her. Or it may be that he thinks that she
thinks that he is mean, when he just wants to be careful; that he
is cruel, when he just wants to be firm; that he is selfish when
he just does not want to be used as a doormat.

His wife may feel that he thinks that she thinks he is selfish
when all she wants is to get him to be a little less reserved. She
may think that he thinks that she thinks he is cruel, because she
feels he always takes everything she says as an accusation. She
may think that he thinks he understands her, when she thinks
he has not begun to see her as a real person, and so on.

One sees both that this area is the very heart of many relationships, and that we have in fact very little systematic and
scientifically tested information about it. But let us first of all
think about the problem a little further.

Reprinted by permission of the authors and the publisher from Ronald
D. Laing, H. Phillipson, and A. R. Lee, *Interpersonal Perception, A Theory and a
Method of Research,* New York, Springer Publishing Co., 1966.

One or both persons in a twosome may spiral off into third, fourth, even fifth levels of what we have suggested may be called metaperspectives. Such a spiral develops, for instance, whenever two persons mistrust each other.

We do not know how people resolve mistrust that takes on this formal structure, but we know that such mistrust is common, and that it sometimes seems to go on endlessly. Logically, the possibilities are that it may end by unilateral or bilateral disarmament; by unilateral separation or mutual divorce; or by a parametric change occurring. Let us consider a simplified version of this spiral.

Jack and Jill are ostensibly in love, and each feels he or she loves the other, but Jack is not sure whether Jill loves Jack, and Jill is not sure whether Jack loves Jill. Jack feels he loves Jill, but does not know whether Jill really believes in his love. Jill feels she loves Jack, but is not sure whether Jack believes she loves him. How can each prove to the other that each loves the other?

Suppose that Jack is what is psychiatrically termed paranoid. This term is a rather inadequate descriptive generalization for certain regularities in Jack's experience and actions, one of which is a persistent tendency to mistrust certain significant others. He persistently refuses to infer from Jill's behaviour towards him, however loving, that she "really" loves him, but believes, despite evidence from Jill's manifest behaviour (he may sooner or later have to invent her "behaviour") that she loves Tom, Dick or Harry. A curious feature of Jack's tendency to attribute to Jill a lack of love for him and a love for Tom, Dick or Harry (for reasons we do not pursue at present) often seems to be that he tends to make this attribution in inverse proportion to Jill's testimony and actions to the contrary.

Jack may reason "Look at all the things that Jill is doing to try to prove to me that she loves me. If she really loved me she would not have to be so obvious about it and try so hard. The fact that she is trying so hard proves she is pretending. She must be trying to cover up her feelings—she must be trying to cover up her true feelings. She probably loves Tom."

At this point Jill is in a double-bind.[1] If she tries to act even more loving, she further activates Jack's assumption that she is pretending. If, on the other hand, she pretends to act less loving and more aloof then she certainly will activate his view that she does not love him. He then can say: "See, I told you so, she really doesn't love me. Look at how aloof she has become."

Jack's phantasy coefficient in his experience of Jill rises as his perception of her tends to discount his phantasy of her.

Thus, the *issue* that he is preoccupied with is love. The *direction* of this issue is Jill's love for Jack. His prototypical expectation is that Jill does not love him. For Jack this issue shapes every other issue in that he coordinates his whole field of experience and his whole field of action around this issue. Now, let us suppose that Jill feels she loves Jack, but realizes that he thinks she does not. The situation then is: Jack thinks Jill does not love him. Jill thinks she loves Jack, but Jill realizes that Jack thinks that she does not love him.

Now, Jack may decide to resolve his mistrust by various moves that one generally regards as part of the paranoid strategy. He may pretend to Jill that he does think she loves him, so that, in his view of her, she will think she has fooled him. He will then mount evidence (she has exchanged glances with a man, she smiled at a man, her walk gives her away because it is the way a prostitute walks, etc.) that seems to him to substantiate his secretly held view that she does not love him. But as his suspicion mounts, he may discover that the evidence he has accumulated suddenly looks very thin. This does not prove, however, that his attribution is incorrect; it proves that he has not taken into account how clever she is. In other words, he invents a meta-metaperspective for her, to cap his metaperspective. Thus, he reasons: "I have not been smart enough. She realizes that I am suspicious so she is not giving anything away. I had better bluff her by pretending to some suspicions that I do not feel, so that she will think I'm on the wrong track." So he pretends to her that he thinks she is having an affair with Tom, when he "knows" that she is having an affair with Dick.

---

[1] G. Bateson, D. D. Jackson, J. Haley, and J. H. Weakland, "Toward a Theory of Schizophrenia," *Behav. Sci.*, 1 (1956), 251–264.

This type of reflection occurs empirically in almost the "pure" form outlined above. This aspect of the paranoid's strategy has still not been adequately explored, but even less is known about how Jack's behaviour and experience is really influenced by and influences Jill and others.

Another form of unilateral spiral is the spiral of concern. Here, the decisive direction of issue is Jill's view of Jack's view of Jill's act towards Jack. (I want you to know I love you.) The persons in whom we see this in purest form are, in clinical terms, depressed and/or obsessional.

However, I may act not only on my own experience but on the other person's experience, by acting on the other so that he will experience me and himself as I wish him to do and act in the way that will enable me to experience him in the way I wish. Reciprocally, the other is experiencing and acting in relation to me, so that I am subject to his action as he is to mine.

We saw in Chapter I how Peter may attempt to control the situation by acting directly on Paul, so that Paul will act towards Peter in a way which Peter wishes, and that this may be either so that he, Peter, can continue to experience himself and Paul suitably, or so that he can be experienced by Paul as he wishes to be. In a system constantly sustained by two agents and comprising nothing other than their behaviour and experience, action either "internally" on self or outwardly through behaviour on the other is the medium for effecting change or for negating change. If it is a steady state that is desired, then, in his dyadic system, it is by *action* by each on self and on other that the steady state of the system is maintained.

Let us consider the way a husband's behaviour towards his wife functions in terms of the husband-and-wife conceived *as a system*.

Husband acts on wife so that wife will experience husband's actions in a particular way. But wife has to *act* in such a way before the husband can realize that she experiences his act conjunctively or disjunctively to his intention; thus, husband's behaviour towards wife affects her experience of him, which, mediated back to him by her behaviour towards him, in turn influences his experience of her. Through this circuit he may feel that his experience is directly related to her experience. For instance, let us say he has acted in some way that he meant to be helpful, but she feels is unhelpful and even cruel. Through the circuit of B and E he then may feel that he *has* been unkind, so that his own self-experience is now implicated. In order to keep his own self-experience and self-identity as he wants it (I am a helpful person, now I feel unhelpful and even cruel), he has to initiate another dyadic circuit by actions towards *her*, by saying, for instance, "I'm sorry," and making amends, reparation, and so on.

We see that in a dyadic system, there is no isolated individual person. The one person, in order to maintain *his own* self-identity, has to *act towards the other*, and however adroit a strategist he may be, he can never rely on controlling the other. She wishes to see herself as kind, but he feels her to be cruel. He wants to be helpful; she finds him a nuisance. Each person has to act outwardly in order to achieve and maintain his or her own inner peace. At best this intimate intermeshed coexistence can be reciprocally confirmatory; at worst it is a mish-mash in which both can lose themselves.

If the other is at one and the same time a threat and necessary to self's identity, then he or she may require to be permanently disarmed and controlled.

There are a number of ways of doing this. We have mentioned some of them. One acts towards the other to control his experience; through his experience, his behaviour; through his behaviour one's experience of his behaviour; fiinally, by a sort of ellipsis, through one's experience of the other's experience, one's experience of oneself. What I think you think of me reverberates back to what I think of myself, and what I think of myself in turn affects the way I act towards you. This influences in turn how you feel about yourself and the way you act towards me, and so on. One may, however, seek to eliminate this dyadic circuit, at any rate from one's own point of view. If one can act upon one's *own* experience of the other, so that one can shape to one's own desire the way one sees the other and hence the way one supposes the other sees oneself, is it worth the bother to act toward the other in order to shape the other's experience? Perhaps not, if it could work. Action towards the other would then be only a gesture performed before a mirror.

Let us consider one facet of an extremely simplified dyadic phantasy system, reverberating around the issue of greed and meanness.

Jack feels Jill is greedy. Jill feels Jack is mean. That is, Jack feels Jill wants too much from him whereas Jill feels Jack does not give her enough. Moreover Jack feels that Jill is mean as well as greedy. And Jill feels that Jack is greedy as well as mean. Each feels that the other has and is withholding what he or she needs. Moreover, Jack does not feel he is either greedy or mean himself, nor does Jill. Jack, however, realizes that Jill thinks he is mean, and Jill realizes that Jack thinks she is greedy. In view of the fact that Jack feels he is already overgenerous, he resents being regarded as mean. In view of the fact that Jill feels that she puts up with so little, she resents being regarded as greedy. Since Jack feels generous but realizes that Jill thinks he is mean, and since Jill feels deprived and realizes that Jack thinks she is greedy, each resents the other and retaliates. If, after all I've put up with, you feel that I'm greedy, then I'm not going to be so forbearing in the future. If, after all I've given you, you feel I'm mean, then you're not getting anything from me any more. The circle is whirling and becomes increasingly vicious. Jack becomes increasingly exhausted by Jill's greed and Jill becomes increasingly starved by Jack's meanness. Greed and meanness are now so confused in and between each and both that they appear to take on a life of their own. Like two boxers dominated by the fight that they are themselves fighting, the dyad, the system, the marriage, becomes "the problem" to each of the persons who comprise it, rather than they themselves. Jack and Jill are not divorced from each other, but they are divorced from the system that their own interaction and interexperience has generated, which now presents itself to each of them as a container, a mechanical machine in which both are being mangled. Each has now become caught and entangled in the properties of a system or a relationship that is experienced by *both* as a prison. Each may now experience the system as a third party—in phantasy terms, a container, a persecuting machine, a suffocating prison, something one is inside, in which one cannot move or breathe, in which one is entangled. Only when it is impossible to live in an impossible situation any more may the process be reversed. It is just from the experience of the *common situation, now shared,* that a ray of deliverance may be glimpsed.

Jack and Jill in the above example are much more in touch with each other than usually is the case. On the level of direct perspective that each has of self and other, they are in disagreement. However, each realizes how the other feels. That is, each person's metaperspective is in play, and is correct. Furthermore, each realizes that he or she is understood, in so far as one's point of view is at least recognized. That is, no disjunction is postulated between direct and meta, or between meta-meta and metalevels of experience.

Now, in the terms of the present discussion:

a) *understanding* can be defined as the conjunction between the metaperspective of one person and the direct perspective of the other;

b) *being understood* is the conjunction between the meta-meta-perspective of the one person and the metaperspective of the other.

c) the *feeling* of being understood is the conjunction of one's own direct perspective with one's *own* meta-metaperspective.

There is a peculiar satisfaction in feeling that one understands another person, and in feeling that one is being understood.

Patently, however, two people may neither understand each other completely nor wish to. They may understand each other while supposing that they do not understand. Understanding may be greater over some issues than in others. The relationship may be relatively symmetrical, in that each understands the other to about the same extent over the same issues, or it may be lopsided, one person, in Jung's sense, being the container and the other the contained. The feeling of being understood entails feeling that the other person's *meta*perspective is correct; in other words, that one's own meta-metafeeling corresponds to one's own direct perspective. One is now operating between all three levels. The feeling of being understood or misunderstood may be desired or feared. Its presence may be comforting or disconcerting. Its presence may mean a sense of being together, its absence a sense of solitude.

People will vary as to whether or not they would rather be understood or understand. An important aspect of each person's *self*-concept is the extent to which he feels capable of being understood. An important aspect of one's image of the other is the extent to which one feels the other can or does understand oneself.

Whether or not it is easier to make guesses between second and first order perspectives, or between third and second order perspectives, is an interesting question, and one towards which our method can contribute an answer.

We must remember that some people feel extremely persecuted because they persist in attributing to the others a capacity to know what is going on in them far higher than the others actually do possess. This may be because they grew up with another who had such an ability (e.g., identical twin), or who in fact laid claims to such understanding. In intergroup and international as well as in interpersonal dyadic systems, the desires to be understood in some respects, the fears of being known in others, the efforts taken towards being understood, and the precautions taken against being known, together with the complementary manoeuvers to achieve knowledge of the other, legitimately and illegitimately (espionage), quite evidently play a large part.

From the point of view of the subject, the starting point is often between the second and third order level of perspective. Jill thinks that Jack thinks that she does not love him, that she neglects him, that she is destroying him, and so on, although she says she does not think that she is doing any of these things. In this position, it is open to Jill to do a number of things. She may constantly complain to Jack that Jack does not realize how much she is doing for him, and that he is always sorry for himself. He may protest that he thinks she is doing all sorts of things for him, but she does not believe him. She may express fears lest he think that she thinks that he is ungrateful to her for all she is doing, when she wants him to know that she does *not* think that he thinks she thinks he thinks that she does not do enough. Here, the *initial* situation from Jill's point of view is: Jill thinks that Jack thinks that Jill neglects him. One move that the other may make in order to break such a unilateral spiral is to break into it at one level of perspective. Thus, Jill thinks Jack does not believe that Jill loves Jack. Jack's move may be to say: "But I *do* believe you *do*." This direct contradiction, in this case intended as reassurance, is usually thought by psychiatrists, psychoanalysts, marriage counsellors, and so on to be ineffective.

A way to enter such a situation therapeutically is to get both Jack and Jill to define their criteria for generosity and to define how their parents defined generosity. One discovers that Jack's father treated his mother very differently than Jill's father treated her mother. Jack's father was too poor to have brought home enough money to make his family feel secure against the possibility of being evicted or not having enough food. Jack remembers vividly how his mother complained to his father about his inadequate income. From this Jack developed the viewpoint that if his father had simply made enough money his mother would have been eternally grateful. Since he is now successful financially, he expects Jill to be eternally grateful to him for providing her with a security that his mother never had. On the other hand, Jill has come from a wealthy family in which there was never any comparable issue of financial insecurity. In Jill's family, consideration, love and kindness were expressed through the giving of gifts, the remembering of anniversaries, etc. She had learned to take it for granted that the man will provide her with an economically secure home. What she looks for are the little niceties which she feels indicate true considerateness, kindness and love. For Jack these niceties are irrelevant; they are minor details, trivia by comparison to the other things he does for the family. However, if each can discover his or her own and the other's value system and thereby see the conjunctions and discrepancies between them, it becomes possible for each to explain himself or herself to the other. It is now, for the first time, feasible for Jack to say: "Well, if it really is that important to you that I remember your birthday, I'll do my darndest to try." It is now possible for Jill to "appreciate" Jack more as a provider in the family. If bitterness and revenge (I am going to hurt you for the hurt you have done to me) have not intensified too much, it may still be relatively simple for each to satisfy the other's expectations according to their idiosyncratic value systems. Such an incredibly simple move can sometimes produce very powerful effects, particularly, early in a relationship. Once a history has been developed of pain and misery, the matter becomes correspondently more complex and difficult to reorient.

There are innumerable such unilateral and bilateral spirals as well as those of giving-taking, trust-mistrust, indifference and concern. There are "ascending" manic" spirals (I'm happy that you're happy I'm happy), and "descending" "depressive" ones (I'm sad that you're sad, etc.); all are in a sense "obsessive." Such spirals can be attempts to get out of a *false or untenable position*. The danger to the persons involved is that the next *move* may be catastrophic. It may be the *last move ever;* it may be the end of the relationship, or the end of the world.

Here we are particularly concerned with how such a unilateral spiral functions in the dyad system. After the twists of the spiral have been extended to a third, even fourth, level, at some point a relatively steady state of reciprocal mistrust, precarious happiness, common misery or terror becomes established. It may be that the only hope at the precatastrophic position is to make a move to change the whole axis of orientation, to change the issue, both in content and direction, and one person has to make the change initially.

Psychoanalytic interpretations often have this form.

Thus, Jack maintains that the issue is: does Jill love Jack, or Tom, Dick or Harry? An analytic interpretation to Jack might be that the "real" or more basic issue is: does *Jack* love Jill, or Tom, Dick or Harry? That is, the analyst (Freud in the Schreber case) registers that in Jack's view the issue is whether or not Jill is unfaithful to him, but feels that Jack should come to examine both the nature of his relation to *Jill* (rather than Jill's relation to him) and of *his* relation to Tom (rather than Jill's relation to Tom). That is, in the twosome Jack and Jill, the analyst would wish to change Jack's axis of orientation away from his attempt to infer the quality of Jill's experience of him *from* the testimony of her behavior towards him *to* the nature of his feelings about Jill and Tom. The analyst's thesis in this case might be expressed as: Jack attributes to Jill's feelings towards Tom what he is afraid to infer about his own feelings about Tom, if he were to examine his own behavior.

A family therapist would feel that it was insufficient to relate to Jack alone in such an interpersonal nexus. He would wish to observe directly how Jack, Jill, Tom, Dick or Harry all relate to one another. In the course of his close examinations of how Jill, for instance, actually behaves with Jack and with Tom, Dick or Harry, he may discover that she indeed is much more demonstrative with them than she is with Jack. And this might even fit her idea of how a wife should be. Jack, however, may feel that Jill's increased demonstrativeness to them is proof that she loves these other men more than himself. One such wife in therapy stated: "But of course I make a bigger fuss over your friends than I do over you. When I am with your friends I put on my social self. When I am with you I'm my real self." The implication being that she saw it as her duty to act in a "charming" way in social situations, but with her own husband she felt able to "be herself." Said she, "Would you want me to act with you, too?" Said he, "No I just would prefer that you would stop acting with others and be your natural self all the time."

Another form of reciprocal alienation gives rise to some very strange situations. Let us suppose again that the pivotal issue between two persons is love. Then my concern may be my love for you, or your love for me. My concern, however, may not be whether I love you or you love me, but whether you need my love. Similarly, your concern may not be whether you love me, or whether I love you, but whether I need your love.

This is a common issue in modern marriage, how common one does not know. Neither party is concerned so much about direct perspectives or direct issues, but about a second or third level. In these terms, I do not want someone to love or someone to love me, but I need someone to need me, and the other is someone who needs me to need her. This reciprocal dependence on the other's dependence is a form of reciprocity tending towards a spiral effect wherein each may become reciprocally more estranged from the act of directly giving or receiving love, and each in greater and greater alienation may even suppose that this is to grow deeper and deeper "in love."

This can be elevated to a system of rights and obligations. If each person is concerned about what the other thinks, feels, does, he may come to regard it as his *right* to expect the other to be concerned about him, and to be under an obligation to feel concern toward the other in turn. I make no move without feeling it as my right that you should be happy or sad, proud or ashamed, of what I do. And I regard you as callous if you do not concern yourself about my concern for you when you do anything.

My need has then ceased to be a matter of direct loving and being loved. My need is for the *other's* need of me. His or her need is that I need him or her. It is my need to be needed by the other. My desire is no longer to love and to be loved. My solicitude is not for another, but for another to want me. My want is a want to be wanted; my longing, a longing to be longed for. And in the same way, my emptiness is that the other does not require me to fulfill him or her. Similarly the other wants to be wanted by me, longs to be longed for by me.

The most natural thing in the world is the desire to love and to be loved. Which is the greater misfortune, to love without being loved or to be loved without loving? Very few people would admit to wanting either contingency. Yet we find people driving themselves into such situations all the time. Why? We say it is "compulsive." We are fortunately not trying to explain the why of this, but to describe the what. And one of the most hellish whirligigs of our contemporary interpersonal alienation is that of two alienated loves, two self-perpetuating solitudes, each in emptiness feeding on the other's emptiness, an inextricable and timeless confusion, tragic and comic—the ever fertile soil of endless recrimination and desolation.

Questions
for
Reflection
and
Discussion
Section Four

1. Have you known people who seem to fit each of Horney's interpersonal life-styles: going *toward* others; going *against* others; and going *away from* others? In a rather general way, how would you tend to characterize your own interpersonal life-style?

2. What is your own personal, honest reaction to Berne's description of the game he calls, "If It Weren't For You"? How does thinking about it make you feel? Do you believe you have ever participated in playing this game?

3. When two persons participate in the type of game described by Berne, is it necessarily true that both are equally responsible for what is occurring? Can only one person be blamed for such interaction? Can a person unknowingly participate in another's game? Do you think you have ever done so? Do you think you are partially responsible if you suffered undesirable consequences because of such participation?

4. Have you ever known anyone who seemed constantly to put you on the defensive—to imply somehow that you were inferior or had done something wrong? How did he compare with Palmer's description of Stanley? Can you suggest reasons why some people behave this way?

5. Have you ever caught yourself saying something like this: "I wonder what he thought I meant when I said he didn't really like me very well"? Have you been able to talk

about such thoughts and feelings with the other person, as suggested by Laing, Phillipson, and Lee?

6. How is it possible for two people to have differing views regarding the relationship between the two of them? Has this happened to you? How did you know it to be true? How far apart were your views of the relationship? Did it make much difference to you? Share these ideas with one of your classmates and ask that person to describe similar situations they have experienced; then check your view of your relationship to this person with their view of it. Discuss this difference—its causes, meaning, and significance.

INTERPERSONAL
SEMANTICS
SECTION FIVE

In every human relationship, words play an important part. They are among the tools used to establish bonds between people and may clarify or obscure ideas, unify or alienate people. The use of words has been cited as the distinguishing characteristic that sets man apart from other animals.

Semantics has long been considered the science of the relationship between words and meaning. Etymologists and philologists trace the historical development of languages while linguists concentrate their attention on language families, dialects, and grammatical structures. The standard dictionary is the result of concerted attention to man's usage of words as a means of assessing categories of meanings.

The emphasis of semantics on the symbol-referent relationship was expanded to include the human variables in usage by Count Alfred Korzybski (1877–1950). Korzybski attempted to formulate how language works, what its possibilities are, and what pitfalls it conceals. His insights, labeled "general semantics," focused attention on the behavioral implications of language.

Korzybski's life and theoretic contributions, both subjects of considerable academic controversy, are treated by Stuart Chase in the first article in this section. Mr. Chase has contributed greatly to a public awareness and appreciation of general semantics in his two widely read volumes, *The Tyranny of Words* and *The Power of Words*.

S. I. Hayakawa has been a major figure in giving general

semantics academic respectability in opposition to the faddists and cultists who seized upon Korzybski's system as an easy answer to a view of the world. Hayakawa's writing has concentrated upon the everyday problems and pitfalls resulting from our language behavior. He conceptualized general semantics as "the study between language, thought, and behavior: between *how we talk,* therefore *how we think,* and therefore *how we act.*"[1]

In the essay presented here, Hayakawa has concerned himself with but one of the possible uses of language—eliciting desired responses from others. He recognizes that speech may also be for phatic purposes (words used primarily to establish some union or relationships between people), for rhetorical allusions, and for reporting the world around us. Here he is discussing how language can be used to "make things happen."

The final article in this section, by the late Dr. Irving Lee of Northwestern University, is the result of keen observation, over a five-year period, of people trying to work together in committees and conferences. He watched conflicts arise and noted the techniques used to avert problems. His findings provide a theoretical foundation for helping us understand how misunderstanding occurs.

We have used the term "interpersonal semantics" in an attempt to focus attention upon the implications of our language usage on our interpersonal relationship. The words that we use constitute an important variable in our attempts to communicate.

[1] S. I. Hayakawa, *The Use and Misuse of Language,* Greenwich, Conn., Fawcett, 1962, p. vii.

Stuart Chase
Eminent Semanticists

Alfred Korzybski, who died in 1950, was the originator of what he called "General Semantics," a discipline which took the study of language and meaning into some pretty deep mathematical and neurological waters. It is still early to tell whether his contribution was as epoch-making as some starry-eyed followers believe, but it was unquestionably an important addition to the whole subject of communication. In the next chapter we shall look rather closely at his special contribution, and meanwhile observe him here as an individual.

I shall never cease to be grateful for the wholesome shock my nervous system received when I first read Korzybski's magnum opus, *Science and Sanity*. It forced me to realize some of the unconscious assumptions imbedded in the language which I as a writer had been calmly accepting. Nature, he said, does not work the way our language works; and he proceeded to give some suggestions for a closer relationship.

As I knew him in his later years—he was 70 when he died—he had the general aspect of an amiable Buddha, bald as a newel post, with kindly, intelligent eyes behind vast, round spectacles, and with a rich Polish accent. He wore as a kind of uniform a khaki shirt, open at the throat, which sometimes kept him out of hotel dining rooms. He was rude, formidable, over-verbalized and strangely appealing—for all I know, an

From *Power of Words*, copyright, 1953, 1954 by Stuart Chase. Reprinted by permission of Harcourt, Brace and World, Inc.

authentic genius. Poland has produced more than her share of mathematical philosophers.

Piecing together parts of his background, we note that he was a count from a proud and ancient family, with an estate in the country and large properties in Warsaw. Trained as a chemical engineer at the Warsaw Polytechnic Institute, he read widely in law, mathematics, and philosophy. He was also, we are told, handsome and a bit wild, the traditional young nobleman. In World War I he served on the Grand Duke's staff, was three times wounded, and then came to America as an artillery expert for the Czarist Russian Army. He added English to his five Continental languages; and while he never got his phonemes straight, he acquired great fluency and came to prefer it. He wrote his books and articles in English and thought in this language. In 1919 he married a talented American painter.

He published two books and a score of papers, all hard to read. It took me two years of reasonably steady application to bulldoze my way through *Science and Sanity*, and I do not think this sluggish pace was altogether my fault. By a curious paradox, Korzybski, who had dedicated his life to clearing communication lines, had the utmost difficulty in clearing his own—at least in English prose. When he conducted an oral seminar, with a full display of kinesics and his extraordinary accent, the line was far more open. I can see him now, reaching stout, muscular arms into the air and wiggling two fingers of each hand to make the "quote" sign, somewhat the way Churchill made the "V" sign. In semantics the quote sign around a word usually means: "Beware, it's loaded!"

"Time-Binding"

Korzybski's chief claim to fame will rest, I think, on *Science and Sanity*, difficult as it is. His earlier book, *The Manhood of Humanity*, is shorter and easier to read. Its thesis is that man is distinguished from the rest of earth's creatures by his language and the ability to pass down what he learns from one generation to the next. Even the most intelligent elephant has to begin over with each generation. "The proper life of man *as man,* is not life-in-space like that of the animals, but life-in-time. . . . Bound-up time is literally the core and substance of civilization."

This passing-down process, to which Korzybski gives the curious name "time-binding," we described earlier when discussing the culture concept, noting that the invention of writing greatly speeded it. Scientists generally confirm the thesis. Both the anthropologists and such sociologists as W. F. Ogburn anticipated Korzybski. He believed, however that the theory was new. Once the idea was mastered, he thought, the race would achieve "manhood," become fully mature, and shake off its infantilisms, verbal and otherwise.

*All through history man has been groping to find his place . . .
to discover his role in the "nature of things." To this end he must
first discover himself and his "essential nature" . . . then perhaps
our civilizations will pass by peaceful evolution from their childhood
to the manhood of humanity.*

Cultural change, unfortunately, can go downhill as well as up, but the opportunity is undeniably there to find our manhood, as knowledge about nature and human nature accumulates. This aspiration Korzybski shares, however, with many earlier writers and idealists—the early Utopians, for instance, and H. G. Wells. I myself used to cherish a private dream which I called "the man on the cliff." He was boldly outlined against the sky—the man we all might be if we put accumulated knowledge really to work.

Following *The Manhood of Humanity,* Korzybski spent ten years of intensive work writing *Science and Sanity.* It was published in 1933 at the bottom of the depression—hardly an auspicious year to bring out a book, especially a costly one. In it Korzybski explored relativity, quantum theory, colloid chemistry, biology, neurology, psychology, psychiatry, mathematical logic, and what was then available by other students of communication and semantics. Later, he urged his classes to read Whorf on linguistics. The question he set himself to answer was how the structure of language could be brought closer to the structure of the space-time world. He cited the new talk of physicists, following the Einstein revolution. If scientists could teach themselves to communicate more clearly, why should not the rest of us do likewise?

Definitions

Before summarizing what Korzybski discovered, let us glance at some of his forerunners in the field of semantics. The word first appeared in dictionaries about fifty years ago, defined as "studies having to do with signification or meaning." The International Society for General Semantics has issued two short, comprehensive definitions, as follows:

Semantics . . . *The systematic study of meaning.*

General Semantics . . . *The study and improvement of human evaluative processes with special emphasis on the relation to signs and symbols, including language.*

Note the accent on "evaluation" in defining General Semantics, and the absence of the word "is" in defining both. Whenever we become conscious about the meaning of a context— "What is the Senator trying to say?" . . . "How can I tell her more clearly?" . . . "What kind of double talk is that?" —we are practicing elementary semantics.

The goals of General Semantics are three:

1. To help the individual evaluate his world. As our environment grows more and more complex, greater precision is needed to interpret it.
2. To improve communication between A and B, also within and between groups of all sizes.
3. To aid in clearing up mental illness. In Chapter 24, we will describe the brilliant work of Dr. Douglas Kelley with battle shock cases during the last war.

Dictionary definitions are useful, but the semanticists make no obeisances to verbal absolutes. David Guralnik, who supervised a recent drastic revision of Webster, reported that his friends were shocked at his temerity.[1] He was shattering their faith in the infallibility of "the dictionary," and probably, by extension, of the Scriptures and other sacred writs. Dictionaries, like certain brands of cigarettes, he said, are supposed to be untouched by human hands. Another serious difficulty was what he called the "semantic merry-go-round that leads the reader a wild chase from one entry to another only to bring him back in a mad finish to his starting point." "*Gangrene:* mortification of a part of the body. . . . *Mortification:* gangrene." He had to be careful, too, of his etymologies, avoiding anything that might suggest Mark Twain's famous derivation of *Middletown* from *Moses*—you drop the "oses" and add the "iddletown."

From Aristotle to Bertrand Russell

Resolved to refuse the logic of Aristotle, Korzybski goes so far as to call General Semantics "a non-Aristotelian system," and invents the symbol, A, to abbreviate "non-Aristotelian." We must give Aristotle his due, however; for along with his creative curiosity about nature, he was also genuinely curious about the power of words. Linguistics, cultural anthropology, and relativity being two thousand years away, he sometimes mistook the peculiar structure of his own Greek for the universal laws of thought, a most natural error.

Aristotle's formal logic—which we shall look at in the next chapter*—was a great achievement for the time, but today it is hardly more useful than the medicine of Galen. Galen has passed respectably into the history of medicine; but Aristotle's logic continues to distort our use of reason. It is still taught in the universities, still in active use by philosophers, lawyers, theologians, and essayists. A standard political speech would be impossible without the aid of its simple two-valued syllogisms.

One of the first students to question the Aristotelian logic

[1] Paper read before Rowfant Club, reprinted by World Publishing Company, 1953.

* See pp. 244–257 of this volume.—Editors' note.

was Bishop William of Occam, who insisted that "entities are not to be multiplied beyond what is necessary." This principle was nicknamed in academic circles "Occam's razor," because it sheared off lush verbalisms. The Bishop was troubled by the clouds of entities, essences, classes, and Absolutes released by the Aristotelian laws. The Bacons, both Roger and Francis, were likewise skeptical. It was Galileo, of course, who broke clean away from Aristotle by substituting experiment and observation for *a priori* reasoning. Instead of deriving the number of teeth in a horse's mouth by logic, it is better to go out in the barn and count them.

A fascinating book might be written on the history of the revolt against language. The age of scientific inquiry, following Galileo, saw an increasing number of first-rate minds questioning the validity of verbal processes. In the last hundred years the critics include Jeremy Bentham, William James, Alexander Bryan Johnson, George Herbert Mead, John Dewey, Ludwig Wittgenstein, Bertrand Russell, F. C. S. Schiller, Rudolf Carnap, E. T. Bell.

Allen Upward, a British philologist pursued the word "idealism" all over Western cultures in an attempt to get at its meaning.[2] His initial bouts with the dictionary were unsatisfactory, thus:

> Mind, *defined as thoughts, sentiments, et cetera.*
>
> Thought, *defined as operations of the mind, ideas, images formed in the mind.*

Combining the two, Upward gets a kind of recurring decimal: Mind equals thought equals images formed in the images formed in the images . . . the same tautology we observed with gangrene-mortification.

H. G. Wells was a searching questioner of verbal processes. In 1891, just turned thirty, he wrote a monograph called "Scepticism of the Instrument," in which he quoted a geologist on rock classifications: "They pass into one another by insensible gradations"—a phrase not lightly to be dismissed.

[2] *The New Word.* Michell Kennerley, 1910.

This is true, said Wells, of most things in nature. "Every species is vague, every term goes cloudy at its edges, and so in my way of thinking, relentless logic is only another phrase for a stupidity—for a sort of intellectual pigheadedness."

Bronislaw Malinowski, the anthropologist, reported that it was impossible for him to learn a native language unless he spent considerable time in hunting, fishing, and living the lives of the people who spoke it. This sequence illustrates again the intimate connection between language and culture. People talk what they do; that is how talking began.

Lady Viola Welby published *What is Meaning?* in 1903, shortly before Einstein announced his first great work on relativity. A serious student of language and communication, she was perhaps the founder of modern semantics. A few years later Bertrand Russell and A. N. Whitehead, in their profound work. *Principia Mathematica,* were forced to deal with language and verbal logic, as well as mathematical symbols. They evolved what they called the Theory of Types, to offset "illegitimate totalities" concealed in language. Here is an example:

```
+---------------------+
|                     |
|                     |
|    All statements   |
|    in this square   |
|    are false        |
|                     |
|                     |
|                     |
+---------------------+
```

If we suppose the proposition inside the square to be true, we must conclude it is false. But if we begin by supposing it false, we have to end by finding it true. The "illegitimate totality" in this logical run-around is the little word "all." The "all" must be limited so that a statement about that totality must itself fall outside the totality. *Principia Mathematica,* is an excellent example of scientists in the throes of trying to remove shackles imposed by their mother tongue.

The Meaning of Meaning

A very important landmark in semantic history was the publication in 1921 of *The Meaning of Meaning* by C. K. Ogden and I. A. Richards. The approach was more literary than mathematical, but the conclusions paralleled those of Bridgman, Korzybski, Whorf. It is always exciting when tunnelers from different sides of a mountain manage to meet in the center.

Ogden and Richards present us with the famous triangle where the *event,* or object in nature, is called the "referent"; the brain is the area of "reference"; and the word is the "symbol." The sign comes to us from an object, say a dog; we proceed counterclockwise and refer to memory traces in the brain; presently, we utter the word "dog."

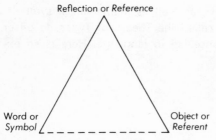

Reflection or *Reference*

Word or Symbol   Object or *Referent*

The lesson of the triangle is to keep the object in mind as one talks, to **find the referent** of one's discourse. Too much human talk, as Occam noted, razor in hand, is in abstract terms, where the mind manipulates the words, but loses sight of the space-time events to which the words refer. On this high level logic can be vigorously employed, but it is the logic of Zeno proving that the tortoise can outrun Achilles, the logic of the number of angels that can dance on a pin, the logic of the inside of the square, cited by Russell.

Let us imagine a high-level discussion between A and B about dogs. "All dogs are trustworthy," says A, with a dog lover's rapt expression. "Try trusting one of them with a five-dollar steak," says B, with a dog hater's glare. The difference can develop into a stupendous row on this "all dogs" level. But if A and B can come down to an inspection of some actual dogs, they will find, of course, that $Rover_1$ is so savage he must be constantly chained up; that $Rover_2$ is so gentle he is welcome at a catshow; and that $Rover_3$ to $Rover_n$ are at various stations of trustworthiness between these limits. The variations could be plotted to form the standard frequency distribution curve. By finding the referent down below, A and B avoid a meaningless battle up above. Agreement can be reached in ordinary affairs, as well as in science, when both A and B can point to the same dog, pat his head and say, "You see what I mean?" Up on the high level, anything can happen. "The ablest logicians," say Ogden and Richards, "are precisely those who are led to evolve the most fantastic systems by the aid of their verbal technique. . . ."

Find the Referent

"All dogs" cause trouble enough, but where are the referents for those higher and vaguer terms which form the common coin of discussion in political and economic affairs? Newspapers today in America carry many words like these below. What do they mean? What can A and B both point to so they may come to some agreement?

American Way	Leftist, Rightist
Appeasement	Loyalty, Security
Balanced Budget	Monopoly
Big Business	New Deal
Bureaucracy	Politicians
Communism	Socialized Medicine
Creeping Socialism	Spending
Democracy	Statism
Fascism	Subversives
Free Enterprise	Totalitarianism
Free World	Wall Street
Government Interference	Welfare State
Labor Agitators	

Two or more Americans can start an argument on any of these terms which may rage for hours without a referent in sight, beyond "Uh, I knew a man whose brother had it straight that—" Yet below and behind these words are events and issues of the first importance which Americans must face.

Every item in the above list belongs in Korzybski's upraised fingers: "Quote—unquote. Beware, it's loaded!" They are in marked contrast to such low-order terms as 100° F., my cat Boots, pure oxygen, the key of C♯ minor, 40 mph. When I was writing *The Tyranny of Words,* everybody was talking, if not shouting loudly, about "Fascism." I asked a hundred persons from various walks of life to tell me what they meant by Fascism. They shared a common dislike for the term, but no two agreed what it meant. There were fifteen distinguishable concepts in the answers submitted. This gave an idea of the chaos involved in high-order terms.

Today Fascism is out of style, and everybody is talking about "Communism." Reporters from the *Capital Times* in Madison, Wisconsin (1953), asked almost 200 persons on the street to answer the question: "What is a Communist?" Here are some of the replies:

Farmer: "They are no good to my notion. I can't figure out what they are."

Stenographer: "If a person didn't have a religion I would be tempted to believe he was a Communist."

Housewife: "I really don't know what a Communist is. I think they should throw them out of the White House."

High-school student: "A Communist is a person who wants war."

Office worker: "Anyone that stands for things that democracy does not."

Not only was there no agreement, but 123 out of 197 persons interviewed frankly admitted *they did not know what a Communist is.* All this came at a time when Congressional investigations were flooding the newspapers with the "Communist Menace" inside America. The danger of drowning we know about; but where shall the wayfaring citizen point to the specific danger of Communism within our borders, in the light of this exhibit?

We will analyze a number of these terms in the pages to follow. Here we repeat the admonition: "Beware, they're loaded!" Find the referent; keep your eye on that dog.

The Semantics of Poetry

In addition to *The Meaning of Meaning*, with its insistence on the referent, Ogden and Richards have each done sound work in communication; Ogden in Basic English, his partner as a writer and lecturer on poetry and criticism. Richards, who has taught at Harvard since 1939, constantly emphasizes the importance of communication and the difficulty of conveying complex meanings. Poetry, of course, tries to convey the most complex meanings expressible in language, and when it succeeds can wield great power.

A measure of its failures appears in Richards' famous study, *Practical Criticism*. He tells how he presented a variety of poems unsigned, to a large and able class for evaluation. Not only did these readers disagree, sometimes diametrically, about every poem, but they often failed to comprehend either its sense or its intention. (None of the poems was especially obscure. What these readers would make of samples of "modern" poetry is past imagining!)

The poet's intention, says Richards, is the first thing for the reader to consider. What is he trying to say? Richards lists ten difficulties the reader meets; for instance, the tendency to "stock responses . . . whenever a poem seems to, or does, involve views and emotions already fully prepared in the reader's mind, so that . . . the button is pressed." Another difficulty Richards calls "doctrinal adhesions," meaning ideological preconceptions in the reader. The whole study illustrates in a startling way what can happen to messages when they reach the semantic decoder.

Common experience is needed to understand any message. "In difficult cases the vehicle of communication must inevitably be complex. . . . What would be highly ambiguous by itself becomes definite in a suitable contéxt. . . . Even in such shallow communication as . . . merely making out the letters in a handwriting this principle is all-important. . . .

"Difficulty of communication . . . should not be confused with the difficulty of the matter communicated. . . . Some very difficult calculations, for example, can be communicated with ease."[3] "The view that meanings belong to words in their own right," says Richards scornfully, "is a branch of sorcery, a relic of the magical theory of names."[4] He pretty well demolishes the one-proper-meaning superstition when he says: "What a word means is the missing parts of the contexts from which it draws its delegated efficiency."

Richards and Ogden in their side of the mountain emphasized language and the arts. Korzybski in his emphasized the language of science. The tunnelers met and let in light from both directions. They meet for us who read them, though I believe the two schools were not in the closest harmony.

The Last Twenty Years

Science and Sanity made readers slowly, partly because reading rates were slow. Gradually, however, a large circle of interest was built up. My book, *The Tyranny of Words,* published in 1938, was the first attempt to interpret both semantics and Korzybski's General Semantics for the layman. Other interpretations soon appeared. The total influence of *Science and Sanity* must now be very comfortable, both in America and abroad. The rancor of some of its critics would indicate this, if nothing else.

S. I. Hayakawa's *Language in Action,* a Book-of-the-Month, appeared in 1941, a clear and readable exposition of semantics. Irving J. Lee of Northwestern University, Wendell Johnson of Iowa State, Anatol Rapoport of the University of Chicago, among others, have contributed important books to the gathering literature.

[3] *Principles of Literary Criticism.* Harcourt, Brace, 1924, 1928.
[4] *Philosophy of Rhetoric.* Oxford University Press, 1935.

Two organizations were founded, the Institute of General Semantics, now under the direction of M. Kendig, through which Korzybski conducted his famous seminars; and the International Society for General Semantics, which, among other activities, publishes the quarterly journal *ETC*, well edited by Hayakawa. Many local groups have been formed. By 1953 courses were being given in more than one hundred American universities, especially favored by speech departments, while a number of elementary schools were experimenting with semantic methods to make children better masters of their language.

Stuart Chase
Korzybski's Contribution

Korzybski often used the simile of the map. A map of the territory, he says, useful as it may be to travelers, is not the territory. Similarly, language is not the world around us, but rather an indispensable guide to that world. The map, however, is worthless if it shows the traveler a structure different from the terrain he sets out upon. Structure in this context means order and relations, what comes after what. If the order of cities on our map does not agree with the order on the territory, we may find ourselves driving to Montreal when we hoped to go to Chicago—in which case it would be better to steer by the sun.

However detailed the map may be, it can never tell *all* about the territory. Similarly, language cannot tell "all" about an event; some characteristics will always be omitted. At the end of every verbal definition, if it is pushed far enough, there are undefined terms; we reach the silent level where we can point, but we cannot say. If there is nothing to point to, the communication line may break. This is one reason why the modern physicists were driven to devise operational definitions.

Apple₁ and Apple₂

Korzybski places an apple on the table and asks us to describe it. We can say it is round, red, appetizing, with a short

From *Power of Words*, copyright, 1953, 1954 by Stuart Chase. Reprinted by permission of Harcourt, Brace and World, Inc.

stem, and one worm hole. But carefully as we may observe it, in the laboratory or out we can never tell *all* the characteristics of the apple, especially as we approach the submicroscopic level. What all the billions of atoms are up to nobody knows except in the most general, statistical way.

Korzybski sets another apple beside the first, of similar shape and color. Is it identical? We are inclined to think so, but looking more closely we see that the stem is shorter, the red color is less vivid, and there are two worm holes instead of one. $Apple_2$ is not $apple_1$. By the same token, $amoeba_2$ is not $amoeba_1$; $Adam_2$ is not $Adam_1$. Nothing in nature is ever identical with anything else if the observations are carried far enough. Beware of false identifications, says Korzybski; you will only confuse yourself and your hearers. Beware of thinking of "Baptists," "Americans," "businessmen," "workers," as identical. Whatever characteristics they may have in common, they have others which are different. Frank Costello and President Eisenhower are both "Americans."

But certainly an object is identical with itself. Or is it? Let us leave the apple on the table for a month. Is it the "same" apple; is $apple_{Oct. 1}$ the same as $apple_{Nov. 1}$? Obviously not; the clear skin has turned brown and wrinkled, and the firm flesh, soft and rotten. $Apple_1$ accordingly is a *process,* changing its characteristics imperceptibly in a minute, slightly in a day, drastically in a month. Nothing in nature is quite what it was a moment ago. Even the Matterhorn wears slowly away, as rock avalanches come down the *couloirs.* Diamonds last longer than apples, but not forever. Some of the new isotypes have a half life of only a few seconds. Be careful of thinking of apples, diamonds, people, or nations as unchanging events. Remember to correct the verbal map which implies that they do not change. Said Korzybski:

The only possible link between the objective world and the verbal world is structural. If the two structures are similar, then the empirical world becomes intelligible to us—we "understand," can adjust ourselves. . . . If the two structures are not similar . . . we do not "know," we do not "understand," the given problems are "unintelligible" to us . . . we do not know how to adjust ourselves.

Korzybski, as we have said, was profoundly influenced by the new language of science. Thermodynamics, he observed, could not have been built on such loose terms as "hot" and "cold"; a language showing minute quantitative changes and relations had to be developed. Also science could not have advanced without Arabic numerals and their invaluable zero. "Every child is now more skillful in arithmetic than great experts before the decimal system."

Our languages, continues Korzybski, are full of primitive metaphysical concepts, and the effect is like emery dust in a delicate machine. Whorf, we remember, came to a similar conclusion. General Semantics seeks to substitute a good lubricant for the emery. "We usually have sense enough to fit our shoes to our feet, but not sense enough to revise older methods of orientation to fit the facts."

Stop, Look, and Listen

How shall we go about revising older methods? Korzybski suggests five little warning signals in our talking and writing:

(1) the symbol *etc.* to remind us of characteristics left out;
(2) *index numbers* to break up false identifications;
(3) *dates* to remind us that objects are in process, in a state of constant change;
(4) *hyphens* to show that events are connected and nature is all of a piece;
(5) *quotes* to remind us that the term we are using is high up the abstraction ladder, and so, "Beware, it's loaded!"

When I first collected and listed these warning signals from the pages of *Science and Sanity,* I thought them rather elementary. Yet I have been using them constantly in my thinking for fifteen years. They work, and their very simplicity makes them the easier to employ.

Etc.

By writing, or by thinking, *etc.* after a statement, we remind ourselves that characteristics have been left out; we have not told *all*. The semantic quarterly is called *ETC,* and thereby warns the reader that it is not the sum total of wisdom.

William James once put it this way: "The word 'and' trails along after every sentence." Forgetting this, we become candidates for the know-it-all fraternity. *Etc.* helps us to keep alert in complicated territory, to delay the dogmatic cocksure response.

Advertisers may tell us about a beautiful streamlined television set with polished walnut cabinet which is being practically given away. The natural reaction of an experienced shopper is: "What are they *not* telling us?" He is using the equivalent of *etc.* on the advertising copy, wondering about the characteristics left out.

In employing this warning signal, however, a warning is in order. Never expect to round up *all* the missing characteristics, or, as we have seen, they are unlimited. Look for enough major characteristics to make a reasonable decision. You will need only a few for a commercial television set, more for a conclusion about U.S. policy in China.

Index Numbers

We have been using these little signals in past chapters, and they serve to remind us of the diversity of nature, and of the diversities among human beings: $Adam_1$ is not $Adam_2$. They are useful to break up stereotypes, fixed ideas, and ideological convictions about "Catholics," "Yankees," "women," "Jews," "Negroes," "Japs," "Wall Streeters." How often do we say, "Politicians are no good, look at Pendergast," then in the next breath praise the integrity of Senator Douglas? $Politician_1$ is not $politician_2$.

Index numbers keep us out of the pitfalls of formal logic. Here are Aristotle's three famous laws:

1. *The law of identity.* A is A.
2. *The law of the excluded middle.* Everything is either A or not-A.
3. *The law of contradiction.* Nothing is both A and not-A.

The letter A is the letter A, all right, and the word "Apple" is the word "Apple," with five letters and phonemes all correct. The law of identity works satisfactorily with words in our heads, but for events outside our heads, such as Korzybski's apple, it does not work without extensive qualification. $Apple_1$ is *not* $Apple_2$. An object is not even identical with itself over a period of time. The fresh sweet apple rots away.

Aristotle's second and third laws are full of mantraps. Take, for instance, the distinction between plants and animals—A and not-A. There is a little organism called *euglena,* which becomes green in abundant sunlight and behaves like a "plant," but when the sunlight disappears, it digests carbohydrates like an "animal." Euglena is thus either a "plant" or an "animal," depending on the time of day. Or, perhaps better, it is neither plant nor animal, it falls outside the categories. Medical history shows authentic cases of men being converted into women surgically, and vice versa. In 1953 the newspapers made much of an attractive young woman who was recently a man. The person has been both a "man" and a "woman," thus denying the law of contradiction.

Formal logic starts with language and tries to force nature into its verbal categories. The scientist starts with a wordless observation of nature, and then tells what he observes, constructing new categories as needed. Index numbers help us begin the analysis at the right end.

Dates

Korzybski's time signal is especially useful for events in process, where the change is clearly recognizable. Seeing the date, one stops and reflects that the situation *now* is not what it was a hundred years ago, or a year ago, or ten minutes ago. $Britain_{1066}$ is not $Britain_{1920}$, and $Britain_{1939}$ is not $Britain_{1953}$. $America_{1783}$ is not $America_{1953}$, and to speak of "The American Way" as something fixed and unchangeable is to speak nonsense.

Appending a date helps to break up slogan thinking: "That's the way it's always been and always will be"; "Once a Communist, always a Communist"; "The leopard cannot change its spots" . . . It offers a personal reminder that one is himself a process, and if he feels badly now he may not feel badly tomorrow. It helps deliver one from fixed ideas, and replaces static concepts with dynamic ones.

Hyphens

Nature is all of a piece, but language divides it. This is, on the whole, a necessary procedure, enabling us to grasp one thing at a time. We must be careful not to mistake the verbal categories, however, for the real thing. Korzybski suggests that hyphens on the page, or in the mind, help us to remember. Instead of "body and mind" it is closer to reality to write *body-mind*; to write *space-time, psycho-logics*.

Quotes

The book you are reading is full of examples of this warning signal of Korzybski's. I try to put quotation marks around abstract terms which are easy to misunderstand. The quotes bid the reader slow down, remember that the term means different things to different people, look carefully to the context. Words like "free enterprise," "statism," "appeasement," vary for every user, depending on his past experience. We gave a current list of them on page 239.

Words like "water," "trees," "houses," "motorcars," are closer to referents, and quotes are seldom needed—except as I set them off in this sentence. For terms like "the flowers in that vase," "my 1954 Chevrolet," the communication line is about as clear as it can get; the referent is being pointed to.

Why use abstractions at all, when they can be so dangerous to understanding? Why not always point to what you are talking about? Well, why use water at all when you can drown in it? Without abstractions we could not think in a human way. The problem is to be aware of them, to remember what level the discourse is on, and the quote signs help that awareness.

Abstraction Ladder

We have spoken repeatedly of levels of abstraction, or abstraction ladders. Here is one ladder, starting with the space-time event.

That apple there on the table
Apples-in-general
Apples as part of the term "fruit"
Foodstuffs
Living standards
Economic goods
Economic systems

When discussing economic systems, it is a good idea to see that apple from time to time, and other tangible products at the bottom of the ladder. Some economists apparently do not eat.

Here is another ladder, beginning at the top and working downward:

Mountains. What can be said about mountains which applies in all cases? Almost nothing. They are areas raised above other areas on land, under the sea, on the moon. The term is purely relative at this stage; something higher than something, farther from the center.

Snow-capped mountains. Here on a lower rung we can say a little more. The elevations must be considerable, except in polar regions—at least 15,000 feet in the tropics. The snow forms glaciers which wind down the sides. They are cloud factories, producing severe storms, and they require special techniques for climbing.

The Swiss Alps. These are snow-capped mountains about which one can say a good deal. The location can be described, also geology, glacier systems, average elevation, climatic conditions, first ascents, and so on.

The Matterhorn. Here we can be even more specific. It is a snow-capped mountain 14,780 feet above the sea, shaped like a sharp wedge, constantly subject to avalanches of rock and ice. It has four faces, four ridges, three glaciers; was first climbed by the Whymper party in 1865, when four out of seven were killed—and so on. We have dropped down to a specific space-time event.

To the question whether it is "safe" to climb the Matterhorn, Leslie Stephen, one of the greatest of the Alpinists, gave two answers of large semantic importance in 1871, long before the word appeared in the dictionary.

Statement 1. "There is no mountain in the Alps which cannot be climbed by a party of practised mountaineers with guides, in fine weather and under favorable conditions of the snow, with perfect safety."

Statement 2. "There is no mountain in the Alps which may not become excessively dangerous if the climbers are inexperienced, the guides incompetent, the weather bad and the snow unfavorable. . . . There are circumstances under which the Righi is far more dangerous than the Matterhorn under others. Any mountain may pass from the top to the bottom of the scale of danger . . . in a day or sometimes in an hour."

Stephen gives us an unforgettable example of the dangers of generalization. The "Matterhorn" in the morning is not the "Matterhorn" in the afternoon. A is not A. $Matterhorn_1$ is an easy day for a woman climber; $Matterhorn_2$ is certain death for the best climber who ever lived.

"Lazy Boy"

Korzybski shows how language manufactures substantives out of adjectives, often with unfortunate results. Here is a boy who persists in getting up late in the morning. Soon his parents are calling him "a naturally lazy boy," a boy characterized by a thing called "laziness." "Laziness" is akin to "badness" in the American culture, and warrants drastic correction. The parents try hard words, then cuffs and whippings. The boy becomes deranged and unmanageable. Fortunately, a doctor is called in and finds, after an examination, that the patient's glands are seriously out of order. He proceeds to correct the condition, and the boy gets up on time. By identifying their son with "laziness," a substantive, the parents might well have ruined him for life.

People are labeled "troublemaker," "Red," "good guy," "bad girl," and action is taken on that one characteristic, rather than on the many characteristics which every individual possesses. You pass in society not for the person you are, but as a labeled dummy. U.S. congressional committees have been pasting the label "Communist Sympathizer" on many loyal Americans, to the extreme damage of both the citizen and the community. Korzybski would have us tear off the labels and look at the real person.

Twenty-One Statements in General Semantics

To the second edition of *Science and Sanity*, Korzybski contributed an introduction which summarized the main principles of General Semantics. I have cast his list into the following twenty-one propositions or statements, trying to make a fair and objective digest. The reader is urged to consult the volume for himself, in case I have erred.

In any scientific endeavor, we borrow foundations from those who have gone before—a part of the process of "time-binding." All the propositions put forth by Korzybski are built on groundwork laid by earlier scientists. Nobody makes unsupported inventions nowadays. The first twelve statements seem to me to rely heavily on the work of preceding scientists, while the last nine are more Korzybski's own. Certainly he stated them uniquely. The five warning signals were of course his own, and I have added them, along with some personal comments, to some of the statements.

1. *No two events in nature are identical.* This proposition is

accepted by modern scientists. It runs counter to the "is of identity" in Indo-European languages and to the "A is A" of formal logic. (As a warning signal, we use *index numbers*.)

2. *Nature works in dynamic processes.* Accepted by modern scientists and by some schools of philosophy. It disagrees with the linear, cause-and-effect structure of our language. (Warning signals: *dates* and *hyphens*.)

3. *Events flow into one another in nature by "insensible grada-tions."* Nature is all of a piece, though our language tends to separate it into classes. (Korzybski suggests the use of *hyphens* to join events—such as body-mind.)

4. *Nature is best understood in terms of structure, order, relation-ships.* Einstein helped to establish this through the principles of relativity. Indo-European languages, with substantives, enti-ties, absolutes, are at odds with the proposition.

5. *Events in nature are four-dimensional.* Modern physicists, as well as the Hopi Indians, think in terms of space-time. Some other languages are structured for three dimensions, and those who speak them have difficulties with the concept of time.

6. *Events have unlimited characteristics.* Our languages leave many of them out and thus may often distort a judgment. (Korzybski suggests "*etc.*" as a warning signal.)

7. *There is no simultaneity in nature.* Western languages as-sume it as a matter of course; modern physicists do not.

8. *There are no abstract qualities outside our heads.* But language may create verbal spooks which seem to be moving out there. Philosophers back to Bishop Occam have been aware of this difficulty. (*Quotes* give a warning.)

9. *Natural "laws" are at best only high probabilities.* Most scientists are now committed to probability theory. The struc-ture of English, among other languages, favors absolute laws and eternal principles.

10. *Multivalued logic is cardinal in understanding and explain-ing nature.* Indo-European languages tend to force us into two-valued thinking, fortified by formal logic. (Korzybski suggests the use of *indexes* and *etc.* as warning signals.)

11. *A word is not a thing but an artificial symbol.* This has

long been known, but the language structure still objectifies words and encourages word magic. (*Quotes* help to offset this danger.)

12. *A fact is not an inference: an inference is not a value judgment.* The distinction is well known to the law, but not to the laity, and vast semantic confusion results. The distinction may be illustrated by three statements:

(1) This train is going at 20 miles an hour. A *fact*.
(2) At this rate we'll be an hour late. An *inference*.
(3) This lousy railroad is never on time! A *value judgment*.[1]

Asked to define an event, most of us jump to the level of value judgment. A proper identification begins at the other end, with the facts.

Now let us list the nine statements which seem more uniquely Korzybski's.

13. *A map is not the territory.* Our words are not nature, but their structure should correspond to the structure of nature if we are to understand our world.

14. *The language of mathematics contains structures which correspond to the structure of nature.* Korzybski expected a crop of young geniuses in physics as a result of the new talk— and sure enough, they appeared.

15. *"Reality" is apperceived on three levels: macroscopic, microscopic, submicroscopic.* This point is not unique with Korzybski, but his emphasis is unique.

16. *The systems of Aristotle, Euclid, and Newton are now special cases, and outmoded as general systems.* Korzybski does not hold that these three great men were wrong, only that their "laws" cover less territory than was formerly supposed.

17. *Extensional, or objective, thinking is clearer and more accurate than intensional, or thinking inside one's skull.* This is another way of saying "find the referent"— a phrase which Korzybski did not like to use.

18. *At the end of all verbal behavior are undefined terms.*

---

[1] If we carry this series one step farther, we have what Dr. Melvin Thorner calls a "purposeful communique"; for instance: "Passengers should avoid the unreliable railroad."

This is the point where the senses must pick up the signs from nature. Korzybski has emphasized this "unspoken level" more forcefully than any other student.

19. *Language is self-reflexive.* It is possible to make statements about a statement about a statement indefinitely. (No apologies to Gertrude Stein.)

20. *Man, alone among earth's creatures, "binds time";* that is, profits by the experience of past generations. This was well known and obvious long before Korzybski, but uniquely phrased by him. (Not included in his list directly.)

21. *The nervous system can be consciously reoriented to improve evaluation.* Science can restore sanity. Korzybski deeply believed this, titled his book as a result of it, but his proof is not conclusive. If the proposition turns out to be true it may add considerably to his stature. Delayed response, the use of the warning signals, awareness of abstractions, and the rest, do improve evaluation without question. But does the use of General Semantics *retrain the whole nervous system,* so that improved evaluation becomes as automatic as the knee jerk? Psychiatrists are skeptical. Korzybski has been called a "thwarted psychiatrist," perhaps with justice.

A Critical Evaluation

It seems plain that while General Semantics has made important contributions to the study of communication it has not seized the leadership. Compared with cultural anthropology, with linguistics, cybernetics, the work of Shannon, it is more a point of view than a rigorous scientific discipline.

Korzybski "brought together a useful way of thinking and talking about human thinking and talking," says Irving J. Lee. At his death in 1950, "he had devised and explained the principles; he had not established a training-testing program with equal thoroughness." He inaugurated no clinic for practicing his methods, no controlled experiments to validate them. There are few reliable case studies of effects on individual persons or groups, in the sense that clinical psychologists make case studies.

Korzybski was something of a prima donna, and he had a few unfortunate prejudices. He was overcritical of the work of others in his field. I felt the sting of this criticism from time to time, though I had done my best to make his work more widely known. At one point the whole movement seemed to be heading toward a cult, with disciples who knew the lingo, but little else. This danger I believe has been safely passed.

Sometimes it seemed as if the originator of General Semantics were trying to set up a one-man philosophy in the great tradition, which would supersede the system of Aristotle, Aquinas, or Hegel. Yet the scientific method, upon which he constantly relied, is incompatible with one-man philosophies. Korzybski could not have it both ways. If he had been more of a scientist he would have written a shorter and better structured book and given himself more time to inaugurate the research which Professor Lee calls for. He would thus have allayed a good deal of frustration in persons like myself who were trying to understand him.

Despite the frustration, some of us kept at it, and rich was our reward. Doors which had been closed began to open; the world took on a new dimension. Among the semanticists who have been carrying on since his death are objective scholars, shy of cults and revelations. They will succeed, I believe, in steering General Semantics into the moving front of the social sciences, where it belongs. Korzybski included in his approach both the natural sciences, represented by physics, and the social sciences, represented by psychology. One of his favorite phrases was "organism-as-a-whole." He did not station himself behind any of the verbal partitions.

Twenty years of General Semantics have demonstrated that one's evaluation of men and events can be sharpened by its use, that certain mental blocks can be remedied, that one's speaking and writing can be clarified.

Students of General Semantics report a better ability to listen, a reduction in the terrors of stage fright, help in cases of stuttering. General Semantics can aid in teaching children, and in bringing "backward" scholars up to mark. It has led to a healthy re-examination of verbal proof and exerted some influence on the law. It promotes techniques of agreement, and encourages a new appraisal of philosophies formulated before Einstein. Perhaps best of all, General Semantics helps the student know what he does not know.

This is no small contribution for one person to make. We owe Korzybski a good deal, not only for what he discovered or highlighted, but for the furor created by his personality. He lit fires, started controversies, caused people to look to their terms, and so gave a much-needed impetus to the whole subject of communication.

"What is the difference, Count Korzybski, between man and other living creatures?" he was sometimes asked. His eyes would gleam behind the great round spectacles and his deep voice with its rolling accent would reply: "A quar-rter-r- of an inch of cor-rtex."

S. I. Hayakawa
The Language
of Social Control

*The effect of a parade of sonorous phrases upon human
conduct has never been adequately studied.*
—Thurman W. Arnold

*Yet the layman errs in his belief that this lack of precision
and finality is to be ascribed to the lawyers. The truth
of the matter is that the popular notion of the possibilities
of legal exactness is based upon a misconception. The
law always has been, is now, and will ever continue
to be, largely vague and variable. And how could this
well be otherwise? The law deals with human relations
in their most complicated aspects. The whole confused,
shifting helter-skelter of life parades before it—more
confused than ever, in our kaleidoscopic age.*
—Jerome Frank

Making Things Happen

The most interesting and perhaps least understood relationship
between words and the world is that between words and future
events. When we say, for example, "Come here!" we are not
describing the extensional world about us, nor are we merely
expressing our feelings; we are trying to *make something hap-*

From *Language in Thought and Action*, 2nd Edition, by S. I. Hayakawa,
copyright 1941, 1949, © 1963, 1964 by Harcourt, Brace and World, Inc. and
reprinted with their permission.

pen. What we call "commands," "pleas," "requests," and "orders" are the simplest ways we have of making things happen by means of words.

There are, however, more roundabout ways. When we say, for example, "Our candidate is a great American," we are of course making an enthusiastic purr about him, but we may also be influencing other people to vote for him. Again, when we say, "Our war against the enemy is God's war. God wills that we must triumph," we are saying something which, though unverifiable, may influence others to help in the prosecution of the war. Or if we merely state as a fact, "Milk contains vitamins," we may be influencing others to buy milk.

Consider, too, such a statement as "I'll meet you tomorrow at two o'clock in front of the Palace Theater." Such a statement about *future* events can only be made, it will be observed, in a system in which symbols are independent of things symbolized. The future, like the recorded past, is a specifically human dimension. To a dog, the expression "hamburger *tomorrow*" is meaningless—he will look at you expectantly, hoping for the extensional meaning of the word "hamburger" to be produced *now*. Squirrels, to be sure, store food for "next winter," but the fact that they store food regardless of whether or not their needs are adequately provided for demonstrates that such behavior (usually called "instinctive") is governed neither by symbols nor by other interpreted stimuli. Human beings are unique in their ability to react meaningfully to such expressions as "next Saturday," "on our next wedding anniversary," "twenty years after date I promise to pay," "some day, perhaps five hundred years from now." That is to say, maps can be made, even though the territories they stand for are not yet actualities. Guiding ourselves by means of such maps or territories-to-be, we can impose a certain predictability upon future events.

With words, therefore, we influence and to an enormous extent *control future events.* It is for this reason that writers write; preachers preach; employers, parents, and teachers scold; propagandists send out news releases; statesmen give addresses. All of them, for various reasons, are trying to influence our conduct—sometimes for our good, sometimes for their own.

These attempts to control, direct, or influence the future actions of fellow human beings with words may be termed *directive uses of language.*

Now it is obvious that if directive language is going to direct, it cannot be dull or uninteresting. If it is to influence our conduct, it *must* make use of every affective element in language: dramatic variations in tone of voice, rhyme and rhythm, purring and snarling, words with strong affective connotations, endless repetition. If meaningless noises will move the audience, meaningless noises must be made; if facts move them, facts must be given; if noble ideals move them, we must make our proposals appear noble; if they will respond only to fear, we must scare them stiff.

The nature of the affective means used in directive language is limited, of course, by the nature of our aims. If we are trying to direct people to be more kindly toward each other, we obviously do not want to arouse feelings of cruelty or hate. If we are trying to direct people to think and act more intelligently, we obviously should not use subrational appeals. If we are trying to direct people to lead better lives, we use affective appeals that arouse their finest feelings. Included among directive utterances, therefore, are many of the greatest and most treasured works of literature: the Christian and Buddhist scriptures, the writings of Confucius, Milton's *Areopagitica,* and Lincoln's Gettysburg Address.

There are, however, occasions when it is felt that language is not sufficiently affective by itself to produce the results wanted. We supplement directive language, by *nonverbal affective appeals* of many kinds. We supplement the words "Come here" by gesturing with our hands. Advertisers are not content with saying in words how beautiful their products will make us; they supplement their words by the use of colored inks and by pictures. Newspapers are not content with saying that communism is a menace; they supply political cartoons depicting communists as criminally insane people placing sticks of dynamite under magnificent buildings labeled "American way of life." The affective appeal of sermons and religious exhortations may be supplemented by costumes, incense, processions, choir music, and church bells. A political candidate seeking office reinforces his speech-making with a considerable array of non-verbal affective appeals: brass bands, flags, parades, picnics, barbecues, and free cigars.[1] Often a candidate's smile or, as in the case of President Kennedy, his wife's appearance and charm may be a powerful influence upon the voter.

Now, if we want people to do certain things and if we are indifferent as to *why they do them,* then no affective appeals need be excluded. Some political candidates want us to vote for them regardless of our reasons for doing so. Therefore, if we hate the rich, they will snarl at the rich for us; if we dislike strikers, they will snarl at the strikers; if we like clambakes, they will throw clambakes; if the majority of us likes hillbilly music, they may say nothing about the problems of government, but travel among their constituencies with hillbilly bands. Again, many business firms want us to buy their products regardless of our reasons for doing so; therefore, if delusions and fantasies will lead us to buy their products, they will seek to produce delusions and fantasies; if we want to be popular with the other sex, they will promise us popularity; if we like pretty girls in bathing suits, they will associate pretty girls in bathing suits with their products, whether they are selling shaving

[1] The following are excerpts from reports of the Republican National Convention of 1948:

"There on the stage a gigantic photograph of the candidate, tinted somewhat too vividly, gazed steadily out over the throngs. Around the balcony hung other photographs: the Dewey family playing with their Great Dane; the Deweys at the circus; Dewey on the farm. Dewey infantrymen passed out soft drinks and small favors to gawking visitors and gave every 200th visitor a door prize. William Horne, a Philadelphia bank employee, was clocked in as the 45,000th visitor and got a sterling silver carving aid." *Time* (July 5, 1948).

"Over loudspeakers of the Bellevue-Stratford came a constant stream of official exhortations against undue crowding at the entrance to the Dewey headquarters. The warnings were part of the game, but they were also justified. Why wouldn't the Dewey headquarters be jammed when prizes—from chewing gum and pocket combs to silk lingerie and dresses—were being doled out with the largess of a radio quiz show? At one point the Dewey people even staged a fashion show, complete with eight bathing beauties. A bewildered foreign newspaperman asked a fellow-reporter, "How can I explain to France what this has to do with electing a President?' . . . The Stassen managers appeared to be saving up their circus talent for Convention Hall, where it turned out to be considerable, ranging from an Indian chief in full regalia to a shapely girl in sailor pants who did a nautical rumba on the rostrum." *Nation* (July 3, 1948)

cream, automobiles, summer resorts, ice-cream cones, house paint, or hardware. Only the law keeps them from presenting pretty girls without bathing suits. The records of the Federal Trade Commission, as well as the advertising pages of many magazines, show that some advertisers will stop at practically nothing.

The Promises of Directive Language

Almost all directive utterances say something about the future. They are "maps," either explicitly or by implication, of *"territories" that are to be.* They direct us to do certain things with the stated or implied promise that if we do these things, certain consequences will follow: "If you adhere to the Bill of Rights, your civil rights too will be protected." "If you vote for me, I will have your taxes reduced." "Live according to these religious principles, and you will have peace in your soul." "Read this magazine, and you will keep up with important current events." "Take Lewis's Licorice Liver Pills and enjoy that glorious feeling that goes with regularity." Needless to say, some of these promises are kept, and some are not. Indeed, we encounter promises daily that are obviously incapable of being kept.

There is no sense in objecting as some people do to advertising and political propaganda—the only kind of directives they worry about—on the ground that they are based on "emotional appeals." Unless directive language has affective power of some kind, it is useless. We do not object to campaigns that tell us, "Give to the Community Chest and enable poor children to enjoy better care," although that is an "emotional appeal." Nor do we resent being reminded of our love of home, friends, and nation when people issue moral or patriotic directives at us. The important question to be asked of any directive utterance is, "Will things happen as promised if I do as I am directed to do? If I accept your philosophy, shall I achieve peace of mind? If I vote for you, will my taxes be reduced? If I use Lifeguard Soap, will my boy friend really come back to me?"

We rightly object to advertisers who make false or misleading claims and to politicians who ignore their promises, although it must be admitted that, in the case of politicians, they are sometimes compelled to make promises that later circumstances prevent them from keeping. Life being as uncertain and as unpredictable as it is, we are constantly trying to find out what is going to happen next, so that we may prepare ourselves. Directive utterances undertake to tell us how we can bring about certain desirable events and how we can avoid undesirable events. If we can rely upon what they tell us about the future, the uncertainties of life are reduced. When, however, directive utterances are of such a character that things do *not* happen as predicted—when, after we have done as we were told, the peace in the soul has not been found, the taxes have not been reduced, the boy friend has not returned, there is disappointment. Such disappointments may be trivial or grave; in any event, they are so common that we do not even bother to complain about some of them. They are, nevertheless, all serious in their implications. *Each of them serves, in greater or lesser degree, to break down that mutual trust that makes cooperation possible and knits people together into a society.*

Every one of us, therefore, who utters directive language, with its concomitant promises, stated or implied, is morally obliged to be as certain as he can, since there is no absolute certainty, that he is arousing no false expectations. Politicians promising the immediate abolition of poverty, national advertisers suggesting that tottering marriages can be restored to bliss by a change in the brand of laundry detergent used in the family, newspapers threatening the collapse of the nation if the party they favor is not elected—all such utterers of nonsense are, for the reasons stated, menaces to the social order. It does not matter much whether such misleading directives are uttered in ignorance and error or with conscious intent to deceive, because the disappointments they cause are all similarly destructive of mutual trust among human beings.

The Foundations of Society

But propaganda, no matter how persuasive, does not create society. We can, if we wish, ignore its directives. We come now to *directive utterances that we cannot ignore if we wish to remain organized in our social groups.*

What we call society is a vast network of mutual agreements. We agree to refrain from murdering our fellow citizens, and they in turn agree to refrain from murdering us; we agree to drive on the right-hand side of the road, and others agree to do the same; we agree to deliver specified goods, and others agree to pay us for them; we agree to observe the rules of an organization, and the organization agrees to let us enjoy its privileges. This complicated network of agreements, into which almost every detail of our lives is woven and upon which most of our expectations in life are based, consists essentially of *statements about future events which we are supposed, with our own efforts, to bring about.* Without such agreements, there would be no such thing as society. We would all be huddling in miserable and lonely caves, not daring to trust anyone. With such agreements, and a will on the part of the vast majority of people to live by them, behavior begins to fall into relatively predictable patterns; cooperation becomes possible; peace and freedom are established.

Therefore, in order that we shall continue to exist as human beings, we *must* impose patterns on each other. We must make citizens conform to social and civic customs; we must make husbands dutiful to their wives; we must make soldiers courageous, judges just, priests pious, and teachers solicitous for the welfare of their pupils. In early stages of culture the principal means of imposing patterns of behavior was, of course, physical coercion. But such control can also be exercised, as human beings must have discovered extremely early in history, by *words*—that is, by directive language. Therefore, directives about matters which society as a whole regards as essential to its own safety are made especially powerful, so that no individual in that society will fail to be impressed with a sense of his obligations. To make doubly sure, society further reinforces the directives by the assurance that punishment, possibly including imprisonment and death, may be visited upon those who fail to heed the words.

Directives with Collective Sanction

These directive utterances with collective sanction, which try to impose patterns of behavior upon the individual in the interests of the whole group, are among the most interesting of linguistic events. Not only are they usually accompanied by ritual; they are usually the central purpose of ritual. There is probably no kind of utterance that we take more seriously, that affects our lives more deeply, that we quarrel about more bitterly. Constitutions of nations and of organizations, legal contracts, and oaths of office are utterances of this kind; in marriage vows, confirmation exercises, induction ceremonies, and initiations, they are the essential constituent. Those terrifying verbal judges called *laws* are simply such directives, accumulated, codified, and systematized through the centuries. In its laws, society makes its mightiest collective effort to impose predictability upon human behavior.

Directive utterances made under collective sanction may exhibit any or all of the following features:

1. Such language is almost always phrased in *words that have affective connotations,* so that people will be appropriately impressed and awed. Archaic and obsolete vocabulary or stilted phraseology quite unlike the language of everyday life is employed. For example: "Wilt thou, John, take this woman for thy lawful wedded wife?" "This lease, made this tenth day of July, A.D. One Thousand Nine Hundred and Sixty-three, between Samuel Smith, hereinafter called the Lessor, and Jeremiah Johnson, hereinafter called Lessee, WITNESSETH, that Lessor, in consideration of covenants and agreements hereinafter contained and made on the part of the Lessee, hereby leases to Lessee for a private dwelling, the premises known and described as follows, to wit . . ."

2. Such directive utterances are often accompanied by *appeals to supernatural powers,* who are called upon to help us carry out the vows, or to punish us if we fail to carry them out. An oath, for example, ends with the words, "So help me God." Prayers, incantations and invocations accompany the utterance

of important vows in practically all cultures from the most primitive to the most civilized. These further serve, of course, to impress our vows on our minds.

3. The *fear of direct punishment* is also invoked. If God does not punish us for failing to carry out our agreements, it is made clear either by statement or implication that our fellow men will. For example, we all realize that we can be imprisoned for desertion, nonsupport, or bigamy; sued for "breach of contract"; "unfrocked" for activities contrary to priestly vows; "cashiered" for "conduct unbecoming an officer"; "impeached" for "betrayal of public trust"; hanged for "treason."

4. The formal and public utterance of the vows may be preceded by *preliminary disciplines* of various kinds: courses of training in the meaning of the vows one is undertaking; fasting and self-mortification, as before entering the priesthood; initiation ceremonies involving physical torture, as before induction into the warrior status among primitive peoples or membership in college fraternities.

5. The utterance of the directive language may be accompanied by other *activities or gestures calculated to impress the occasion on the mind.* For example, everybody in a courtroom stands up when a judge is about to open a court; huge processions and extraordinary costumes accompany coronation ceremonies; academic gowns are worn for commencement exercises; for many weddings, an organist and a soprano are procured and special clothes are worn.

6. The uttering of the vows may be immediately followed by *feasts, dancing, and other joyous manifestations.* Again the purpose seems to be to reinforce still further the effect of the vows. For example, there are wedding parties and receptions, graduation dances, banquets for the induction of officers and, even in the most modest social circles, some form of "celebration" when a member of the family enters into a compact with society. In primitive cultures, initiation ceremonies for chieftains may be followed by feasting and dancing that last for several days or weeks.

7. In cases where the first utterance of the vows is not made

a special ceremonial occasion, the effect on the memory is usually achieved by *frequent repetition*. The flag ritual ("I pledge allegiance to the flag of the United States of America . . .") is repeated daily in most schools. Mottoes, which are briefly stated general directives, are repeated frequently; sometimes they are stamped on dishes, sometimes engraved on a warrior's sword, sometimes inscribed in prominent places such as on gates, walls, and doorways, where people can see them and be reminded of their duties.

The common feature of all these activities that accompany directive utterances, as well as of the affective elements in the language of directive utterances, is the deep effect they have on the memory. Every kind of sensory impression from the severe pain of initiation rites to the pleasures of banqueting, music, splendid clothing, and ornamental surroundings may be employed; every emotion from the fear of divine punishment to pride in being made the object of special public attention may be aroused. This is done in order that the individual who enters into his compact with society—that is, the individual who commits himself to the "map" of the not-yet-existent "territory" —shall never forget to try to bring that "territory" into existence.

For these reasons, such occasions as when a cadet receives his commission, when a Jewish boy has his *bar mitzvah,* when a priest takes his vows, when a policeman receives his badge, when a foreign-born citizen is sworn in as a citizen of the United States, or when a president takes his oath of office— these are events one never forgets. Even if, later on, a person realizes that he has not fulfilled his vows, he cannot shake off the feeling that he should have done so. All of us, of course, use and respond to these ritual directives. The phrases and speeches to which we respond reveal our deepest religious, patriotic, social, professional, and political allegiances more accurately than do the citizenship papers or membership cards that we may carry in our pockets or the badges that we may wear on our coats. A man who has changed his religion after reaching adulthood will, on hearing the ritual he was accustomed to hearing in childhood, often feel an urge to return to his earlier form of worship. In such ways, then, do human beings use words to reach out into the future and control each other's conduct.

It should be remarked that many of our social directives and many of the rituals with which they are accompanied are antiquated and somewhat insulting to adult minds. Rituals that originated in times when people had to be scared into good behavior are unnecessary to people who already have a sense of social responsibility. For example, a five-minute marriage ceremony performed at the city hall for a mature, responsible couple may "take" much better than a full-dress church ceremony performed for an infantile couple. In spite of the fact that the strength of social directives obviously lies in the willingness, the maturity, and the intelligence of the people to whom the directives are addressed, there is still a widespread tendency to rely upon the efficacy of ceremonies as such. This tendency is due, of course, to a lingering belief in word-magic, the notion that, by *saying* things repeatedly or in specified ceremonial ways, we can cast a spell over the future and force events to turn out the way we said they would. ("There'll always be an England!") An interesting manifestation of this superstitious attitude towards words and rituals is to be found among those members of patriotic societies who seem to believe that the way to educate school children in democracy is to stage bigger and better flag-saluting ceremonies and to treble the occasions for singing "God Bless America."

What Are "Rights"?

What, extensionally, is the meaning of the word "my" in such expressions as "my real estate," "my book," "my automobile"? Certainly the word "my" describes no characteristics of the objects named. A check changes hands and "your" automobile becomes "mine" but no change results in the automobile. What has changed?

The change is of course, in *our social agreements covering our behavior* toward the automobile. Formerly, when it was "yours," you felt free to use it as you liked, while I did not. Now that it is "mine," I use it freely and you may not. The meaning of "yours" and "mine" lies not in the external world, but in *how we intend to act.* And when society as a whole recognizes my "right of ownership" (by issuing me, for example, a certificate of title), it agrees to protect me in my intentions to use the automobile and to frustrate, by police action if necessary, the intentions of those who may wish to use it without my permission. Society makes this agreement with me in return for my obeying its laws and paying my share of the expenses of government.

Are not, then, all assertions of ownership and statements about "rights" directives? Cannot, "This is *mine,*" be translated, "I am going to use this object; you keep your hands off"? Cannot, "Every child has a *right* to an education," be translated, "*Give* every child an education"? And is not the difference between "moral rights" and "legal rights" the difference between agreements which people believe *ought* to be made, and those which, through collective legislative sanction, *have been* made?

Directives and Disillusionment

A few cautions may be added before we leave the subject of directive language. First, it should be remembered that, since words cannot "say all" about anything, the promises implied in directive language are never more than "outline maps" of "territories-to-be." The future will fill in those outlines, often in unexpected ways. Sometimes the future will bear no relation to our "maps" at all, in spite of all our endeavors to bring about the promised events. We swear always to be good citizens, always to do our duty, and so on, but we never quite succeed in being good citizens *every* day of our lives or in performing *all* our duties. A realization that directives cannot *fully* impose any pattern on the future saves us from having impossible expectations and therefore from suffering needless disappointments.

Secondly, one should distinguish between directive and informative utterances, which often look alike. Such statements as "A boy scout is clean and chivalrous and brave" or "Policemen are defenders of the weak" *set up goals* and do not necessarily describe the present situation. This is extremely important, because all too often people understand such definitions as descriptive and are then shocked and disillusioned when they encounter a boy scout who is not chivalrous or a policeman who is a bully. They decide that they are "through with the boy scouts" or "disgusted with all policemen," which, of course, is nonsense. They have, in effect, inferred an informative statement from what is to be taken only as a very general directive.

A third source of disappointment and disillusionment arising from the improper understanding of directives results from reading into directives promises that they do not make. A common instance is provided by advertisements of the antiseptics and patent medicines which people buy under the impression that the cure or prevention of colds was promised. Because of the rulings of the Federal Trade Commission the writers of these advertisements carefully avoid saying that their preparations will prevent or cure anything. Instead, they say that they "help reduce the severity of the infection," "help relieve the symptoms of a cold," or "help guard against sniffling and other discomforts." If after reading these advertisements you feel that prevention or cure of colds has been promised, you are exactly the kind of sucker they are looking for. (Of course, if you buy the product knowing clearly what was promised and what was not, that is a different matter.)

Another way of reading into directives things that were not said is by believing promises to be more specific and concrete than they really are. When, for example, a candidate for political office promises to "help the farmer," and you vote for him, and then you discover that he helps the *cotton* farmer without helping the *potato* farmer (and you grow potatoes—you cannot exactly accuse him of having broken his promise. Or, if another candidate promises to "protect union labor," and you vote for him, and he helps to pass legislation that infuriates the officials of your union (he calls it "legislation to protect union members from their own racketeering leadership")—again you cannot exactly accuse him of having broken his promise, since his action may well have been sincerely in accord with his notion of "helping union labor." The ambiguities of campaign oratory are notorious.

Politicians are often accused of breaking their promises. No doubt many of them do. But it must be remarked that they often do not promise as much as their constituents think they do. The platforms of the major parties are almost always at high levels of abstraction ("they mean all things to all men," as the cynical say), but they are often understood by voters to be more specific and concrete (i.e., at lower levels of abstraction) than they are. If one is "disillusioned" by the acts of a politician, sometimes the politician is to blame, but sometimes the voter is to blame for having had the illusion to start with—or, as we shall say, for having *confused different levels of abstraction.* What is meant by this expression will be more fully explained in ensuing chapters.

Irving J. Lee
They Talk
Past Each Other

*"It takes," says Thoreau, in the noblest and most useful
passage I remember to have read in any modern author,
"two to speak truth—one to speak and another to hear."
—Robert Louis Stevenscn, "Truth of Intercourse," Virginibus
Puerisque, J. M. Dent & Sons, 1925, p. 32.*

How Misunderstanding Happens

The one thing people tend to take for granted when talking to
others is that they understand each other. It is rare, indeed, in
a meeting to have someone hold up his own argument long
enough to say, "I think you said. . . . Did you?" or "Was I right
in thinking you meant . . . ?" We found people ever so eager to
parry what a man says without ever wondering whether that is
what the man said.

In the give-and-take of talk things go fast, and one is so
busy organizing his reply that he doesn't take the time to make
sure he knows what he is replying to. This is unfortunate because it often means that, instead of talking with others, people
talk past or by-pass each other.

Note some by-passings.

*1. The British Staff prepared a paper which they wished to
raise as a matter of urgency, and informed their American*

"They Talk Past Each Other" from *How to Talk with People* by Irving J. Lee.
Copyright, 1952 by Harper & Row, Publishers, Inc. Reprinted by permission of
the publisher.

colleagues that they wished to "table it." To the American staff
"tabling" a paper meant putting it away in a drawer and
forgetting it. A long and even acrimonious argument ensued
before both parties realised that they were agreed on the merits
and wanted the same thing.[1]

2. I remember a worrisome young man who, one day, came
back from the X-ray room wringing his hands and trembling
with fear. "It is all up with me," he said. "The X-ray man said I
have a hopeless cancer of the stomach." Knowing that the
roentgenologist would never have said such a thing, I asked,
"Just what did he say?" and the answer was on dismissing him,
the roentgenologist said to an assistant, "N.P." In Mayo clinic
cipher this meant "no plates," and indicated that the X-ray man
was so satisfied with the normal appearance of the stomach on
the X-ray screen that he did not see any use in making films. But
to the patient, watching in an agony of fear for some portent of
disaster, it meant "nothing possible": in other words that the
situation was hopeless![2]

3. A foreman told a machine operator he was passing: "Better
clean up around here." It was ten minutes later when the foreman's
assistant phoned: "Say, boss, isn't that bearing Sipert is working
on due up in engineering pronto?"

"You bet your sweet life it is. Why?"

"He says you told him to drop it and sweep the place up. I
thought I'd better make sure."

"Listen," the foreman flared into the phone, "get him right
back on that job. It's got to be ready in twenty minutes."

. . . What [the foreman] had in mind was for Sipert to gather
up the oily waste, which was a fire and accident hazard. This
would not have taken more than a couple of minutes, and there
would have been plenty of time to finish the bearing. Sipert,
of course, should have been able to figure this out for himself—
except that something in the foreman's tone of voice, or in his
own mental state at the time, made him misunderstand the

[1] Winston Churchill, "The Second World War," Vol. III, Book II, *The New York Times*, February 28, 1950, p. 31.
[2] Walter C. Alvarez, *Nervousness, Indigestion and Pain*, Paul B. Hoeber, Inc., 1943, p. 74.

foreman's intent. He wasn't geared to what the foreman had said.[3]

4. Lady recently ordered some writing paper at a department store and asked to have her initials engraved thereon. The salesgirl suggested placing them in the upper right-hand corner or the upper left-hand corner, but the customer said no, put them in the center. Well, the stationery has arrived, every sheet marked with her initials equidistant from right and left and from top and bottom.[4]

5. In a private conversation with Mr. Molotov, it became apparent that another difficult misunderstanding in language had arisen between ourselves and the Russians. At the San Francisco Conference when the question of establishing a trusteeship system within the United Nations was being considered, the Soviet delegation had asked Mr. Stettinius what the American attitude would be toward the assumption by the Soviet Union of a trusteeship. Mr. Stettinius replied in general terms, expressing the opinion that the Soviet Union was "eligible" to receive a territory for administration under trusteeship. Mr. Molotov took this to mean we would support a Soviet request for a trusteeship.[5]

In each case a word or phrase or sentence was used one way by the speaker and interpreted in another way by the listener. This is possible because words are versatile. Except for those intended for highly specialized purposes (like tetrasporangium, icosahedron, bisulfite), it is not unusual to find most words put to rather varied uses. A seventh-grade class in English was able to make up thirty sentences in which the word "set" was used differently each time. Even "word" is listed in sixteen different ways in *The American College Dictionary*.

The naïve speaker of a language usually has the feeling that, in general, words have a meaning, and he is seldom conscious of the great "area" of meaning for all except highly technical words. It is in this respect that the student's observation first needs

[3] *The Foreman's Letter*, National Foreman's Institute, Inc., February 8, 1950, p. 3.

[4] "The Talk of the Town," *The New Yorker*, January 28, 1950, p. 21. Reprinted by permission. Copyright, 1950, The New Yorker Magazine, Inc.

[5] James F. Byrnes, *Speaking Frankly*, Harper & Brothers, 1947, p. 96.

widening and sharpening. Frequently we have tried to "build vocabularies" by adding more units or words. But to push first the addition of more vocabulary units in order to increase the number of words may interfere with, rather than help, effective mastery of language. This is the process that produces a Mrs. Malaprop. Most frequently the student needs first to know well the various areas of use of the units he is already familiar with; he needs to be made conscious of the great diversity of uses or meanings for commonly used words. He must be made aware, for example, that the statement "The children did not count" can mean that they did not utter the words for the numbers in a series, or that the children were not considered. Ordinarily we just don't believe without considerable careful examination that for the five hundred most used words in English (according to the Thorndike Word Book) the Oxford Dictionary records and illustrates from our literature 14,070 separate meanings.[6]

At different times the same words may be used differently.

When Francis Bacon referred to various people in the course of his Essays as indifferent, obnoxious, and officious, he was describing them as "impartial," submissive," and "ready to serve." When King James II observed that the new St. Paul's Cathedral was amusing, awful, and artificial, he implied that Sir Christopher Wren's recent creation was "pleasing, awe-inspiring, and skilfully achieved." When Dr. Johnson averred that Milton's Lycidas was "easy, vulgar, and therefore disgusting," he intended to say that it was "effortless, popular, and therefore not in good taste."[7]

The role of experience also affects the varieties of usage. Brander Matthews provided an example from a dinner-party conversation:

The second topic . . . was a definition of the image called up in our several minds by the word forest. Until that evening I had never thought of forest as clothing itself in different colors and taking on different forms in the eyes of different men; but I then discovered that even the most innocent word may don strange

[6] Charles C. Fries, "Using the Dictionary," *Inside the ACD*, October, 1948, p. 1.
[7] Simeon Potter, *Our Language*, Pelican Books, 1950, p. 116.

disguises. To Hardy forest suggested the sturdy oaks to be assaulted
by the woodlanders of Wessex; and to Du Maurier it evoked the
trim and tidy avenues of the national domain of France. To Black
the word naturally brought to mind the low scrub of the so-called
deer-forests of Scotland; and to Gosse it summoned up a view
of the green-clad mountains that towered up from the Scandinavian
fiords. To Howells it recalled the thick woods that in his youth
fringed the rivers of Ohio; and to me there came back swiftly
the memory of the wild growths bristling up unrestrained by man,
in the Chippewa Reservation which I had crossed fourteen years
before in my canoe trip from Lake Superior to the Mississippi.
Simple as the word seemed, it was interpreted by each of us in
accord with his previous personal experience.[8]

This conclusion about the range and possible uses of a word
is easily verified. When it is forgotten, a listener just as easily
comes to believe that (1) there is but one way to use a word—
his—and (2) the speaker is doing with his words what the listener would were the listener doing the talking.

Can you see these beliefs at work in the examples given
above?

In short, what you understand by any word or statement
may not be what someone else intends to say. In a way, this is
so obvious that most of us feel no obligation to think more
about it. However, when one is aware of the fact it does not
necessarily follow that he will act in terms of it. And there is
some evidence that, unless people can be made sensitive to
the possibility of by-passing, they make only meager efforts to
stop it.

It Takes Two to Make Communication

I have no wish here to give comfort to the bore who gets so
much pleasure squelching discussions with his defiant "Define

---

[8] Brander Matthews, *These Many Years: Recollections of a New Yorker*,
Charles Scribner's Sons, 1917, pp. 287–288. Quoted from the essay by Allen
Walker Read, "Linguistic Revision as a Requisite for the Increasing of Rigor in
Scientific Method," read at the Third Congress on General Semantics, July 22,
1949.

your terms." His maneuver results in shifting the burden in communication to the other fellow. Both must be brought into the act. We would have the listener work just a bit, too. So we urge him to state his notion of what was being said. Incidentally, that bore may sometimes be routed with this: "What definition of my words have you in mind? Perhaps we are thinking together after all."

The "plain-talk" and "say-it-in-simple-words" teachers have been in vogue but they haven't been especially helpful. They, too, tend to put the emphasis on one side of the communication line. Putting the burden for understanding on the speaker is a kind of implied invitation to the listener to sit back and contentedly assume he has nothing to do but wait his turn. And besides, even the simple words have uses which too frequently vary between man and man.

We once observed eight meetings of a group of nine men, who functioned as a standing committee in a corporation having wide public responsibilities. Five had taken one or more courses and had studied some of the books on "talking plainly." One of the items checked had to do with "the assumption of understanding." Can men be differentiated according to their readiness to believe they know what the other fellow is referring to? We looked in their replies for such indications as *questions* for assurance that the asker is "with" the speaker, *qualifications* like "If I understand what you say" or "If I know what you mean . . . ," *invitations* like "Correct me if I'm off the beam" or "Tell me whether I answered what you intended to say. . . ."

We were hardly prepared to find that four of the "plain-talk students" did the least amount of questioning, qualifying, inviting, etc. This may, of course, be an accident. Before a conclusion worth much can be drawn we should have a broader sampling of the population. And before a cause can be assigned with confidence much more investigation would be needed. Nevertheless, *these particular men,* knowing the ways to "plainness" and using them, tended to think they had done enough when they spoke so. They seemed to focus attention on *their* talking. They made no comparable effort to look to the character of what they heard.

I am not at all arguing that this finding in these particular cases means that training in plain talking makes for poor listening. I am trying to suggest only that training in the explicit effort at understanding may be a difficult sort of thing and may not automatically carry over from other training.

Cardinal Manning once said something relevant:

I have no doubt that I will hear that I am talking of what I do not understand; but in my defence I think I may say, I am about to talk of what I do not understand for this reason: I cannot get those who talk about it to tell me what they mean. I know what I mean by it, but I am not at all sure that I know what they mean by it; and those who use the same words in different senses are like men that run up and down the two sides of a hedge, and so can never meet.

It is helpful to think of the radio in this. The performer in the studio can talk his heart out, but if the man in the easy chair is tuned in elsewhere it really makes no difference what is being said. Unless the receiver is on the same wave length, the character of what is sent out hardly governs the communication process.[9]

This is not to imply that a speaker cannot help by putting what he has to say in clear, listenable language. Anything he does to define, simplify, amplify, illustrate, is all to the good. But it is only part of the process. The listener has a job to do, too. He must make the effort to come to terms with the speaker to keep from assuming that he inevitably knows what the speaker has in mind. At the very least he might temper his arrogance with a question now and then just to make sure.

It takes two to make communication.

Are You on His Communication Line?

The preceding pages of this chapter were mimeographed and given to three groups, one meeting for study of the Bible, one

[9] This image is well developed in the article by Charles T. Estes, "Speech and Human Relations in Industry," *The Quarterly Journal of Speech,* April, 1946, pp. 160–169.

considering matters of policy in a business corporation, and one working on problems in the administration of a college fraternity. Every member of each group read a portion out loud. We then talked about the main point—it takes two to make communication. We agreed that this was rather simple stuff and that we would try to talk with the possibility of by-passing in mind. We agreed, further, that no one of us would be insulted if asked to clarify or "talk some more" on any doubtful point. Nor would anyone feel hesitant about trying to get on the same wave length with anyone else. We gave each a small card with the inscription, "Are you on *his* communication line?"

What happened?

In each case the business of the meeting was slowed down. Only half as many items on the agenda could be covered. There was a certain amount of unfruitful wrangling about small points. Some members became tongue-tied in the face of so much freedom. Others became impatient with what seemed a waste of time, this trying to get to the speaker. The first sessions were always the worst. Most members felt comfortable only after the second or third.

And then we came upon something interesting. A man was being listened to. He found that others were actually waiting until he finished. He felt flattered in turn by the fact that another was trying to reach him rather than argue at him. He found himself trying to make his points so that his hearers would have less trouble with them. They were trying harder to read the cards he was putting on the table. The ornery member, normally so quick to doubt, stayed to question. The timid member found that the social pressure about the participation was all on his side.

We are inclined to think that the long-run results were worth the time and trouble.

The Purist's Dogma

In a number of experimental discussion groups generous enough to submit to such instruction there was a curious resistance to this seemingly obvious doctrine. I would be asked questions like these: Do you mean to say that a word doesn't have some definite, accurate meaning of its own regardless of the person who uses it? Isn't there a right or correct use for each word? If somebody fails to use a word exactly isn't he violating some rule in rhetoric or grammar?

How did these people come under the spell of the purist's dogma? Were they remembering some menacing drillmaster with a word list asking "What is the meaning of _____?" Or had they been badgered by vocabulary tests with entries like *glabrous heads: bald, over-sized, hairy, square, round; his stilted manner: irresolute, improper, cordial, stiffly formal* with instructions to circle the meaning? Or maybe they grew up when Alexander Woollcott was campaigning against certain current usage. He fought the use of "alibi" as a synonym for excuse; he wanted it saved for its "elsewhere" sense. He sneered when "flair" was used in the sense of knack or aptitude. He wanted it reserved for "capacity to detect." He and the traditional handbooks had a long list of such "reservations."

Or maybe they got their moorings from the pronouncements of Richard Grant White, who once said, "There is a misuse of words that can be justified by no authority, however great, and by no usage, however general." Or maybe they got no further in *Through the Looking Glass* than

"... How old did you say you were?"

Alice made a short calculation, and said, "Seven years and six months."

"Wrong!" Humpty Dumpty exclaimed triumphantly. *"You never said a word like it!"*

"I thought you meant 'How old are you?'" Alice explained.

"If I'd meant that, I'd have said it," said Humpty Dumpty.

Regardless of the source, they used this dogma as the basis for a theory of their own about the cause of misunderstanding. If a speaker didn't use a word correctly it was only natural if a listener who did know the exact meaning was misled. Just get people to use words in their right meaning and then everyone will understand everyone else.

Indeed, this might be a way—but how can we do it? Who

has the authority to declare *the* correct use and who has the time to learn it? There are more than 600,000 words in the Merriam-Webster unabridged dictionary and perhaps half as many more in the technical vocabularies of medicine, engineering, law, etc. And when the dictionary gives several meanings, which is *the* one? And just how is anyone going to curb those who, like Humpty Dumpty, would have their own ways with words:

"... Impenetrability! That's what I say!"

"Would you tell me please," said Alice, "what that means?"

"Now you talk like a reasonable child," said Humpty Dumpty, looking very much pleased. "I meant by 'impenetrability' that we've had enough of that subject, and it would be just as well if you'd mention what you mean to do next, as I suppose you don't mean to stop here all the rest of your life."

"That's a great deal to make one word mean," Alice said in a thoughtful tone.

"When I make a word do a lot of work like that," said Humpty Dumpty, "I always pay it extra."

And what is more crucial, why do we look at words alone? Are words not most often used with other words in phrases, clauses, sentences? May not the setting affect the word?

We tried to get around this ill-advised zeal for exactness by suggesting that a word might be compared with a tool which can be used in a variety of ways. Thus, a screwdriver might be designed to drive screws, but once available it can be used to stir paint, jimmy a tight window, or, lacking any other weapon, to defend oneself with. You might, if you wish, insist that the screw function is the "right" or "correct" one and that a pistol is a much more effective weapon. But your insistence will hardly stop me from using the screwdriver in these other ways if I find it convenient or necessary to do so. A carpenter with a full rack of tools may have good reason for reserving each for but one use but if some other purpose is served there is nothing in the nature of the tool which could prevent that other use. The desire for the restriction, then, is personal rather than functional.

Within limits, especially in technical disciplines, it is possible to standardize word usage. One is usually safe in assuming that the workers in specialized areas will conform to some established, stipulated word usages. In the military establishment and in legal affairs, for example, it is often possible as well as necessary to insist that particular words be used in particular ways.

Once outside the range of the specialist's interests, however, we are wise if we expect words to be used variously. A speaker's concern at any moment is not to use a word but to make a statement. In his eagerness to speak his piece he is more concerned with his continuous expression than with his total effect. If he happens to range outside his listeners' conventional usage, they will get nowhere lamenting his lexicographical heresy. And if they do not get to his usage they are likely to assume that he said what he never intended to.

We have come to see wisdom in this advice: Never mind what words mean. What did *he* mean?

It may take time to find out what a man means. It may demand a patient listening and questioning. It may be an unexciting effort. But it should help to bring people into an area of awareness which they are too often on the outside of. Mr. Justice Jackson's experience in a situation more momentous than anything we were exposed to adds to our confidence in the advice:

It was my experience with the Soviet lawyers at Nürnberg that the most important factor in collaboration with the Soviet was patiently and persistently to make sure, when a proposition is first advanced, that it is thoroughly understood and that both sides are using their words to express the same sense. When this was done, the Soviet lawyers kept their agreements with us quite as scrupulously as American lawyers would. They may or may not regard that as a compliment, but my intentions are good. But it was my experience that it took infinite patience with them, as they thought it took infinite patience with us, to get to a point where there was a real meeting of minds as distinguished from some textual abstract formula which both could accept only because concretely it meant nothing or meant different things to each. And I have sometimes wondered how much misunderstanding could have been avoided if arrangement between the two countries had not often been concluded so hurriedly, in the stress of events, that this time-consuming and dreary process of reducing generalities to concrete agreements was omitted.[10]

[10] Excerpt from address by Mr. Justice Robert H. Jackson at the Bar Dinner of the New York County Lawyers' Association, December 8, 1949.

Questions
for
Reflection
and
Discussion
Section Five

1. What are the most recent "god" and "devil" terms that have entered our vocabularies?
2. Chase notes that general semantics "is more a point of view than a rigorous scientific discipline." Do you agree? Can it ever be more?
3. Hayakawa discusses the "directive" use of language. What are the other uses of language that have been mentioned in this text?
4. What are the intrinsic dangers in using words for control? What about the alternatives?
5. A number of news commentators and politicians have popularized the concept of "empty rhetoric." How can this concept be explained from a semanticist's point of view?
6. What are some commonly used words that are especially susceptible to being misunderstood? Are Lee's suggestions for listening and clarifying realistic?

INTERPERSONAL CONTEXTS
SECTION SIX

We each become a different person as we move from one situation to another. This changing of roles is an essential facet of societal pressures. We behave differently in the college classroom than we do at a party; we communicate differently with our parents than with our peers; we may be more formal in the presence of strangers or people with whom we feel ill at ease.

Contextual variables concern the *who, where,* and *when* of communication. Understanding the expectancies of the situation may define our role for us and account for our varying communication behaviors.

Erving Goffman has been the leading analyst of the varieties of behavior in different settings. In the essay presented here he is concerned with what he calls "focused interaction," that is, "concerned with clusters of individuals who extend one another a special communication license and sustain a special type of mutual activity that can exclude others who are present in the situation." This type of communication can be contrasted to the unintentional communication always occurring when people are together. The "face engagement" is a special category of communication context that involves mutual engagement and is purposive in nature.

The article by Leon Festinger is a research-oriented report on the state of findings in informal settings. Some of the pressures that affect communication are identified with potential consequences cited. A series of interrelated hypotheses are reported.

The final article applies the psychological factors present in all interpersonal encounters to behaviors in small groups. Jon Eisenson, J. Jeffery Auer, and John V. Irwin have prepared an excellent synthesis of the research findings pertinent to the psychology of group discussion. Since the discussion group is often a critical testing ground of our communication capabilities, this theory has particular significance.

Erving Goffman
Face
Engagements

1. Civil Inattention

When persons are mutually present and not involved together in conversation or other focused interaction, it is possible for one person to stare openly and fixedly at others, gleaning what he can about them while frankly expressing on his face his response to what he sees—for example, the "hate stare" that a Southern white sometimes gratuitously gives to Negroes walking past him.[1] It is also possible for one person to treat others as if they were not there at all, as objects not worthy of a glance, let alone close scrutiny. Moreover, it is possible for the individual, by his staring or his "not seeing," to alter his own appearance hardly at all in consequence of the presence of the others. Here we have "nonperson" treatment; it may be seen in our society in the way we sometimes treat children, servants, Negroes, and mental patients.[2]

Currently, in our society, this kind of treatment is to be contrasted with the kind generally felt to be more proper in most situations, which will here be called "civil inattention." What seems to be involved is that one gives to another enough visual notice to demonstrate that one appreciates that the other is present (and that one admits openly to having seen him), while

Reprinted with permission of The Macmillan Company from *Behavior in Public Places* by Erving Goffman. © by The Free Press, a Division of The Macmillan Company, 1963.

[1] J. H. Griffin, *Black Like Me* (Boston: Houghton Mifflin, 1961), pp. 54, 128.
[2] *The Presentation of Self*, pp. 151–153.

at the next moment withdrawing one's attention from him so as to express that he does not constitute a target of special curiosity or design.

In performing this courtesy the eyes of the looker may pass over the eyes of the other, but no "recognition" is typically allowed. Where the courtesy is performed between two persons passing on the street, civil inattention may take the special form of eyeing the other up to approximately eight feet, during which time sides of the street are apportioned by gesture, and then casting the eyes down as the other passes—a kind of dimming of lights. In any case, we have here what is perhaps the slightest of interpersonal rituals, yet one that constantly regulates the social intercourse of persons in our society.

By according civil inattention, the individual implies that he has no reason to suspect the intentions of the others present and no reason to fear the others, be hostile to them, or wish to avoid them. (At the same time, in extending this courtesy he automatically opens himself up to a like treatment from others present.) This demonstrates that he has nothing to fear or avoid in being seen and being seen seeing, and that he is not ashamed of himself or of the place and company in which he finds himself. It will therefore be necessary for him to have a certain "directness" of eye expression. As one student suggests, the individual's gaze ought not to be guarded or averted or absent or defensively dramatic, as if "something were going on." Indeed, the exhibition of such deflected eye expressions may be taken as a symptom of some kind of mental disturbance.[3]

Civil inattention is so delicate an adjustment that we may expect constant evasion of the rules regarding it. Dark glasses, for example, allow the wearer to stare at another person without that other being sure that he is being stared at.[4] One person

[3] M. D. Riemer, "Abnormalities of the Gaze—A Classification," *Psychiatric Quarterly*, 29 (1955), 659–672.

[4] A notable observer of face-to-face conduct, the novelist William Sansom, disputes this point in "Happy Holiday Abroad," in *A Contest of Ladies* (London: Hogarth Press, 1956), p. 228:

Slowly he walked the length of the beach, pretending to saunter studying each bather sideways from behind his black spectacles. One would think

can look at another out of the corner of his eyes. The fan and parasol once served as similar aids in stealing glances, and in polite Western society the decline in use of these instruments in the last fifty years has lessened the elasticity of communication arrangements.[5] It should be added, too, that the closer the onlookers are to the individual who interests them, the more exposed his position (and theirs), and the more obligation they will feel to ensure him civil inattention. The further they are from him, the more license they will feel to stare at him a little.

In addition to these evasions of rules we also may expect frequent infractions of them. Here, of course, social class subculture and ethnic subculture introduce differences in patterns, and differences, too, in the age at which patterns are first employed.

The morale of a group in regard to this minimal courtesy of civil inattention—a courtesy that tends to treat those present merely as participants in the gathering and not in terms of other social characteristics—is tested whenever someone of very divergent social status or very divergent physical appearance is present. English middle-class society, for example, prides itself in giving famous and infamous persons the privilege of being civilly disattended in public, as when the Royal children manage to walk through a park with few persons turning around to

---

such dark glasses might conceal the inquisitive eye: but Preedy knew better, he knew they do the opposite, as soon as they are swivelled anywhere near the object it looks like a direct hit. You cannot appear to glance just beyond with your dark guns on.

[5] See P. Binder, *Muffs and Morals* (New York: Morrow, n.d.), Chap. 9, "Umbrellas, Walking-Sticks, and Fans," pp. 178–196. The author suggests, p. 193:

Another quizzing fan [in eighteenth-century England] had an inset of mica or gauze, so that a lady might cunningly use her fan as a lorgnette while her face appeared to be screened from view. This type of fan was intended for use at a risqué play, where modesty required some equivalent to the earlier facemask.

Successful devices of this kind must incorporate three features: the user must be able to look at the other, be able to give the appearance of not being ashamed of being seen by the other, and be able to conceal that he is in fact spying. Children in Shetland Isle primary schools handle visiting strangers with something like a fan—but one that fails in the last two counts—by shyly hiding their faces behind their two hands while peeking out at the visitor from a crack between two fingers.

stare. And in our own American society, currently, we know that one of the great trials of the physically handicapped is that in public places they will be openly stared at, thereby having their privacy invaded, while, at the same time, the invasion exposes their undesirable attributes.[6]

The act of staring is a thing which one does not ordinarily do to another human being; it seems to put the object stared at in a class apart. One does not talk to a monkey in a zoo, or to a freak in a sideshow—one only stares.[7]

An injury, as a characteristic and inseparable part of the body, may be felt to be a personal matter which the man would like to keep private. However, the fact of its visibility makes it known to anyone whom the injured man meets, including the stranger. A visible injury differs from most other personal matters in that anyone can deal with it regardless of the wish of the injured person; anyone can stare at the injury or ask questions about it, and in both cases communicate to and impose upon the injured person his feelings and evaluations. His action is then felt as an intrusion into privacy. It is the visibility of the injury which makes intrusion into privacy so easy. The men are likely to feel that they have to meet again and again people who will question and stare, and to feel powerless because they cannot change the general state of affairs. . . .[8]

Perhaps the clearest illustration both of civil inattention and of the infraction of this ruling occurs when a person takes advantage of another's not looking to look at him, and then finds that the object of his gaze has suddenly turned and caught the illicit looker looking. The individual caught out may then shift his gaze, often with embarrassment and a little shame, or he may carefully act as if he had merely been seen in the moment of observation that is permissible; in either case we see evidence of the propriety that should have been maintained.

[6] See the very useful paper by R. K. White, B. A. Wright, and T. Dembo, "Studies in Adjustment to Visible Injuries: Evaluation of Curiosity by the Injured," *Journal of Abnormal and Social Psychology*, 43 (1948), 13–28.

[7] *Ibid.*, p. 22.

[8] *Ibid.*, pp. 16–17.

To behave properly and to have the *right* to civil inattention are related: propriety on the individual's part tends to ensure his being accorded civil inattention; extreme impropriety on his part is likely to result in his being stared at or studiously not seen. Improper conduct, however, does not automatically release others from the obligation of extending civil inattention to the offender, although it often weakens it. In any case, civil inattention may be extended in the face of offensiveness simply as an act of tactfulness, to keep an orderly appearance in the situation in spite of what is happening.

Ordinarily, in middle-class society, failure to extend civil inattention to others is not negatively sanctioned in a direct and open fashion, except in the social training of servants and children, the latter especially in connection with according civil inattention to the physically handicapped and deformed. For examples of such direct sanctions among adults one must turn to despotic societies where glancing at the emperor or his agents may be a punishable offense,[9] or to the rather refined rules prevailing in some of our Southern states concerning how much of a look a colored male can give to a white female, over how much distance, before it is interpreted as a punishable sexual advance.[10]

Given the pain of being stared at, it is understandable that staring itself is widely used as a means of negative sanction, socially controlling all kinds of improper public conduct. Indeed it often constitutes the first warning an individual receives that he is "out of line" and the last warning that it is necessary to give him. In fact, in the case of those whose appearance tests to the limit the capacity of a gathering to proffer civil inattention, staring itself may become a sanction against staring. The autobiography of an ex-dwarf provides an illustration:

There were the thick-skinned ones, who stared like hill people come down to see a traveling show. There were the paper-peekers, the furtive kind who would withdraw blushing if you caught them

[9] R. K. Douglas, *Society in China* (London: Innes, 1894), p. 11.

[10] See, for example, the notable Webster-Ingram case reported November 12–13, 1952 (AP). In many societies in Africa and Asia, a similar taboo exists regarding glances that males cast females.

at it. There were the pitying ones, whose tongue clickings could almost be heard after they had passed you. But even worse, there were the chatterers, whose every remark might as well have been "How do you do, poor boy?" They said it with their eyes and their manners and their tone of voice.

I had a standard defense—a cold stare. Thus anesthetized against my fellow man, I could contend with the basic problem— getting in and out of the subway alive.[11]

2. The Structure of Face Engagements

When two persons are mutually present and hence engaged together in some degree of unfocused interaction, the mutual proffering of civil inattention—a significant form of unfocused interaction—is not the only way they can relate to one another. They can proceed from there to engage one another in focused interaction, the unit of which I shall refer to as a *face engagement* or an *encounter*.[12] Face engagements comprise all those instances of two or more participants in a situation joining each other openly in maintaining a single focus of cognitive and visual attention—what is sensed as a single *mutual activity*, entailing preferential communication rights. As a simple example —and one of the most common—when persons are present together in the same situation they may engage each other in a talk. This accreditation for mutual activity is one of the broadest of all statuses. Even persons of extremely disparate social positions can find themselves in circumstances where it is fitting

[11] H. Viscardi, Jr., *A Man's Stature* (New York: John Day, 1952), p. 70, as cited in B. A. Wright, *Physical Disability—A Psychological Approach* (New York: Harper & Bros., 1960), p. 214.

[12] The term "encounter," which is much the easier of the two to use, has some common-sense connotations that ought here to be ruled out. First, the term is sometimes used to refer to mediated, as well as to direct, contact between two persons, as when persons have correspondence with each other. Secondly, the term is sometimes used with an implication of there having been difficulty or trouble during the interaction, as in the phrase "run-in." Finally, the term is sometimes used to cover occasions which bring two persons into easy access to each other, regardless of how many times they may come together in a joint conversation during this time, as in the phrase, "I next encountered him at the Jones's party." I have attempted to consider the internal dynamics of encounters in "Fun in Games" in *Encounters*, pp. 17–81.

to impute it to one another. Ordinarily the status does not have a "latent phase" but obliges the incumbents to be engaged at that very moment in exercising their status.

Mutual activities and the face engagements in which they are embedded comprise instances of small talk, commensalism, love-making, gaming, formal discussion, and personal servicing (treating, selling, waitressing, and so forth). In some cases, as with sociable chats, the coming together does not seem to have a ready instrumental rationale. In other cases, as when a teacher pauses at a pupil's desk to help him for a moment with a problem he is involved in, and will be involved in after she moves on, the encounter is clearly a setting for a mutual instrumental activity, and this joint work is merely a phase of what is primarily an individual task.[13] It should be noted that while many face engagements seem to be made up largely of the exchange of verbal statements, so that conversational encounters can in fact be used as the model, there are still other kinds of encounters where no word is spoken. This becomes very apparent, of course, in the study of engagements among children who have not yet mastered talk, and where, incidentally, it is possible to see the gradual transformation of a mere physical contacting of another into an act that establishes the social relationship of jointly accrediting a face-to-face encounter.[14] Among adults, too, however, nonverbal encounters can be observed: the significant acts exchanged can be gestures[15] or even, as in board and card games, moves. Also, there are certain close comings-together over work tasks which give rise to a single focus of visual and cognitive attention and to intimately coordinated contributions, the order and kind of contribution being determined by shared appreciation of what the task-at-the-moment requires as the next act. Here, while no word of direction or sociability may be spoken, it will be understood that lack of

[13] Suggested by Arthur Stinchcombe.

[14] See, for example, the early study by A. Beaver, *The Initiation of Social Contacts by Preschool Children* (New York: Bureau of Publications, Teachers College, Columbia University, Child Development Monographs, No. 7, 1932), pp. 1–14.

[15] D. Efon, *Gesture and Environment* (New York: King's Crown Press, 1941), p. 38.

attention or coordinated response constitutes a breach in the mutual commitment of the participants.[16]

Where there are only two participants in a situation, an encounter, if there is to be one, will *exhaust* the situation, giving us a *fully-focused gathering*. With more than two participants, there may be persons officially present in the situation who are officially excluded from the encounter and not themselves so engaged. These unengaged[17] participants change the gathering into a *partly-focused* one. If more than three persons are present, there may be more than one encounter carried on in the same situation—a *multifocused* gathering. I will use the term *participation unit* to refer both to encounters and to unengaged participants; the term *bystander* will be used to refer to any individual present who is not a ratified member of the particular encounter

---

[16] The kind of intimate coordination consequent on involvement in the same task is nicely described in F. B. Miller, " 'Situational' Interactions—A Worthwhile Concept?" *Human Organization,* 17 (Winter, 1958–59), 37–47. After pointing out the differences between this kind of focused interaction and the kind necessarily involving speech or gestures, the writer does not, however, go on to consider the similarities, such as the fact that withdrawal of attention, or ineptness, can give rise to the same kind of corrective social control in both cases. A well-described illustration of a task activity as an engagement may be found in T. Burling, *Essays on Human Aspects of Administration* (New York State School of Industrial and Labor Relations, Cornell University, Bulletin 25, August, 1953), pp. 10–11:

> What is actually happening is that the changing needs of the patient, as they develop in the course of the operation, determine what everybody does. When a surgical team has worked long enough together to have developed true teamwork, each member has such a grasp of the total situation and of his role in it that the needs of the patient give unequivocal orders. A small artery is cut and begins to spurt. In a chain-of-command organization the surgeon would note this and say to the assistant, "Stop that bleeder." The assistant, in turn, would say to the surgical nurse, "Give me a hemostat," and thus, coordinated effort would be achieved. What actually happens is that the bleeder gives a simultaneous command to all three members of the team, all of whom have been watching the progress of the operation with equal attention. It says to the surgeon, "Get your hand out of the way until this is controlled." It says to the instrument nurse, "Get a hemostat ready," and it says to the assistant, "Clamp that off." This is the highest and most efficient type of cooperation known. It is so efficient that it looks simple and even primitive. It is possible only where every member of the team knows not only his own job thoroughly, but enough about the total job and that of each of the other members to see the relationship of what he does to everything else that goes on.

[17] An "unengaged" participant may of course be involved in a task or other main focus of attention and hence not be "disengaged" in the situation.

in question, whether or not he is currently a member of some other encounter.

In our society, face engagements seem to share a complex of properties, so that this class of social unit can be defined analytically, as well as by example.

An encounter is initiated by someone making an opening move, typically by means of a special expression of the eyes but sometimes by a statement or a special tone of voice at the beginning of a statement.[18] The engagement proper begins when this overture is acknowledged by the other, who signals back with his eyes, voice, or stance that he has placed himself at the disposal of the other for purposes of a mutual eye-to-eye activity—even if only to ask the initiator to postpone his request for an audience.

There is a tendency for the initial move and the responding "clearance" sign to be exchanged almost simultaneously, with all participants employing both signs, perhaps in order to prevent an initiator from placing himself in a position of being denied by others. Glances, in particular, make possible this effective simultaneity. In fact, when eyes are joined, the initiator's first glance can be sufficiently tentative and ambiguous to allow him to act as if no initiation has been intended, if it appears that his overture is not desired.

Eye-to-eye looks, then, play a special role in the communication life of the community, ritually establishing an avowed openness to verbal statements and a rightfully heightened mutual relevance of acts.[19] In Simmel's words:

[18] When the individual is socially subordinated to the one to whom he is about to initiate an encounter overture, he may be required to use a minimal sign so that the superior can easily continue to overlook it, or can respond to it at his own convenience. For example, *Esquire Etiquette* (New York: Lippincott, 1953), p. 24, in listing the habits of a good secretary, includes "waiting to be recognized, when she has stepped in to speak to you, before interrupting whatever you are doing." In such cases the fiction is maintained that the superordinate alone can initiate an engagement. The classic case here is the mythical butler who coughs discreetly so that his master will take note of his presence and allow him to deliver a message.

[19] In face engagements embodying a formal sports activity, opening moves may take other forms, as when boxers touch gloves, or swordsmen touch foils, in order to establish a sporting bracket or frame, as it were, around the oncoming encounter. Where participants know each other well, clearance signs

Of the special sense-organs, the eye has a uniquely sociological function. The union and interaction of individuals is based upon mutual glances. This is perhaps the most direct and purest reciprocity which exists anywhere. This highest psychic reaction, however, in which the glances of eye to eye unite men, crystallizes into no objective structure; the unity which momentarily arises between two persons is present in the occasion and is dissolved in the function. So tenacious and subtle is this union that it can only be maintained by the shortest and straightest line between the eyes, and the smallest deviation from it, the slightest glance aside, completely destroys the unique character of this union. No objective trace of this relationship is left behind, as is universally found, directly or indirectly, in all other types of associations between men, as, for example, in interchange of words. The interaction of eye and eye dies in the moment in which directness of the function is lost. But the totality of social relations of human beings, their self-assertion and self-abnegation, their intimacies and estrangements, would be changed in unpredictable ways if

---

may be taken for granted, and the initiator may pause slightly or in other ways slightly modify his opening action, as a courtesy, and then proceed as if clearance had been granted.

Interestingly enough, some face engagements are of the kind in which coordination of activity is typically embodied in the usual ritual brackets of eye-recognition and exchange of words, but which, under special circumstances, are carefully initiated, maintained, and terminated *without* usual verbal or gestural overlay. Thus, in many mental hospitals, patients expect to be able to call on *any* patient who is smoking for a light, regardless of how withdrawn or regressed the smoker may appear to be. The gestured request for a light seems to be invariably complied with, but very often the complier addresses himself to the technical task alone, declining any other kind of negotiation or business. A similar kind of deritualized encounter is found where a man holds a door open for a woman he does not know, under circumstances that could imply an overture or could bring home undesirable facts about the woman for being in the region; under such circumstances the male may be careful to proffer civil inattention even while nicely adjusting his physical behavior to the movements of the woman. Emily Post, *Etiquette* (New York: Funk and Wagnalls, 1937), p. 26, suggests a similar courtesy:

Lifting the hat is a conventional gesture of politeness shown to strangers only, not to be confused with bowing, which is a gesture used to acquaintances and friends. In lifting his hat, a gentleman merely lifts it slightly off his forehead—by the brim of a stiff hat or by the crown of a soft one—and replaces it; he does not smile or bow, nor does he even look at the object of his courtesy. No gentleman ever subjects a lady to his scrutiny or his apparent observation if she is a stranger.

*there occurred no glance of eye to eye. This mutual glance
between persons, in distinction from the simple sight or observation
of the other, signifies a wholly new and unique union between
them.*[20]

It is understandable, then, that an individual who feels he
has cause to be alienated from those around him will express
this through some "abnormality of the gaze," especially averting of the eyes.[21] And it is understandable, too, that an individual who wants to control others' access to him and the information he receives may avoid looking toward the person who is
seeking him out. A waitress, for example, may prevent a waiting customer from "catching her eye" to prevent his initiating
an order. Similarly, if a pedestrian wants to ensure a particular
allocation of the street relative to a fellow pedestrian, or if a
motorist wants to ensure priority of his line of proposed action
over that of a fellow motorist or a pedestrian, one strategy is to
avoid meeting the other's eyes and thus avoid cooperative
claims.[22] And where the initiator is in a social position requiring him to give the other the formal right to initiate all encounters, hostile and teasing possibilities may occur, of which
Melville's *White Jacket* gives us an example:

*But sometimes the captain feels out of sorts, or in ill-humour, or
is pleased to be somewhat capricious, or has a fancy to show a
touch of his omnipotent supremacy; or, peradventure, it has so*

[20] From his *Soziologie*, cited in R. E. Park and E. W. Burgess, *Introduction
to the Science of Sociology* (2nd. ed.; Chicago: University of Chicago Press,
1924), p. 358. An interesting statement of some of the things that can be
conveyed through eye-to-eye contact alone is given by Ortega y Gasset in his
Man and People (New York: Norton, 1957), pp. 115–117. He implies that there
is a whole vocabulary of glances, describing several of them.

[21] M. D. Riemer, "The Averted Gaze," *Psychiatric Quarterly*, 23 (1949),
108–115. It would be very interesting to examine techniques employed by the
blind and the dumb to provide functional substitutes for clearance cues and
other eye contributions to the structure of face-to-face communication.

[22] The general point behind this example has been made by T. C. Schelling
in his analysis of the bargaining power of the individual who can convincingly
commit himself to a line of action, in this case by communicating his inability to
receive demands and threats through messages See Schelling's "An Essay on
Bargaining." *The American Economic Review*, 46 (1956), 281–306, esp. pp.
294–295.

happened that the first lieutenant has, in some way, piqued or offended him, and he is not unwilling to show a slight specimen of his dominion over him, even before the eyes of all hands; at all events, only by some one of these suppositions can the singular circumstance be accounted for, that frequently Captain Claret would pertinaciously promenade up and down the poop, purposely averting his eye from the first lieutenant, who would stand below in the most awkward suspense, waiting the first wink from his superior's eye.

"Now I have him!" he must have said to himself, as the captain would turn toward him in his walk; "now's my time!" and up would go his hand to his cap; but, alas! the captain was off again; and the men at the guns would cast sly winks at each other as the embarrassed lieutenant would bite his lips with suppressed vexation.

Upon some occasions this scene would be repeated several times, till at last Captain Claret, thinking that in the eyes of all hands his dignity must by this time be pretty well bolstered, would stalk toward his subordinate, looking him full in the eyes; whereupon up goes his hand to the cap front, and the captain, nodding his acceptance of the report, descends from his perch to the quarter-deck.[23]

As these various examples suggest, mutual glances ordinarily must be withheld if an encounter is to be avoided, for eye contact opens one up for face engagement. I would like to add, finally, that there is a relationship between the use of eye-to-eye glances as a means of communicating a request for initiation of an encounter, and other communication practices. The more clearly individuals are obliged to refrain from staring directly at others, the more effectively will they be able to attach special significance to a stare, in this case, a request for an encounter. The rule of civil inattention thus makes possible, and "fits" with, the clearance function given to looks into others' eyes. The rule similarly makes possible the giving of a special function to "prolonged" holding of a stranger's glance, as when

[23] Herman Melville, *White Jacket* (New York: Grove Press, n.d.), p. 276.

unacquainted persons who had arranged to meet each other manage to discover one another in this way.[24]

Once a set of participants have avowedly opened themselves up to one another for an engagement, an eye-to-eye ecological huddle tends to be carefully maintained, maximizing the opportunity for participants to monitor one another's mutual perceivings.[25] The participants turn their minds to the same subject matter and (in the case of talk) their eyes to the same speaker, although of course this single *focus* of attention can shift within limits from one topic to another and from one speaker or target to another.[26] A shared definition of the situation comes to pre-

[24] Evelyn Hooker, in an unpublished Copenhagen Address, August 14, 1961, titled "The Homosexual Community," suggests: "It is said by homosexuals that if another catches and holds the glance, one need know nothing more about him to know that he is one of them."

[25] This may not be a universal practice. According to an early report on the Northwest Coast Amazons:

When an Indian talks he sits down, no conversation is ever carried on when the speakers are standing unless it be a serious difference of opinion under discussion; nor, when he speaks, does the Indian look at the person addressed, any more than the latter watches the speaker. Both look at some outside objects. This is the attitude also of the Indian when addressing more than one listener, so that he appears to be talking to some one not visibly present.

(T. Whiffen, *The North-West Amazons* [London: Constable, 1915], p. 254.) In our own society, however, we can readily understand that when convicts are forbidden to talk to one another but desire to do so, they can effectively shield their joint involvement by talking without moving their lips and without looking at each other. See, for example, J. Phelan, *The Underworld* (London: Harrap, 1953), pp. 7–8 and 13. We can also understand that when technical considerations prevent eye-to-eye accessibility (as in the case of a surgical nurse receiving orders from a surgeon who must not take his eyes from the surgical field), considerable discipline will be required of the recipient if communication is to be maintained. Finally, we can appreciate that the blind will have to learn to act as if the speaker is being watched, even though in fact the blind recipient could as well direct his sightless gaze anywhere. In the latter connection see H. Chevigny, *My Eyes Have a Cold Nose* (New Haven: Yale University Press, 1962). p. 51.

[26] Cf. R. F. Bales *et al.*, "Channels of Communication in Small Groups," *American Sociologic Review,* 16 (1951), 461–468, p. 461:

The conversation generally proceeded so that one person talked at a time, and all members in the particular group were attending the same conversation. In this sense, these groups might be said to have a "single focus," that is, they did not involve a number of conversations proceeding at the same time, as one finds at a cocktail party or in a hotel lobby. The single focus

vail. This includes agreement concerning perceptual relevancies and irrelevancies, and a "working consensus," involving a degree of mutual considerateness, sympathy, and a muting of opinion differences.[27] Often a group atmosphere develops—

---

is probably a limiting condition of fundamental importance in the generalizations reported here.

To this the caution should be added that the multiple focuses found in places like hotel lobbies would occur simultaneously with unfocused interaction.

[27] Hence, as Oswald Hall has suggested to me, when closeness and sympathy are to be held to a minimum, as when a butler talks to a house guest, or an enlisted man is disciplined by an officer, eye-to-eye communion may be avoided by the subordinate holding his eyes stiffly to the front. An echo of the same factor is to be found even in mediated conversation, where servants are obliged to answer the telephone by saying "Mrs. So-and-So's residence" instead of "Hello."

This tendency for eye-to-eye looks to involve sympathetic accommodation is nicely suggested in Trotsky's description of street disturbances during the "five days" in *The History of the Russian Revolution*, trans. Max Eastman (New York: Simon and Schuster, 1936), 1, 109:

> In spite of the auspicious rumors about the Cossacks, perhaps slightly exaggerated, the crowd's attitude toward the mounted men remains cautious. A horseman sits high above the crowd; his soul is separated from the soul of the demonstrator by the four legs of his beast. A figure at which one must gaze from below always seems more significant, more threatening. The infantry are beside one on the pavement—closer, more accessible. The masses try to get near them, look into their eyes, surround them with their hot breath. A great rôle is played by women workers in the relation between workers and soldiers. They go up to the cordons more boldly than men, take hold of the rifles, beseech, almost command: "Put down your bayonets —join us." The soldiers are excited, ashamed, exchange anxious glances, waver; someone makes up his mind first, and the bayonets rise guiltily above the shoulders of the advancing crowd. The barrier is opened, a joyous and grateful "Hurrah!" shakes the air.

A more formalized version of the same tendency is described as obtaining among the Bedouins. See A. Musīl, *The Manners and Customs of the Rwala Bedouins* (New York: American Geographical Society, Oriental Explorations and Studies Studies No. 6, 1928), p. 455:

> A salutation, if returned, is a guarantee of safety in the desert, *as-salâm salâme*. If a stranger travels unaccompanied by a ḥawi through the territory of a tribe unknown to him and salutes someone—be it only a little girl— and is saluted in return, he may be reasonably certain that he will be neither attacked nor robbed, for even a little girl with all her kin will protect him. Should the fellow tribesmen of the girl attack and rob him, mâḥûd, he has only to ask the help of her kinsfolk, who must take his part. The girl is the best witness: "A traveler saluted me at such and such a place, of about such and such an age, dressed thus and so, riding on a she-camel," of which she also gives a description. Frequently even an enemy saves himself in this manner when hotly pursued. Realizing that he cannot escape, he suddenly changes his course, returns by a roundabout

what Bateson has called ethos.[28] At the same time, a heightened
sense of moral responsibility for one's acts also seems to develop.[29] A "we-rationale" develops, being a sense of the single

way to the camp of his pursuers, salutes a child, and, taking its hand, allows
himself to be led to the tent of the parents. The adult Bedouins, being
more cautious, do not answer at once when saluted by a man they do
not know. Especially if two or three are riding together and approach a
camp at night, the guard replies to their salute thus:
"Ye are outlawed; I shall not return your salutation; tarâkom mwaṣṣedîn
w-lâ 'alejkom radd as-salâm." For an outlawed one, mwassed, is treated like
an enemy to whom a salutation is of no use whatever.
Because of the obligation of considerateness among members of an engagement, and especially between a speaker and the particular member to whom
he addresses his remarks, individuals sometimes "talk into the air" or mutter,
pointedly addressing their remarks to no one, or to a child or pet. The person
for whose benefit the remarks are intended may thus be half forced into the
role of overhearer, allowing greater liberties to be taken with him than could
be comfortably managed in direct address.
[28] G. Bateson, Naven (Cambridge: Cambridge University Press, 1936), pp.
119–120:
When a group of young intellectual English men or women are talking and
joking together wittily and with a touch of light cynicism, there is
established among them for the time being a definite tone of appropriate
behavior. Such specific tones of behavior are in all cases indicative of an
ethos. They are expressions of a standardised system of emotional attitudes.
In this case the men have temporarily adopted a definite set of sentiments
towards the rest of the world, a definite attitude towards reality, and they
will joke about subjects which at another time they would treat with
seriousness. If one of the men suddenly intrudes a sincere or realist remark
it will be received with no enthusiasm—perhaps with a moment's silence and
a slight feeling that the sincere person has committed a solecism. On another
occasion the same group of persons may adopt a different ethos; they may
talk realistically and sincerely. Then if the blunderer makes a flippant joke
it will fall flat and feel like a solecism.
[29] And so we find that bringing someone into a face engagement can be
used by the initiator as a form of social control, as when a teacher stops a
student's sotto voce comments by looking him in the eye and saying, "What
did you say?" or when failure to accord civil inattention is handled as Norman
Mailer describes in his novel The Deer Park (New York: Signet Books, 1957)
p. 212:
Beda [a celebrity] looked at a woman who had been staring at him
curiously, and when he winked, she turned away in embarrassment. "Oh
God, the tourists," he said.
Interestingly enough, since joint participation in an encounter allows participants
to look fully at each other—in fact, enjoins this to a degree—we find that one
strategy employed by an individual when he is caught out by the person he is
staring at is to act as if this staring were the first move in an overture to
engagement, thereby ratifying and legitimating the failure to accord civil
inattention.

thing that we the participants are avowedly doing together at the time. Further, minor ceremonies are likely to be employed to mark the termination of the engagement and the entrance and departure of particular participants (should the encounter have more than two members). These ceremonies, along with the social control exerted during the encounter to keep participants "in line," give a kind of ritual closure to the mutual activity sustained in the encounter. An individual will therefore tend to be brought all the way into an ongoing encounter or kept altogether out of it.[30]

Engagements of the conversational kind appear to have, at least in our society, some spatial conventions. A set of individuals caused to sit more than a few feet apart because of furniture arrangements will find difficulty in maintaining informal talk;[31] those brought within less than a foot and a half of each other will find difficulty in speaking directly to each other, and may talk at an off angle to compensate for the closeness.[32]

---

[30] One well-established way of confirming and consolidating a leave-taking is for the leave-taker to move away physically from the other or others. In places like Shetland Isle this can cause a problem when two persons pause for a moment's sociability and then find that their directions of movement do not diverge sharply. If the two persons walk at a normal pace, they find themselves attempting to close out the encounter while still having easy physical access to each other. Sometimes one individual offers an excuse to break into a run; sometimes, even if it takes him out of his way, he may take a path diverging sharply from that taken by his erstwhile coparticipant.

[31] R. Sommer, "The Distance for Comfortable Conversation: A Further Study," *Sociometry*, 25 (1962), 111–116. See also his "Studies in Personal Space," *Sociometry*, 22 (1959), 247–260.

[32] See E. T. Hall, *The Silent Language* (New York: Doubleday, 1959), pp. 204–206. In B. Schaffner, ed., *Group Processes*, Transactions of the Fourth (1957) Conference (New York: Josiah Macy, Jr. Foundation, 1959), p. 184, R. Birdwhistell comments as follows in a symposium discussion:

It appears that Americans, when standing face to face, stand about arm's length from each other. When they stand side by side, the distance demanded is much less. When " middle majority Americans" stand closer than this in a face-to-face position they will either gradually separate or come toward each other and begin to emit signs of irritation. However, if they are put in a situation in which they are not required to interact—say on a streetcar— they can stand quite close, even to the point of making complete contact.

The amount of this territory seems to vary culturally. So, there can be a situation where two or three ethnic groups occupy different territories, that is, varying amounts of personal space. For example, put together a

In brief, then, encounters are organized by means of a special set of acts and gestures comprising communication about communicating. As a linguist suggests:

There are messages primarily serving to establish, to prolong, or to discontinue communication, to check whether the channel works ("Hello, do you hear me?"), to attract the attention of the interlocutor or to confirm his continued attention ("Are you listening?" or in Shakespearean diction, "Lend me your ears!"— and on the other end of the wire "Um-hum").[33]

Everyday terms refer to different aspects of encounters. "Cluster," "knot," "conversational circle"—all highlight the physical aspects, namely, a set of persons physically close together and facially oriented to one another, their backs toward those who are not participants. "Personal encounter" refers to the unit in terms of the opportunity it provides or enforces for some kind of social intimacy. In the literature, the term "the interaction" is sometimes used to designate either the activity occurring within the cluster at any one moment or the total activity occurring from the moment the cluster forms to the moment at which it officially disbands. And, of course, where spoken messages are exchanged, especially under informal circumstances, the terms "chat," "a conversation," or "a talk" are employed.

It may be noted that while all participants share equally in

Southeastern European Jew (who occupies about half the area of personal space) and a middle class American and a high degree of irritation results, particularly if the middle class American keeps drifting around to the side, in order not to be insulting, and the Southeastern European Jewish man tries to move around to get face-to-face relationship. You get an actual dance, which very often turns into what is practically a fight.

From all of this it follows that among persons arranged in a discussion circle, persons adjacent to each other may tend not to address remarks to each other, except to pass side comments, since a voice full enough to embrace the circle would be too full for the distance between them. For experimental evidence, see B. Steinzor, "The Spatial Factor in Face to Face Discussion Groups," *Journal of Abnormal and Social Psychology,* 45 (1950), 552–555.

[33] R. Jakobson, "Closing Statement: Linguistics and Poetics," in T. A. Sebeok, ed., *Style in Language* (New York: Wiley, 1960), p. 355. Cf. the concept of metacommunication in J. Ruesch and G. Bateson, *Communication* (New York: Norton, 1951).

the rights and obligations described, there are some rights that may be differentially distributed within an encounter. Thus, in spoken encounters, the right to listen is one shared by all, but the right to be a speaker may be narrowly restricted, as, for example, in stage performances and large public meetings. Similarly, children at the dinner table are sometimes allowed to listen but forbidden to talk;[34] if not forbidden to talk, they may be "helped out" and in this way denied the communication courtesy of being allowed to finish a message for themselves.[35] And in other engagements, one category of participant may be allowed to say only "Yes, sir," or "No, sir," or restricted to the limited signalling that a modulation of applause allows. The differential rights of players vis-à-vis kibitzers in games provide another example.

When the communication of a face engagement has been established between two or more individuals, the resulting state of ratified mutual participation can last for varying periods. When a clearly defined task is involved, the engagement may last for hours. When no apparent work or recreational task is involved, and what is perceived as sociability alone holds the participants, certain durations seem to be favored. The contact may be very brief, as brief, in fact, as the opening meeting of eyes itself. In our own middle-class society there are "chats," where two individuals pause in their separate lines of action for what both recognize to be a necessarily brief period of time; there are greetings, whereby communion is established and maintained long enough for the participants to exchange brief interpersonal rituals; and, briefest of all, there are recognitional or "friendly" glances. (Of course, a recognitional glance may be merely the first interchange in an extended greeting, and a greeting merely the opening phase of a chat, but these extensions of coparticipation are not always found.) Except for the ritual of civil inattention, the mere exchange of friendly glances is perhaps the most frequent of our interpersonal rituals.

Encounters of an obligatory kind are linked to the world of

[34] J. H. S. Bossard, "Family Modes of Expression," *American Sociological Review*, 10 (1945), 226–237, p. 229.
[35] *Ibid.*

domestic convivial occasions. In some social circles, a guest entering a party has a right to be greeted by the host or hostess and conveyed into the proceedings in visible contact with the authorizing person, this encounter thereby legitimating and celebrating the newcomer's participation in the occasion. His departure may be marked with the same kind of ceremony, officially bringing his participation to an end.[36] The occasion then closes in and over the place he has left, and if he should have to return for something he has forgotten, embarrassment is likely to be felt, especially if the ethos of the occasion has changed, and especially if marked ceremonial attention had been given his leave-taking.[37]

Encounters, of course, tend to be taken as an expression of the state of a social relationship. And, as will be considered later, to the degree that contact is practical, it may have to be made so as not to deny the relationship.[38] Further, each engagement tends to be initiated with an amount of fuss appropriate to the period of lapsed contact, and terminated with the amount appropriate to the assumed period of separation. There results a kind of tiding over, and a compensation for the diminishing effects of separation.[39] At a party, then, a version of Mrs. Post's ruling is likely to prevail:

[36]Here there is an interesting difference between Anglo-American and French custom; in France, the entering or departing person ratifies his entrance or departure not only through contact with the person managing the occasion but often also by a hand-shaking engagement with some or all of the other guests present.

[37] The same sort of embarrassment occurs when a member of an organization, who has been given a farewell party and gift to mark a termination of his membership and to set the stage for the group's developing a new relation to a substitute, then finds that he must remain with or return to the organization. He finds that the group has "worked through" his membership, leaving him present but socially not there.

[38] Face engagements, of course, are not the only kinds of contact carrying ceremonial functions. Gifts, greeting cards, and salutatory telegrams and telephone calls also serve in this way. Each social circle seems to develop norms as to how frequently and extensively these ought to be employed to affirm relationships among geographically separated people, depending on the costs faced by each group in using these several devices. Just as friends at the same social party are obliged to spend at least a few moments chatting together, so a husband out of town on business may be considered "in range" and be obliged to telephone home in the evening.

[39] E. Goffman, "On Face-Work," *Psychiatry*, 18 (1955), 229.

In meeting the same person many times within an hour or so, one does not continue to bow after the second, or at most third meeting. After that one either looks away or merely smiles.[40]

The same mere smile between the same two persons newly coming within range of each other in a foreign country may constitute a grievous affront to their relationship.

I have suggested that a face engagement is a sufficiently clear-cut unit that an individual typically must either be entirely within it or entirely outside it. This is nicely borne out by the trouble caused when a person attempts to be half-in and half-out. None the less, there are communication arrangements that seem to lie halfway between mere copresence and full scale coparticipation, one of which should be mentioned here. When two persons walk silently together down the street or doze next to each other at the beach, they may be treated by others as "being together," and are likely to have the right to break rather abruptly into spoken or gestured communication, although they can hardly be said to sustain continuously a mutual activity. This sense of being together constitutes a kind of lapsed verbal encounter, functioning more as a means of excluding nonmembers than as a support for sustained focused interaction among the participants.[41]

Persons who can sustain lapsed encounters with one another are in a position to avoid the problem of "safe supplies" during spoken encounters—the need to find a sufficient supply of inoffensive things to talk about during the period when an official state of talk prevails. Thus, in Shetland Isle, when three or four women were knitting together, one knitter would say a word, it would be allowed to rest for a minute or two, and then another knitter would provide an additional comment. In the same manner a family sitting around its kitchen fire would look into the flames and intersperse replies to statements with periods of observation of the fire. Shetland men used for the same purpose

---

[40] Emily Post, *Etiquette, op. cit.,* p. 29.

[41] Being "with" someone at a given moment is to be distinguished from the party relationship of having "come with" someone to the occasion, the latter representing a preferential claim as to whom one will leave with, be loyal to, and the like.

the lengthy pauses required for the proper management of their pipes.

To these comments on the structure of engagements I would like to add a brief remark on the information that encounters convey to the situation as a whole. In an earlier section, it was suggested that an individual divulges things about himself by his mere presence in a situation. In the same way, he gives off information about himself by virtue of the encounters in which others do or do not see him. Involvement in focused interaction therefore inevitably contributes to unfocused interaction conveying something to all who are present in the situation at large.

In public places in our society, what is conveyed by being in or out of encounters differs appreciably according to sex and the periods of the week. Morning and lunchtime are times when anyone can appear alone almost anywhere without this giving evidence of how the person is faring in the social world; dinner and other evening activities, however, provide unfavorable information about unaccompanied participants, especially damaging in the case of female participants. Weekend nights, and ceremonial occasions such as Thanksgiving, Christmas, and, especially, New Year's Eve, are given special weight in this connection, being times when an unengaged individual in a semipublic place may feel very much out of place.

It should be added, finally, that in so far as others judge the individual socially by the company he is seen in, for him to be brought into an engagement with another is to be placed in the position of being socially identified as the other is identified.

3. Accessibility

In every situation, those present will be obliged to retain some readiness for potential face engagements. (This readiness has already been suggested as one way in which situational presence is expressed.) There are many important reasons why the individual is usually obliged to respond to requests for face engagements. In the first place, he owes this to himself because often it will be through such communication that his own interests can be served, as when a stranger accosts him to tell him he has dropped something, or that the bridge is out. For similar reasons he owes this accessibility to others present, and to persons not present for whom those present may serve as a relay. (The need for this collective solidarity is heightened in urban living, which brings individuals of great social distance within range of one another.) Further, as previously suggested, participation in a face engagement can be a sign of social closeness and relatedness; when this opportunity to participate is proffered by another, it ought not to be refused, for to decline such a request is to reject someone who has committed himself to a sign of desiring contact. More than this, refusal of an offer implies that the refuser rejects the other's claim to membership in the gathering and the social occasion in which the gathering occurs. It is therefore uncommon for persons to deny these obligations to respond.

Although there are good reasons why an individual should keep himself available for face engagements, there are also good reasons for him to be cautious of this.

In allowing another to approach him for talk, the individual may find that he has been inveigled into a position to be attacked and assaulted physically. In societies where public safety is not firmly established, especially in places such as the desert, where the traveler is for long periods of time remote from any source of help, the danger that a face engagement may be a prelude to assault becomes appreciable, and extensive avoidance practices or greetings at a distance tend to be employed.[42] Here, of course, the "physical safety" component of civic order and the communication component overlap. But apart from this extreme, we should see that when an individual opens himself up to talk with another, he opens himself up to pleadings, commands, threats, insult, and false information. The mutual considerateness characteristic of face engagements reinforces these dangers subjecting the individual

---

[42] The case of desert contacts is vividly described in a short story by Paul Bowles, "The Delicate Prey," in *The Delicate Prey and Other Stories* (New York: Random House, 1950), pp. 277–289, esp. pp. 279–280.

to the possibility of having his sympathy and tactfulness exploited, and causing him to act against his own interests.

Further, words can act as a "relationship wedge"; that is, once an individual has extended to another enough consideration to hear him out for a moment, some kind of bond of mutual obligation is established, which the initiator can use in turn as a basis for still further claims; once this new extended bond is granted, grudgingly or willingly, still further claims for social or material indulgence can be made. Hence, in one important example, a man and a woman can start out as strangers and, if conditions are right, progress from an incidental encounter to matrimony. We need only trace back the history of many close relationships between adults to find that something was made of face engagements when it need not have been. Of course, persons usually form "suitable" relationships, not allowing casual encounters to be a wedge to something else. But there is sufficient slippage in systems of conviviality segregation to give mothers concern about their daughters and to provide one of the basic romantic themes of light fiction.

I have suggested some reasons why individuals, at least in our own society, are obliged to keep themselves available for face engagements, and I have also suggested some of the dangers persons open themselves up to in so doing. These two opposing tendencies are reconciled in society, apparently, by a kind of implicit contract or gentleman's agreement that persons sustain: given the fact that the other will be under some obligation, often unpleasant, to respond to overtures, potential initiators are under obligation to stay their own desires. A person can thus make himself available to others in the expectation that they will restrain their calls on his availability and not make him pay too great a price for his being accessible. Their right to initiate contact is checked by their duty to take his point of view and initiate contact with him only under circumstances that he will easily see to be justified; in short, they must not "abuse" their privileges.

This implicit communication contract (and the consequence of breaking it) receive wide mythological representation, as in our own "cry wolf" tale. Understandably, infractions of the rule against undesired overture do cause some anxiety, for the recipient must either accede to the request or demonstrate to himself and the others present that his availability for face engagements was not part of his character but a false pose, to be maintained only when no price was involved in maintaining it.

In noting the implicit contract that makes persons present delicately accessible and inaccessible to each other, we can go on to note a basic margin of appetite and distaste to be found in social situations. The reasons why individuals are obliged to restrain themselves from making encounter overtures provide many of the reasons why they might want to do so. And the obligation to be properly accessible often covers a desire to be selectively quite unavailable. Hence, many public and semi-public places, such as cocktail lounges and club cars, acquire a special tone and temper, a special piquancy, that blurs the communication lines, giving each participant some desire to encroach where perhaps he does not have a right to go, and to keep from being engaged with others who perhaps have a right to engage him. Each individual, then, is not only involved in maintaining the basic communication contract, but is also likely to be involved in hopes, fears, and actions that bend the rules if they do not actually break them.

It has been suggested, then, that as a general rule the individual is obliged to make himself available for encounters even though he may have something to lose by entering them, and that he may well be ambivalent about this arrangement. Here mental patients provide a lesson in reverse, for they can show us the price that is paid for declining to make oneself available and force us to see that there are reasons why someone able to be accessible should be willing to pay the price of remaining inaccessible.

In brief, a patient who declines to respond to overtures is said to be "out of contact," and this state is often felt to be full evidence that he is very sick indeed, that he is, in fact, cut off from all contact with the world around him. In the case of some "organic" patients, this generalization from inaccessibility appears quite valid, as it does with certain "functionals." There are patients, for example, who, before admission had progressively withdrawn from responding to such things as the telephone and doorbell and, once in the hospital, decline all staff overtures for engagement, this being but one instance of a general withdrawal of concern for the life about them.

In the case of other patients, however, refusal to enter proffered engagements cannot be taken as a sign of unconcern for the gathering, but rather as a sign of alienation based on active feelings such as fear, hate, and contempt, each of which can be understandable in the circumstances, and each of which can allow the patient to show a nice regard for other situational proprieties.

Thus, there are patients who coldly stare through direct efforts to bring them into a state of talk, declining all staff overtures however seductive, teasing, or intensive who will none the less allow themselves face engagements carefully initiated and terminated by themselves without the usual courtesies. Still other patients who are out of contact to most persons on the ward will engage in self-initiated encounters with a small select number of others by means of coded messages, foreign language, whispering, or the exchange of written statements. Some patients, unwilling to engage in spoken encounters with anyone will be ready to engage in other types of encounters, such as dancing or card playing. Similarly, I knew a patient who often blankly declined greetings extended him by fellow-patients on the grounds, but who could be completely relied upon not to miss a cue when performing the lead in a patient dramatic production.

As might then be expected, a patient declining to conduct himself properly in regard to face engagements might be well conducted in regard to unfocused interaction.[43] One illustration was provided by a patient I observed, a young woman of thirty-two, who at one point in her "illness" was ready to han-

---

[43] Manner books contain the same suggestion. See, for example, *Good Manners* (New York: L. M. Garrity and Co., 1929), p. 31:

Many people whose "acting" manners are good have poor "talking" manners. They may be gossipy or they may tell off-color stories; or say things that hurt people's feelings, or they may chatter on so continuously that no one else can get a word in "edgewise."

dle her dress and deportment with all the structured modesty that is required of her sex, while at the same time her language was foul. During another phase of her illness, this patient, in the company of a friendly nurse, enjoyed shopping trips to the neighboring town, during which she and her keeper got wry pleasure from the fact that the patient was "passing" as a "normal" person. Had anyone made an opening statement to the patient, however, the masquerade would have been destroyed, for this was a time when the patient was mute in all verbal interaction or, at best, spoke with very great pressure.

A touching illustration of the same difference in capacity for focused and unfocused interaction was provided at Central Hospital by patients who were fearful and anxious of their whole setting, but who none the less made elaborate efforts to show that they were still what they had been before coming to the hospital and that they were in poised, business-like control of the situation. One middle-aged man walked busily on the grounds with the morning newspaper folded under one arm and a rolled umbrella hooked over the other, wearing an expression of being late for an appointment. A young man, having carefully preserved his worn grey flannel suit, bustled similarly from one place he was not going to another. Yet both men stepped out of the path of any approaching staff person, and painfully turned their heads away whenever someone proffered an exchange or greeting of some kind, for both employed the tack of being mute with many of the persons whom they met. The management of a front of middle-class orientation in the situation, in these circumstances, was so precarious and difficult that (for these men) it apparently represented the day's major undertaking.[44] In other cases, of course, it is not fear that seems to account for the inaccessibility of otherwise properly mannered persons, but rather hostility: to acknowledge a staff overture is partly to acknowledge the legitimacy of the staff

[44] Just as it is evident that the individual may comply with rules regarding unfocused interaction while failing to comply with regulations regarding focused interaction, so cases can be found of mental patients who dress in a spectacularly improper manner but who are none the less ready to be socially tractable as conversationalists. Here are two pieces of evidence in favor of distinguishing conceptually between focused and unfocused interaction.

person making the overture, and if he is a serious worthy person then so must be his implied contention that the individual with whom he is initiating contact, namely, oneself, is a mental patient properly confined to a mental ward. To strengthen one's feeling that one is really sane, it may thus seem reasonable to disdain encounters in which the opposite will be assumed—even though this results in exactly the kind of conduct, namely, inaccessibility, that confirms the hospital's view that one is mentally ill.

A final point about accessibility should be mentioned. As previously suggested, conversational engagements are often carried out as involvements subordinated to some other business at hand, just as side involvements, such as smoking, are often carried out as activities subordinated to a conversational main involvement. The question arises as to the limits placed upon this coexistence in middle-class society. There are, for example, records of middle-class Navy personnel postponing a visit to the "head" until others have left so as not to have to defecate while being accessible to others for talk. I have also been told by a middle-class informant that she was always uneasy about painting her toenails while in the presence of her husband, since the painting involved too much attention to leave her sufficiently respectful of the talk.

4. Leave-Taking Rights

Just as the individual is obliged not to exploit the accessibility of others (else they have to pay too large a price for their obligation to be accessible), so he is obliged to release those with whom he is engaged, should it appear, through conventional cues, that they desire to be released (else they have to pay too great a price for their tact in not openly taking leave of him). A reminder of these rules of leave-taking can be found in elementary school classrooms where leave-taking practices are still being learned, as, for example, when a teacher, having called a student to her desk in order to correct his exercise book, may have to turn him around and gently propel him back to his seat in order to terminate the interview.

The rights of departure owed the individual, and the rule of tactful leave-taking owed the remaining participants, can be in conflict with each other. This conflict is often resolved, in a way very characteristic of communication life, by persons active in different roles tacitly cooperating to ease leave-taking. Thus, business etiquette provides the following lesson:

> on when to go—*your exit cues are many. They range from clear-cut closing remarks, usually in the form of a "thank you for coming in," to a vacant and preoccupied stare. But in any case they should come from the interviewer. It should not be necessary for him to stand, abruptly; you should have been able to feel the good-bye in the air far enough in advance to gather up your gear, slide forward to the edge of your chair and launch into a thank-you speech of your own. Nor should it be necessary to ask that embarrassing question, "Am I taking too much of your time?"; if that thought crosses your mind, it's time to go.*[45]

In fact, persons can become so accustomed to being helped out by the very person who creates the need for help, that when cooperation is not forthcoming they may find they have no way of handling the incident. Thus, some mental patients may characteristically hold a staff person in an encounter regardless of how many hints the latter provides that termination ought now to occur. As the staff person begins to walk away, the patient may follow along until the locked door is reached, and even then the patient may try to accompany him. At such times the staff person may have to hold back the patient forcibly, or precipitously tear himself away, demonstrating not merely that the patient is being left in the lurch, but also that the staff show of concern for the patient is, in some sense, only a show. Pitchmen and street stemmers initiate a similar process; they rely on the fact that the accosted person will be willing to agree to a purchase in order not to have to face being the sort of person who walks away from an encounter without being officially released.

[45] *Esquire Etiquette, op. cit.,* p. 59.

Leon Festinger
Informal
Social Communication

The importance of strict theory in developing and guiding programs of research is becoming more and more recognized
today. Yet there is considerable disagreement about exactly
how strict and precise a theoretical formulation must be at
various stages in the development of a body of knowledge.
Certainly there are many who feel that some "theorizing" is too
vague and indefinite to be of much use. It is also argued that
such vague and broad "theorizing" may actually hinder the
empirical development of an area of knowledge.

On the other hand there are many who express dissatisfaction with instances of very precise theories which do exist here
and there, for somehow or other a precise and specific theory
seems to them to leave out the "real" psychological problem.
These persons seem to be more concerned with those aspects
of the problem which the precise theory has not yet touched.
From this point of view it is argued that too precise and too
strict theorizing may also hinder the empirical development of
an area of knowledge.

It is probably correct that if a theory becomes too precise too
early it can have tendencies to become sterile. It is also probably correct that if a theory stays too vague and ambiguous for
too long it can be harmful in that nothing can be done to dis-

From Leon Festinger, "Informal Social Communication," *The Psychological
Review*, Vol. 57, 1950, pp. 271–282. Copyright 1950 by the American Psychological Association and reproduced by permission.

prove or change it. This probably means that theories, when vague, should at least be stated in a form which makes the adding of precision possible as knowledge increases. It also probably means that theory should run ahead, but not too far ahead, of the data so that the trap of premature precision can be avoided. It certainly means that theories, whether vague or precise, must be in such a form that empirical data can influence them.

This article is a statement of the theoretical formulations which have been developed in the process of conducting a program of empirical and experimental research in informal social communication. It has grown out of our findings thus far and is in turn guiding the future course of the research programs.[1] This program of research concerns itself with finding and explaining the facts concerning informal, spontaneous communication among persons and the consequences of the process of communication. It would seem that a better understanding of the dynamics of such communication would in turn lead to a better understanding of various kinds of group functioning. The theories and hypotheses presented below vary considerably in precision, specificity and the degree to which corroborating data exist. Whatever the state of precision, however, the theories are empirically oriented and capable of being tested.

Since we are concerned with the spontaneous process of communication which goes on during the functioning of groups we must first differentiate the variety of types of communication which occur according to the theoretical conditions which give rise to tendencies to communicate. It is plausible to assume that separating the sources or origins of pressures to communicate that may act on a member of a group will give us fruitful areas to study. This type of differentiation or classification is, of course, adequate only if it leads to the separation of conceptually clear areas of investigation within which communication can be organized into statable theoretical and empirical laws.

We shall here deal with those few of the many possible

[1] This research program consists of a number of coordinated and integrated studies, both in the laboratory and in the field. It is being carried out by the Research Center for Group Dynamics under contract N6onr—23212 NR 151–698 with the Office of Naval Research.

sources of pressures to communicate in which we have thus far been able to make theoretical and empirical progress. We shall elaborate on the theory for regarding them as giving rise to pressures to communicate and on specific hypotheses concerning the laws of communication which stem from these sources.

I. Pressures Toward Uniformity in a Group

One major source of forces to communicate is the pressure toward uniformity which may exist within a group. These are pressures which, for one reason or another, act toward making members of a group agree concerning some issue or conform with respect to some behavior pattern. It is stating the obvious, of course, to say that these pressures must be exerted by means of a process of communication among the members of the group. One must also specify the conditions under which such pressures toward uniformity arise, both on a conceptual and an operational level so that in any specific situation it is possible to say whether or not such pressures exist. We shall, in the following discussion, elaborate on two major sources of pressures toward uniformity among people, namely, social reality and group locomotion.

1. Social reality. Opinions, attitudes, and beliefs which people hold must have some basis upon which they rest for their validity. Let us as a start abstract from the many kinds of bases for the subjective validity of such opinions, attitudes, and beliefs one continuum along which they may be said to lie. This continuum we may call a scale of degree of physical reality. At one end of this continuum, namely, complete dependence upon physical reality, we might have an example such as this: A person looking at a surface might think that the surface is fragile or he might think that the surface is unbreakable. He can very easily take a hammer, hit the surface, and quickly be convinced as to whether the opinion he holds is correct or incorrect. After he has broken the surface with a hammer it will probably make little dent upon his opinion if another person should tell him that the surface is unbreakable. It would thus seem that where there is a high degree of dependence upon

physical reality for the subjective validity of one's belief or opinions the dependence upon other people for the confidence one has in these opinions or beliefs is very low.

At the other end of the continuum, where the dependence upon physical reality is low or zero, we might have an example such as this: A person looking at the results of a national election feels that if the loser had won, things would be in some ways much better than they are. Upon what does the subjective validity of this belief depend? It depends to a large degree on whether or not other people share his opinion and feel the same way he does. If there are other people around him who believe the same thing, then his opinion is, to him, valid. If there are not others who believe the same thing, then his opinion is, in the same sense, not valid. Thus where the dependence upon physical reality is low the dependence upon social reality is correspondingly high. An opinion, a belief, an attitude is "correct," "valid," and "proper" to the extent that it is anchored in a group of people with similar beliefs, opinions, and attitudes.

This statement, however, cannot be generalized completely. It is clearly not necessary for the validity of someone's opinion that everyone else in the world think the way he does. It is only necessary that the members of that group to which he refers this opinion or attitude think the way he does. It is not necessary for a Ku Klux Klanner that some northern liberal agree with him in his attitude toward Negroes, but it is eminently necessary that there be other people who also are Ku Klux Klanners and who do agree with him. The person who does not agree with him is seen as different from him and not an adequate referent for his opinion. The problem of independently defining which groups are and which groups are not appropriate reference groups for a particular individual and for a particular opinion or attitude is a difficult one. It is to some extent inherently circular since an appropriate reference group tends to be a group which does share a person's opinions and attitudes, and people tend to locomote *into* such groups and *out of* groups which do not agree with them.

From the preceding discussion it would seem that if a discrepancy in opinion, attitude, or belief exists among persons who are members of an appropriate reference group, forces to communicate will arise. It also follows that the less "physical reality" there is to validate the opinion or belief, the greater will be the importance of the social referent, the group, and the greater will be the forces to communicate.

2. Group locomotion. Pressures toward uniformity among members of a group may arise because such uniformity is desirable or necessary in order for the group to move toward some goal. Under such circumstances there are a number of things one can say about the magnitude of pressures toward uniformity.

(a) They will be greater to the extent that the members perceive that group movement would be facilitated by uniformity.

(b) The pressures toward uniformity will also be greater, the more dependent the various members are on the group in order to reach their goals. The degree to which other groups are substitutable as a means toward individual or group goals would be one of the determinants of the dependence of the member on the group.

We have elaborated on two sources of pressure toward uniformity among members of groups. The same empirical laws should apply to communications which result from pressures toward uniformity irrespective of the particular reasons for the existence of the pressures. We shall now proceed to enumerate a set of hypotheses concerning communication which results from pressures toward uniformity.

II. Hypotheses About Communication Resulting from Pressures Toward Uniformity

Communications which arise from pressures toward uniformity in a group may be seen as "instrumental" communications. That is, the communication is not an end in itself but rather is a means by which the communicator hopes to influence the person he addresses in such a way as to reduce the discrepancy that exists between them. Thus we should examine the determinants of: (1) when a member communicates, (2) to whom he communicates, and (3) the reactions of the recipient of the communication.

(1) Determinants of the magnitude of pressure to communicate:

Hypothesis 1a: The pressure on members to communicate to others in the group concerning "item x" increases monotonically with increase in the perceived discrepancy in opinion concerning "item x" among members of the group.

Remembering that we are considering only communication that results from pressures toward uniformity, it is clear that if there are no discrepancies in opinion, that is, uniformity already exists in the group, there will be no forces to communicate. It would be plausible to expect the force to communicate to increase rapidly from zero as the state of affairs departs from uniformity.

Hypothesis 1b: The pressure on a member to communicate to others in the group concerning "item x" increases monotonically with increase in the degree of relevance of "item x" to the functioning of the group.

If "item x" is unimportant to the group in the sense of not being associated with any of the values or activities which are the basis for the existence of the group, or if it is more or less inconsequential for group locomotion, then there should be few or no forces to communicate even when there are perceived discrepancies in opinion. As "item x" becomes more important for the group (more relevant), the forces to communicate when any given magnitude of perceived discrepancy exists, should increase.

Corroborative evidence for this hypothesis is found in an experiment by Schachter (8) where discussion of the same issue was experimentally made relevant for some groups and largely irrelevant for others. It is clear from the data that where the discussion was relevant to the functioning of the group there existed stronger forces to communicate and to influence the other members. Where the issue is a relevant one the members make longer individual contributions to the discussion and there are many fewer prolonged pauses in the discussion.

Hypothesis 1c: The pressure on members to communicate to others in the group concerning "item x" increases monotonically with increase in the cohesiveness of the group.

Cohesiveness of a group is here defined as the resultant of all the forces acting on the members to remain in the group. These forces may depend on the attractiveness or unattractiveness of either the prestige of the group, members in the group, or the activities in which the group engages. If the total attraction toward the group is zero, no forces to communicate should arise; the members may as easily leave the group as stay in it. As the forces to remain in the group increase (given perceived discrepancies in opinion and given a certain relevance of the item to the functioning of the group) the pressures to communicate will increase.

Data from an experiment by Back (1) support this hypothesis. In this experiment groups of high and low cohesiveness were experimentally created using three different sources of attraction to the group, namely, liking the members, prestige attached to belonging, and possibility of getting a reward for performance in the group activity. For each of the three types of attraction to the group the more cohesive groups were rated as proceeding at a more intense rate in the discussion than the corresponding less cohesive groups. In addition, except for the groups where the attraction was the possibility of reward (perhaps due to wanting to finish and get the reward) there was more total amount of attempted exertion of influence in the highly cohesive groups than in the less cohesive groups. In short, highly cohesive groups, having stronger pressures to communicate, discussed the issue at a more rapid pace and attempted to exert more influence.

(2) Determinants of choice of recipient for communications:

Hypothesis 2a: The force to communicate about "item x" to A PARTICULAR MEMBER of the group will increase as the discrepancy in opinion between that member and the communicator increases.

We have already stated in Hypothesis 1a that the pressure to communicate in general will increase as the perceived nonuniformity in the group increases. In addition the force to communicate will be strongest toward those whose opinions are most different from one's own and will, of course, be zero towards those in the group who at the time hold the same opinion as the communicator. In other words, people will tend to communicate to those within the group whose opinions are most different from their own.

There is a clear corroboration of this hypothesis from a number of studies. In the previously mentioned experiment by Schachter (8) the distribution of opinions expressed in the group was always as follows: Most of the members' opinions clustered within a narrow range of each other while one member, the deviate, held and maintained an extremely divergent point of view. About five times as many communications were addressed to the holder of the divergent point of view as were addressed to the others.

In an experiment by Festinger and Thibaut (5) the discussion situation was set up so that members' opinions on the issue spread over a considerable range. Invariably 70 to 90 per cent of the communications were addressed to those who held opinions at the extremes of the distribution. The curve of number of communications received falls off very rapidly as the opinion of the recipient moves away from the extreme of the distribution. The hypothesis would seem to be well substantiated.

Hypothesis 2b: The force to communicate about "item x" to A PARTICULAR PERSON will decrease to the extent that he is perceived as not a member of the group or to the extent that he is not wanted as a member of the group.

From the previous hypothesis it follows that communications will tend to be addressed mainly toward those with extreme opinions within the group. This does not hold, however, for any arbitrarily defined group. The present hypothesis, in effect, states that such relationships will apply only within *psychological* groups, that is, collections of people that exist as groups psychologically for the members. Communications will tend not to be addressed towards those who are not members of the group.

The study by Schachter (8) and the study by Festinger and Thibaut (5) both substantiate this hypothesis. In Schachter's experiment those group members who do not want the person holding the extremely divergent point of view to remain in the group tend to stop communicating to him towards the end of the discussion. In the experiment by Festinger and Thibaut, when the subjects have the perception that the persons present include different kinds of people with a great variety of interests, there tends to be less communication toward the extremes in the last half of the discussion after the rejection process has had time to develop. In short, communication towards those with different opinions decreases if they are seen as not members of the *psychological* group.

Hypothesis 2c: The force to communicate "item x" to a particular member will increase the more it is perceived that the communication will change that member's opinion in the desired direction.

A communication which arises because of the existence of pressures toward uniformity is made in order to exert a force on the recipient in a particular direction, that is, to push him to change his opinion so that he will agree more closely with the communicator. If a member is perceived as very resistant to changing his opinion, the force to communicate to him decreases. If it seems that a particular member will be changed as the result of a communication so as to increase the discrepancy between him and the communicator, there will exist a force not to communicate to him. Thus under such conditions there will be tendencies *not* to communicate this particular item to that member.

There is some corroboration for this hypothesis. In a face-to-face verbal discussion where a range of opinion exists, the factors which this hypothesis points to would be particularly important for those members whose opinions were near the middle of the range. A communication which might influence the member at one extreme to come closer to the middle might at the same time influence the member at the other extreme to move farther away from the middle. We might then expect from this hypothesis that those holding opinions in the middle of the existing range would communicate less (because of the conflict) and would address fewer communications to the whole group (attempting to influence only one person at a time).

A number of observations were conducted to check these derivations. Existing groups of clinical psychologists who were engaging in discussions to reconcile their differences in ratings of applicants were observed. Altogether, 147 such discussions were observed in which at least one member's opinion was in the middle of the existing range. While those with extreme opinions made an average of 3.16 units of communication (number of communications weighted by length of the communication), those with middle opinions made an average of only 2.6 units of communication. While those with extreme opinions addressed 38 per cent of their communications to the whole group, those with middle opinions addressed only 29 per cent of their communications to everyone.

(3) Determinants of change in the recipient of a communication:

Hypothesis 3a: The amount of change in opinion resulting from receiving a communication will increase as the pressure towards uniformity in the group increases.

There are two separate factors which contribute to the effect stated in the hypothesis. The greater the pressure towards uniformity, the greater will be the amount of influence exerted by the communications and, consequently, the greater the magnitude of change that may be expected. But the existence of pressures toward uniformity will not only show itself in increased attempts to change the opinions of others. Pressures toward uniformity will also produce greater readiness to change in the members of the group. In other words, uniformity may be achieved by changing the opinions of others and/or by changing one's own opinions. Thus we may expect that with increasing pressure towards uniformity there will be less resistance to change on the part of the members. Both of these factors will contribute to produce greater change in opinion when the pressure toward uniformity is greater.

There is evidence corroborating this hypothesis from the experiment by Festinger and Thibaut (5). In this experiment three degrees of pressure towards uniformity were experimentally induced in different groups. Irrespective of which of two problems were discussed by the group and irrespective of whether they perceived the group to be homogeneously or heterogeneously composed, the results consistently show that high pressure groups change most, medium pressure groups change next most, and low pressure groups change least in the direction of uniformity. While the two factors which contribute to this effect cannot be separated in the data, their joint effect is clear and unmistakable.

Hypothesis 3b: The amount of change in opinion resulting from receiving a communication will increase as the strength of the resultant force to remain in the group increases for the recipient.

To the extent that a member wishes to remain in the group, the group has power over that member. By power we mean here the ability to produce real change in opinions and attitudes and not simply change in overt behavior which can also be produced by means of overt threat. If a person is unable to leave a group because of restraints from the outside, the group can then use threats to change overt behavior. Covert changes in opinions and attitudes, however, can only be produced by a group by virtue of forces acting on the member to remain in the group. Clearly the maximum force which the group can successfully induce on a member counter to his own forces can not be greater than the sum of the forces acting on that member to remain in the group. The greater the resultant force to remain in the group, the more effective will be the attempts to influence the member.

This hypothesis is corroborated by two separate studies. Festinger, Schachter and Back (4) investigated the relationship between the cohesiveness of social groups in a housing project (how attractive the group was for its members) and how effectively a group standard relevant to the functioning of the group was maintained. A correlation of .72 was obtained between these two variables. In other words, the greater the attractiveness of the group for the members, the greater was the amount of influence which the group could successfully exert on its members with the result that there existed greater conformity in attitudes and behavior in the more cohesive groups.

Back (1) did a laboratory experiment specifically designed to test this hypothesis. By means of plausible instructions to the subjects he experimentally created groups of high and low cohesiveness, that is, conditions in which the members were strongly attracted to the group and those in which the attraction to the group was relatively weak. The subjects, starting with different interpretations of the same material, were given an opportunity to discuss the matter. Irrespective of the source of the attraction to the group (Back used three different types of attraction in both high and low cohesive conditions) the subjects in the high cohesive groups influenced each other's opinions more than the subjects in the low cohesive groups. In short, the greater the degree of attraction to the group, the greater the amount of influence actually accomplished.

Hypothesis 3c: The amount of change in opinion resulting from receiving a communication concerning "item x" will decrease with increase in the degree to which the opinions and attitudes involved are anchored in other group memberships or serve important need satisfying functions for the person.

If the opinion that a person has formed on some issue is supported in some other group than the one which is at present attempting to influence him, he will be more resistant to the attempted influence. Other sources of resistance to being influenced undoubtedly come from personality factors, ego needs and the like.

Specific evidence supporting this hypothesis is rather fragmentary. In the study of social groups in a housing project by Festinger, Schachter and Back (4), the residents were asked whether their social life was mainly outside the project or not. Of those who conformed to the standards of their social groups within the project about 85 per cent reported that their social life was centered mainly within the project. Less than 50 per cent of those who did not conform to the standards of the project social group, however, reported that their social life was centered mainly in the project. It is likely that they were able to resist the influences from within the project when their opinions and attitudes were supported in outside groups.

The experiments by Schachter (8) and by Festinger and Thibaut (5) used the same discussion problem in slightly different situations. In the former experiment subjects identified themselves and verbally supported their opinions in face-to-face discussion. In the latter experiment the subjects were anonymous, communicating only by written messages on which the sender of the message was not identified. Under these latter conditions many more changes in opinion were observed than under the open verbal discussion situation even though less time was spent in discussion when they wrote notes. This difference in amount of change in opinion is probably due to the ego defensive reactions aroused by openly committing oneself and supporting one's opinions in a face-to-face group.

(4) Determinants of change in relationship among members:

Hypothesis 4a: The tendency to change the composition of the psychological group (pushing members out of the group) increases as the perceived discrepancy in opinion increases.

We have already discussed two of the responses which members of groups make to pressures toward uniformity, namely, attempting to influence others and being more ready to be influenced. There is still a third response which serves to move toward uniformity. By rejecting those whose opinions diverge from the group and thus redefining who is and who is not in the psychological group, uniformity can be accomplished. The greater the discrepancy between a person's opinion and the opinion of another, the stronger are the tendencies to exclude the other person from the psychological group.

There is evidence that members of groups do tend to reject those whose opinions are divergent. In the study of social groups within a housing project Festinger, Schachter and Back (4) found that those who did not conform to the standards of their social group were underchosen on a sociometric test, that is, they mentioned more persons as friends of theirs than they received in return. Schachter (8) did an experiment specifically to test whether or not members of groups would be rejected simply for disagreeing on an issue. Paid participants in the groups voiced divergent or agreeing opinions as instructed. In all groups the paid participant who voiced divergent opinion on an issue was rejected on a postmeeting questionnaire concerning whom they wanted to have remain in the group. The same paid participants, when voicing conforming opinions in other groups, were not rejected.

Hypothesis 4b: When nonconformity exists, the tendency to change the composition of the psychological group increases as the cohesiveness of the group increases and as the relevance of the issue to the group increases.

We have previously discussed the increase in forces to communicate with increase in cohesiveness and relevance of issue. Similarly, these two variables affect the tendency to reject persons from the group for nonconformity. Theoretically we should expect any variable which affected the force to communicate (which stems from pressures toward uniformity) to affect also the tendency to reject nonconformers in a similar manner. In others words, increases in the force to communicate concerning an item will go along with increased tendency to reject persons who disagree concerning that item.

The previously mentioned experiment by Schachter (8) was designed to test this hypothesis by experimentally varying cohesiveness and relevance in club groups. In this experiment the more cohesive groups do reject the nonconformer more than the less cohesive groups and the groups where the issue is relevant reject the nonconformer more than groups where the issue is not very relevant to the group functioning. Those groups where cohesiveness was low and the issue was not very relevant show little, if any, tendency to reject the deviate.

III. Forces to Change One's Position in a Group

Another important source of forces to communicate are the forces which act on members of groups to locomote (change their position) in the group, or to move from one group to another. Such forces to locomote may stem from the attractiveness of activities associated with a different position in the group or from the status of that position or the like. Thus a new member of a group may wish to become more central in the group, a member of an organization may wish to rise in the status hierarchy, a member of a business firm may want to be promoted or a member of a minority group may desire acceptance by the majority group. These are all instances of forces to locomote in a social structure.

It is plausible that the existence of a force acting on a person in a specific direction produces behavior in that direction. Where locomotion in the desired direction is not possible, at least temporarily, there will exist a force to communicate in that direction. The existence of a force in a specific direction will produce behavior in that direction. One such kind of behavior is communication. This hypothesis is not very different from the hypothesis advanced by Lewin (6) to account for the superior recall of interrupted activities.

An experiment by Thibaut (9) tends to corroborate this theoretical analysis. In his experiment he created two groups, one of high status and privileged, the other of low status and underprivileged. These two groups, equated in other respects, functioned together so that the members of the high status group could play an attractive game. The low status group functioned merely as servants. It was clear that forces were acting on the members of the low status group to move into the other group. As the privileged position of the high status group became clearer and clearer the amount of communication from the low status team to the high status group increased. The number of communications from members of the high status group to the low status group correspondingly decreased. When, in some groups, the status and privilege relationship between the two teams was reversed toward the end of the experimental session, thus reducing the forces to locomote into the other group, the number of communications to that other group correspondingly decreased.

Further corroboration is found in a preliminary experiment, mainly methodologically oriented, conducted by Back *et al.*

(2). In this experiment new items of information were planted with persons at various levels in the hierarchy of a functioning organization. Data on transmission of each of the items of information were obtained through cooperators within the organization who were chosen so as to give adequate coverage of all levels and all sections within it. These cooperators recorded all instances of communication that came to their attention. Of seventeen acts of communication recorded in this manner, eleven were directed upwards in the hierarchy, four toward someone on the same level and only two were directed downwards. The existence of forces to move upward in such a hierarchical organization may be taken for granted. The great bulk of the communications recorded went in the same direction as these forces to locomote.

In considering communication among members of differentiated social structures it is important also to take into account restraints against communication.

Infrequent contact in the ordinary course of events tends to erect restraints against communication. It is undoubtedly easier to communicate a given item to a person whom one sees frequently or to a person to whom one has communicated similar items in the past. The structuring of groups into hierarchies, social clusters, or the like, undoubtedly tends to restrict the amount and type of contact between members of certain different parts or levels of the group and also undoubtedly restricts the content of the communication that goes on between such levels in the ordinary course of events. These restrictions erect restraints against certain types of communication.

There are some data which tend to specify some of the restraints against communication which exist. In the study of the communication of a spontaneous rumor in a community by Festinger, Cartwright *et al.* (3) it was found that intimacy of friendship tended to increase ease of communication. Persons with more friends in the project heard the rumor more often than those with only acquaintances. Those who had few friends or acquaintances heard the rumor least often. At the same time this factor of intimacy of friendship was not related to how frequently they relayed the rumor to others. In other words, it was not related to forces to communicate but seemed to function only as a restraint against communicating where friendship did not exist.

There is also some evidence that the mere perception of the existence of a hierarchy sets up restraints against communication between levels. Kelley (7) experimentally created a two-level hierarchy engaging in a problem-solving task during which they could and did communicate within levels and between levels. Control groups were also run with the same task situation but with no status differential involved between the two subgroups. There was more communication between subgroups under these control conditions than where there was a status differential involved.

It seems that, in a hierarchy, there are also restraints against communicating hostility upwards when the hostility is about those on upper levels. In the same experiment by Kelley there was much criticism of the *other group* expressed by both high status and low status members. The proportion of these critical expressions which are directed upward by the low status group is much less, however, than the proportion directed downward by the high status groups.

IV. Emotional Expression

An important variety of communications undoubtedly results from the existence of an emotional state in the communicator. The existence of joy, anger, hostility and the like seems to produce forces to communicate. It seems that communications resulting from the existence of an emotional state are consummatory rather than instrumental.

By an instrumental communication we mean one in which the reduction of the force to communicate depends upon the effect of the communication on the recipient. Thus in communication resulting from pressures toward uniformity in a group, the mere fact that a communication is made does not affect the force to communicate. If the effect has been to change the recipient so that he now agrees more closely with the communicator, the force to communicate will be reduced. If the recipient changes in the opposite direction, the force to communicate to him will be increased.

By a consummatory communication we mean one in which the reduction of the force to communicate occurs as a result of the expression and does not depend upon the effect it has on the recipient. Certainly in the case of such communications the reaction of the recipient may introduce new elements into the situation which will affect the force to communicate, but the essence of a consummatory communication is that the simple expression does reduce the force.

Specifically with regard to the communication of hostility and aggression, much has been said regarding its consummatory nature. The psychoanalytic theories of catharsis, in particular, develop the notion that the expression of hostility reduces the emotional state of the person. There has, however, been very little experimental work done on the problem. The previously mentioned experiment by Thibaut in which he created a "privileged-underprivileged" relationship between two equated groups has some data on the point. There is evidence that those members of the "underprivileged" groups who expressed their hostility toward the "privileged" groups showed less residual hostility toward them in post-experimental questionnaires. There is, however, no control over the reactions of the recipients of the hostile communications nor over the perceptions of the communicators of what these reactions were. An experiment is now in progress which will attempt to clarify some of these relationships with both negative and positive emotional states.

V. Summary

A series of interrelated hypotheses has been presented to account for data on informal social communication collected in the course of a number of studies. The data come from field studies and from laboratory experiments specifically designed to test the hypotheses.

Three sources of pressures to communicate have been considered:

1. Communication arising from pressures toward uniformity in a group. Here we considered determinants of magnitude of the force to communicate, choice of recipient for the communication, magnitude of change in recipient and magnitude of tendencies to reject nonconformers.

2. Communications arising from forces to locomote in a social structure. Here we considered communications in the direction of a blocked locomotion and restraints against communication arising in differentiated social structures.

3. Communications arising from the existence of emotional states. In this area data are almost completely lacking. Some theoretical distinctions were made and an experiment which is now in progress in this area was outlined.

Bibliography

1. Back, K. The exertion of influence through social communication. *J. abn. soc. Psychol.* 1950.

2. ———; Festinger, L.; Hymovitch, B.; Kelley, H. H.; Schachter, S.; & Thibaut, J. The methodological problems of studying rumor transmission. *Human Relations,* 1950.

3. Festinger, L.; Cartwright, D.; *et al.* A study of a rumor: its origin and spread. *Human Relations,* 1948, **1,** 464–486.

4. ———; Schachter, S.; & Back, K. *Social pressures in informal groups: a study of a housing project.* New York: Harper & Bros., 1950.

5. ———; & Thibaut, J. Interpersonal communication in small groups. *J. abn. soc. Psychol.* 1950.

6. Lewin, K. Formalization and progress in psychology. In *Studies in Topological and Vector Psychology 1, Univ. Ia. Stud. Child Welf.,* 1940, **16,** No. 3.

7. Kelley, H. H. Communication in experimentally created hierarchies. *Human Relations,* 1950.

8. Schachter, S. Deviation, rejection, and communication. *J. abn. soc. Psychol.,* 1951.

9. Thibaut, J. An experimental study of the cohesiveness of underprivileged groups. *Human Relations,* 1950, **3.**

Jon Eisenson,
J. Jeffery Auer, and
John V. Irwin
**Psychology of
Group Discussion**

Preliminary Definitions

First of all, a few definitions are in order. What do we mean by
a group? And what is its social function? Social psychologists
distinguish between primary and secondary groups. The latter
term refers to large and artificial categories, created by the accident of circumstance or even by the imagination: persons "belonging to" nations or local communities, ethnic or religious
aggregates, socio-economic classes, or those who have merely
paid their dues to a single organization. Our concern is not
with these secondary groups, but with primary ones. Cooley
(1909, p. 23) was perhaps the first to describe them: "By primary groups I mean those characterized by intimate face-to-
face association and cooperation. They are primary in several
senses, but chiefly in that they are fundamental in forming the
social nature and ideals of the individual. The result of intimate
association, psychologically, is a certain fusion of individualities
in a common whole, so that one's very self, for many purposes
at least, is the common life and purpose of the group. Perhaps
the simplest way of describing this wholeness is by saying that
it is 'we'; it involves the sort of sympathy and mutual identification for which 'we' is the natural expression."

Cooley's description still provides a standard frame of reference for investigations of primary groups and their behavior.

From *The Psychology of Communication* by Jon Eisenson, J. Jeffery Auer
and John V. Irwin. Copyright, © 1963 by Meredith Corporation. Reprinted by
permission of Appleton-Century-Crofts.

The possibility of interaction through direct communication, of course, is a key element of the primary group. Homans (1950, p. 1) makes it central in his definition: "a number of persons who communicate with one another over a span of time, and who are few enough so that each person is able to communicate with all others, not at secondhand, through other people, but face-to-face."

A Concept of the Group

Any concept of the group must account for the nature of membership and common and differentiating group characteristics.

Individuals in Groups

The most important thing to remember about groups is that they are made up of people. Thus, we first consider the relations of individuals to groups.

1. *Each individual lives in a society that is built upon group organization.* Although humans consider themselves to be individuals, they seldom act completely independently. Instead they enter into formal or informal group relationships, not merely for social convenience, but because human beings are increasingly dependent upon structured groups and collective action for their economic, political, and cultural sustenance. In modern society the "survival of the fittest" theory applies as much or more to groups than to individuals.

2. *Each individual belongs to overlapping groups.* "We are all bundles of hyphens" is one way of generalizing about the multiple groups to which each individual belongs in his various social roles as wage earner, churchgoer, citizen, voter, parent, etc. Intellectually, emotionally, and often financially, individuals contribute to these groups and, in turn, are influenced by them. Only a few fortunate persons find all of their group memberships compatible; more often they are "at war with themselves" in a battle of conflicting loyalties.

3. *Each individual is sometimes apart from all groups.* As he participates in any one group, he must react to its pressures in

consonance with his other group relationships. To make this intricate adjustment of conflicting psychological forces, the individual must try to stand apart from all of his affiliations. The decisions he reaches in this state of temporary isolation may seem to him to be independently arrived at, but they are nonetheless achieved in the shadow of the groups to which he belongs.

Similarities Among Groups

Whether formal or informal, any group consists of persons who are at a particular time organized in a special way for a common purpose. In certain aspects, therefore, all groups are similar.

1. *Groups are usually built around common interests.* Though on many matters members of a group may disagree, even violently, their existence as a group requires that at least temporarily they must agree on the main purpose for which they are organized. This fact alone is usually responsible for developing cohesiveness among members and group loyalties. Both cohesion and loyalty may disappear, of course, if the common interest is lost.

2. *Groups commonly determine their own membership.* Persons who do not share a group's common interests are seldom knowingly invited to join; groups tend to think non-believers are nuisances. And persons who cannot "see the light" tend to agree. Thus a sense of unity is maintained, at least on the group's main interest or cause, and differences are limited to ways and means of achieving it.

3. *Groups tend to be dynamic rather than static.* Those that are literally static seldom survive in a competitive society. Instead, groups maintain their vitality by recruiting new converts, or by redefining or replacing old objectives. Even groups determined to maintain the status quo need to be dynamic in developing new methods for resisting change.

4. *Groups usually try to transmit their sense of values.* Social and cultural values, especially, are transmitted through group struc-

tures, rather than by individuals. Though not done intentionally, this still tends to give stability to a group, even across spatial and temporal divisions.

5. *Groups tend to influence an individual's "life's chances."* An individual's normal expectations for health, education, wealth, occupation, and cultural values—what the sociologist calls "life's chances"—are often determined by the groups he is "born into" or succeeds in entering. Thus a person's group memberships may provide a basis for a fairly reliable prediction of what social or professional opportunities will be open to him, and how he will react to them.

Differential Characteristics of Groups

Although we have identified some features common to all groups, certain differentiating aspects must also be noted. It has often been said that an individual in a group tends to behave just as he would when alone, only more so. This observation assumes that formal and informal groups are composed of like-minded individuals, and that it is therefore possible to think of group behavior as the composite projection of the behaviors of the individuals composing it. This does not mean that a "group personality" or a "group mind" exists as an entity apart from individual members. It does mean, however, that certain behaviors may be identified as characteristic for members of particular groups. For convenience in distinguishing among groups, analyzing them, and sometimes for predicting their probable behavior, seven specific characteristics have been isolated in the research literature on groups.

1. *Group conformity.* Most individuals tend to behave, as we noted in our discussion of motivation in Chapter 14, in ways that will gain recognition, admiration, respect, or approval. This desire for acceptance and status is especially strong when it concerns groups to which we belong; through trial and error we learn that one way of gaining acceptance is by conforming to the standards and mores of the group. Thus it is that group opinion often influences belief and behavior more than does

expert opinion, and that a tendency to conform is common enough to be called a characteristic of groups. The degree of conformity, in turn, determines how free members feel to express their own opinions, and how freely these expressions will be accepted by the group. In psychological literature it is common to call the group atmosphere "permissive" when little conformity is demanded, "autocratic" when independent judgment is discouraged.

2. *Group prejudices.* Though we often believe that other persons are prejudiced, few of us willingly admit to prejudices of our own which make us intolerant of the race, religion, social status, or nationality of others. In general we find prejudice most apparent among cohesive groups of like-minded people, and it is intensified when they are in the group environment.

3. *Group resistance to change.* New concepts seldom win complete and immediate acceptance, particularly when they lead to social changes. True as this is for individuals, it is even truer for individuals in the company of their fellows. Thus, another important index to a group's behavior is the degree to which it resists change, either within the group or in its relations with other groups. Equally characteristic may be the group's strategy of resistance. On the other hand, groups may also follow particular patterns in accepting, or bringing about, change. In effecting change, for example, a group may follow the dictate of a leader, establish a consensus, and so on.

4. *Group structure.* One of the focal points of recent small group research has been the status of individuals within the group, and their relations with other members, both directly and through subgroups. In some large groups, of course, subgroups develop not only because of common interests, but because the work of the parent organization may be more efficiently performed by smaller task forces, or because it is more convenient to have a number of smaller meetings than one large one. Inevitably the activities of the subgroups and their relationships to the parent organization may profoundly affect the ways in which members (a) communicate with each other, (b) interact, and (c) control each other's and the group's behavior. When group processes break down, the first step in understand-

ing why, and in restoring them, may be to make a careful analysis of the structure of the group.

5. *Group values.* Another characteristic differentiating groups is the set of values or ideals it endorses or maintains. An analysis of these values—and of the probable attitudes and beliefs giving rise to them—will aid in understanding a group's behavior. Such an analysis may also serve to explain one group's feelings of hostility or aggressive behavior toward another. Finally, an understanding of those values cherished by a group may provide a basis for predicting its behavior, especially in terms of the programs or propositions it will accept and support.

6. *Group patterns of decision.* By common practice a group may follow a more or less constant procedure in decision-making, and this will reflect another behavioral facet. Some groups are autocratically led by one individual and decisions are made by *authority.* More democratic groups conclude discussions by counting votes, determining majorities, and deciding by *enumeration.* In other groups the establishment of conflicting beliefs or alternate courses of action results in a yielding by each subgroup of some portion of its position, and a decision by the method of *compromise.* Under the most favorable conditions of all, a group establishes a true synthesis of the views of its whole membership and makes its decision by *consensus.* The climate requisite for reaching a consensus, or sometimes even for full discussion before compromise or enumeration, seldom exists when groups feel outside pressures, work in a state of tension, or are hurried by a deadline.

7. *Group patterns of discussion.* All of the preceding characteristics of a group's behavior will be reflected in the nature and effectiveness of its communication patterns. A given group, for example, may condone or encourage noncomformity, be relatively free of prejudice, welcome change, discourage the creation of subgroups, place a high value on individual feelings, and settle its differences by majority rule. In such an extremely congenial combination of characteristics one might confidently expect well-tempered, logical, and uninhibited discussion. With the change of even a single factor in the group's characteristic behavior, however—such as the development of a

sudden desire for close conformity, or the establishment of cliques within the group—the group's patterns of communication might be significantly altered.

The Group as a Communication Unit

We have defined the group as, among other things, a formal or informal organization which makes discussion possible. Discussion may be defined as social interaction through face-to-face communication. Combining the elements of both these definitions *we can define group discussion as a planned, but relatively informal, meeting in which those who attend are invited to join in purposeful talk about a topic or problem of common interest, under the guidance of a leader, chairman, or moderator.* Several components of this definition should be singled out for comment. They constitute elements that appear to be requisites for successful discussion. Because, as we shall note later, there are potentially disruptive forces at work in many groups, we cannot say that communication will necessarily be successful when these elements are present. We do believe that *at least* these five elements must be present for effective communication in group situations. We came to this conclusion after a careful examination of the experimental and expositional literature on discussion.

1. *Planning* in advance, rather than relying upon spontaneous combustion, seems essential for profitable discussion. Often a designated leader takes the initiative for this planning, but it is best done when several members of the group share in formulating goals and procedures.

2. *Informality* usually encourages greater participation than does a rigid atmosphere, and the size of the group and the physical arrangements should be controlled to that end. The best description of this element is organized informality.

3. *Participation* to the fullest extent of each member's capacity to contribute is essential for good discussion. The basic assumptions of the discussion method are that each member may have something valuable to contribute, and that the best way to

discover right solutions is through cooperative pooling of all available information, evaluation, and judgment.

4. *Purpose* is a requisite for profitable talk of any kind, and especially for discussion. In some circumstances simple pleasantries or even socially useful talk may have a point, but group discussions are intended to be learning or problem-solving experiences.

5. *Leadership,* of some sort, is necessary for successful group discussion. This may be exercised by a prescribed individual such as the chairman of a committee or the senior member present, or it may be diffused among several members. In small groups whose members know each other, the functions of leadership may be shared by all participants.

We conclude these comments on the group as a communication unit by citing a few examples of discussion situations. Customarily we regard discussion as a method for learning and for problem-solving. Within each category there may be more specific purposes.

1. *Learning groups* may be concerned only with exchanging facts and opinions, as in typical classroom and study groups, workshops, and many professional conferences. Also basically learning situations, though designed so that members can form individual attitudes, are discussions centering on social and political problems, "Great Books" study groups, and so on. Another type of learning is involved when a discussion group's purpose is to release tensions and develop understandings, as in family councils, some labor-management grievance discussions, and group therapy sessions.

2. *Problem-solving groups* may engage in various types of work projects, but are most commonly concerned with reaching group decisions of some sort, as in legislative and business organization committees, international conferences, and the like. Occasionally a group goes beyond the task of finding a solution and also has administrative functions, including the determination of action steps to put the solution into operation, as with steering committees, executive councils, and boards of directors.

These examples do not exhaust the possible applications of the discussion method but are illustrative only. When we speak of communicating groups in this chapter we will mean any of the varieties of learning and problem-solving situations we have listed. The most distinguishing characteristic of all of them is that they involve face-to-face discussion, direct communication and interaction.

The three aspects of group discussion most thoroughly explored by experimentation are those involving the function of group leadership, the operation of psychological forces within groups, and the behavioral results of discussion. We now report on each of these topics.

A Concept of Leadership in Discussion Groups

Attempts to analyze the nature of leadership are at least as old as Moses, and have ranged from the glib assertion that "leaders are born, not made" to controlled studies of traits, methods, and effects of leaders. For those wishing to pursue this topic we have cited some of these studies in the comments that follow.

The Behavior of Leaders

Despite extensive research efforts to discover whether there are qualities common to all leaders, the facts are still elusive. (Beer, et al., 1959; Browne and Cohn, 1958; Stodgill, 1948; Zeleny, 1939.) The precise nature of leadership—significant in all social and political structures—remains to be defined, though certain generalizations may be made. We know, for example, that those regarded as leaders are likely to be either very skilled in interpersonal relations or very adept in manipulating and controlling the behavior of others. We also know that many accepted leaders obtain their status through personal prestige, while others have it because they are feared. And we know that some persons exercise leadership because it is inherent in the positions they hold, while others become leaders without official sanction. Seldom, however, do we identify a complex of qualities making up what might be called a "leadership personality." We find instead that quite different sets of traits, skills, and techniques, exercised by different people, bring similar results; and that some leaders are effective in one situation but fail in another.

We conclude, therefore, that (a) leadership is not a stable quality, identifiable in all recognized leaders or in all situations, and (b) we need to study leaders and their functions in various situations to learn what they do, what groups expect of them, and how they influence behavior. Recent investigations of such questions suggest that there are significant theoretical considerations:

1. *A group's characteristics determine its concept of leadership.* We have suggested that a group profile may be drawn from an analysis of seven differential characteristics. The particular combination of these appears to determine whether a group conceives of its leaders as benevolent despots who make all decisions and initiate all actions, as mere presiding officers for discussions in which group members decide matters for themselves, or as something in between.

2. *A group's concept of leadership influences the techniques of its leaders.* If members of a group behave as though they want someone to tell them what to think or do, someone is likely to do just that. Even the leader who attempts to create a permissive atmosphere and encourage free participation in decision-making may, if the members fail to respond promptly, succumb to the temptation to tell them what to do.

3. *A leader's personality and emotional needs determine his concept of leadership.* The personality of a leader may be as influential in determining the nature of his leadership behavior as the characteristics of the group. If, for example, he likes being a "boss," and likes the emotional satisfaction that autocratic behavior sometimes brings, he will find it convenient to mistrust the group's intelligence and intentions and conclude that he must dominate it—for its own good! On the other hand, if he draws emotional security from cooperative efforts, he will try to encourage the group and guide it toward reliance upon its own judgments.

4. *A leader's concept of leadership influences his choice of techniques.* Even unconsciously, a leader tends to determine first the kind of behavior he hopes for from his group; then he discovers and uses appropriate techniques of leadership. One leader may think his proper function is to "run things." He will then see that a rigid agenda is drawn up for every discussion, leaving nothing to chance; he will interpose his own opinions frequently, and use techniques of positive suggestion to win their acceptance. Another leader, democratically inclined, may think his proper function is to encourage and assist the group to run itself. He will then urge members to develop their own agenda, accepting even spontaneous changes; he will keep his own opinions in the background, try to remove any obstacles in the way of free member participation, and assist the group in synthesizing its own views.

Many persons in government, education, and business believe that the discussion method is important not only as a democratic method of solving problems, but also for improving interpersonal relations, and a large body of psychological research supports their view. It follows, therefore, that these persons are concerned with developing democratic rather than autocratic leadership. Despite some significant experimentation with training procedures there are still many questions to be explored. Here are a few of them.

1. How much advance planning and structuring of the group process is consistent with democratic leadership?

2. How far can a laissez-faire-inclined leader go in encouraging a group to determine its own procedures and make its own decisions—and mistakes—without actually creating conflict and frustration?

3. How much should the leader let himself be influenced by a desire for efficiency and economy of time and energy in achieving group goals?

4. How much attention can the leader focus on the process of problem-solving and upon interpersonal relations without jeopardizing adequate attention to the problem under discussion?

5. How can the leader discover and employ techniques that

will give the group the benefit of his knowledge and ability and yet maintain a permissive climate for unrestricted member participation?

These questions may seem to imply a sharp distinction between leadership and membership, or followership. This is not our intention. Actually there should be no differences in the way all members, including the nominal leader, if any, view the purposes and goals of group discussion. Observations of groups in action suggest that they are most effective when everyone undertakes such responsibilities as these:

1. Help to develop and maintain group values and standards.

2. Contribute to the maintenance of group cohesiveness and morale.

3. Participate in setting general and specific group goals.

4. Try to make the enterprise truly a group one by building a permissive atmosphere for free discussion.

5. Understand and try to accommodate the emotional needs and tensions of other members.

6. Direct motivational drives of members into channels that will be productive in accomplishing group goals.

7. Employ appropriate skills and techniques for effective, intelligent and responsible communication within the group.

8. Take part in an evaluation of the group's progress toward its goals and the effectiveness of its behavior.

The alert reader will note that this list of every-member responsibilities is similar to those commonly assigned to nominal leaders. This similarity is intentional. It underscores the notion that what may be called the leadership function in a group should be shared.

The Leadership Function

Our preference for the term "leadership function" rather than "functions of leaders" derives from our conviction that it is more important that the tasks of leadership be performed in a group than it is to designate who should do them. It may well be that the group leader, chairman, or moderator, is normally assumed to be responsible for all necessary leadership tasks.

But it is likely that the experience of group discussion will be more satisfying psychologically when the leader shares this responsibility with qualified members, or when they exercise initiative in undertaking these tasks themselves. Indeed, one of the obligations of leadership is undoubtedly to train and encourage members to assume as many of the necessary leadership functions as they can.

Many of those who write about group discussion find it convenient to divide the leadership function into two types of activity: (a) those tasks related to *group functioning*, i.e., building, strengthening, and maintaining the group process by channeling interpersonal behavior into productive activity, and (b) those pertaining to *problem-solving*, i.e., locating, defining, investigating, analyzing, and solving the problem. In sharing the leadership function through the performance of these tasks individual members are often said to be undertaking task-related roles. A typical list of these member roles begins with those related to group functioning:

1. *The morale builder* encourages individual contributions to the discussion, creates a receptive atmosphere for new facts and opinions, and commends those who deserve it.

2. *The conciliator* recognizes differences of opinion, tries to anticipate conflicts and relieve tensions by focusing attention on common goals and emphasizing cohesiveness.

3. *The compromiser* tries to reconcile conflicting views, even if it means modifying his own opinions, and seeks to evolve a consensus, or at least a harmonious middle ground.

4. *The expediter* tries to facilitate the discussion process, assisting members in clarifying and communicating their ideas, rephrasing, repeating when necessary, and otherwise improving the level of communication.

5. *The standard-setter* helps maintain a high level of group achievement in the quality of reasoning that leads to solving the group's problem.

6. *The process observer* usually does not take an active part in the discussion but attempts to view it objectively, so that he may both make useful suggestions to the leader and help members evaluate their own contributions.

The second category of member roles includes those related to problem-solving:

1. *The inquirer* is concerned with discovering, disclosing, and analyzing the raw materials of reasoning, facts, and opinions.

2. *The contributor* tries to provide the raw materials of reasoning by submitting factual information or considered opinions about facts.

3. *The elaborator* attempts to translate generalizations into concrete examples, define ambiguities, and project the probable effects of proposed solutions upon future group behavior.

4. *The reviewer* tries to clarify relations among ideas presented, trace conceptual patterns, and reorient the group position in terms of agreed-upon objectives.

5. *The evaluator* weighs the group's thinking in terms of its own standards, raising questions about the evidence and argument presented in the discussion, or about practical applications of proposed solutions.

6. *The energizer* keeps the discussion moving toward its goal by redirecting the attention and arousing the interests of members, and channeling their motivational drives.

7. *The group recorder* performs a secretarial function, summarizing the discussion, noting agreements and open questions, and reporting decisions.

Sometimes these leadership functions must be directed toward modifying the behavior of members whose only contributions to the group are negative and disruptive of the communication process. Among such members are *dominators,* who assert real or alleged authority, demand attention, and behave aggressively in other ways; *blockers,* often frustrated dominators, who stubbornly resist all group efforts when their own authority is challenged; *cynics,* who, when they fail to block the group's will, rationalize by denigrating the group process; *security-seekers* whose emotional needs for sympathy or recognition are stronger than their identification with the group's goals; and *lobbyists* whose concern for items on their own private—and sometimes hidden—agendas blinds them to the group's needs.

There is no magic, of course, in the labels we have given to these roles in which members share the leadership function. A different set might be equally useful in identifying and evaluating different functional contributions in group discussions.

Psychological Forces in Discussion Groups

We are now ready to sum up the applications of what we have said in this chapter. For convenience we shall do this in terms of a series of psychological forces that research has shown to be significant in face-to-face discussion situations. As before, we will cite representative studies to serve as a point of departure for those who wish to pursue this topic further.

Cohesiveness

Our earlier comments on the concept of the group should have at least implied the importance of cohesiveness in discussion groups. Cartwright and Zander (1953) have distinguished three meanings for this term: "(a) attraction to the group, including resistance to leaving it; (b) morale, or the level of motivation of the members to attack their tasks with zeal; and (c) coordination of the efforts of members." Representative studies by Festinger (1951), Fouriezos, *et al.* (1950), Stotland (1959), and Torrance (1957) lend support to this description of cohesiveness and underscore its significance. They indicate that unless members have a psychological sense of identification with each other and are motivated to work enthusiastically together on a common task, group structure tends to disintegrate, resistance to change increases, values come into conflict, and patterns of discussion break down.

The leadership of a group, of course, can be a vital element in creating and maintaining cohesiveness. In terms of the four functional psychological factors we discussed in the last chapter, the leader should be concerned with keeping the *attention* of the group focused upon its task; creating a common ground of *interest* among members; channeling the strongest *motivation* for each member into a desire to achieve the group's goals and support its values; and guiding the discussion so that *learning* will be reinforced.

Goals

While we have referred first to cohesiveness among the special forces operating in discussion groups, we could almost as logically have started with the establishment of group goals, so closely are they associated. In practice, the discovery of common individual goals (learning about a subject, solving a problem, and so on) may be what attracts people to each other and causes them to form a group. It may also happen that the achievement of a group goal eliminates the chief reason for cohesiveness, and the group will break up unless further common interests are developed. Gerard (1957), Harnack (1955), and Keltner (1947) have shown experimentally the importance to the individual's role in the group process of clarifying goals and also of recognizing obstacles in the way of them. It is an obvious function of leadership to aid in this process of goal identification and then to turn the motivational drives of members toward achieving the goals.

Interaction

This term covers a variety of factors affecting the communicative behavior of a group of individuals. Kimball Young (1958, pp. 225–242) regards communication structure, power relationships, interpersonal relations, and size of a group as the most important ones. Much of our previous discussion can conveniently be summarized under these headings.

In the last chapter we noted that the communication structure of any group involves a speaker and his message, and his listeners and their responses. In a discussion group it is better to think of the messages and responses of speakers-listeners, since members take these roles alternately. Thus it is important that every participant understand and apply what is known about the functional psychological factors of attention and perception, interest, motivation, and learning and remembering. Training for discussion speaker-listeners should also include appropriate applications of these factors in performing the various member roles related to group functioning and problem-solving.

On a more sophisticated level of training for participation in group discussion the studies of discrete classifications of member contributions should be consulted. In an early investigation Simpson (1938) identified various types of member contributions and, with more refined techniques for observing and recording, Bales (1950) evolved a classification of twelve categories of messages in discussion. In highly condensed form these classes are: *A. Positive Reactions:* 1. shows solidarity, 2. shows tension release, 3. agrees; *B. Attempted Answers:* 4. gives suggestions, 5. gives opinion, 6. gives orientation; *C. Questions:* 7. asks for orientation, 8. asks for opinion, 9. asks for suggestion; *D. Negative Reactions:* 10. disagrees, 11. shows tension, 12. shows antagonism. The use of the Bales categories for quantifying contributions, and of special techniques such as those suggested by Brandenburg and Neal 1953) for judging their quality, provide the basis for much of the experimental research on discussion.

When discussion theorists speak of power relationships, they have in mind the various factors that appear to give special potency to the contributions of individual members. In many respects their observations parallel our treatment in the last chapter of impressiveness as a functional factor in learning and remembering. One series of studies reported by Lippitt, *et al.* (1952) established a number of indexes for measuring attributed power (reported about an individual by other members) and manifest power (observations of influential behavior by an individual). Subsequent investigations have focused sharply on the nature and operation of such power-producing factors as status, prestige, reinforcement, and different styles of leadership. (Gerard, 1957; Oakes, *et al.,* 1960; Torrance, 1957; Utterback, 1958; Wischmeier 1955.)

In discussing the concepts of the group and of group leadership we have identified many interpersonal relationships which are fundamental to healthy interaction. Psychologists have given perhaps more attention to the question of how group members react to each other as persons than to any other aspect of communicative behavior in discussion. In addition to pertinent studies already cited, we suggest the scope of this topic by noting research exploring various significant continua such as certainty-uncertainty, agreement-disagreement (Simpson, 1960), cooperation-competition (Smith, *et al.*, 1957), and like-dislike (Moreno and Jennings, 1938).

The variable of group size also affects interpersonal relations in discussion. In terms of the differential characteristics we considered earlier, it can be generalized that as the size of a discussion group increases, conformity tends to lessen and resistance to change to increase, more conflicting subgroups are likely to emerge, consensus is harder to achieve, and the opportunity for individual contribution is limited. It is also apparent that increased size requires more complex, and perhaps more directive, leadership functions, and this in turn may result in less member satisfaction with the group process and product. The maximum size for informal group discussions has long been regarded as fifteen to twenty persons, and for effective committee work Slater (1958) supports the conclusion of Bales (1954) that five is probably the optimum number, with a range from three to seven. The relative efficiency of these numbers may, of course, be affected by other factors, such as the nature of the problem being discussed, the amount of experience members have had in working with each other, and various kinds of outside pressures.

Behavioral Results of Discussion

Many of the studies reported in this chapter have utilized special methods for measuring the impact of discussion upon individual behavior by modifying attitudes and beliefs. We have already called particular attention to the quantifying procedures of Bales. Bass, *et al.* (1957) refined objective methods for studying group behavior, and have applied them to a number of variables, including the effect of motivation upon consistency of performance (Bass, 1959). Glanzer and Glaser (1959) reported special techniques for studying group structure as well as behavior, and Roby (1957) evolved a model for measuring complex variables in discussion. Dickens (1955) proposed statistical procedures for quantifying "spread-of-participation," and Matthews and Bendig (1955) for establishing an "index of agreement" on discussion outcomes. These reports should be among those consulted by persons interested in methods for measuring behavior in discussion groups.

Throughout this chapter we have dealt with the most significant psychological variables in the group discussion situation, and in most instances the research studies cited have measured the impact of discussion on behavior in terms of attitudes, beliefs, and opinions. It is beyond the purpose of this book to summarize all of the studies on the behavioral results of discussion, but from those cited, and supporting ones not reported here, we submit these general conclusions:

1. In many investigations it has been found that even relatively short discussions may significantly change the attitudes of as many as forty per cent of the participants. It has also been demonstrated that discussion can significantly change the overt behavior patterns of group members. The changes in attitudes may be in various directions if the problem discussed has several alternative solutions.

2. It has been found that members of discussion groups who have arrived at a consensus are more likely to feel personal involvement in the problem and greater responsibility for the decision than are members of a co-acting audience.

3. While the contributions of various group members obviously vary in both quantity and quality, experimental programs do establish that individuals may be trained to greater effectiveness in general participation and in leadership functions.

4. Even without discussion, it has been found that on matters involving judgment the group average is superior to the majority of individual judgments, although there will naturally always be some individuals who are superior to the average. Group conclusions reached after discussion are superior to individual conclusions whenever these factors are important: a variety of points of view on a problem, a large number of suggestions for its solution, or a large number of effective criticisms for alternate solutions.

5. In various experiments where it is possible to determine "right" answers by other means, it has been demonstrated that those who reach such conclusions through discussion tend to hold them more tenaciously than do individuals who have

"wrong" answers. Research has also shown that discussion groups are more likely to accept sound suggestions than to reject them; more likely to reject bad ones than to accept them.

6. None of the available evidence suggests that the discussion method is a panacea. Discussion groups are made up of individuals who—even when in a permissive atmosphere and encouraged to proceed logically, efficiently, and responsibly—are still subject to limitations in attention and perception, fluctuations in interest, conflicts among motivational drives, and variations in the capacity for learning and remembering.

References

Auer, J. J. Recent literature in discussion. *Quart. J. Spch,* 1953, **39,** 95–98.

Bales, R. F. *Interaction process analysis.* Reading, Mass.: Addison-Wesley, 1950.

Bales, R. F. In conference. *Harvard Bus. Rev.,* 1954, **32,** 44–50.

Barnlund, D. C. Consistency of emergent leadership in groups with changing tasks and members. *Spch Monogr.,* 1962, **29,** 45–52.

Bass, B. M.; Gaier, E. L.; Farese, F. J.; & Flint, A. W. An objective method for studying behavior in groups. *Psychol. Rep.,* 1957, **3,** 265–280.

Bass, B. M. Effects of motivation on consistency of performance in groups. *Educ. psychol. Measmt,* 1959, **19,** 247–252.

Beer, M.; Buckhout, R.; Horowitz, M. W.; & Levy, S. Some perceived properties of the difference between leaders and nonleaders. *J. Psychol.,* 1959, **47,** 49–56.

Bradenburg, E., & Neal, P. A. Graphic techniques for evaluating discussion and conference procedures. *Quart. J. Spch,* 1953, **39,** 201–208.

Browne, C. G., & Cohn, T. S. (Eds.) *The study of leadership.* Danville, Ill.: Interstate Printers and Publishers, 1958.

Cartwright, D., & Zander, A. (Eds.) *Group dynamics: research and theory.* New York: Harper & Row, 1953. Pp. 73–85.

Cleary, J. W. A bibliography of rhetoric and public address. Annually in *Spch Monogr.,* 1957 ff., **25** ff.

Cooley, C. H. *Social organization.* New York: Scribner's, 1909.

Dickens, M. A statistical formula to quantify the "spread-of-participation" in group discussion. *Spch Monogr.*, 1955, **22**, 28–30.

Festinger, L. Architecture and group membership. *J. soc. Issues*, 1951, **7**, 152–163.

Fouriezos, N. T.; Hutt, M. L.; & Guetzkow, H. Measurement of self-oriented needs in discussion groups. *J. abnorm. soc. Psychol.*, 1950, **45**, 682–690.

Gerard, H. B. Some effects of status, role clarity, and group goal clarity upon the individual's relations to group processes. *J. Pers.*, 1957, **25**, 475–488.

Glanzer, M., & Glaser, R. Techniques for the study of group structure and behavior. *Psychol. Bull.*, 1959, **56**, 317–332.

Haberman, F. W. A bibliography of rhetoric and public address. Annually, 1948–1956, in *Quart. J. Spch*, **34–36**; in *Spch Monogr.*, **18–24**.

Haiman, F. S. Materials in groups dynamics. *Quart. J. Spch*, 1954, **40**, 201–206.

Harnack, R. V. An experimental study of the effects of training in the recognition and formulation of goals upon intragroup cooperation. *Spch Monogr.*, 1955, **22**, 31–38.

Homans, G. C. *The human group.* New York: Harcourt, Brace & World, 1950.

Keltner, J. W. Goals, obstacles, and problem formulation in group discussion. *Quart. J. Spch*, 1947, **33**, 468–473.

Lippitt, R.; Polansky, N.; Redl, F.; & Rosen, S. The dynamics of power. *Human Relat.*, 1952, **5**, 37–64.

Matthews, J., & Bendig, A. W. The index of agreement: a possible criterion for measuring the outcome of group discussion. *Spch Monogr.*, 1955, **22**, 39–42.

Moreno, J. L., & Jennings, H. H. Statistics of social configurations. *Sociometry*, 1938, **1**, 342–374.

Oakes, W. F.; Droge, A. E.; & August, B. Reinforcement effects on participation in group discussion. *Psychol. Rep.*, 1960, **7**, 503–514.

Roby, T. B. On the measurement and description of groups. *Behav. sci.*, 1957, **2**, 119–127.

Simpson, R. H. *A study of those who influence and of those who are influenced in discussion.* New York: Teachers College, Columbia University, 1938.

Simpson, R. H. Attitudinal effects of small group discussions: shifts on certainty-uncertainty and agreement-disagreement continua. *Quart. J. Spch,* 1960, **46,** 415–418.

Slater, P. E. Contrasting correlates of group size. *Sociometry,* 1958, **21,** 129–130.

Smith, A. J., Madde, H. E., & Sobol, R. Productivity and recall in cooperative and competitive discussion groups. *J. Psychol.,* 1957, **43,** 193–204.

Stodgill R. M. Personal factors associated with leadership: a survey of the literature. *J. Psychol.,* 1948, **25,** 35–71.

Stotland, E. Determinants of attraction to groups. *J. soc. Psychol.,* 1959, **49,** 71–80.

Strodtbeck, F. L., & Hare, A. P. Bibliography of small group research. *Sociometry,* 1954, **17,** 107–178.

Torrance, E. P. Group decision-making and disagreement. *Social Forces,* 1957, **35,** 314–318.

Utterback, W. E. The influence of style and moderation on the outcomes of discussion. *Quart. J. Spch,* 1958, **44,** 149–152.

Wischmeier, R. R. Group-centered and leader-centered leadership: an experimental study. *Spch Monogr.,* 1955, **22,** 43–48.

Young, K. *Social psychology.* (3rd ed.) New York: Appleton-Century-Crofts, 1958.

Questions
for
Reflection
and
Discussion
Section Six

1. What are some characteristics of "face engagements" in our Western culture that have different significance in other parts of the world? Consider such factors as eye contact, gestures, and personal encounter.
2. What are the interpersonal clues and cues that determine the formality of a given social situation?
3. Do groups have "normative" (collective) norms or individual norms? What are these norms based upon? What are the effects of these norms?
4. You have just been elected chairman of a small group. You know that your career depends upon your success at this task. The members of the group will vote at the end of the year to either extend your assignment or dismiss you. What things would you consider in trying to lead this group, and in establishing an open atmosphere for communication among the leader and the members? Defend your reasons for choosing this approach.
5. Analyze a real-life group in terms of the sources of pressure, both external and internal, that affect the behaviors of the members.
6. What dimensions do you feel are important in asserting the effectiveness or success of a group? How might these dimensions be measured?

INTERPERSONAL BARRIERS
SECTION SEVEN

There are certain potential barriers between people that limit the possibility of establishing effective interpersonal relationships. Some of these barriers have been identified in other sections of this book: language differences, environmental differences, negative orientations toward others, and distortions of interpersonal perception. For the most part the barriers previously discussed have been those which originate in a social milieu, that is, the larger social context. For example, language differences and negative attitudes toward people in general are more the product of one's social environment than the result of the interaction between two people.

In this section we are primarily concerned with barriers between two people that result from their direct contact or interaction. The barriers to be discussed include: (1) a person's lack of awareness of the ways in which he communicates his attitude *toward the other person* when he thinks he is communicating his attitude toward the topic they are discussing; (2) lack of understanding of ways in which communication behavior increases a person's defensiveness; and (3) insensitivity to factors which decrease or increase the degree of interpersonal trust.

Each of these barriers is highly personal in its origin. One's attitude toward another person, one's need to be defensive in his presence, and one's readiness to trust that person are heavily influenced by two factors: one's own internal sense of security, and the way in which the other person affects this sense of security.

Much is still unknown about these personal barriers to human relationships. Behavioral science in these areas is still in the exploratory stage. The articles included in this section must be viewed as tentative statements of principles in need of further investigation. However, each article focuses upon a problem which is obviously important, and useful insights into these problems is provided.

The article by Roethlisberger describes a communication event in which one of the persons involved ignores factors directly influencing his personal relationship to the other person. In this case, the listener hears *attitude* much louder than the intended message of the speaker.

Gibb's article on defensive communication identifies two categories of behavior: (1) that which produces a "defensive" climate; and (2) that which results in a "supportive" climate. Six types of interpersonal behavior which can increase a person's need to be defensive are described in some detail.

The article on interpersonal trust identifies characteristic ways in which we must be perceived by others if we expect them to trust us. Factors which cause distrust are discussed, along with situational conditions which limit the degree of interpersonal trust likely to occur.

F. J. Roethlisberger
Barriers to Communication Between Men

In thinking about the many barriers to personal communication, particularly those that are due to differences of background, experience, and motivation, it seems to me extraordinary that any two persons can ever understand each other. Such reflections provoke the question of how communication is possible when people do not see and assume the same things and share the same values.

On this question there are two schools of thought. One school assumes that communication between A and B, for example, has failed when B does not accept what A has to say as being fact, true, or valid. The goal of communication is to get B to agree with A's opinions, ideas, facts, or information.

The position of the other school of thought is quite different. It assumes that communication has failed when B does not feel free to express his feelings to A because B fears they will not be accepted by A. Communication is facilitated when on the part of A or B or both there is *a willingness to express and accept differences.*

As these are quite divergent conceptions let us explore them further with an example. Bill, an employee, is talking with his boss in the boss's office. The boss says, "I think, Bill, that this is the best way to do your job." Bill says, "Oh yeah!" According

Reprinted by permission from *ETC.: A Review of General Semantics*, Vol. IX, No. 2; copyright 1952, by the International Society for General Semantics. This paper was presented originally on October 11, 1951, at Northwestern University's Centennial Conference on Communications.

to the first school of thought, this reply would be a sign of poor communication. Bill does not understand the best way of doing his work. To improve communication, therefore, it is up to the boss to explain to Bill why his way is the best.

From the point of view of the second school of thought, Bill's reply is neither a sign of good nor bad communication. Bill's response is indeterminate. What Bill means, the boss has an opportunity to find out if he so desires. Let us assume that this is what he chooses to do, i.e., find out what Bill means. So this boss tries to get Bill to talk more about his job while he (the boss) listens.

For purposes of simplification, I shall call the boss representing the first school of thought "Smith" and the boss representing the second school of thought "Jones." In the presence of the so-called same stimulus, each behaves differently. Smith chooses to *explain*, Jones chooses to *listen*. In my experience Jones's response works better than Smith's. It works better because Jones is making a more proper evaluation of what is taking place between him and Bill than Smith is. Let us test this hypothesis by continuing with our example.

The Assumptions, Perceptions, and Feelings of Smith[1]

Smith assumes that he understands what Bill means when Bill says, "Oh yeah!" so there is no need to find out. Smith is sure that Bill does not understand why this is the best way to do his job, so Smith has to tell him. In the process let us assume Smith is logical, lucid, and clear. He presents his facts and evidence well. But, alas, Bill remains unconvinced. What does Smith do? Operating under the assumption that what is taking place between him and Bill is something essentially logical, Smith can draw only one of two conclusions: (1) either he has not been clear enough, or (2) Bill is too damned stupid to understand. So either he has to "spell out" his case in words of fewer and fewer syllables, or give up. Smith is reluctant to do the latter, so he continues to explain. What happens?

[1] For the concepts I use to present my material I am greatly indebted to some very interesting conversations I had with my friend, Irving Lee.

If Bill still does not accept Smith's explanation of why this is the best way for him to do his job, a pattern of interacting feelings is produced of which Smith is often unaware. The more Smith cannot get Bill to understand him, the more frustrated Smith becomes and the more Bill becomes a threat to his logical capacity. Since Smith sees himself as a fairly reasonable and logical chap, this is a difficult feeling to accept. It is much easier for him to perceive Bill as uncooperative or stupid. This perception, however, will affect what Smith says and does. Under these pressures Bill comes to be evaluated more and more in terms of Smith's values. By this process Smith tends to treat Bill's values as unimportant. He tends to deny Bill's uniqueness and difference. He treats Bill as if he had little capacity for self-direction.

Let us be clear. Smith does not see that he is doing these things. When he is feverishly scratching hieroglyphics on the back of an envelope, trying to explain to Bill why this is the best way to do his job, Smith is trying to be helpful. He is a man of good will and he wants to set Bill straight. This is the way Smith sees himself and his behavior. But it is for this very reason that Bill's "Oh yeahs" are getting under Smith's skin. "How dumb can a guy be?"

Unfortunately, Bill will hear this more than Smith's "good intentions." Bill will feel misunderstood. He will not see Smith as a man of good will trying to be helpful. Rather he will perceive him as a threat to his self-esteem and personal integrity. Against this threat Bill will feel the need to defend himself at all cost. Not being as logically articulate as Smith, Bill expresses this need by saying, "Oh yeah!"

The Assumptions, Perceptions, and Feelings of Jones

Let us leave this sad scene between Smith and Bill, which I fear is going to terminate by Bill either leaving in a huff or being kicked out of Smith's office. Let us turn for a moment to Jones and see what he is assuming, seeing, hearing, feeling, doing, and saying when he interacts with Bill.

Jones, it will be remembered, does not assume that he

knows what Bill means when he says "Oh yeah," so he has to find out. Moreover, he assumes that when Bill said this, he had not exhausted his vocabulary or his feelings. Bill may not necessarily mean one thing; he may mean several different things. So Jones decides to listen.

In this process Jones is not under any illusion that what will take place will be essentially logical. Rather, he is assuming that what will take place will be primarily an interaction of feelings. Therefore, he cannot ignore the feelings of Bill, the effect of Bill's feelings upon him, or the effect of his feelings upon Bill. He cannot ignore his relationship to Bill. He does not assume that Bill's attitude toward him makes no difference to what Bill will hear or accept. Therefore, Jones will be paying strict attention to all of the things Smith has ignored. Jones will be addressing himself to Bill's feelings, his own, and the interactions between them.

Jones will, therefore, realize that he had ruffled Bill's feelings with his comment, "I think, Bill, this is the best way to do your job." So instead of trying to get Bill to understand him, he decides to try to understand Bill. He does this by encouraging Bill to speak. Instead of telling Bill how he should feel or think, he asks Bill such questions as, is this what you feel, is this what you see, is this what you assume? Instead of ignoring Bill's evaluations as irrelevant, not valid, inconsequential, or false, he tries to understand Bill's reality as Bill feels it, perceives it, and assumes it to be. As Bill begins to open up, Jones's curiosity is piqued by this process. Instead of seeing Bill as stupid, he perceives Bill as quite an interesting guy.

This is what Bill hears. Therefore, Bill feels understood and accepted as a person. He becomes less defensive. He is in a better frame of mind to explore and re-examine his own perceptions, feelings, and assumptions. In this process he perceives Jones as a source of help. Bill feels free to express his differences. He feels that Jones has some respect for his capacity for self-direction. These positive feelings toward Jones make Bill more inclined to say, "Well, Jones, I don't quite agree with you that this is the best way to do my job, but I'll tell you what I'll do. I'll try to do it that way for a few days, and then I'll tell you what I think."

Conclusions

I grant that my two orientations do not work themselves out in practice in quite as simple or neat a fashion as I have been able to work them out on paper. Bill could have responded to Smith in many other ways. He might even have said, "O.K., boss, I agree that your way of doing my job is better." But Smith still would not have known how Bill felt when he made this statement or whether Bill was actually going to do his job differently. Likewise, Bill could have responded to Jones in a way different from my example. In spite of Jones's attitude, Bill might still be reluctant to express himself freely to his boss.

The purpose of my examples has not been to demonstrate the right or wrong way of doing something. My purpose has been to provide something concrete to point to when I make the following generalizations:

1. Smith represents to me a very common pattern of misunderstanding. It does not arise because Smith is not clear enough in expressing himself. It arises because of Smith's misevaluation of what is taking place when two people are talking together.

2. Smith's misevaluation of the process of personal communication consists of certain very common assumptions. Three of these very common assumptions are (a) that what is taking place is something essentially logical; (b) that words in themselves apart from the people involved mean something; (c) that the purpose of the interaction is to get Bill to see things from Smith's point of view.

3. Because of these assumptions, a chain reaction of perception and negative feelings is engendered which blocks communication. By ignoring Bill's feelings and by rationalizing his own, Smith ignores his relationship to Bill as one of the most important determinants of the communication. As a result, Bill hears Smith's *attitude* more clearly than the logical content of

Smith's words. Bill feels that his individual uniqueness is being denied. His personal integrity being at stake, he becomes defensive and belligerent. As a result, Smith feels frustrated. He perceives Bill as stupid. As a result he says and does things which only provoke more defensiveness on the part of Bill.

4. In the case of Jones, I have tried to show what might possibly happen if we made a different evaluation of what is taking place when two people are talking together. Jones makes a different set of assumptions. He assumes (a) that what is taking place between him and Bill is an interaction of sentiments; (b) that Bill—not his words in themselves—means something; (c) that the object of the interaction is to give Bill an opportunity to express freely his differences.

5. Because of these assumptions, a psychological chain reaction of reinforcing feelings and perceptions is set up which facilitates communication between him and Bill. When Jones addresses himself to Bill's feelings and perceptions from Bill's point of view, Bill feels understood and accepted as a person; Bill feels free to express his differences. Bill sees Jones as a source of help; Jones sees Bill as an interesting person. Bill in turn becomes more cooperative.

6. If I have identified correctly these very common patterns of personal communication, then some interesting hypotheses can be stated:

(a) Jones's method works better than Smith's not because of any magic, but because Jones has a better map than Smith of the process of personal communication.

(b) The practice of Jones's method, however, is not merely an intellectual exercise. It depends upon Jones's capacity and willingness to see and accept points of view different from his own, and to practice this orientation in a face-to-face relationship. This practice involves an emotional as well as an intellectual achievement. It depends in part upon Jones's awareness of himself; it depends in part upon the practice of a skill.

(c) Although our colleges and universities try to get students to appreciate intellectually points of view different from their own, very little is done to help them to implement this general intellectual appreciation in a simple face-to-face relationship—

at the level of a skill. Most universities train their students to be logical, lucid, and clear. Very little is done to help them to listen more skillfully. As a result, our educated world contains too many Smiths and too few Joneses.

(d) The biggest block to personal communication is man's inability to listen intelligently, understandingly, and skillfully to another person. This deficiency in the modern world is widespread and appalling. In our universities, as well as elsewhere, too little is being done about it.

In conclusion, let me apologize for acting toward you like Smith. But who am I to violate a long-standing academic tradition!

Jack R. Gibb
Defensive Communication

One way to understand communication is to view it as a people process rather than as a language process. If one is to make fundamental improvement in communication, he must make changes in interpersonal relationships. One possible type of alteration—and the one with which this paper is concerned—is that of reducing the degree of defensiveness.

Definition and Significance

Defensive behavior is defined as that behavior which occurs when an individual perceives threat or anticipates threat in the group. The person who behaves defensively, even though he also gives some attention to the common task, devotes an appreciable portion of his energy to defending himself. Besides talking about the topic, he thinks about how he appears to others, how he may be seen more favorably, how he may win, dominate, impress, or escape punishment and/or how he may avoid or mitigate a perceived or an anticipated attack.

Such inner feelings and outward acts tend to create similarly defensive postures in others; and, if unchecked, the ensuing circular response becomes increasingly destructive. Defensive behavior, in short, engenders defensive listening, and this in turn produces postural, facial, and verbal cues which raise the defense level of the original communicator.

Reprinted by permission of the author and publisher from Jack R. Gibb, "Defensive Communication," *The Journal of Communication*, Vol. 11, No. 3 (September, 1961), 141–148.

Defense arousal prevents the listener from concentrating upon the message. Not only do defensive communicators send off multiple value, motive, and affect cues, but also defensive recipients distort what they receive. As a person becomes more and more defensive, he becomes less and less able to perceive accurately the motives, the values, and the emotions of the sender. The writer's analyses of tape recorded discussions revealed that increases in defensive behavior were correlated positively with losses in efficiency in communication.[1] Specifically, distortions became greater when defensive states existed in the groups.

The converse, moreover, also is true. The more "supportive" or defense reductive the climate the less the receiver reads into the communication distorted loadings which arise from projections of his own anxieties, motives, and concerns. As defenses are reduced, the receivers become better able to concentrate upon the structure, the content, and the cognitive meanings of the message.

Categories of Defensive and Supportive Communication

In working over an eight-year period with recordings of discussions occurring in varied settings, the writer developed the six pairs of defensive and supportive categories presented in Table 2. Behavior which a listener perceives as possessing any

TABLE 2   CATEGORIES OF BEHAVIOR CHARACTERISTIC OF SUPPORTIVE AND DEFENSIVE CLIMATES IN SMALL GROUPS

Defensive Climates	Supportive Climates
1. Evaluation	1. Description
2. Control	2. Problem orientation
3. Strategy	3. Spontaneity
4. Neutrality	4. Empathy
5. Superiority	5. Equality
6. Certainty	6. Provisionalism

[1] J. R. Gibb, "Defense Level and Influence Potential in Small Groups," in L. Petrullo and B. M. Bass (eds.), *Leadership and Interpersonal Behavior* (New York: Holt, Rinehart and Winston, Inc., 1961), pp. 66–81.

of the characteristics listed in the left-hand column arouses defensiveness, whereas that which he interprets as having any of the qualities designated as supportive reduces defensive feelings. The degree to which these reactions occur depends upon the personal level of defensiveness and upon the general climate in the group at the time.[2]

Evaluation and Description

Speech or other behavior which appears evaluative increases defensiveness. If by expression, manner of speech, tone of voice, or verbal content the sender seems to be evaluating or judging the listener, then the receiver goes on guard. Of course, other factors may inhibit the reaction. If the listener thought that the speaker regarded him as an equal and was being open and spontaneous, for example, the evaluativeness in a message would be neutralized and perhaps not even perceived. This same principle applies equally to the other five categories of potentially defense-producing climates. The six sets are interactive.

Because our attitudes toward other persons are frequently, and often necessarily, evaluative, expressions which the defensive person will regard as nonjudgmental are hard to frame. Even the simplest question usually conveys the answer that the sender wishes or implies the response that would fit into his value system. A mother, for example, immediately following an earth tremor that shook the house, sought for her small son with the question: "Bobby, where are you?" The timid and plaintive "Mommy, I didn't do it" indicated how Bobby's chronic mild defensiveness predisposed him to react with a projection of his own guilt and in the context of his chronic assumption that questions are full of accusation.

Anyone who has attempted to train professionals to use information-seeking speech with neutral affect appreciates how difficult it is to teach a person to say even the simple "who did

---

[2] J. R. Gibb, "Sociopsychological Processes of Group Instruction," in N. B. Henry (ed.), *The Dynamics of Instructional Groups* (Fifty-ninth Yearbook of the National Society for the Study of Education, Part II, 1960), pp. 115–135.

that?" without being seen as accusing. Speech is so frequently judgmental that there is a reality base for the defensive interpretations which are so common.

When insecure, group members are particularly likely to place blame, to see others as fitting into categories of good or bad, to make moral judgments of their colleagues, and to question the value, motive, and affect loadings of the speech which they hear. Since value loadings imply a judgment of others, a belief that the standards of the speaker differ from his own causes the listener to become defensive.

Descriptive speech, in contrast to that which is evaluative, tends to arouse a minimum of uneasiness. Speech acts which the listener perceives as genuine requests for information or as material with neutral loadings is descriptive. Specifically, presentations of feelings, events, perceptions, or processes which do not ask or imply that the receiver change behavior or attitude are minimally defense producing. The difficulty in avoiding overtone is illustrated by the problems of news reporters in writing stories about unions, communists, Negroes, and religious activities without tipping off the "party" line of the newspaper. One can often tell from the opening words in a news article which side the newspaper's editorial policy favors.

Control and Problem Orientation

Speech which is used to control the listener evokes resistance. In most of our social intercourse someone is trying to do something to someone else—to change an attitude, to influence behavior, or to restrict the field of activity. The degree to which attempts to control produce defensiveness depends upon the openness of the effort, for a suspicion that hidden motives exist heightens resistance. For this reason attempts of nondirective therapists and progressive educators to refrain from imposing a set of values, a point of view, or a problem solution upon the receivers meet with many barriers. Since the norm is control, noncontrollers must earn the perceptions that their efforts have no hidden motives. A bombardment of persuasive "messages" in the fields of politics, education, special causes, advertising, religion, medicine, industrial relations and guidance has bred cynical and paranoidal responses in listeners.

Implicit in all attempts to alter another person is the assumption by the change agent that the person to be altered is inadequate. That the speaker secretly views the listener as ignorant, unable to make his own decisions, uninformed, immature, unwise, or possessed of wrong or inadequate attitudes is a subconscious perception which gives the latter a valid base for defensive reactions.

Methods of control are many and varied. Legalistic insistence on detail, restrictive regulations and policies, conformity norms, and all laws are among the methods. Gestures, facial expressions, other forms of nonverbal communication, and even such simple acts as holding a door open in a particular manner are means of imposing one's will upon another and hence are potential sources of resistance.

Problem orientation, on the other hand, is the antithesis of persuasion. When the sender communicates a desire to collaborate in defining a mutual problem and in seeking its solution, he tends to create the same problem orientation in the listener; and, of greater importance, he implies that he has no predetermined solution, attitude, or method to impose. Such behavior is permissive in that it allows the receiver to set his own goals, make his own decisions, and evaluate his own progress—or to share with the sender in doing so. The exact methods of attaining permissiveness are not known, but they must involve a constellation of cues and they certainly go beyond mere verbal assurances that the communicator has no hidden desires to exercise control.

Strategy and Spontaneity

When the sender is perceived as engaged in a stratagem involving ambiguous and multiple motivations, the receiver becomes defensive. No one wishes to be a guinea pig, a role player, or an impressed actor, and no one likes to be the victim of some hidden motivation. That which is concealed, also, may appear larger than it really is with the degree of defensiveness of the listener determining the perceived size of the suppressed element. The intense reaction of the reading audience to the material in the *Hidden Persuaders* indicates the prevalence of defensive reactions to multiple motivations behind strategy. Group members who are seen as "taking a role," as feigning emotion, as toying with their colleagues, as withholding information, or as having special sources of data are especially resented. One participant once complained that another was "using a listening technique" on him!

A large part of the adverse reaction to much of the so-called human relations training is a feeling against what are perceived as gimmicks and tricks to fool or to "involve" people, to make a person think he is making his own decision, or to make the listener feel that the sender is genuinely interested in him as a person. Particularly violent reactions occur when it appears that someone is trying to make a stratagem appear spontaneous. One person has reported a boss who incurred resentment by habitually using the gimmick of "spontaneously" looking at his watch and saying, "My gosh, look at the time—I must run to an appointment." The belief was that the boss would create less irritation by honestly asking to be excused.

Similarly, the deliberate assumption of guilelessness and natural simplicity is especially resented. Monitoring the tapes of feedback and evaluation sessions in training groups indicates the surprising extent to which members perceive the strategies of their colleagues. This perceptual clarity may be quite shocking to the strategist, who usually feels that he has cleverly hidden the motivational aura around the "gimmick."

This aversion to deceit may account for one's resistance to politicians who are suspected of behind-the-scenes planning to get his vote, to psychologists whose listening apparently is motivated by more than the manifest or content-level interest in his behavior, or to the sophisticated, smooth, or clever person whose "oneupmanship" is marked with guile. In training groups the role-flexible person frequently is resented because his changes in behavior are perceived as strategic maneuvers.

In contrast, behavior which appears to be spontaneous and free of deception is defense reductive. If the communicator is seen as having a clean id, as having uncomplicated motivations, as being straightforward and honest, and as behaving spontaneously in response to the situation, he is likely to arouse minimal defense.

Neutrality and Empathy

When neutrality in speech appears to the listener to indicate a lack of concern for his welfare, he becomes defensive. Group members usually desire to be perceived as valued persons, as individuals of special worth, and as objects of concern and affection. The clinical, detached, person-as-an-object-of-study attitude on the part of many psychologist-trainers is resented by group members. Speech with low affect that communicates little warmth or caring is in such contrast with the affect-laden speech in social situations that it sometimes communicates rejection.

Communication that conveys empathy for the feelings and respect for the worth of the listener, however, is particularly supportive and defense reductive. Reassurance results when a message indicates that the speaker identifies himself with the listener's problems, shares his feelings, and accepts his emotional reactions at face value. Abortive efforts to deny the legitimacy of the receiver's emotions by assuring the receiver that he need not feel bad, that he should not feel rejected, or that he is overly anxious, though often intended as support giving, may impress the listener as lack of acceptance. The combination of understanding and empathizing with the other person's emotions with no accompanying effort to change him apparently is supportive at a high level.

The importance of gestural behavioral cues in communicating empathy should be mentioned. Apparently spontaneous facial and bodily evidences of concern are often interpreted as especially valid evidence of deep-level acceptance.

Superiority and Equality

When a person communicates to another that he feels superior in position, power, wealth, intellectual ability, physical characteristics, or other ways he arouses defensiveness. Here as with the other sources of disturbance whatever arouses feelings of inadequacy causes the listener to center upon the affect loading of the statement rather than upon the cognitive elements. The receiver then reacts by not hearing the message, by forgetting it, by competing with the sender, or by becoming jealous of him.

The person who is perceived as feeling superior communicates that he is not willing to enter into a shared problem-solving relationship, that he probably does not desire feedback, that he does not require help, and/or that he will be likely to try to reduce the power, the status, or the worth of the receiver.

Many ways exist for creating the atmosphere that the sender feels himself equal to the listener. Defenses are reduced when one perceives the sender as being willing to enter into participative planning with the mutual trust and respect. Differences in talent, ability, worth, appearance, status, and power often exist, but the low defense communicator seems to attach little importance to these distinctions.

Certainty and Provisionalism

The effects of dogmatism in producing defensiveness are well known. Those who seem to know the answers, to require no additional data, and to regard themselves as teachers rather than as co-workers tend to put others on guard. Moreover, in the writer's experiment, listeners often perceived manifest expressions of certainty as connoting inward feelings of inferiority. They saw the dogmatic individual as needing to be right, as wanting to win an argument rather than solve a problem, and as seeing his ideas as truths to be defended. This kind of behavior often was associated with acts which others regarded as attempts to exercise control. People who were right seemed to have low tolerance for members who were "wrong"—i.e., who did not agree with the sender.

One reduces the defensiveness of the listener when he communicates that he is willing to experiment with his own behavior, attitudes, and ideas. The person who appears to be taking provisional attitudes, to be investigating issues rather than taking sides on them, to be problem solving rather than debating, and to be willing to experiment and explore tends to communicate that the listener may have some control over the shared quest or the investigation of the ideas. If a person is genuinely searching for information and data, he does not resent help or company along the way.

Conclusion

The implications of the above material for the parent, the teacher, the manager, the administrator, or the therapist are fairly obvious. Arousing defensiveness interferes with communication and thus makes it difficult—and sometimes impossible—for anyone to convey ideas clearly and to move effectively toward the solution of therapeutic, educational, or managerial problems.

Kim Giffin and
Bobby R. Patton
**Personal Trust
in Human Interaction**

Let us suppose that we are members of the Board of Directors
of a large metropolitan hospital. Each of us is a specialist in a
particular field: the handling of finances, the administration of
hospital personnel, the care and use of hospital equipment, etc.
Varying conditions call for group decisions involving special
items of information from each of us. Does it appear that the
amount of trust we have in each other makes a difference as
we communicate these items of information and guide our actions accordingly? While the answer is obvious, only recently
has research been conducted on this significant variable in human communication.

The ultimate objective of research on human behavior is to
determine the relationship between two (or more) behavioral
elements; an example of two such behavioral elements might
be (1) instructional communication on the part of a job supervisor, and (2) the implementation of these instructions on the
part of an employee. However, the determination of the *attitude*
of the employee toward the supervisor (for example, the degree to which the employee *trusts* the supervisor) is also of importance because the use of such a construct as "trust" can
explain the relationship between the two behavioral elements.

The concept of trust is identified as a "construct" because it is
an attitude which cannot be observed *per se;* it can only be inferred from observed behavior of two types: (1) the degree to
which the instructions were followed, or (2) responses on an introspective questionnaire or interview schedule. A danger for a
behavioral scientist is that he may confuse his thinking by fail-

ing to recognize the limited research value of construct-measurement, and by confusing the construct itself with behavioral reality.

It is important to distinguish the difference between an attitude of trust (the introspective orientation which is a potential for action) and the action itself (trusting behavior). It is commonly accepted that one's attitude toward another person may not always be reflected by one's observable actions. Thus, behavior which may appear to be based upon an attitude of trust may not always be so, and an attitude of trust may not always be reflected by observable trusting behavior. For example, what may appear to be trusting behavior may be exhibited by a small child ignorantly following his unthinking brother across an expressway, or a person refraining from demonstrating distrustful behavior toward a revered person, such as a bishop, for moral reasons.

The Concept of Trusting Behavior

Traditionally trust has been viewed as a somewhat mystical and intangible factor defying careful definition. Dictionary definitions include such synonyms as "confidence," "reliance," "expectation," and "hope." One dictionary states as its first definition of trust: "Reliance on the integrity, justice, etc., of a person, or on some quality or attribute of a thing; confidence." These definitions are imprecise and unsuitable for scientific investigation.

In his pioneering research on trust and suspicion, Morton Deutsch noted the importance of trust to an understanding of social life and personality development. In an attempt to define *trusting behavior* operationally in the interpersonal situation, Deutsch noted that trusting behavior involves more than predictability—expectation is also involved. He noted that risk or personal inolvement is requisite and that, when trust is not fulfilled, the trusting individual suffers an unpleasant consequence which is greater than the gain he would have received if the trusted person had proven to be reliable.[1]

[1] M. Deutsch, "Trust and Suspicion," *Journal of Conflict Resolution*, 2 (1958), 265–279.

In a recent summary of literature pertaining to a theory of interpersonal trust, Kim Giffin indicated that the following elements are requisite for a condition of interpersonal trusting behavior:

(1) A person (P) *is relying* upon another person (O).
(2) P *is risking* something he values.
(3) P *is attempting* to achieve a desired goal.[2]

Each of these elements is requisite for a trusting situation; it should be noted that each of the elements in *trusting behavior* can, when present, be ascertained by a competent observer.

A logical approach for research on trust in human interaction is to determine interrelationships between the four variables identified in the paradigm above: (1) characteristics of P; (2) P's perception of O; (3) P's perception of the degree of risk he is taking; and (4) P's perception of the value of the goal he is attempting to achieve. This schema will be employed in the sections that follow.

Personality Dimensions of Trusting Person (P)

The degree of trust P has for O in an interaction situation can be viewed as the index of his degree of fear or anxiety regarding possible interaction with O. If P trusts O only to a very small degree in such a setting, his attitude may be defined in terms of fear. If there is no reason (as perceived by others) for P's lack of trust of O, such fear may be viewed as irrational or unreasonable. Such unreasonable or unfounded fear of O in a communication setting has been defined by Giffin and Bradley as "speech anxiety."[3]

Personality variables which are correlated with lack of trust of others are P's (1) self-concept, (2) anxiety tendency, (3) degree of personal flexibility, and (4) degree of motivation to avoid failure (M_{nf}) compared with his motivation to succeed (M_s).

[2] K. Giffin, "The Contributions of Studies of Source Credibility to a Theory of Interpersonal Trust in the Communication Process," *Psychological Bulletin*, **68** (1967), 104–120.

[3] K. Giffin and K. Bradley, "Group Counseling for Speech Students with Low Self-Confidence: An Approach and a Rationale," *Journal of Communication*, in press.

Self-Concept and Trust of Others

It is almost without question in our Western culture that nothing is quite so important as one's concept of oneself. This cultural trait places severe emphasis on one's ability to protect his self-concept. We know that many times people have given up material wealth, personal health, and even their lives to preserve a self-image.

One's cognition of oneself is obtained, in part, by personal sensory perception, and also, in part, by checking with other people. Social psychologists in the tradition of Charles H. Cooley and George Herbert Mead hold that a person's impressions of his mind, self, and consciousness emerge as internalizations of concepts evolved from social interaction. According to this line of reasoning, a person *needs to interact* with others in order to verify his own view of himself.

In a well-known essay Leon Festinger elaborated on this theory. He identified a continuum on one end of which he placed "physical reality" and on the other "social reality." Social reality included (among other things) appropriate social behavior. An opinion of oneself as a social being, according to Festinger's line of reasoning, is perceived by the individual as valid to the extent it is "anchored in" (reflected by) an approved reference group. Thus, the validation of one's perception of himself socially requires feedback from other people. However, if an adequate "social self" is highly desired, but if there is considerable question in a person's mind about his social quality, he is not likely to expose himself via communication with others. In fact, he will likely *fear* communication situations.[4]

Initial studies support the relationship between fear of interaction and "self-concept" of the communicator.[5] Although most of the available evidence comes from studies which must be viewed as more exploratory than definitive, existing re-

[4] L. Festinger, "Informal Social Communication," *Psychological Review,* 57 (1950), 271–282.

[5] L. Crowell, A. Katcher, and S. Miyamota, "Self-Concepts of Communication Skill and Performance in Small Group Discussion," *Speech Monographs,* 22 (1955), 20–27; and E. Bormann and G. Shapiro, "Perceived Confidence as a Function of Self-Image," *Central States Speech Journal, 13* (1962), 253–256.

search data tend to indicate that *P's trust of O in an interaction is a function of P's self-concept.*

Both Heider's balance theory and Festinger's theory of cognitive dissonance would lead us to suspect that a person with very high self-concept would not fear exposure of himself in his interaction with others, and if an attack upon his self-image occurred, he would likely disparage the source of the attack. Very likely he would filter such information, accepting only that which tended to agree with (confirm) his high self-concept, and rejecting that which disconfirmed it. Exactly the same reasoning would lead a person with low self-concept to accept information which *confirms his low opinion of himself,* and reject information which would tend to raise it.

An experiment by Deutsch and Solomon supports this suggestion; although parts of their data are subject to more than one interpretation, they found fairly clear evidence that subjects with a low concept of their ability to do "flexible thinking" viewed low evaluations of themselves from others more favorably than they viewed high evaluations.[6] Thus, it appears that *persons with low self-concept will give more attention to information confirming their low self-concept, and less attention to information disconfirming it.*

In our culture a low self-concept and confirmation of it, even if thought to be valid, is not pleasant. Thus, the individual with low self-esteem would likely pay more attention to information which confirms low self-concept, but be unhappy about it. He would *fear* confirmation of *his fears.* When possible, he will likely try to avoid communication situations in which he perceives himself exposed to such possible confirmation. It is surprising to find that the relationship between self-concept and avoidance of interaction situations has received little formal investigation; early indications found in exploratory studies have not been pursued.[7] Because of the lack of pertinent research

[6] M. Deutsch and L. Solomon, "Reactions to Evaluations by Others as Influenced by Self-Evaluations," *Sociometry, 22* (1959), 93–112.

[7] S. Ainsworth, "A Study of Fear, Nervousness, and Anxiety in the Public Speaking Situation," (Unpublished Ph.D. dissertation, Northwestern University, 1949). And G. Law and B. Sheets, "The Relation of Psychometric Factors to Stage Fright," *Speech Monographs, 18* (1951), 266–271

evidence, the relationship is here stated in tentative terms: It appears that *persons with low self-concept will tend to avoid inter- action situations.*

In terms of interpersonal relationships, the protection of one's self-image is closely linked with trust in those with whom one interacts. Self-confidence in interpersonal relations can be conceptualized as willingness to expose one's self-concept to evaluation by others. This line of reasoning exposes a related question: Will P's trust of O be increased as he perceives O in- creasing trust in him? Perhaps trust in the communication proc- ess is literally a three-way thoroughfare: (1) confidence (trust) in oneself, (2) trust extended to the others present, and (3) per- ceived trust extended by others.

Carl Rogers uses the term "acceptance behavior" to refer to a therapist's behavior which is perceived by the client as indica- tive of trust on the part of the therapist *toward the client*. He cites evidence that the patient's perception of such trusting be- havior is related to a patient's willingness to expose himself for therapy (trust in the therapist).[8]

Certain assumptions have to be made in order to accept studies of mental patients as supportive evidence of a principle of human relationships between people who are thought to be normal. However, there is additional support from Jack Gibb's study of quite normal subjects. He found that six types of non- accepting behavior on the part of others caused increased de- fensive behavior on the part of the individual. This defensive behavior included postural, facial, and verbal cues of the fear aroused, withdrawal tendencies, and *distortion* of the messages received. The nonaccepting behaviors on the part of others, which produced these defensive behaviors in the individual, included communication identified as (1) evaluative, (2) con- trol-oriented, (3) strategy-oriented, (4) neutral (detached), (5) expressive of superiority feelings, and (6) certainty-oriented (dogmatic).[9]

[8] C. Rogers, *On Becoming a Person*, New York, Houghton-Mifflin, 1961, pp. 39–58.

[9] J. Gibb, "Defensive Communication," *Journal of Communication*, 11 (1961), 141–148.

In view of these findings, it seems appropriate to suggest that *trust of others in a given interaction situation is a function of perceived acceptance by valued others.*

Theorists of child and personality development postulate the development of a basic attitude of trust in a child as the first necessary step toward the development of a mature person. An infant's orientation toward the world is gained through the way in which his needs are met. If his desires and needs are fulfilled, he finds the world a reliable, stable, good place which can be trusted or relied upon to fulfill his needs.[10]

A healthy child has a positive self-concept. The development of self-concept is based in part upon communication with other people. A theoretical basis rests in Mead's conceptualization of the communication process as essential for the development of the "self."[11] In this sense the "self" that an individual perceives is largely determined by his interaction with the world, primarily through interpersonal communication. Not only is one's self-concept largely formed through social interaction, but this interaction allows continued validation of one's "self" through the process of checking with others. This human need to evaluate one's own opinions and abilities is described by Festinger in his theory of social comparison.[12]

Kim Giffin and Mary Heider presented an analysis of the relationship of communication suppression in childhood to trust of others in interaction situations. Communication in child development was given the role of providing the opportunity for the child to relate to the world, to develop trust of others, to initiate interaction, and to develop a positive self-concept. Parental suppression of a child's communication was conceptualized as a negative reaction on the part of a parent (or parent surrogate) to a child's attempt to express himself.[13]

[10] L. Stone and J. Church, *Childhood and Adolescence,* New York, Random House, 1957.

[11] G. Mead, *Mind, Self and Society,* Chicago, University of Chicago Press, 1934.

[12] L. Festinger, "A Theory of Social Comparison Processes," *Human Relations,* 7 (1954), 117–140.

[13] K. Giffin and M. Heider, "The Relationship between Speech Anxiety and the Suppression of Communication in Childhood," *The Psychiatric Quarterly Supplement, Part 2* (1967), Utica, N.Y., State Hospitals Press.

An exploratory study of the relationship between parental communication suppression and a person's fear of others in interaction settings showed significant correlations. It appears that if a child's communication receives negative feedback, negative feelings about himself are likely to follow. Continued attempts at self-expression, met by parental suppression, are likely to produce an undesirable self-concept. It is likely that the child will tend to guard against situations where he is expected to reveal a part of himself and to avoid interaction which might validate a negative self-concept. As communication lessens, a positive self-concept disappears, and the child's social health is undermined.[14] These tentative findings support the conclusion that *self-concept is a function of degree of parental approval of childhood attempts to engage in interaction.*

Anxiety Tendency and Trust of Others

If a personality test contains a factor identified as anxiety-tendency, or tendency to worry, or just degree of "social adjustment," it is reasonable to attempt to determine if it correlates with trust of others. Such a study remains to be done. However, studies have been made which correlate general anxiety with a construct thought to be related to trust of others: speech anxiety. Positive correlations have been found by a number of studies reviewed by Clevenger.[15] In general, positive relationships have been found between degree of speech anxiety and scores on a number of introspective personal adjustment measures: Social Adjustment scores on the Minnesota Personality Scale; number of friends and degree of shyness, seclusiveness, withdrawal, and inhibition; degree of introversion, neuroticism, submissiveness, and self-confidence on the Bernreuter Scales; amount of depression and psychasthenia (a neurosis characterized by morbid anxieties) on the Minnesota Multiphasic Per-

14 M. Heider, "An Investigation of the Relationship between Speech Anxiety in Adults and Their Indication of Parental Communication Suppression during Childhood," (Unpublished M.A. thesis, The University of Kansas, 1968).

15 T. Clevenger, Jr., "A Synthesis of Experimental Research in Stage Fright," *Quarterly Journal of Speech, 45* (1959), 134–145.

sonality Inventory; social adjustment scores on the Bell Adjustment Inventory; and anxiety scores on the Taylor Manifest Anxiety Scale. These findings are still somewhat inconclusive, and improved measurement instruments are needed; however, existing evidence supports the principle that *trust of others in interaction is a function of P's anxiety tendency.*

Authoritarianism and Trust of Others

The mass of research employing the F scale developed by Adorno and others indicates consistent differences between low and high F-scale scorers in their behavior in social situations and in their responses to various questionnaires. High scorers tended to be more authoritarian, less intellectually sophisticated, less liberal politically, more cynical, and more prejudiced against minority groups.[16] In a study reported by Deutsch, he had his subjects play an interpersonal game in which they were required, in one situation, to choose between trusting and suspecting another person; in the second situation, subjects were required to choose between acting in a trustworthy manner and an untrustworthy manner. Subjects who were more trusting were more likely to be trusted, indicating that behavior toward another person tends to be congruent with what one expects from him. The F-scale scores of the players correlated significantly with game behavior; subjects with low F scores tended to be trusting and trustworthy, whereas subjects with high F scores tended to be more suspicious and untrustworthy. The importance of these correlations is the demonstration of a relationship between trusting behavior and a measurable personality dimension known as "authoritarianism."[17]

Although Deutsch inferred the presence of an attitude of trust from the presence of cooperative behavior, and although there has been adverse criticism of the validity of the F-scale,

---

[16] R. Christie and P. Cook, "A Guide to Published Literature Relating to the Authoritarian Personality through 1956," *Journal of Psychology, 45* (1958), 171–199.

[17] M. Deutsch, "Trust, Trustworthiness, and the F Scale," *Journal of Abnormal and Social Psychology, 61* (1960), 138–140.

research to date indicates that *trust of others in human interaction is a function of personal dogmatism.*

Personal Motivation and Trust of Others

We have indicated that the trusting person hopes to achieve some *goal*. It appears that the person with low motivation generally would not care much about such a goal. On the other hand, it appears that the person with high motivation would care a lot about the goals achievable via interpersonal communication. Two definable and measureable personality characteristics which are related to motivation are: (1) motivation to achieve success; and (2) motivation to avoid failure.

According to Atkinson and Feather, motivation to achieve success is one of a class of motives described as approach tendencies, the aim of which is to maximize satisfaction.[18] Achievement motivation is the tendency to approach situations in which one can achieve success and is designated as M_s. Motivation to avoid failure is one of a class of motives described as avoidance tendencies, the aim of which is to minimize psychological discomfort. Motivation to avoid failure is the tendency to avoid undertaking an activity which may lead to a failure, and is designated as M_{af}. This avoidance tendency always resists the influence of motivation to achieve success. When M_s is greater than M_{af} in a person, he is achievement-oriented. When M_{af} is greater than M_s in a person, he is failure-oriented.

The achievement-oriented person is generally attracted to activities requiring skill; he accepts a 50–50 risk and is enthusiastic and fairly confident when approaching a task in which the possibility of success is ambiguous. The failure-oriented person, on the other hand, resists activities in which his skill will be compared to the skill of others, and would never undertake an activity the outcome of which is uncertain if it were not for powerful social forces. His anxiety in competitive situations is symptomatic of his resistance to participation.

Giffin and Masterson presented a theoretical model of the re-

[18] J. Atkinson and N. Feather, "Introduction and Overview," *A Theory of Achievement Motivation*, New York, Wiley, 1966, pp. 3–10.

lationships between M_s and M_{af} in determining speech anxiety. Its major hypothesis was that when M_{af} is greater than M_s, a person will indicate a greater degree of introspectively measured speech anxiety.[19] The available evidence tends to support this conclusion: A person's trust of others in interaction settings is a function of the relationship between his M_s and M_{af} index.

Perceived Characteristics of Person Trusted (O)

The way in which P's perceptions of O influences his trust of O has been of major concern to many scholars. In his *Rhetoric* Aristotle suggested that ethos, the estimation of a speaker by a listener, is based upon the listener's perception of three characteristics of the speaker: (1) intelligence (correctness of opinions), (2) character (honesty), and (3) goodwill (favorable intention regarding the listener).

Carl Hovland and his associates defined source credibility as the resultant value (combined effect) of "(1) . . . the extent to which a communicator is perceived to be a source of valid assertions (his 'expertness') and (2) the degree of confidence in the communicator's intent to communicate the assertions he considers most valid (his 'trustworthiness')."[20] It is clear that these writers were discussing interpersonal perceptions. However, they seemed to combine the factors of character and goodwill under the single concept of perceived intent to be a reliable communicator.

In clarity of conceptualization, it appears that Aristotle's separation of reliability and intentions is a valid and fundamental one. A person may be perceived as having high general reliability (high "quality" of character), and at the same time be perceived as opposed to the desired goals of the potentially trusting person; that is, his reliability is high and positive, but his intentions are negative.

[19] K. Giffin and S. Masterson, "A Theoretical Model of the Relationships between Motivation and Self-Confidence in Communication," *Communication Spectra '67: Proceedings of the 1967 Annual Conference of the National Society for the Study of Communication*, Flint, Michigan, NSSC, 1968, pp. 311–316.

[20] C. Hovland, I. Janis, and H. Kelley, *Communication and Persuasion*, New Haven, Yale University Press, 1953, p. 21.

In the studies of trusting behavior there is some evidence that the trusted person's intentions are perceived as a separate variable. Deutsch and his colleagues found that cooperation was increased when a person communicated (1) his intention of reciprocating trust, (2) the conditions under which he intended to try to restore trust when it had been violated, and (3) conditions under which he intended to reciprocate trust.[21] Additional support for the importance of the trusted person's intentions has been reported by Jack Gibb. Gibb found that trust is increased by communication which showed a person's intentions to be (1) non-evaluative, (2) problem-oriented rather than oriented toward social control, (3) spontaneous rather than strategic, (4) empathic rather than neutral, (5) on an equal basis rather than on an unequal one, and (6) provisional or tentative rather than certain.[22]

In a detailed analysis of the studies of interpersonal perceptions as they relate to interpersonal trust, Giffin concluded that interpersonal trust appears to be influenced by P's perceptions of the following characteristics of O:

(1) *expertness* relevant to the topic under discussion: This expertise may be in the form of quantity of pertinent information, degree of ability or skill, or validity of judgment.
(2) *reliability:* This may be perceived as dependability, predictability, consistency, or intentions of O regarding the goals or objectives of P.
(3) *dynamism:* behavior perceived as more active than passive and more open or frank than closed or reserved.[23]

Each of these three characteristics of O may be perceived directly by P.

Study of the relationship between P's perception of O (as a person to be trusted) and the conformity-influence of others present has been begun. Initial support for the probability of such a relationship comes from studies which were not specifi-

21 Deutsch, 1958, *Ibid.*

22 Gibb, *Ibid.*

23 K. Giffin, "The Contributions of Studies of Source Credibility to a Theory of Interpersonal Trust in the Communication Process," *Psychological Bulletin, 68* (1967), 104–120.

cally concerned with interpersonal trust: they are known as studies of conformity-influence. This influence is the social pressure within a group which tends psychologically to force the individuals within that group to behave similarly.

If the members of a group behave as if they trust a specified person (O), any one person (P) in the group may infer that the other members perceive in O high degrees of expertness, reliability, or dynamism; P can draw such an inference from his perception of the behavior of the other groups members *even without any direct perception of O!* An exploratory study by Tubbs tends to support the statement that P's trust of O is a function of P's perception of trust of O by other members of an interacting group.[24]

Related hypotheses may be developed which are concerned with P's perception of O's (1) expertness, (2) reliability, and (3) dynamism, as each relates to P's perception of the trust placed in O by other group members. An additional set of sub-hypotheses concern selected characteristics of the specified reference group. Social conformity influence has been shown to be influenced by each of the following conditions: (1) degree of agreement (e.g., unanimity) on an expressed opinion; (2) size of group; (3) degree of difficulty of decision required; (4) degree of general credibility of group opinion expressed; (5) degree of attractiveness of reference group to P; and (6) degree of interdependency of group members. Thus, there are at least eighteen possible hypotheses relevant to the relationships between P's perceptions of O's expertness, reliability, and dynamism, and these six group member variables; such studies have been begun.

The study of P's perceptions and trust of O under *conditions of communication denial* (of P by O) have barely begun. Communication denial should not be confused with interpersonal disagreement. When two people expose and discuss a disagreement between them, communication can be efficient and productive. However, when P attempts to communicate with O, and then O tries to refuse to give any response at all, two basic

[24] S. Tubbs, "The Influence of Majority Opinion and Game-Playing Behavior on Interpersonal Trust" (Unpublished doctoral dissertation, University of Kansas, 1969).

principles of interpersonal communication are at work: (1) all attempts to initiate interpersonal communication carry an implied request: "Please validate me" and (2) in an interpersonal situation neither person *cannot not* communicate on the meta-communicational level. Thus, efforts by O to ignore P's attempts to communicate with O carry a message to P, *whether or not* O wishes to convey such a message, and that message constitutes a denial of P's right to communicate with O (at this time, on this topic). Such a denial implies an invalidation of P; it denies his existence on a functional, interpersonal level.

A current investigation by members of The University of Kansas Communication Research Center staff (Giffin, Downs, Groginsky, Poore, and Falzer) involves the following hypothesis. Denial of P's attempts to communicate with O decreases P's trust of O. In this particular research effort, the subjects are college students; the research questions are as follows:

(a) When college students perceive denial by university officials of attempts by college students to communicate with university officials, a specific pattern of escalation of these communication attempts will occur.

(b) When college students perceive denial by university officials of repeated communication attempts by college students, increased social alienation of these students will occur.

Findings to date support this tentative line of reasoning. Additional hypotheses for this series of studies are being developed; they involve investigation of forms of escalation of communication efforts in response to perceived communication denial.

Perceived Risk in Trusting Situations

In the introductory section we indicated that one of the essential elements in a condition of trusting behavior was that the trusting person (P) is risking something he values. Relevant research has indicated that (at least) three variables influence the degree of perceived risk P is willing to take when trusting O: (1) P's power over O (specifically, P's capability of retaliation if O violates P's trust in O, (2) O's possibility of gain by violating P's trust of O, and (3) the presence of an external threat to both P and O.

The Trusting Person's Power over the Person Trusted

Power is here defined as ability to influence another person's behavior; this ability may involve "leadership," authority, persuasion, use of sanctions, or physical control. Solomon has reported evidence that when a person (P) has such power over another (O), P apparently tends to trust O more.[25] In addition, findings by Loomis tend to show that when P believes he can *retaliate to a violation* of his trust of O, P tends to trust O more; in a sense, P has thus threatened to use power to diminish his degree of reliance upon O, that is, P has diminished his perceived risk in that trusting situation.[26] Further research is needed, but findings to date indicate that *P's trust of O is a function of P's perceptions of O's responsiveness to P's leadership behavior.*

Possibility of Gain Through Trust Violation

In a risk situation where P perceives that O can gain no significant advantage by violation of P's trust in O, it appears that P will tend to trust O more than he will where gain by trust-violation is possible. At the present time research is being planned to test this hypothesis: *P's trust of O is a function of P's perception of O's opportunity to achieve personal gain through violation of P's trust in O.*

Presence of External Threat

It is commonly believed that two or more persons will trust each other more when together they are faced with an external

[25] L. Solomon, "The Influence of Some Types of Power Relationships and Game Strategies upon the Development of Interpersonal Trust," *Journal of Abnormal and Social Psychology, 61* (1960), 223–230.

[26] J. Loomis, "Communication, the Development of Trust and Cooperative Behavior," *Human Relations, 12* (1959), 305–315.

threat; "joining hands in the face of a common enemy" is a well-known principle of human behavior. Inferential evidence of an apparent increase of one person's trust of another in the presence of a disliked third person was obtained by Farr.[27] Available evidence indicates that *P's trust of O is a function of the existence of an external threat to both P and O (as perceived by P).*

Perceived Value of Goal Desired

We have previously suggested that one requisite element for a condition of interpersonal trust is that P (the trusting person) is attempting to achieve some desired goal. The degree to which this goal is desired by P should have some relevance to the amount of trust P is willing to place in O. In an interaction situation, this goal may be a desire on the part of P to (1) exchange information with O, (2) change O's attitude and/or related behavior, or (3) establish a warm interpersonal relationship with O.

Regardless of the type of interaction goal, it would seem that *the magnitude of importance* attached to such a goal would influence P's willingness to increase his personal risk. Deutsch explored this relationship, but did not subject it to sophisticated investigation.[28] Further exploratory studies should be made regarding the following hypothesis: *P's trust of O is a function of the magnitude of the importance to P of the goal which P can achieve only by trusting O.*

Conclusions

Personal trust in human interaction has been discussed in terms of four variables: (1) personality characteristics of P; (2) the characteristics of O as perceived by P; (3) degree of risk in the

---

[27] J. Farr, "The Effects of a Disliked Third Person upon the Development of Mutual Trust," a paper read to the American Psychological Associate Conference, New York, September, 1957.

[28] M. Deutsch, "The Effect of Motivational Orientation upon Trust and Suspicion," *Human Relations,* 13 (1960), 123–139.

trusting situation as perceived by P; and (4) P's perception of the value of the goal he is attempting to achieve. Relevant research which has been completed was reviewed, and research in progress was summarized along with the identification of ten tentative conclusions.

At the present time the interaction situation which appears to provide optimal potential for personal trust is the following: P (the trusting person has a high self-concept, low general anxiety tendency, low degree of authoritarianism, and degree of motivation to succeed (M_s) which is greater than his motivation to avoid failure (M_{af}); O (the person being trusted) is perceived by P as having high degrees of (relevant) expertise, reliability, and dynamism; the members of a reference group thought to be relevant by P indicate similar perceptions of O; the trusting situation is perceived by P as involving low risk because (1) P has power of retaliation over O if P's trust in O is violated, (2) O has no possibility of personal gain by violation of P's trust, and (3) there is the presence of an external threat to both P and O; and P perceives high value in the goal he is attempting to achieve. The relationship of each of these variables to personal trust in human interaction is in need of further research.

Questions
for
Reflection
and
Discussion
Section Seven

1. Make notes on how you think "Bill" feels after the interview described by Roethlisberger? With another member of your class, role-play the interview between "Smith" and "Bill." Use your own words, but in general follow the plot. Now, compare your feelings with your notes made previously. Discuss these feelings with your classmate.

2. Select a teacher with whom you currently are having difficulty. Note the degree to which this difficulty is due to your relationship with this teacher (or to lack of understanding of the conceptual or cognitive work in the course). If you can, arrange an interview with this teacher and try to find out what he (or she) actually thinks about the nature of your relationship. To what extent does the viewpoint expressed by this teacher limit the possibility of your working well together? To what extent does *your* view of the relationship limit or handicap such working together?

3. In Gibb's article note carefully the effect of dogmatic communication behavior. How can one be forthright, open, and honest without being dogmatic?

4. Suppose "persuasion" is defined as supplying another person with reasons for thinking, believing, or acting in some particular way. How can you be persuasive without arousing defensiveness on the part of the other person?

5. Can you make a reasonable distinction between a trusting *attitude* and trusting *behavior*? Does the distinction you have made satisfy you? Select a classmate toward whom you have

a positive, warm, friendly feeling; note the nature and degree of trust you feel toward this person. Now ask him (or her) to borrow half of the money you have with you. Tell him you trust him and just feel like doing a good turn today. *Now,* note your feelings of tension as you await his response —is there a feeling of anxiety? Also, note your feelings to the actual response. What does trusting behavior really require on your part?

6. Can you recall a situation in which you did not feel very trustful of a person, but decided to rely upon his expertness, reliability, or dynamism because *other* people seemed to be willing to do so? Do you think that your behavior in such a case could properly be called "conformity" behavior?

GUIDELINES
TO
EFFECTIVE
INTERPERSONAL
COMMUNICATION
SECTION EIGHT

Much of the literature on interpersonal relationships is analytical or descriptive. Personality factors which are helpful or not have been described; relationships which are satisfying or not satisfying have been analyzed. However, in such writings only *by implication* are suggestions made which might help a person to achieve more effective interpersonal relations.

We have been able to find a few essays which give specific suggestions for improving our interpersonal relationships. Only a small number of these suggestions have been treated in significant detail. These suggestions may be summarized under three general directives: (1) Try to be helpful to the other person as he tries to achieve some interpersonal goal; (2) when working with others, try to give fair consideration both to the personal needs and the task orientation of the other person; and (3) try to focus upon goals which you can *share* with others; that is, goals which, if achieved, benefit both of you, thus avoiding emphasis on goals which place you in direct opposition to others.

The three essays presented in this section treat each of these suggestions in some detail. The first, by Carl Rogers, gives specific suggestions for one who would like to become more helpful to other persons, particularly those who ask for help. Although Rogers's comments were originally intended for persons working with clinical patients, they have since been recognized as valuable for any person who would like to be helpful to ordinary people who have common problems. Emphasis is placed on being empathic, having nonpossessive regard for the other person, and being open and frank in showing one's true feelings and reactions.

The article by Bales suggests ways in which members of decision-making groups can achieve a balance between requisite task-oriented behavior and behavior which gives appropriate consideration to the personal needs of the members. The concept of "dual leadership" is presented wherein separate role-functions are performed to help the group achieve both of these requirements.

The article by Buchanan shows the value of emphasizing shared or "superordinate" goals, that is, objectives felt to be important by *both* members of the interaction. There is danger of producing irreducible discord by emphasizing individual goals upon which members disagree. Alert and informed persons are highly sensitive to attempts to persuade or manipulate them; disagreements which are impossible to resolve may be minimized by avoiding behavior which produces polarization. Emphasis on targets which are mutually desired can significantly improve one's interpersonal relations.

Carl R. Rogers
The Characteristics of
a Helping Relationship

*I have long had the strong conviction—some might say
it was an obsession—that the therapeutic relationship
is only a special instance of interpersonal relationships
in general, and that the same lawfulness governs all
such relationships. This was the theme I chose to work
out for myself when I was asked to give an address to
the convention of the American Personnel and Guidance
Association at St. Louis, in 1958.*

*Evident in this paper is the dichotomy between the
objective and the subjective which has been such an
important part of my experience during recent years.
I find it very difficult to give a paper which is either
wholly objective or wholly subjective. I like to bring the
two worlds into close juxtaposition, even if I cannot fully
reconcile them.*

My interest in psychotherapy has brought about in me an interest in every kind of helping relationship. By this term I mean
a relationship in which at least one of the parties has the intent
of promoting the growth, development, maturity, improved
functioning, improved coping with life of the other. The other,
in this sense may be one individual or a group. To put it in

Reprinted by permission of the publisher from *On Becoming a Person*,
Boston, Houghton Mifflin, 1961, pp. 39–58.

another way, a helping relationship might be defined as one in which one of the participants intends that there should come about, in one or both parties, more appreciation of, more expression of, more functional use of the latent inner resources of the individual.

Now it is obvious that such a definition covers a wide range of relationships which usually are intended to facilitate growth. It would certainly include the relationship between mother and child, father and child. It would include the relationship between the physician and his patient. The relationship between teacher and pupil would often come under this definition, though some teachers would not have the promotion of growth as their intent. It includes almost all counselor–client relationships, whether we are speaking of educational counseling, vocational counseling, or personal counseling. In this last-mentioned area it would include the wide range of relationships between the psychotherapist and the hospitalized psychotic, the therapist and the troubled or neurotic individual, and the relationship between the therapist and the increasing number of so-called "normal" individuals who enter therapy to improve their own functioning or accelerate their personal growth.

These are largely one-to-one relationships. But we should also think of the large number of individual–group interactions which are intended as helping relationships. Some administrators intend that their relationship to their staff groups shall be of the sort which promotes growth, though other administrators would not have this purpose. The interaction between the group therapy leader and his group belongs here. So does the relationship of the community consultant to a community group. Increasingly the interaction between the industrial consultant and a management group is intended as a helping relationship. Perhaps this listing will point up the fact that a great many of the relationships in which we and others are involved fall within this category of interactions in which there is the purpose of promoting development and more mature and adequate functioning.

The Question

But what are the characteristics of those relationships which *do* help, which do facilitate growth? And at the other end of the scale is it possible to discern those characteristics which make a relationship unhelpful, even though it was the sincere intent to promote growth and development? It is to these questions, particularly the first, that I would like to take you with me over some of the paths I have explored, and to tell you where I am, as of now, in my thinking on these issues.

The Answers Given by Research

It is natural to ask first of all whether there is any empirical research which would give us an objective answer to these questions. There has not been a large amount of research in this area as yet, but what there is is stimulating and suggestive. I cannot report all of it but I would like to make a somewhat extensive sampling of the studies which have been done and state very briefly some of the findings. In so doing, oversimplification is necessary, and I am quite aware that I am not doing full justice to the researches I am mentioning, but it may give you the feeling that factual advances are being made and pique your curiosity enough to examine the studies themselves, if you have not already done so.

Studies of Attitudes

Most of the studies throw light on the attitudes on the part of the helping person which make a relationship growth-promoting or growth-inhibiting. Let us look at some of these.

A careful study of parent–child relationships made some years ago by Baldwin and others (1) at the Fels Institute contains interesting evidence. Of the various clusters of parental attitudes toward children, the "acceptant–democratic" seemed most growth-facilitating. Children of these parents with their warm and equalitarian attitudes showed an accelerated intellectual development (an increasing I.Q.), more originality, more emotional security and control, less excitability than children from other types of homes. Though somewhat slow initially in social development, they were, by the time they reached school age, popular, friendly, nonaggressive leaders.

Where parents' attitudes are classed as "actively rejectant" the children show a slightly decelerated intellectual development, relatively poor use of the abilities they do possess, and some lack of originality. They are emotionally unstable, rebellious, aggressive, and quarrelsome. The children of parents with other attitude syndromes tend in various respects to fall in between these extremes.

I am sure that these findings do not surprise us as related to child development. I would like to suggest that they probably apply to other relationships as well, and that the counselor or physician or administrator who is warmly emotional and expressive, respectful of the individuality of himself and of the other, and who exhibits a nonpossessive caring, probably facilitates self-realization much as does a parent with these attitudes.

Let me turn to another careful study in a very different area. Betz and Whitehorn (2, 18) investigated the degree of success achieved by young resident physicians in working with schizophrenic patients on a psychiatric ward. They chose for special study the seven who had been outstandingly helpful, and seven whose patients had shown the least degree of improvement. Each group had treated about fifty patients. The investigators examined all the available evidence to discover in what ways the A group (the successful group) differed from the B group. Several significant differences were found. The physicians in the A group tended to see the schizophrenic in terms of the personal meaning which various behaviors had to the patient, rather than seeing him as a case history or a descriptive diagnosis. They also tended to work toward goals which were oriented to the personality of the patient, rather than such goals as reducing the symptoms or curing the disease. It was found that the helpful physicians, in their day by day interaction, primarily made use of active personal participation—a person-to-person relationship. They made less use of procedures which could be classed as "passive permissive." They were even less likely to use such procedures as interpretation, instruction or advice, or emphasis upon the practical care of the patient. Finally, they were much more likely than the B group to develop a relationship in which the patient felt trust and confidence in the physician.

Although the authors cautiously emphasize that these findings relate only to the treatment of schizophrenics, I am inclined to disagree. I suspect that similar facts would be found in a research study of almost any class of helping relationship.

Another interesting study focuses upon the way in which the person being helped perceives the relationship. Heine (11) studied individuals who had gone for psychotherapeutic help to psychoanalytic, client-centered, and Adlerian therapists. Regardless of the type of therapy, these clients report similar changes in themselves. But it is their perception of the relationship which is of particular interest to us here. When asked what accounted for the changes which had occurred, they expressed some differing explanations, depending on the orientation of the therapist. But their agreement on the major elements they had found helpful was even more significant. They indicated that these attitudinal elements in the relationship accounted for the changes which had taken place in themselves: the trust they had felt in the therapist; being understood by the therapist; the feeling of independence they had had in making choices and decisions. The therapist procedure which they had found most helpful was that the therapist clarified and openly stated feelings which the client had been approaching hazily and hesitantly.

There was also a high degree of agreement among these clients, regardless of the orientation of their therapists, as to what elements had been unhelpful in the relationship. Such therapist attitudes as lack of interest, remoteness or distance, and an over-degree of sympathy, were perceived as unhelpful. As to procedures, they had found it unhelpful when therapists had given direct specific advice regarding decisions or had emphasized past history rather than present problems. Guiding suggestions mildly given were perceived in an intermediate range—neither clearly helpful nor unhelpful.

Fiedler, in a much quoted study (7), found that expert therapists of differing orientations formed similar relationships with their clients. Less well known are the elements which characterized these relationships, differentiating them from the relationships formed by less expert therapists. These elements are: an ability to understand the client's meanings and feelings; a sensitivity to the client's attitudes; a warm interest without any emotional over-involvement.

A study by Quinn (14) throws light on what is involved in understanding the client's meanings and feelings. His study is surprising in that it shows that "understanding" of the client's meanings is essentially an attitude of *desiring* to understand. Quinn presented his judges only with recorded therapist statements taken from interviews. The raters had no knowledge of what the therapist was responding to or how the client reacted to his response. Yet it was found that the degree of understanding could be judged about as well from this material as from listening to the response in context. This seems rather conclusive evidence that it is an attitude of wanting to understand which is communicated.

As to the emotional quality of the relationship, Seeman (16) found that success in psychotherapy is closely associated with a strong and growing mutual liking and respect between client and therapist.

An interesting study by Dittes (4) indicates how delicate this relationship is. Using a physiological measure, the psychogalvanic reflex, to measure the anxious or threatened or alerted reactions of the client, Dittes correlated the deviations on this measure with judges' ratings of the degree of warm acceptance and permissiveness on the part of the therapist. It was found that whenever the therapist's attitudes changed even slightly in the direction of a lesser degree of acceptance, the number of abrupt GSR deviations significantly increased. Evidently when the relationship is experienced as less acceptant the organism organizes against threat, even at the physiological level.

Without trying fully to integrate the findings from these

various studies, it can at least be noted that a few things stand out. One is the fact that it is the attitudes and feelings of the therapist, rather than his theoretical orientation, which is important. His procedures and techniques are less important than his attitudes. It is also worth noting that it is the way in which his attitudes and procedures are *perceived* which makes a difference to the client, and that it is this perception which is crucial.

"Manufactured" Relationships

Let me turn to research of a very different sort, some of which you may find rather abhorrent, but which nevertheless has a bearing upon the nature of a facilitating relationship. These studies have to do with what we might think of as manufactured relationships.

Verplanck (17), Greenspoon (8) and others have shown that operant conditioning of verbal behavior is possible in a relationship. Very briefly, if the experimenter says "Mhm," or "Good," or nods his head after certain types of words or statements, those classes of words tend to increase because of being reinforced. It has been shown that using such procedures one can bring about increases in such diverse verbal categories as plural nouns, hostile words, statements of opinion. The person is completely unaware that he is being influenced in any way by these reinforcers. The implication is that by such selective reinforcement we could bring it about that the other person in the relationship would be using whatever kinds of words and making whatever kinds of statements we had decided to reinforce.

Following still further the principles of operant conditioning as developed by Skinner and his group, Lindsley (12) has shown that a chronic schizophrenic can be placed in a "helping relationship" with a machine. The machine, somewhat like a vending machine, can be set to reward a variety of types of behaviors. Initially it simply rewards—with candy, a cigarette, or the display of a picture—the lever-pressing behavior of the patient. But it is possible to set it so that many pulls on the lever may supply a hungry kitten—visible in a separate enclosure—with a drop of milk. In this case the satisfaction is an altruistic one. Plans are being developed to reward similar social or altruistic behavior directed toward another patient, placed in the next room. The only limit to the kinds of behavior which might be rewarded lies in the degree of mechanical ingenuity of the experimenter.

Lindsley reports that in some patients there has been marked clinical improvement. Personally I cannot help but be impressed by the description of one patient who had gone from a deteriorated chronic state to being given free grounds privileges, this change being quite clearly associated with his interaction with the machine. Then the experimenter decided to study experimental extinction, which, put in more personal terms, means that no matter how many thousands of times the lever was pressed, no reward of any kind was forthcoming. The patient gradually regressed, grew untidy, uncommunicative, and his grounds privileges had to be revoked. This (to me) pathetic incident would seem to indicate that even in a relationship to a machine, trustworthiness is important if the relationship is to be helpful.

Still another interesting study of a manufactured relationship is being carried on by Harlow and his associates (10), this time with monkeys. Infant monkeys, removed from their mothers almost immediately after birth, are, in one phase of the experiment, presented with two objects. One might be termed the "hard mother," a sloping cylinder of wire netting with a nipple from which the baby may feed. The other is a "soft mother," a similar cylinder made of foam rubber and terry cloth. Even when an infant gets all his food from the "hard mother" he clearly and increasingly prefers the "soft mother." Motion pictures show that he definitely "relates" to this object, playing with it, enjoying it, finding security in clinging to it when strange objects are near, and using that security as a home base for venturing into the frightening world. Of the many interesting and challenging implications of this study, one seems reasonably clear. It is that no amount of direct food reward can take the place of certain perceived qualities which the infant appears to need and desire.

Two Recent Studies

Let me close this wide-ranging—and perhaps perplexing—sampling of research studies with an account of two very recent investigations. The first is an experiment conducted by Ends and Page (5). Working with hardened chronic hospitalized alcoholics who had been committed to a state hospital for sixty days, they tried three different methods of group psychotherapy. The method which they believed would be most effective was therapy based on a two-factor theory of learning; a client-centered approach was expected to be second; a psychoanalytically oriented approach was expected to be least efficient. Their results showed that the therapy based upon a learning theory approach was not only not helpful, but was somewhat deleterious. The outcomes were worse than those in the control group which had no therapy. The analytically oriented therapy produced some positive gain, and the client-centered group therapy was associated with the greatest amount of positive change. Follow-up data, extending over one and one-half years, confirmed the in-hospital findings, with the lasting improvement being greatest in the client-centered approach, next in the analytic, next the control group, and least in those handled by a learning theory approach.

As I have puzzled over this study, unusual in that the approach to which the authors were committed proved *least* effective, I find a clue, I believe, in the description of the therapy based on learning theory (13). Essentially it consisted (a) of pointing out and labeling the behaviors which had proved unsatisfying, (b) of exploring objectively with the client the reasons behind these behaviors, and (c) of establishing through reeducation more effective problem-solving habits. But in all of this interaction the aim, as they formulated it, was to be impersonal. The therapist "permits as little of his own personality to intrude as is humanly possible." The "therapist stresses personal anonymity in his activities, i.e., he must studiously avoid impressing the patient with his own (therapist's) individual personality characteristics." To me this seems the most likely clue to the failure of this approach, as I try to interpret the facts in the light of the other research studies. To withhold one's self as a person and to deal with the other person as an object does not have a high probability of being helpful.

The final study I wish to report is one just being completed by Halkides (9). She started from a theoretical formulation of mine regarding the necessary and sufficient conditions for therapeutic change (15). She hypothesized that there would be a significant relationship between the extent of constructive personality change in the client and four counselor variables: (a) the degree of empathic understanding of the client manifested by the counselor; (b) the degree of positive affective attitude (unconditional positive regard) manifested by the counselor toward the client; (c) the extent to which the counselor is genuine, his words matching his own internal feeling; and (d) the extent to which the counselor's response matches the client's expression in the intensity of affective expression.

To investigate these hypotheses she first selected, by multiple objective criteria, a group of ten cases which could be classed as "most successful" and a group of ten "least successful" cases. She then took an early and late recorded interview from each of these cases. On a random basis she picked nine client—counselor interaction units—a client statement and a counselor response—from each of these interviews. She thus had nine early interactions and nine later interactions from each case. This gave her several hundred units which were now placed in random order. The units from an early interview of an unsuccessful case might be followed by the units from a late interview of a successful case, etc.

Three judges, who did not know the cases or their degree of success, or the source of any given unit, now listened to this material four different times. They rated each unit on a seven point scale, first as to the degree of empathy, second as to the counselor's positive attitude toward the client, third as to the counselor's congruence or genuineness, and fourth as to the degree to which the counselor's response matched the emotional intensity of the client's expression.

I think all of us who knew of the study regarded it as a very bold venture. Could judges listening to single units of inter-action possibly make any reliable rating of such subtle qualities as I have mentioned? And even if suitable reliability could be obtained, could eighteen counselor–client interchanges from each case—a minute sampling of the hundreds or thousands of such interchanges which occurred in each case—possibly bear any relationship to the therapeutic outcome? The chance seemed slim.

The findings are surprising. It proved possible to achieve high reliability between the judges, most of the inter-judge correlations being in the 0.80's or 0.90's, except on the last variable. It was found that a high degree of empathic under-standing was significantly associated, at a .001 level, with the more successful cases. A high degree of unconditional positive regard was likewise associated with the more successful cases, at the .001 level. Even the rating of the counselor's genuineness or congruence—the extent to which his words matched his feel-ings—was associated with the successful outcome of the case, and again at the .001 level of significance. Only in the investi-gation of the matching intensity of affective expression were the results equivocal.

It is of interest too that high ratings of these variables were not associated more significantly with units from later inter-views than with units from early interviews. This means that the counselor's attitudes were quite constant throughout the interviews. If he was highly empathic, he tended to be so from first to last. If he was lacking in genuineness, this tended to be true of both early and late interviews.

As with any study, this investigation has its limitations. It is concerned with a certain type of helping relationship, psycho-therapy. It investigated only four variables thought to be significant. Perhaps there are many others. Nevertheless it represents a significant advance in the study of helping rela-tionships. Let me try to state the findings in the simplest possible fashion. It seems to indicate that the quality of the counselor's interaction with a client can be satisfactorily judged on the basis of a very small sampling of his behavior. It also means that if the counselor is congruent or transparent, so that his words are in line with his feelings rather than the two being discrepant; if the counselor likes the client, unconditionally; and if the counselor understands the essential feelings of the client as they seem to the client—then there is a strong probability that this will be an effective helping relationship.

Some Comments

These then are some of the studies which throw at least a measure of light on the nature of the helping relationship. They have investigated different facets of the problem. They have approached it from very different theoretical contexts. They have used different methods. They are not directly comparable. Yet they seem to me to point to several statements which may be made with some assurance. It seems clear that relationships which are helpful have different characteristics from relationships which are unhelpful. These differential characteristics have to do primarily with the attitudes of the helping person on the one hand and with the perception of the relationship by the "helpee" on the other. It is equally clear that the studies thus far made do not give us any final answers as to what is a helping relationship, nor how it is to be formed.

How Can I Create a Helping Relationship?

I believe each of us working in the field of human relationships has a similar problem in knowing how to use such research knowledge. We cannot slavishly follow such findings in a mechanical way or we destroy the personal qualities which these very studies show to be valuable. It seems to me that we have to use these studies, testing them against our own experience and forming new and further personal hypotheses to use and test in our own further personal relationships.

So, rather than try to tell you how you should use the findings I have presented, I should like to tell you the kind of questions which these studies and my own clinical experience raise for me, and some of the tentative and changing hypotheses which guide my behavior as I enter into what I hope may be helping relationships, whether with students, staff, family, or clients. Let me list a number of these questions and considerations.

1. Can I *be* in some way which will be perceived by the other person as trustworthy, as dependable or consistent in some deep sense? Both research and experience indicate that this is very important, and over the years I have found what I believe are deeper and better ways of answering this question. I used to feel that if I fulfilled all the outer conditions of trustworthiness—keeping appointments, respecting the confidential nature of the interviews, etc.—and if I acted consistently the same during the interviews, then this condition would be fulfilled. But experience drove home the fact that to act consistently acceptant, for example, if in fact I was feeling annoyed or skeptical or some other nonacceptant feeling, was certain in the long run to be perceived as inconsistent or untrustworthy. I have come to recognize that being trustworthy does not demand that I be rigidly consistent but that I be dependably real. The term "congruent" is one I have used to describe the way I would like to be. By this I mean that whatever feeling or attitude I am experiencing would be matched by my awareness of that attitude. When this is true, then I am a unified or integrated person in that moment, and hence I can *be* whatever I deeply *am*. This is a reality which I find others experience as dependable.

2. A very closely related question is this: Can I be expressive enough as a person so that what I am will be communicated unambiguously? I believe that most of my failures to achieve a helping relationship can be traced to unsatisfactory answers to these two questions. When I am experiencing an attitude of annoyance toward another person but am unaware of it, then my communication contains contradictory messages. My words are giving one message, but I am also in subtle ways communicating the annoyance I feel and this confuses the other person and makes him distrustful, though he too may be un-

aware of what is causing the difficulty. When as a parent or a therapist or a teacher or an administrator I fail to listen to what is going on in me, fail because of my own defensiveness to sense my own feelings, then this kind of failure seems to result. It has made it seem to me that the most basic learning for anyone who hopes to establish any kind of helping relationship is that it is safe to be transparently real. If in a given relationship I am reasonably congruent, if no feelings relevant to the relationship are hidden either to me or the other person, then I can be almost sure that the relationship will be a helpful one.

One way of putting this which may seem strange to you is that if I can form a helping relationship to myself—if I can be sensitively aware of and acceptant toward my own feelings—then the likelihood is great that I can form a helping relationship toward another.

Now, acceptantly to be what I am, in this sense, and to permit this to show through to the other person, is the most difficult task I know and one I never fully achieve. But to realize that this *is* my task has been most rewarding because it has helped me to find what has gone wrong with interpersonal relationships which have become snarled and to put them on a constructive track again. It has meant that if I am to facilitate the personal growth of others in relation to me, then I must grow, and while this is often painful it is also enriching.

3. A third question is: Can I let myself experience positive attitudes toward this other person—attitudes of warmth, caring, liking, interest, respect? It is not easy. I find in myself, and feel that I often see in others, a certain amount of fear of these feelings. We are afraid that if we let ourselves freely experience these positive feelings toward another we may be trapped by them. They may lead to demands on us or we may be disappointed in our trust, and these outcomes we fear. So as a reaction we tend to build up distance between ourselves and others—aloofness, a "professional" attitude, an impersonal relationship.

I feel quite strongly that one of the important reasons for the professionalization of every field is that it helps to keep this distance. In the clinical areas we develop elaborate diagnostic formulations, seeing the person as an object. In teaching and in administration we develop all kinds of evaluative procedures, so that again the person is perceived as an object. In these ways, I believe, we can keep ourselves from experiencing the caring which would exist if we recognized the relationship as one between two persons. It is a real achievement when we can learn, even in certain relationships or at certain times in those relationships, that it is safe to care, that it is safe to relate to the other person for whom we have postive feelings.

4. Another question the importance of which I have learned in my own experience is: Can I be strong enough as a person to be separate from the other? Can I be a sturdy respecter of my own feelings, my own needs, as well as his? Can I own and, if need be, express my own feelings as something belonging to me and separate from his feelings? Am I strong enough in my own separateness that I will not be downcast by his depression, frightened by his fear, nor engulfed by his dependency? Is my inner self hardy enough to realize that I am not destroyed by his anger, taken over by his need for dependence, nor enslaved by his love, but that I exist separate from him with feelings and rights of my own? When I can freely feel this strength of being a separate person, then I find that I can let myself go much more deeply in understanding and accepting him because I am not fearful of losing myself.

5. The next question is closely related. Am I secure enough within myself to permit him his separateness? Can I permit him to be what he is—honest or deceitful, infantile or adult, despairing or over-confident? Can I give him the freedom to be? Or do I feel that he should follow my advice, or remain somewhat dependent on me, or mold himself after me? In this connection I think of the interesting small study by Farson (6) which found that the less well adjusted and less competent counselor tends to induce conformity to himself, to have clients who model themselves after him. On the other hand, the better adjusted and more competent counselor can interact with a client through many interviews without interfering with the freedom of the

client to develop a personality quite separate from that of his therapist. I should prefer to be in this latter class, whether as parent or supervisor or counselor.

6. Another question I ask myself is: Can I let myself enter fully into the world of his feelings and personal meanings and see these as he does? Can I step into his private world so completely that I lose all desire to evaluate or judge it? Can I enter it so sensitively that I can move about in it freely, without trampling on meanings which are precious to him? Can I sense it so accurately that I can catch not only the meanings of his experience which are obvious to him, but those meanings which are only implicit, which he sees only dimly or as confusion? Can I extend this understanding without limit? I think of the client who said, "Whenever I find someone who understands a *part* of me at the time, then it never fails that a point is reached where I know they're *not* understanding me again. . . . What I've looked for so hard is for someone to understand."

For myself I find it easier to feel this kind of understanding, and to communicate it, to individual clients than to students in a class or staff members in a group in which I am involved. There is a strong temptation to set students "straight," or to point out to a staff member the errors in his thinking. Yet when I can permit myself to understand in these situations, it is mutually rewarding. And with clients in therapy, I am often impressed with the fact that even a minimal amount of empathic understanding—a bumbling and faulty attempt to catch the confused complexity of the client's meaning—is helpful, though there is no doubt that it is most helpful when I can see and formulate clearly the meanings in his experiencing which for him have been unclear and tangled.

7. Still another issue is whether I can be acceptant of each facet of this other person which he presents to me. Can I receive him as he is? Can I communicate this attitude? Or can I only receive him conditionally, acceptant of some aspects of his feelings and silently or openly disapproving of other aspects? It has been my experience that when my attitude is conditional, then he cannot change or grow in those respects in which I cannot fully receive him. And when—afterward and sometimes

too late—I try to discover why I have been unable to accept him in every respect, I usually discover that it is because I have been frightened or threatened in myself by some aspect of his feelings. If I am to be more helpful, then I must myself grow and accept myself in these respects.

8. A very practical issue is raised by the question: Can I act with sufficient sensitivity in the relationship that my behavior will not be perceived as a threat? The work we are beginning to do in studying the physiological concomitants of psychotherapy confirms the research by Dittes in indicating how easily individuals are threatened at a physiological level. The psychogalvanic reflex—the measure of skin conductance—takes a sharp dip when the therapist responds with some word which is just a little stronger than the client's feelings. And to a phrase such as, "My you *do* look upset," the needle swings almost off the paper. My desire to avoid even such minor threats is not due to a hypersensitivity about my client. It is simply due to the conviction based on experience that if I can free him as completely as possible from external threat, then he can begin to experience and to deal with the internal feelings and conflicts which he finds threatening within himself.

9. A specific aspect of the preceding question but an important one is: Can I free him from the threat of external evaluation? In almost every phase of our lives—at home, at school, at work—we find ourselves under the rewards and punishments of external judgments. "That's good"; "that's naughty." "That's worth an A"; "that's a failure." "That's good counseling"; "that's poor counseling." Such judgments are a part of our lives from infancy to old age. I believe they have a certain social usefulness to institutions and organizations such as schools and professions. Like everyone else I find myself all too often making such evaluations. But, in my experience, they do not make for personal growth and hence I do not believe that they are a part of a helping relationship. Curiously enough a positive evaluation is as threatening in the long run as a negative one, since to inform someone that he is good implies that you also have the right to tell him he is bad. So I have come to feel that the more I can keep a relationship free of judgment and evaluation, the

more this will permit the other person to reach the point where he recognizes that the locus of evaluation, the center of responsibility, lies within himself. The meaning and value of his experience is in the last analysis something which is up to him, and no amount of external judgment can alter this. So I should like to work toward a relationship in which I am not, even in my own feelings, evaluating him. This I believe can set him free to be a self-responsible person.

10. One last question: Can I meet this other individual as a person who is in process of *becoming,* or will I be bound by his past and by my past? If, in my encounter with him, I am dealing with him as an immature child, an ignorant student, a neurotic personality, or a psychopath, each of these concepts of mine limits what he can be in the relationship. Martin Buber, the existentialist philosopher of the University of Jerusalem, has a phrase, "confirming the other," which has had meaning for me. He says "Confirming means . . . accepting the whole potentiality of the other. . . . I can recognize in him, know in him, the person he has been . . . *created* to become. . . . I confirm him in myself, and then in him, in relation to this potentiality that . . . can now be developed, can evolve" (3). If I accept the other person as something fixed, already diagnosed and classified, already shaped by his past, then I am doing my part to confirm this limited hypothesis. If I accept him as a process of becoming, then I am doing what I can to confirm or make real his potentialities.

It is at this point that I see Verplanck, Lindsley, and Skinner, working in operant conditioning, coming together with Buber, the philosopher or mystic. At least they come together in principle, in an odd way. If I see a relationship as only an opportunity to reinforce certain types of words or opinions in the other, then I tend to confirm him as an object—a basically mechanical, manipulable object. And if I see this as his potentiality, he tends to act in ways which support this hypothesis. If, on the other hand, I see a relationship as an opportunity to "reinforce" *all* that he is, the person that he is with all his existent potentialities, then he tends to act in ways which support *this* hypothesis. I have then—to use Buber's term—confirmed him as a living person, capable of creative inner development. Personally I prefer this second type of hypothesis.

Conclusion

In the early portion of this paper I reviewed some of the contributions which research is making to our knowledge *about* relationships. Endeavoring to keep that knowledge in mind I then took up the kind of questions which arise from an inner and subjective point of view as I enter, as a person, into relationships. If I could, in myself, answer all the questions I have raised in the affirmative, then I believe that any relationships in which I was involved would be helping relationships, would involve growth. But I cannot give a positive answer to most of these questions. I can only work in the direction of the positive answer.

This has raised in my mind the strong suspicion that the optimal helping relationship is the kind of relationship created by a person who is psychologically mature. Or to put it in another way, the degree to which I can create relationships which facilitate the growth of others as separate persons is a measure of the growth I have achieved in myself. In some respects this is a disturbing thought, but it is also a promising or challenging one. It would indicate that if I am interested in creating helping relationships I have a fascinating lifetime job ahead of me, stretching and developing my potentialities in the direction of growth.

I am left with the uncomfortable thought that what I have been working out for myself in this paper may have little relationship to your interests and your work. If so, I regret it. But I am at least partially comforted by the fact that all of us who are working in the field of human relationships and trying to understand the basic orderliness of that field are engaged in the most crucial enterprise in today's world. If we are thoughtfully trying to understand our tasks as administrators, teachers, educational counselors, vocational counselors, therapists, then we are working on the problem which will determine the future of this planet. For it is not upon the physical sciences that the future will depend. It is upon us who are trying to understand and deal with the interactions between human beings—who are trying to create helping relationships. So I hope that the questions I ask of myself will be of some use to you in gaining understanding and perspective as you endeavor, in your way, to facilitate growth in your relationships.

References

1. Baldwin, A. L., J. Kalhorn, and F. H. Breese. Patterns of parent behavior. *Psychol. Monogr.*, 1945, *58*, No. 268, 1–75.

2. Betz, B. J., and J. C. Whitehorn. The relationship of the therapist to the outcome of therapy in schizophrenia. *Psychiat. Research Reports #5. Research techniques in schizophrenia.* Washington, D.C., American Psychiatric Association, 1956, 89–117.

3. Buber, M., and C. Rogers. Transcription of dialogue held April 18, 1957, Ann Arbor, Mich. Unpublished manuscript.

4. Dittes, J. E. Galvanic skin response as a measure of patient's reaction to therapist's permissiveness. *J. Abnorm. & Soc. Psychol.*, 1957, *55*, 295–303.

5. Ends, E. J., and C. W. Page. A study of three types of group psychotherapy with hospitalized male inebriates. *Quar. J. Stud. Alcohol*, 1957, *18*, 263–277.

6. Farson, R. E. Introjection in the psychotherapeutic relationship. Unpublished doctoral dissertation, University of Chicago, 1955.

7. Fiedler, F. E. Quantitative studies on the role of therapists' feelings toward their patients. In Mowrer, O. H. (Ed.), *Psychotherapy: theory and research.* New York: Ronald Press, 1953, Chap. 12.

8. Greenspoon, J. The reinforcing effect of two spoken sounds on the frequency of two responses. *Amer. J. Psychol.*, 1955, *68*, 409–416.

9. Halkides, G. An experimental study of four conditions necessary for therapeutic change. Unpublished doctoral dissertation, University of Chicago, 1958.

10. Harlow, H. F. The nature of love. *Amer. Psychol.*, 1958, *13*, 673–685.

11. Heine, R. W. A comparison of patients' reports on psychotherapeutic experience with psychoanalytic, nondirective, and Adlerian therapists. Unpublished doctoral dissertation, University of Chicago, 1950.

12. Lindsley, O. R. Operant conditioning methods applied to research in chronic schizophrenia. *Psychiat. Research Reports #5. Research techniques in schizophrenia.* Washington, D.C., American Psychiatric Association, 1956, 118–153.

13. Page, C. W., and E. J. Ends. A review and synthesis of the literature suggesting a psychotherapeutic technique based on two-factor learning theory. Unpublished manuscript, loaned to the writer.

14. Quinn, R. D. Psychotherapists' expressions as an index to the quality of early therapeutic relationships. Unpublished doctoral dissertation, University of Chicago, 1950.

15. Rogers, C. R. The necessary and sufficient conditions of psychotherapeutic personality change. *J. Consult. Psychol.,* 1957, *21,* 95–103.

16. Seeman, J. Counselor judgments of therapeutic process and outcome. In Rogers, C. R., and R. F. Dymond (Eds.), *Psychotherapy and personality change.* University of Chicago Press, 1954, Chap. 7.

17. Verplanck, W. S. The control of the content of conversation: reinforcement of statements of opinion. *J. Abnorm. & Soc. Psychol.,* 1955, *51,* 668–676.

18. Whitehorn, J. C., and B. J. Betz. A study of psychotherapeutic relationships between physicians and schizophrenic patients. *Amer. J. Psychiat.,* 1954, *111,* 321–331.

Robert F. Bales
In Conference

*Extensive laboratory research provides "rules of thumb"
for setting up and directing committees with decision-
making responsibilities.*

There is a widespread interest in the process of decision making among executives in business, the military, government,
research, civic affairs—indeed, in every sort of organization set
up to produce anything by cooperation. Technical experts are
called in to give advice; management committees must decide
on basic policies; labor teams must plan and regulate their
work; staff meetings take place daily at every level. Decision
making is the pinpoint focus of the vast social machinery that
makes up our democratic society and its economy.

Most decisions are made "in conference." Then they normally
require a long series of further conferences for their implementation. Probably no serious estimate has ever been made
of the total number of hours American businessmen spend per
year "in conference." But the number must be astronomical.

Committee Operation

Yet think how little we know about the actual operation of a
committee and how little we are able to predict or control its
success or failure. Many a "good idea" has emerged at the other

Reprinted by permission of the publisher from Robert F. Bales, "In Conference," *Harvard Business Review, 32* (March–April 1954), pp. 44–50. © 1954 by
the President and Fellows of Harvard College; all rights reserved.

end of the committee operation as a kind of "bad dream," mangled and amputated in its essentials, patched together with fantasies into a monster that finally dies at the hands of some committee further on down the line. It is no matter for wonder that committee meetings are often viewed with mixed feelings of apprehension and cynical humor.

It is not true, of course, that "nothing good ever comes out of a committee"—not so true, at least, as that nothing good ever reaches practical application without the work of innumerable committees. But the uncertainty whether a particular committee or work group may unexplainably go sour, or simply fail to produce at some critical point, is considerable.

The practical need to reduce this uncertainty and to improve the wisdom of critical decisions is resulting in an increasing amount of scientific research on the underlying problems. Research on decision making is being conducted by groups whose interests range from economics, military and industrial logistics, mathematics and statistics, through formal logic and the theories of information and of communication networks, to conference procedures, the theory of leadership, and social relations.

Direct Experiments

One aspect of this broad front of scientific development is the direct experimental study of committee meetings where decisions are made.

Not many years ago nobody seriously supposed that the subtle aspects of face-to-face human relations could be studied experimentally in the laboratory. All sorts of skeptical objections appeared, even among social scientists, when a few of their more hopeful colleagues began to set up small groups of subjects under laboratory conditions and study social behavior by direct observation. Now a number of such laboratories are in operation, and findings of possible practical importance are beginning to appear.

One of the early installations was set up by the Laboratory of Social Relations at Harvard University in 1947. This laboratory and some of its findings will serve as an illustration of the type of research now going on in a number of centers:

On the third floor of Harvard's Emerson Hall there is a specially designed room for the purpose of observing the operation of committees and similar types of small groups. Containing chairs and a table which can be varied in size, it is well lighted and surfaced in acoustic tile. On one wall is a chalkboard and a large mirror. Behind the mirror is an observation room, for in reality the mirror is a one-way glass through which a team of observers on the other side may watch without disturbing the subjects. While the subject group is aware that it is being watched, the illusion is such that any self-consciousness is only brief and the "mirror" is ignored and soon forgotten.

The groups vary in size from two to seven members, depending on the particular problem under discussion. The problem for discussion may be industrial, governmental, military, or educational in character, but in any case it has to do with administration and requires a decision or recommendation of some kind.

During the discussion the observers behind the "mirror" note the action within the group: who speaks, to whom he speaks, and how he speaks. The actual subject matter is not the primary concern, except as it indicates the speaker's feelings.

An ingenious machine, built by the laboratory, makes it easy for the observer to classify each statement as it is made. Observers are trained until they are able to classify within a second or so any remark that is made into one of 12 descriptive categories. (Originally there were 87 categories of response, but gradually the list has been reduced to 12.) In addition, the conversation is sound-recorded for later checking.

Each experimental group takes part in 4 sessions of 40 minutes each. By the end of this time, an accurate appraisal of the way in which it operates as a group is possible, and the relationships between members can be predicted with some confidence should it ever meet again.

Kinds of Behavior

All the behavior that goes on in a committee (or, indeed, in any verbal interchange) can be viewed as a sequence of questions, answers, and positive and negative reactions to the questions and answers. Three types of questions are distinguished: *asking for information, opinion,* and *suggestion.* Corresponding to these three types of questions are three types of answers: *giving information, opinion,* and *suggestions.* These answers are problem-solving attempts, and they call for reactions. Negative reactions include: *showing disagreement, tension,* or *antagonism.* On the positive side the corresponding reactions include: *showing agreement, tension release,* and *friendly solidarity.* These are the 12 categories of remarks used as a basis of analysis in the Harvard experiments.

Successful Decisions

It is interesting to note that, on the average, about 50% of all remarks made in the meetings are answers while the remaining 50% consist of questions and reactions. Such a 50–50 balance (or something close to it) may be one characteristic of successful communication. Problem-solving attempts are needed to reach a decision, but that is not all. It may well be that if enough time is not regularly allowed also for questioning and reaction to occur in the meeting, the members will carry away tensions that will eventually operate to vitiate an apparently successful but actually superficial decision.

Participation of Members

A decision is not a successful decision unless each member who is supposed to have been involved in its making is actually bound by it in such a way that his later behavior conforms to it.

By and large, members do not seem to feel strongly bound by a decision unless they have participated in making it. However, participation does not necessarily mean that each member has to talk an equal amount. As a matter of fact, even approximate equality of actual talking time among members is very rare; and, when it does appear, it is usually associated with a free-for-all conflict. A moderate gradient among members in talking time is the more usual thing.

More significantly, participation means that the meeting

operates under the presumption that each member has an equal right to ask questions or voice negative or positive reactions to any proposal made, if he wishes, and a right to expect that, if he makes a proposal, it will receive an appropriate reaction from some other member. Because of time exigencies, most members, most frequently, allow a voiced proposal to represent what they themselves would say, and a voiced reaction to represent what they themselves might respond.

On the other hand, it is difficult to know when a member's feelings and interests are being adequately represented and when they are not. The difference is so subtle that he himself is not always able to tell. He may go away dissatisfied without knowing quite why. Hence there is probably no adequate substitute for *some* actual verbal participation of each member. A few words on his part will serve to express and solidify his involvement, and to avoid his subsequent dissatisfaction.

Optimum Balance

There are about twice as many positive reactions in most meetings as there are negative reactions. One might suppose that the more successful the meeting, the fewer negative reactions and the more positive reactions one would find. But the evidence does not support this view. Rather, there appears to be a kind of optimum balance. Departures too far to either side are indicators of trouble.

Disagreement. Rates of disagreement and antagonism that are too high are sure indicators of trouble. Apparently, when ill feeling rises above some critical point, a "chain reaction" or "vicious circle" tends to set in. Logic and the practical demands of the task cease to be governing factors. Such an occurrence is an impressive experience when seen from the perspective of the observer behind the one-way glass in the laboratory:

The observer is unseen by the subjects, cannot communicate with them, and so in a basic sense is "not involved." He knows that no action will be taken on the decision of the committee.

He may have heard the same case discussed hundreds of times before. Nevertheless, he is "caught in the illusion of reality" as the temperature of the group begins to rise.

Suddenly the credulity of the observer is strained beyond some critical point. The illusion that the group is dealing with some external problem breaks. It becomes perfectly transparent—to the observer—that emotions have taken over, and that what one member is saying does not refer at all to some external situation but to himself and the other members present.

"Facts" are unwittingly invented or are falsified. Other facts drop out of sight entirely. When one member insists that "people in his office should be treated like human beings," it is clear that he refers to himself and how he feels he should be treated in this group. When his opponent insists that "trouble-makers should be fired," it is equally clear that he refers to the man who just spoke to him.

The decision, if any, reached by a group in this state has all the characteristics of a "bad dream," indeed.

Agreement. There can also be too many agreements and too few disagreements. This condition may be an indication either of lack of involvement in the practical demands of the task or of an atmosphere so inhibited and constrained that nobody dares risk disagreement. In the ordinary mill run of opinions and suggestions, there is always a certain percentage so unrealistic, exaggerated, or unsuitable that not to disagree means not to solve the problem.

Closely related to the rate of agreement is the rate of suggestion. Groups in a smoothly operating condition tend to show relatively high rates of suggestion, as well as of agreement. But there is a joker in this finding. This condition is an *outcome* of smooth sailing, *not* a way to attain it.

As most people would suppose, giving facts is fairly safe. The probability of arousing disagreement by reviewing the facts of the case is relatively low. But giving opinions is more risky, for in so doing a man gives his inferences and expresses his feelings and values, including his prejudices. Others are more likely to disagree, and the means of resolving disagreements are much more vague and indirect than in the case of disputed facts.

Indeed, a suggestion can cause a real bottleneck. If a man agrees to the suggestion, he must embrace all it implies, or involves. He has bound himself to future action. Most people are quite sensitive to this kind of constriction, even though they know that a decision is necessary. That is why, as the rate of giving suggestions goes up, the rate of negative reactions also tends to increase.

Reducing the Risk

Of course suggestions are necessary before a decision is reached. The decision point is inevitably a crisis point. But this is the risk that all decision-making groups have to take. The wise strategist should seek to reduce his risks to a calculated minimum, which is something quite different from trying to escape them entirely.

But how? The laboratory observations suggest a reasonable solution. Most successful groups go through an ordered series of three phases or stages in the solution of a problem:

(1) They attempt to assemble the largest possible pool of common information about the facts of the case.

(2) They make inferences and evaluations, and try to form common opinions in a general way.

(3) Only in the final phase do they get around to more specific suggestions, after an extensive groundwork has been laid.

Not all groups do this, by any means. Some start the other end to, and some start with an outburst of opinions before they ever look at a fact. Indeed, many of the members are hardly conscious of any difference between a fact and an opinion.

It is probably not any excess of wisdom or extraordinary sensitivity that produces the typical order of stages. It is rather, we may suppose, the "brute logic of natural selection." A suggestion given at a premature stage simply dies for lack of support, or is trampled to death in the general melee. Gradually the discussion is forced back to facts, where agreement can be reached.

In an environment barren of consensus, only a fact can survive; and, where there is hostility, even facts find a slim foothold. But a rich background of common facts lays the groundwork for the development of common inferences and sentiments, and out of these common decisions can grow. No decision rests on "facts" alone, but there is no better starting point. To start the decision-making process at any other point is to multiply the risk of a vicious circle of disagreement—and at no saving of time in the long run.

Dual Leadership

One of the most startling implications of the laboratory research so far is that the concept of "leader," if it is taken too literally, can cause the man who thinks he *is* one to disregard a most important fact—namely, that there is usually *another* leader in the group whom he can overlook only at his peril.

Separate Roles

The laboratory findings, while still tentative, indicate that the man who is judged by the group members to have the "best ideas" contributing to the decision is *not* generally the "best liked." There are two separate roles—that of task leader and that of social leader. If a man comes into a task-leadership position because he is popular or best-liked, he is ordinarily confronted with a choice: (1) If he chooses to try to keep the task leadership of the group, he tends to lose some of his popularity and to collect some dislikes. (2) If he chooses to try to keep his popularity, he tends to lose the task leadership. People differ in the way they solve this dilemma, although most tend to prefer to keep the popularity rather than the task leadership.

The difficulty becomes more acute with time. At the end of the group's first meeting there is 1 chance in 2 that the task leader will be the most liked. At the end of the second meeting the chances are reduced to 1 in 4. At the end of the third they are 1 in 6, and at the end of the fourth they are only 1 in 7.

There are apparently few men who can hold both roles; instead, the tendency is for these positions to be held by two different men. Each is in reality a leader, and each is important to the stability of the group. The task leader helps to keep the group engaged in the work, but the pressure of decision and work tends to provoke irritation and injure the unity of the group. The best-liked man helps to restore this unity and to keep the members of the group aware of their importance as particular individuals, whose special needs and values are respected. These men complement each other, and they are both necessary for smooth operation of a committee.

It is especially important for these two men to recognize each other's roles and in effect to form a coalition. The most stable groups observed have been those in which this coalition has taken place. There are indications that such durable groups as the family and simple small communities are constructed this way, and apparently the coalition also takes place in many administrative staffs, sometimes consciously but more often accidentally.

These findings challenge some very basic concepts of leadership. Millions are spent each year by business, government, and the armed forces in developing means for recognizing leaders, and much has been written about the "characteristics" of leadership. Yet it appears that whatever superior qualities the individual may possess as a simple individual, he may be unable, just because of the way groups work, to maintain a stable leadership position without a co-leader of complementary qualities.

Communication Networks

Significantly, among the half-dozen instances where the observation room and equipment at the Harvard laboratory have been duplicated are several installations by the military:

The Air Force has built a room at Maxwell Field, Alabama, for testing and predicting leadership ability. Other divisions of the

*armed forces are also engaged in the same kind of experimenta-
tion, for one of the most pressing problems they face is the
development of leaders and the selection of personnel who
have to work in small groups—bomber and submarine crews,
intelligence teams, and communications centers—particularly
in situations where immediate processing of information and
rapid but wise decisions are a tactical necessity.*

One of the persistent problems in rapid communications networks such as those found in military defense is how to keep
the actual control over critical decisions in the hands of the person or persons who will later bear the formal responsibility for
the decision. Practically, the decision-making function on the
tactical level tends to gravitate to the person who is at the
center of the communication network, where information about
the tactical situation is immediately available. But this tactical
information center tends not to coincide with the top spot in the
chain of command, where formal authority and responsibility
are centered.

Here again is an instance where it is unrealistic to operate
with a simple notion of a single "leader" in whom all essential
leadership functions can be vested. Although this problem appears most clearly in larger organizations, it is essentially a
large-scale version of the same tendency toward division of
labor in leadership that can be seen in a committee.

Committee Membership

If all this is true, the emphasis should shift from seeking the
ideal leader to trying to compose the ideal total group. Accordingly, at Harvard the next few years will be devoted to observing groups for the specific purpose of assessing the personnel,
and then attempting actually to compose new committees from
them which will function in a predicted way. With the right
kind of assessment of each person's action within a group, it
may be possible to pick, say, two people who would appear to
be complementary leaders, put them with three more "neutral"
people, and thus form a committee which would theoretically

function at a certain predicted level of effectiveness. This at least is a start in the direction of rational composition of total groups.

Optimum Size

Just to take one of the elementary problems, the question of optimum size of a committee has received many interesting answers, but so far they seem to come mostly from numerology rather than from scientific research. For the particular task and time limits given to subjects in the Harvard laboratory, five seems to be the preferred number. Below that size subjects begin to complain that the group is too small, and above it that the group is too large. The fact that there is a distinct "saddle point" at five suggests that the notion of an optimum size is meaningful, if the task, time, and other circumstances are well enough specified. But the optimum size must surely vary according to conditions.

There seems to be a crucial point at seven. Below seven, for the most part, each person in the group says at least something to each other person. In groups over seven the low participators tend to stop talking to each other and center their communications on the few top men. The tendencies toward centralization of communication seem to increase rather powerfully as size increases.

At the same time, there are certain difficulties inherent in groups of as low as two and three members. In a two-man group no majority short of unanimity can form. Each person can exercise a complete veto over the other. One person can exercise power quite as effectively by simply refusing to react as he can by making suggestions, and this tendency toward withdrawal of one member appears with some frequency.

In a three-man group the tendency of two to form a combination against the third seems fairly strong. If this happens, the would-be task leader may be overcautious because he knows that, if his lieutenant disagrees with him, he may be left in the minority. The lieutenant knows he has this power but that, if he exercises it, the third man may step in to take his place. The third man on the outside of the coalition is left powerless whether he agrees or disagrees, so long as the other two agree, and tends either to withdraw or set up a damaging but unsuccessful protest. It is hard for a three-man group to have a "healthy" amount of disagreement. The structure is too sensitive to disagreement, and therefore it tends to an all-or-none extreme.

Recommendations

It is important to realize that basic research is a long, slow process which really cannot be short-cut by concentration on the need for practical results. Some of the generalizations ventured above actually go somewhat beyond the base of firmly established facts, and all of them should be taken with a generous grain of salt in any attempted application since circumstances alter cases. With proper precautions, however, a summary of "rules of thumb" may be helpful in pinpointing some possible applications based on the experience of observing many laboratory groups:

(1) Avoid appointing committees larger than seven members unless necessary to obtain representation of all relevant points of view. Try to set up conditions of size, seating, and time allowed so that each member has an adequate opportunity to communicate directly with each other member.

(2) Avoid appointing committees as small as two or three members if the power problem between members is likely to be critical.

(3) Choose members who will tend to fall naturally into a moderate gradient of participation. Groups made up of all high participators will tend to suffer from competition. Groups made up of all lows may find themselves short on ideas.

(4) Avoid the assumption that a good committee is made up of one good "leader" and several "followers." Try to provide the group with both a task leader and a social leader, who will support each other. It is probably not a bad idea to

include a "humorist" if the social leader does not have a light touch. A few strong but more silent men add judicious balance to the group.

A group of otherwise balanced composition can probably absorb one "difficult" member—one of the type, for example, who talks too much, is short on problem-solving ability, tends to arouse dislikes, and cannot be changed by ordinary social pressures. If such a member must be included, probably the best strategy is to "surround" him.

(5) In actual procedure, start with facts if possible. Even where the facts are thought to be well known to all the members, a short review is seldom a waste of time. A good general procedure is probably to plan to deal with three questions on each major agenda item:

"What are the facts pertaining to the problem?"

"How do we feel about them?"

"What shall we do about the problem?"

This is probably the preferred order. Take time to lay the groundwork before getting to specific suggestions, the third stage. It may be noted, by the way, that the order recommended is the exact opposite of that which is characteristic of formal parliamentary procedure.

(6) Solicit the opinions and experiences of others, especially when disagreements begin to crop up. People often think they disagree when actually they simply are not talking about the same experiences. In such cases they do not draw each other out far enough to realize that, although they are using the same *words,* they are thinking about different *experiences.* Try to get past the words and general statements the other man uses to the experiences he is trying to represent. Members of the group may agree with his experiences.

(7) When somebody else is talking, listen, and keep indicating your reactions actively. Most people are not much good at reading your mind. Besides that, they need the recognition you can give them by your honest reaction, whether positive or negative.

(8) Keep your eyes on the group. When you are talking, talk to the group as a whole rather than to one of your

cronies or to one of your special opponents. Search around constantly for reactions to what you are saying. A good deal of communication goes on at a subverbal level. Nothing tones up the general harmony of a group like a good strong undercurrent of direct eye contact.

(9) When you scent trouble coming up, break off the argument and backtrack to further work on the facts and direct experience. In some instances the best way to get started on a cooperative track again after a period of difficulty is to agree to go out and gather some facts together by direct experience.

(10) Keep your ear to the ground. No recipe or set of rules can substitute for constant, sensitive, and sympathetic attention to what is going on in the relations between members. Do not get so engrossed in getting the job done that you lose track of what is the first prerequisite of success—keeping the committee in good operating condition.

Paul C. Buchanan
How Can We Gain
Their Commitment?

It's my impression—though I have no figures to prove it—that management's faith in communications as a key to organizational effectiveness is not quite so fervent as it was a few years ago. At all events, while most companies now are probably doing a better job of keeping their employees informed, it is doubtful whether many managements would agree that their communications programs have markedly increased employee commitment to organizational goals.

One reason for the often minimal impact of the best-intentioned efforts to "communicate" with employees is the general tendency to view the communications process in terms of "who says what, through what media, to whom, and with what results." Consequently, attempts to improve the effectiveness of employee communications have placed prime emphasis upon improving the *content* (or what is said, printed, or pictured), upon selecting the most appropriate *medium* (or how the message is said, printed, or pictured), and upon specifying the target audience. These are questions with which the communications specialist must rightly concern himself. But this approach overlooks some fundamental aspects of the communications process, about which interesting findings have recently emerged from behavioral science research.

In this article, I shall discuss these findings as they relate to three aspects of the communications process:

Reprinted by permission of the publisher from *Personnel*, January–February 1965. © 1965 by the American Management Association, Inc.

1. The intentions of the sender.
2. The role of the receiver.
3. The relation between the sender and receiver.

First, I shall consider these three aspects separately. I shall then go on to discuss some research that shows the close connection among them and the relevance of these findings to the problem of obtaining commitment in an organization.

1. Intentions of the sender. In general, it can be said that the sender's purpose is to influence the receiver in some manner—to convince him of something, to improve his behavior by providing him relevant information, to change his attitude, to increase his commitment. But *why* does the sender see the need to influence a particular audience in one or another of these ways? The answer to this question is that his action reflects not only the facts he has about the situation, but also the assumption he makes about it.

All too often, we operate from assumptions we have not made explicit and therefore of which we are frequently not aware. As Harold Leavitt has pointed out:

> . . . *if any generalized rule of thumb exists for the prospective behavior changer, it might be this one: Let him examine his own reasons for wanting to effect a particular change before plunging into the effort. Let him examine his own motives. If he does, he may be more likely to effect change successfully because he will be more clearheaded about what he wants to do; or he may alter or give up his efforts altogether.*[1]

Thus, in our examination of the communications process we must take the intentions of the sender into account. I shall return to this point later.

2. The role of the receiver. What are you doing as you read this article? Are you merely "taking in" what I have to say, or are you reacting to it with some ideas of your own? Ordinarily, we think of the receiver of our message as passive, and

[1] H. J. Leavitt, *Managerial Psychology* (Second Edition), University of Chicago Press, Chicago, 1964.

therefore we feel the need to "motivate" him. Some communications studies have shown, however, that, far from being passive, the receiver, too, has purposes that have to be taken into account. Thus, Leon Festinger and Nathan Maccoby, in a recently published study, commented:

Let us first try to understand the . . . behavior of a person who, while strongly committed to an opinion, listens to a vigorous, persuasive communication that attacks that opinion. Certainly, such a listener is not passive. He does not sit there listening and absorbing what is said without any counteraction on his part. Indeed, it is most likely that under such circumstances, while he is listening to the persuasive communication, he is very actively, inside his own mind, counterarguing, derogating the points the communicator makes, and derogating the communicator himself. In other words, we can imagine that there is really an argument going on, and one side being vocal and the other subvocal.

Let us imagine that one could somehow prevent the listener from arguing back while listening to the persuasive communication. If one created such a passive listener, it seems reasonable to expect that the persuasive communication would then have more of an impact. The listener, not able to counterargue, would be more influenced and would be less likely to reject the communication.[2]

The researchers set up a procedure for testing this possibility and ran the test in three different experiments. In all three cases, the results were consistent with the hypothesis.

Not only does the receiver respond to a communiqué in a way that serves his interests, but his interests also influence what it is he reads, hears, or watches. The receiver seeks out information to solve specific problems, to reinforce shaken convictions, to consolidate ones recently acquired, or to explain something he doesn't yet understand.[3] Thus, it happens that

[2] L. Festinger and N. Maccoby, "On Resistance to Persuasive Communications," *Journal of Abnormal & Social Psychology*, April, 1964, pp. 359–366.

[3] R. A. Bauer, "The Obstinate Audience: The Influence Process from the Point of View of Social Communication," *American Psychologist*, May, 1964, pp. 319–329.

what is not said in a company publication is sometimes more important to the employee than what is said. The employee wants to understand the intentions and values that underlie the events management reports, or he wants to check the accuracy of the impressions he has already formed. As a result, he is likely to be actively trying to find out what the intentions of the sender are. If these aren't made clear, they will be guessed at. This is one of the important sources of *noise* in a communications system.

Thus, in understanding what happens in the communications process, we have to take account of the role of the receiver. I shall return to this point later also.

3. The relation between sender and receiver. This relationship is the track on which messages move. Or perhaps it would be more accurate to say that it is the medium through which communication takes place, and that what we usually call media are rather vehicles for transferring ideas, feelings, intentions, and so on, through the medium. We pay attention to this relationship when we talk about credibility, trust, and intention. And it is the relationship between sender and receiver we are concerned about when we try to increase employee commitment to the goals of the organization.

Win-Lose Competition

Now let's take a look at some research findings that, I think, link these three aspects of the communication process together. The studies in question are ones that have explored the effects of intergroup relations upon communications. They have taken the form of a series of experiments in human relations training laboratories in which the training groups (consisting of 8 to 12 members each) were pitted against each other in win-lose competition. In a typical experiment, after each group has worked together for several meetings and its members have smoothed out some of their internal operating difficulties, the members are asked to rate their own group and each of the other groups (in such terms as how good a group it is).

Then, two groups are assigned a common task (such as writing a two-page report on how to improve union-management relations in their company) and are told that the reports will be studied and compared, and that one will be judged better than the other. In other words, they have to work under win-lose conditions.

This experiment has been conducted by a number of psychologists with a variety of groups. Though different types of subjects have been used, the results have been the same. Thus, we can have confidence in the findings, which (insofar as they relate to communications) are as follows:[4]

1. Under conditions of competition, a group demands greater conformity from its own members than it does when it is not in competition with some other group. This conformity takes the form of tolerating fewer *negative* comments about one's own group or its product, and fewer *positive* comments about the competing group or its product. In other words, negative comments about one's own group or its product, and positive comments about the competing group and its product are rejected.

2. In their interactions, each group accentuates the *strengths* of its own position or its product, and the *shortcomings* of the competing group and its product. Desirable characteristics that in fact are common to both groups or to both products are recognized as applying to one's own group only.

3. The comments exchanged between the representatives or members of the competing groups are challenging. They tend to be exaggerated, and gradually to become overly hostile. They leave little room for problem solving.

"We-They" Confrontation

It seems to me that these findings explain at least in part why management finds it so difficult to get commitment from

[4] R. R. Blake and J. S. Mcuton, "The Intergroup Dynamics of Win-Lose Conflict and Problem-Solving Collaboration in Union-Management Relations," in M. Sherif, *Intergroup Relations and Leadership*, John Wiley & Sons, New York, 1962, pp. 98–103.

employees. Far more often than not, the relationship between management and employees is a competitive one. Each side tends to speak of the other as "they," and of themselves as "we." The very form in which the communications problem is commonly stated—we need to get *their* commitment—implies this relationship.

The research results described above suggest that to the extent that a competitive relationship exists between management and employees, an attempt by one group to influence the other will tend to increase each side's commitment to its **own** group and intensify its rejection of the other. Now, notice what happens to intentions: Sensing the negative reactions of the other group, each sees the need to become "persuasive." Thus, sensing the lack of employee commitment, management becomes interested in gaining it; and, sensing management's attempt to persuade them, employees start rumors critical of management. But the greater the effort made by either to support its own cause, the more likely is it that the employees will be confirmed in their belief that management is "trying to put something over on us" and that management, for its part, will see the employees as lacking in commitment to the organization.

So much for the problem. It seems clear that if the relations between sender and receiver are to be improved, some way must be found to reduce intergroup competition. How can this be done?

At first glance, the solution would seem to be an increased exchange of information. But research has shown that this, in itself, is not of much help. Sherif, for example, in an experiment that aimed at improving intergroup relations, found that bringing the members of the two groups together to facilitate informal communication among the members resulted in *increased* hostility.[5] Furthermore, studies of the effects of intercultural exchange programs between nations have found these programs to be of little value in improving international relations. Person-to-person interactions across group lines seem to

---

[5] M. Sherif, *ibid*, pp. 9–13.

make those whose attitudes are already favorable more favorable and those whose attitudes are already unfavorable even more unfavorable. In other words, instead of being altered, attitudes are likely to be intensified through person-to-person interactions.[6]

Ends Defeated by Means

It would seem, therefore, that the greater an organization's need to increase the commitment of its employees, the greater is the likelihood that the usual approaches to obtaining it—more persuasive communications, town hall meetings where top management interacts with employees, and so on—will magnify the problem. So what else might one do?

While the answer to this question is still not very clear, some promising steps have been tried out. One method, which has been used recently in several organizations, consists of bringing the members of the two groups together, as groups, to talk about their relationship: to exchange information on how they view themselves and the other group, and to review happenings that have led each group to view themselves and the other group as they do. Among such groups have been the management committee and the union officers in one plant; a group of headquarters people and a plant management committee; and representatives of two different departments. These mutual explorations of relations, carried out in an atmosphere where there are no operating problems to solve and where time pressures are minimized, appear to be a promising means of developing collaborative working relations between groups in an organization.[7]

"Superordinate" Goals

Why does such talking through of their relationships by members of two groups lead to improvement? The answer seems to lie in the nature of win-lose competition. Win-lose

[6] R. R. Blake, "Psychology and the Crisis of Statesmanship." *American Psychologist*, February, 1959, pp. 87–94.

[7] Blake and Mouton, *op. cit.*, pp. 119–138.

competition implies that if one group is to satisfy more of its needs the other group must thereby fulfill fewer of its needs. Thus, if the company is to make more profits, employees must work harder, be reduced in number, and so on; if the union gets more influence, management will "lose control," or have its "prerogatives" infringed upon. Hence, the goals of the two groups are seen as mutually exclusive.

Sherif has shown, however, that this need not happen. In a series of experiments he set up a situation in which competing groups had what he called "superordinate" goals. By this he means *goals that are desired by both groups, but can be attained by neither side without help from the other.* He found that when such goals could be set up or developed, it was possible to overcome even intense intergroup rivalry and to obtain collaborative relations between the groups—without either group's losing its identity as a group.

In the "talk through" meetings that have resulted in improved intergroup relations in organizations, what seems to have happened is that the groups found that they had, or could develop, "superordinate" goals: When they had the courage to examine their own operation, and allowed themselves to hear the other group, they found that their interpretation of events had been influenced (distorted) by their attitude toward the other group, and that their goals were actually much more "superordinate" than they had realized. After becoming aware of this, and identifying these goals, the groups were able to shift toward a collaborative rather than a competitive relationship with one another. In short, the aim of communication shifted from an attempt on the part of one group to "persuade" or "gain the commitment of" the other, to an attempt to understand themselves and the others, and thus to a form of mutual problem solving.

Obviously, long-rooted habits of thought and organization customs cannot be changed overnight, and I am not suggesting that it is easy to apply the research findings discussed here. Nevertheless, they seem to me to provide a springboard for a challenging new approach to the problem of developing a more productive relationship between employees and the company than generally exists today.

Questions
for
Reflection
and
Discussion
Section Eight

1. Rogers argues that even in an "interpersonal" relationship between a person and a machine, the machine must be trustworthy if the relationship is to be rewarding and continued. Do you believe that trustworthiness is all-important in relationships between people? What other factors are relevant? Which are more important?

2. Do you see a possible analogy between studies of psychotherapist effectiveness involving empathy, unconditional warmth, and genuineness and teacher effectiveness in the classroom? What are the weaknesses or limitations of such an analogy? Can a teacher's role properly be thought to involve a "helping relationship" with his students?

3. For successful decision-making by groups, Bales suggests certain types of communicative behavior by group members. Specifically, what place does *disagreement* between members have in this set of suggestions? How can you avoid harmful effects of disagreement in your relationships with others?

4. Can you see value in Bales's concept of "dual leadership" roles? Can you make a useful application to your participation in a campus group? If you were forced to make a choice, which leadership role would best fit your personality, temperament, and sense of social values?

5. What undesirable or unrealistic effects of "win-lose" competitive situations are cited by Buchanan? How many campus organizations (including classroom settings) appear to be based primarily upon this principle? What negative or

undesirable effects, if any, have you observed as a result? Have you properly assessed such situations for both positive and negative outcomes?

6. Buchanan seems to make a rather strong case against persuasive communication behaviors, particularly when used to control or manipulate the behavior of people. If you have been given the responsibility of being a group's "leader" or of "managing" a company, what does he suggest as alternative behavior? How valuable (valid, viable) do you believe this suggestion to be?

Designed by Michel Craig
Set in Spartan
Composed by V&M Typographical, Inc.
Printed and bound by The Murray Printing Company
HARPER & ROW, PUBLISHERS   70 71 72 73 7 6 5 4 3 2 1